Technology, Work and Globalization

Series Editors
Leslie P. Willcocks, Department of Management, London School of Economics and Political Science, London, UK
Mary C. Lacity, Sam M. Walton College of Business, University of Arkansas, Fayetteville, AR, USA

The Technology, Work and Globalization series was developed to provide policy makers, workers, managers, academics and students with a deeper understanding of the complex interlinks and influences between technological developments, including information and communication technologies, work organizations and patterns of globalization. The mission of the series is to disseminate rich knowledge based on deep research about relevant issues surrounding the globalization of work that is spawned by technology.

Leslie Willcocks · Ilan Oshri · Julia Kotlarsky
Editors

Transformation in Global Outsourcing

Towards Digital Sourcing of IT and Business Services

Editors
Leslie Willcocks
London, UK

Julia Kotlarsky
The University of Auckland Business School
Auckland, New Zealand

Ilan Oshri
The University of Auckland Business School
Auckland, New Zealand

ISSN 2730-6623   ISSN 2730-6631 (electronic)
Technology, Work and Globalization
ISBN 978-3-031-61021-9   ISBN 978-3-031-61022-6 (eBook)
https://doi.org/10.1007/978-3-031-61022-6

© The Editor(s) (if applicable) and The Author(s), under exclusive licence to Springer Nature Switzerland AG 2024

This work is subject to copyright. All rights are solely and exclusively licensed by the Publisher, whether the whole or part of the material is concerned, specifically the rights of translation, reprinting, reuse of illustrations, recitation, broadcasting, reproduction on microfilms or in any other physical way, and transmission or information storage and retrieval, electronic adaptation, computer software, or by similar or dissimilar methodology now known or hereafter developed.
The use of general descriptive names, registered names, trademarks, service marks, etc. in this publication does not imply, even in the absence of a specific statement, that such names are exempt from the relevant protective laws and regulations and therefore free for general use.
The publisher, the authors and the editors are safe to assume that the advice and information in this book are believed to be true and accurate at the date of publication. Neither the publisher nor the authors or the editors give a warranty, expressed or implied, with respect to the material contained herein or for any errors or omissions that may have been made. The publisher remains neutral with regard to jurisdictional claims in published maps and institutional affiliations.

This Palgrave Macmillan imprint is published by the registered company Springer Nature Switzerland AG
The registered company address is: Gewerbestrasse 11, 6330 Cham, Switzerland

If disposing of this product, please recycle the paper.

Preface

As researchers, advisers and practitioners in global sourcing, the lead authors of this book have a combined experience of over 70 years. During that time, we have produced over 40 books and 150 learned articles, and also sought to influence practice through advisory work, conference presentations and numerous media publications, blogs and online panels. In 2007, we also founded an ongoing annual global sourcing workshop designed to explore how new and emerging forms of outsourcing and offshoring challenge sourcing practices and theories, and consequently identify new directions for research and practice. The workshop has brought together viewpoints from various disciplines, including information systems, international business, strategy, operation management and organisational behaviour.

Together we have followed the modern global outsourcing market for information technology and business services from its inception in the 1989–91 period, through its adoption of business process outsourcing, offshoring, application service provision, cloud sourcing and into today's ongoing transformation with the rise of digital technologies and services.

Outsourcing is the handing over to third-party management of activities, processes and/or human resources for required results. There are many other sourcing options, the main ones being in-house delivery, insourcing (buying in external resources but managing them internally), out-tasking (outsourcing on a small scale) renting services, joint ventures, build-operate-transfer models, shared services (delivered internally or by a third party), and, more recently, cloud sourcing and crowdsourcing (see below). The evolution and performance of these models have been fascinating to research and participate in, and our combined experiences have taught us some abiding lessons, especially about outsourcing.

Perennial Lessons

Our first lesson is that **outsourcing is perennially attractive as a sourcing option**, whether in times of economic growth or slowdown, though the reasons for outsourcing will be different. Cost efficiency is invariably the primary reason, at any time, but typically organisations have multiple reasons. For example, to secure fast growth an organisation may use extra services, or ones they have no immediate capability to perform. In a recession, outsourcing could be a management option for reducing costs, and improving operational efficiency. This hardly exhausts the possibilities. We identified over 23 reasons why organisations outsource, and most clients have four to seven objectives informing their decisions. One interesting pattern we have identified is how many organisations evolve their global sourcing strategy. We have always argued that it is risky to outsource a problem, something you do not understand, and/or anything you cannot draw up a detailed contract for. In these circumstance, it is best to bring these things in-house and build up the learning and only selectively outsource commodity services. Over time, as you build up knowledge of a technology, process or service, and as you build an in-house capability to manage external service providers, then it becomes increasingly attractive to outsource that activity. Thus, outsourcing forms part of a much bigger global sourcing strategy that will evolve over time. This observation becomes particularly pertinent as organisations adopt emerging digital technologies, as detailed in section 3 of this book.

The second lesson is that **multisourcing is perennially the dominant client preference**. This sees the adoption of a 'horses for courses' approach with clients selecting the best supplier (external or internal) for a specific, ring-fenced set of activities. The in-house option remains an important part of a multisourcing approach and has received added vitality with emerging 'SMAC/BRAIDA' technologies and services—social media, mobile, analytics, cloud blockchain, robotics, automation of knowledge work (including AI), Internet of Things, digital fabrication and augmented reality. But as we shall see in Chapter 1, cloud computing has seen a big, accelerating growth in outsourcing over the last ten years. Multisourcing also sees a variety of decisions on **location**. There are globally today over 130 viable locations for offshoring and nearshoring. India and the Philippines lead in terms of size and service range, but increasingly clients mitigate risks by spreading outsourced work around several geographical locations and suppliers, and increasingly use nearsourcing as an option in the light of perceived increasing geopolitical risk. A similar pattern can be seen for in-house work and captive centres, which has grown in attraction due to automation making labour outsourcing less necessary, and also the need to learn in-house about how to use and deploy emerging technologies.

Thirdly, the importance of **key internal capabilities** emerges as a fundamental factor in achieving positive global sourcing outcomes. We have noted multiple times the need for in-house business, technology and external service facing capabilities that found a global sourcing, three to five year strategy that can elicit and deliver on business requirements, establish and support the technology trajectory, while optimally leveraging external service provision. These key capabilities are vital for keeping control of an organisation's technology and business process destiny, and ensuring they are aligned with business imperatives. The issue of key internal capabilities reappears several times in this book, not least in chapters dealing with innovation, automation/AI and digital transformation.

Fourthly, right from the early days to the present, **long-term 10-12 year, strategic partnering involving one major supplier, has been very**

oversold. Firstly, in a dynamic, uncertain, increasingly interconnected business and global environment, it is unrealistic to sign deals longer than 3–5 years, not least because the technologies change so rapidly, as do the underlying economics. Secondly, it is difficult to find one supplier who can deliver all of a large organisation's service needs at the right price, and to the required standard. As a result invariably the main supplier sub-contracts parts of the agreed work, this incurs hidden transaction costs, governance and standards issues. Thirdly, it is difficult to write detailed contracts and establish performance metrics for long periods of time. To this day, therefore we see three to five year detailed contracts with regular review clauses, and explicit multisourcing of between 3 and 5 suppliers regarded as the most efficient approach for medium to large organisations.

Fifthly, both clients and suppliers of outsourcing arrangements have long aspired to achieve **innovation**, and **closer partnering** with suppliers much more closely aligned with business goals, and measured on **business outcomes**, and not just service performance. Suppliers have aspired to move further up the value chain going beyond commodity services to strategic relationships, consultancy services, taking over more control of technology platforms. Historically, outsourcing stakeholders have struggled to deliver on these aspirations, though the maturing of global sourcing management practices has made them still challenging, but more realistically attainable in the 2020s, than they were, especially in the 1989–2010 period. Our Chapter 14 points one way forward with vendor innovation ecosystems.

The other thing we have learned is that technological change is a constant backdrop to global sourcing, and in the last ten years, it has been particularly impactful as a factor. With the rise of cloud services, the Internet and SMAC/BRAIDA technologies, we have seen a global outsourcing pivot, from around 2014/15 (see Chapter 1). The fundamental principles for global sourcing do not change, though we have seen some developments and maturing, as we discuss in the sections in this book on governing traditional business services, and advancing sourcing performance. But in a period where clients and vendors alike are running legacy systems, technologies and processes, while still trying to digitalise their businesses, it is important to pick up on the challenges and progress being made. This is accomplished in the final section on shifting from traditional sourcing to digital services. Let us look in more detail at the chapters contained in this volume.

London, UK
Auckland, New Zealand
Auckland, New Zealand

Leslie Willcocks
Ilan Oshri
Julia Kotlarsky

Acknowledgements

We would like to thank all the participants of the Global Sourcing Workshop over the last 16 years, members of the AIS SIG Advances in Sourcing and the participants of the ICIS, ECIS PACIS Sourcing tracks.

Leslie would like to thank all his colleagues at the London School of Economics and Political Science for creating such a congenial environment and the intellectual and social stimulation over many years. Also his wonderful co-workers on global sourcing stretching back to the early 1990s. The list has to include Mary Lacity, Sara Cullen, Ilan Oshri, Julia Kotlarsky, Peter Seddon John Hindle, Wendy Currie, David Feeny, Daniel Gozman and Eleni Lioliou, but in fact there are so many more, and great thanks also to our thoughtful respondents who gave so freely of their time and knowledge, and without which most of the research could not have been done.

We would also like to acknowledge permissions granted to develop versions from or reproduce parts of the following publications:

Chapter 2 is a revised and updated version of Krancher, O., Oshri, I., Kotkarsky, J., & Dibbern, J. (2022). Bilateral, Collective, or Both?

Formal Governance and Performance in Multisourcing. *Journal of the Association of Information Systems*, 23(5), 1211–1234.

Chapter 3 is a revised and updated version of Oshri, I., Dibbern, J., Kotlarsky, J., & Krancher, O. (2019). An information processing view on joint-vendor performance in multi-sourcing: The role of the Guardian. *Journal of Management of Information Systems*, 36(4), 1248–1283.

Chapter 4 is a more developed and updated version of Lioliou, E., Willcocks, L., & Liu, X. (2019). Researching IT multi-sourcing and opportunistic behavior in conditions of uncertainty: A case approach. *Journal of Business Research*, 103, 387–396.

Chapter 5 is updated from an earlier version of Lacity, M., & Willcocks, L. (2017). Conflict resolution in business services outsourcing relationships. *Journal of Strategic Information Systems*, 26, 80–100.

Chapter 6 is an updated version of Brooks, J., Ravishankar, M.N., & Oshri, I. (2020). Paradox and the negotiation of tensions in globally distributed work. *Journal of Information Technology*, 35(3):232–250.

Chapter 7 is an updated version of Oshri, I., Sidhu, J., & Kotlarsky, J. (2019). East, West, Would Home Really Be Best? On Dissatisfaction with Offshore-Outsourcing and Firms' Inclination to Backsource. *Journal of Business Research*, 103, 644–653.

Chapter 8 is a revised and updated version of Brooks, J., Ravishankar, M.N., & Oshri, I. (2021). Status differentials and framing in the implementation of IT-enabled task migration strategies. *Information Systems Journal*, 32(2), 414–439.

Chapter 9 is revised, updated and synthesised from Lacity, M., & Willcocks, L. (2021). Becoming Strategic with Intelligent Automation. *MIS Quarterly Executive*, 20(2), 169–182, and Lacity, M., Willcocks, L., & Gozman, D. (2021). Influencing information systems practice: The action principles approach applied to robotic process and cognitive automation. *Journal of Information Technology*, 36(3), 216–240. https://doi.org/10.1177/0268396221990778.

Chapter 10—An earlier version of this chapter was published as Beulen, E., Plugge, A., & Hillegersberg, J. van (2022). Formal and relational governance of artificial intelligence outsourcing. *Information Systems and e-Business Management,* 20, 719–748. This is a much revised and updated version.

Chapter 11 is a more developed version of a chapter from the authors' textbook: Oshri, I., Kotlarsky, J., Willcocks, L.P. (2023). Internet Delivery Sourcing Models. In I. Oshri, J. Kotlarsky & L.P. Willcocks (Eds.), *The Handbook of Global Outsourcing and Offshoring* (4th ed., pp. 39–65). Palgrave Macmillan.

Chapter 12 is based on the conference paper: He, R.-H., Kotlarsky, J., & Nevo, D. (2021). A Process Perspective on Emerging Value in Tournament-based and Collaborative Crowdsourcing. *Proceedings of the HICSS-54,* Hawaii.

Chapter 13 synthesises and updates a number of research papers and articles by Leslie Willcocks. The notion of the digital flexible organisation first appears in Willcocks, L. (2021). Robo-Apocalypse? Response and outlook on the post-COVID-19 future of work. *Journal of Information Technology,* 36(2), 188–194.

Chapter 14 is based on several studies, and we would like to acknowledge the contributions of Evelien Scherp, Heiner Himmerleich, Hrishi Hrishikesh and Anthony Vlasic to two of these on vendor innovation ecosystems and sustainability. The sections on digital transformation draw upon the original research work of John Hindle of Knowledge Capital Partners and Leslie Willcocks.

Introduction

In Chapter 1—*The Outsourcing Pivot: Advances and Challenges*—we provide a detailed overview and analysis of the nature of this pivot from traditional sourcing to digital services, and the hybrid, changing attributes of global sourcing practices through the mid-2020s. We then focus on advances in the governance of traditional IT and business services.

Advances in the Governance of Traditional IT and Business Services

Chapter 2 looks at the governing mechanisms of **multisourcing** arrangements. Multisourcing has become a dominant outsourcing practice. Yet the extant IS literature offers only limited insights into how to stipulate individual (i.e. vendor) and joint (i.e. the entire vendor network) performance while ensuring governance efficiency. The chapter, by Oliver Krancher, Ilan Oshri, Julia Kotkarsky and Jens Dibbern, sets about examining how these three dimensions of multisourcing success can be achieved through formal governance. Specifically, they consider bilateral outcome control, collective outcome control, and conflict management procedures (amongst vendors) as key formal governance. A pan-European survey of client firms engaged in multisourcing arrangements shows that bilateral outcome control improves individual performance, collective outcome control improves joint performance and governance efficiency, and conflict management procedures contribute positively to all success dimensions. Further, according to the interaction analyses, the benefits of collective outcome control are weakened by bilateral outcome control (for joint performance) and strengthened by conflict management procedures (for all success dimensions). These findings indicate multisourcing clients face delicate trade-offs in deciding whether to follow a bilateral or collective approach. While a bilateral approach centred on bilateral outcome control promises high-quality individual components, a collective approach relying on collective outcome control and conflict management procedures promises a coherent, integrated service with comparatively low governance effort. The chapter provides new insights into how multisourcing governance mechanisms and their interplay affect success in multisourcing.

These authors continue with the multisourcing theme in Chapter 3 which asks: what does **the guardian** do in multisourcing projects? The chapter examines joint vendor performance. Using an Information Processing View, the authors argue that managing interdependencies between multiple vendors imposes substantial information processing (IP) requirements on clients. To achieve high joint performance, clients therefore need to possess sufficient IP capacity. The chapter examines how three sources of IP capacity, two internal (the client's inter-vendor governance and the client's architectural knowledge) and one external (the guardian vendor), work together in realising joint performance. The results show that formal governance and architectural knowledge contribute to joint performance. The guardian vendor contributes to joint performance in settings where the client deploys strong governance but lacks architectural knowledge. This suggests that contrary to common views in the literature, guardian vendors should not be understood as mediators (or single points of contact) who relieve clients from governance efforts. Instead, guardian vendors are more fruitfully understood as architects, who complement the client's governance efforts by compensating for knowledge gaps. Put simply, client firms should consider using a guardian vendor to compensate for weak architectural knowledge while still maintaining strong formal and informal governance of all vendors.

In Chapter 4, Eleni Lioliou, Leslie Willcocks and Xiaohui Liu reflect on IT **multisourcing and opportunistic behaviour of service providers** in conditions of uncertainty. In particular, they focus on a relatively neglected but major driver of opportunistic behaviour, namely the uncertainty surrounding the transaction. Developing an extended transaction cost economics perspective, their investigation looks at the roles of internal and behavioural uncertainty and the occurrence of opportunistic behaviour. The chapter offers a rich multisourcing case study within the financial services sector which is compared and re-analysed against a further detailed case in the literature. It emerges that internal uncertainty creates an 'alignment of actions' problem between outsourcing partners, while behavioural uncertainty can shape an 'alignment of objectives' problem, leading to the occurrence of opportunistic behaviour. The chapter contributes to a more thorough understanding of ways to reduce these uncertainties and facilitate coopetition between multiple vendors.

In Chapter 5, Mary Lacity and Leslie Willcocks focus on the perennial management challenges of **conflict resolution** in business services outsourcing. Many business services outsourcing relationships are strategic, in the sense that they are large, underpin clients' business strategies, and the client can become highly dependent on service provider capabilities and performance. Despite the size and maturity of the BSO market, up to 50% of BSO relationships result in poor outcomes, partly because partners cannot resolve conflicts. The question arises: *"What types of inter-organizational conflicts arise in BSO relationships and how do partners resolve them?"*. Looking at 13 major BSO cases, the authors conceptualise three types of conflicts specific to BSO: commercial conflicts, service conflicts and relationship conflicts. Conflicts as studied here are not minor disagreements, but have a strategic dimension. Commercial conflicts were the most serious because outsourcing relationships are firstly commercial transactions—a provider must earn a profit and a client must meet its economic business case to be viable. Theoretically, the authors found Thomas and Kilmann's typology of conflict resolution styles to be robust enough to characterise the BSO conflict cases, provided a switched style category was included. Consistent with the theory, only the collaborative and switched-to collaborative styles resolved conflicts to the satisfaction of both partners. Novel findings that extend or contest prior theory are identified as part of a future research agenda. For practitioners, the chapter also identifies five effective conflict resolution behaviours.

Moving on from governance issues, the next section of our book looks at recent research-based around progressing global sourcing performance.

Advancing Sourcing Performance

Tensions are a major source of communication problems, coordination issues and conflict in globally distributed work (GDW). In Chapter 6, Jade Brooks, M.N. Ravishankar and Ilan Oshri argue that the extant literature falls short of addressing **tensions in globally distributed work** at two levels. First, it fails to fully account for the intrinsic and entrenched nature of tensions in GDW, suggesting instead that they can be resolved or made to disappear. Second, it does not examine the key interactions between different kinds of tensions. Drawing on qualitative data from a distributed finance organisation and applying concepts from paradox theory, the authors show how globally distributed units negotiate knowledge, power and identity tensions in collaborative work. The findings illuminate how distributed teams address tensions, accommodate contradictory needs and create collaborative opportunities. The chapter synthesise the findings into a model of tension evolution and management in GDW, which shows how defensive behaviours can be turned into collaborative ones.

The apparent abundance of instances of disenchantment with **offshore-outsourcing** leads to the question of why relatively few disappointed firms backsource (i.e. bring back offshored operations in-house). In general, of all sourcing decisions by firms, **backsourcing** is perhaps the most thinly researched and insufficiently understood. In Chapter 7, Ilan Oshri, Jatinder Sidhu and Julia Kotlarsky draw on the behavioural theory of the firm (BTF) to propose a novel model that ascribes differences in firms' inclination to backsource to the level of dissatisfaction from non-attainment of offshoring aspirations. Building on ideas of bounded rationality, problemistic search and satisficing decisions from BTF, the model maintains that offshoring dissatisfaction's effect on backsourcing inclination will depend on managerial expectations regarding technical challenges, financial loss and quality decline following backsourcing, as well as on internal political support and financial slack for backsourcing. Structural equation modelling of data from a cross-industry survey of firms located in the U.S. many other and the U.K. provides support for the theoretical model. The study highlights the importance of recognising the role managerial perceptions/cognitive biases and subgroup political relations can play in shaping firms' backsourcing behaviours.

In globally distributed environments, an **organisational-level decision to migrate IT-enabled tasks** cannot be conflated with the actual execution of strategy since a high-level consensus does not always specify the precise sequencing and pacing of task migration in detail. This absence of operational-level detailing can trigger status-led enactments of power. Drawing on a qualitative case study of a distributed finance function in a global logistics firm, Chapter 8 by Jade Brooks, M.N. Ravishankar and Ilan Oshri, explores how high-status business units frame their task migration actions. This is contrasted with how a low-status support unit frames and accounts for the actions of high-status business units. The authors show how high-status business units frame their own actions as protecting, supporting and monitoring the migrated tasks, while the low-status support unit frames the same set of actions as resisting, interfering and hypercriticising. The authors suggest that during the implementation of task migration strategies, framing and accompanying attributions of a low-status unit consider its weaker position of power and serve to neutralise conflict with the more powerful, higher-status unit.

The remaining six chapters of the book investigate major developments in the transformation of global sourcing from traditional to digital services.

Shifting from Traditional Sourcing to Digital Services

In Chapter 9, Leslie Willcocks and Mary Lacity provide a comprehensive examination of the evolution of **intelligent automation as a sourcing option**. They note that a new sourcing destination was floated in 2012, ostensibly called 'Robotistan'—a fictional place representing the growth of robotic process automation, then subsequently cognitive automation and what has become called artificial intelligence. These are potential machine-based complementors to, and replacements for, the more traditional labour-based models leveraged by global sourcing clients and providers up to then. The chapter includes an assessment of the job implications of automation so far, and into the future. Overall automation is found to be a surprisingly slow evolution with relatively low impacts on most work so far, but adoption and work reorganisation have been accelerating since the pandemic crisis. Drawing on an eight-year longitudinal research base, the authors detail the advances in the technologies and summarise some 39 action principles, that, suitably applied, lead to effective use of these automation technologies, whether by client or provider organisations. The authors point to a range of challenges—organisations struggle to scale their automations. There are problems with integrating automation technologies with existing or new IT and processes, let alone across the enterprise. Management all too often drive their automation and digital transformation strategies from different parts of the organisation. The authors conclude with an agenda for much needed research in this area.

The arrival of **artificial intelligence and algorithms** has engendered much interest in the governance challenges when these are considered as candidates for outsourcing. In Chapter 10, Erik Beulen, Albert Plugge and Jos van Hillegersberg review relevant formal **and relational aspects of AI governance.** They comment that outsourcing emerging technologies, such as artificial intelligence (AI) and algorithms, are expected to impact organisations significantly, due to a tight labour market for AI expertise. However, they remark on a research gap in how formal and relational governance affect vendors who provide AI services, including developing and maintaining algorithms. Based on exploratory research amongst eight suppliers and two market research advisors, the authors conducted 18 expert interviews. They adapted the outsourcing governance model of Lioliou et al. (2014), including their emphasis on the psychological contract and researched how formal contractual and relational governance affect AI and algorithms outsourcing.[1] The results indicate various forms of contractual models in which some cater for clients' needs specifically, e.g. outcome-based, experience-driven Service Level Agreements. The examination provides insights that formal and relational outsourcing governance is complementary in cases where clients and vendors co-develop AI and algorithms. The chapter contributes to the business services literature by exploring differences between vendors in providing AI services and developing and maintaining algorithms. The study points to AI and algorithms outsourcing shifting the emphasis from a transactional type of arrangement to a relational type of outsourcing arrangement. The combination of both formal and relational governance mechanisms positively contributes to sourcing governance, while the innovative character of AI and algorithms strengthens the psychological contract between client and supplier(s).

In Chapter 11, Ilan Oshri, Julia Kotlarsky and Leslie Willcocks look at **Internet service delivery models** and how cloud **services and crowdsourcing** are increasingly popular sourcing models based on Internet delivery of products or services. In practice, these high-level sourcing models can be implemented in different ways in terms of specific operational and commercial aspects of service provision. In this chapter, the authors describe the key principles of these two Internet-based sourcing models and give examples of how they have been adopted by client firms.

Chapter 12 offers a process perspective on emerging value in **tournament-based and collaborative crowdsourcing**. Value, in crowdsourcing, is attributed to outcomes such as reducing costs, improving quality through broad participation, generating alternative solutions with increased creativity and enabling the employment of specialists on an ad hoc basis. These benefits of crowdsourcing typically reflect the focal firm's perspective and are perceived at a single point in time, either prior

---

[1] Lioliou, E., Zimmermann, A., Willcocks, L.P. and Gao, L. (2014). Formal and relational governance in IT outsourcing: substitution, complementarity and the role of the psychological contract. *Information Systems Journal*, 24(6), 503–535. https://Doi.org/10.1111/isj.12038.

to initiating the project or post hoc. In this study, Hi Rui He, Julia Kotlarsky and Dorit Nevo take a longitudinal and stakeholder-centred approach to examine the process of value co-creation through interactions between firm and crowd. In offering a process perspective on emerging value and distinguishing between value for firm and value for crowd, the authors address an observable gap in the literature which lacks an overarching understanding of crowdsourcing value creation.

As intimated above, traditional outsourcing has been predicated largely on a labour-based model. Chapter 13, by Leslie Willcocks, takes a macro-perspective on the **future of work**. Will new advanced technologies, harnessed to improve productivity and cut costs, finally lead to large-scale job loss? How can skills shortages be ameliorated? Would extending the labour market ever further virtually and globally remedy labour problems? What policies towards different forms of labour will be optimal? The chapter finds evidence-based answers to these questions and points to both an emerging way forward—a digitalised flexible labour model—and its inherent challenges. Taking the period to 2030, the chapter investigates first the extent to which digital technologies are likely to replace human labour, the exponential rise in the amount of work to be done, and how far distinctively human skills are future-proofed, and therefore likely to be in short supply. The evidence is then assessed for a permanent switch to home and remote working enabled by emerging technologies. Given the 2020s context, the chapter goes on to assess the business, digital and labour strategies of work organisations and identifies and points to the promise and challenges presented by a dominant, if largely tactical and ad hoc, trend towards a **digitally enabled flexible labour model** heavily dependent on contractual arrangements, and including the leveraging of multiple technological and labour sourcing options.

The post-COVID-19 world has been going through multiple shocks that require executives and decision makers to rethink their sourcing strategies. In Chapter 14, Ilan Oshri, Leslie Willcocks and John Hindle pay close attention to two emerging topics in the business community. The first topic is effective **management of innovation ecosystems** that have become critical for client firm's ability to speed up time-to-market and ensure access to critical skills in a timely manner. The second results from the growing compliance and demands by governments and enterprises to increase **transparency with regard to carbon footprints**. **Sustainability** has taken a central role in corporate responsibility, particularly with regard to environmental issues. As the chapter makes clear, both issues have implications for an organisation's future global sourcing strategies. The chapter subsumes these issues into the all-encompassing one of how organisations are seeking to manage their **digital transformations**. The chapter argues that seven core internal capabilities are required to effectively manage in and leverage digital technologies. While these are being put in place, a global sourcing strategy that navigates between multiple sourcing options can be operationalised. The chapter focuses particularly on the key capability of a digital platform, and its relationship to business strategy and the use of the external services market.

Contents

1 The Global Outsourcing Pivot: Advances and Challenges   1
Leslie Willcocks, Ilan Oshri, and Julia Kotlarsky

Part I   Governing Traditional Outsourcing Services

2 The Governing Mechanisms of Successful
Multisourcing Projects   19
*Oliver Krancher, Ilan Oshri, Julia Kotlarsky,
and Jens Dibbern*

3 What the Guardian Does in Multisourcing Projects   61
*Ilan Oshri, Jens Dibbern, Julia Kotlarsky,
and Oliver Krancher*

4 IT Multisourcing and Opportunistic Behavior
in Conditions of Uncertainty   111
Eleni Lioliou, Leslie Willcocks, and Xiaohui Liu

5   Conflict Resolution in Business Services Outsourcing
    Relationships   147
    Leslie Willcocks and Mary Lacity

Part II Advancing Sourcing Performance

6   Managing Tensions in Globally Distributed Work   205
    Jade Brooks, M. N. Ravishankar, and Ilan Oshri

7   On Dissatisfaction with Offshore-Outsourcing: Is
    Backsourcing the Right Response?   249
    Ilan Oshri, Jatinder Sidhu, and Julia Kotlarsky

8   Status Differentials and Framing
    in the Implementation of Task Migration
    Strategies   281
    Jade Brooks, M. N. Ravishankar, and Ilan Oshri

Part III Shifting from Traditional Sourcing to Digital
         Services

9   The Evolution of Intelligent Automation
    as a Sourcing Option   327
    Leslie Willcocks and Mary Lacity

10 Formal and Relational Outsourcing Governance
    of Artificial Intelligence and Algorithms   355
    Erik Beulen, Albert Plugge, and Jos van Hillegersberg

11 Internet-Based Sourcing: Cloud and Crowdsourcing
    as Delivery Models   393
    Ilan Oshri, Julia Kotlarsky, and Leslie Willcocks

12 A Process Perspective on Emerging Value
    in Tournament-Based and Collaborative Crowdsourcing   425
    Hee Rui He, Julia Kotlarsky, and Dorit Nevo

13 Digitalised Flexible Organisations: Towards
    the Sourcing Future of Work   453
    Leslie Willcocks

14 Emerging Global Sourcing Challenges: Innovation, Net Zero and Digital Transformation   477
   Ilan Oshri, Leslie Willcocks, Heiner Himmerleich, Anthony Vlasic, Hrishi Hrishikesh, and John Hindle

Index   505

Notes on Contributors

Erik Beulen is a Professor of Information Management at the University of Manchester/AMBS, UK. He is also a Professor of Information Management & Digital Transformations at Tilburg University, NL, and the academic director of the executive M.Sc. Information Management & Digital Transformations at TIAS Business School (NL). In addition, he is an external adviser at Bain & Company.

Jade Wendy Brooks is a Lecturer in Information Systems at the University of Auckland Business School, New Zealand. Her research uses mainly qualitative interpretive methods to better understand power (status), knowledge and identity tensions at work. Her research features in scholarly journals such Journal of Information Technology, Information Systems Journal and others.

Jens Dibbern is Professor of Information Systems at the University of Bern, Department of Business Administration in Switzerland. His research focuses on IT sourcing, platform ecosystems, system implementation/use and distributed collaboration. His publications appeared in Information Systems 20 Research (ISR), Management Information Systems Quarterly (MISQ), Journal of Management Information Systems (JMIS), Journal of the Association of Information Systems (JAIS) and others. He has been Associate Editor of MISQ and currently serves as Senior Editor of JAIS and MISQ Executive; he is also department Editor of Business & Information Systems Engineering (BISE).

Hee Rui He is an Associate Professor in Information Systems and Management at the School of Management, Wenzhou Business College, China. He achieved a Ph.D. from Aston University. His research focuses on crowdsourcing, value co-creation and business sustainability.

Heiner Himmerleich is Partner and Director, Technology & Digital Transformation, and Global Segment Leader for Technology Sourcing at BCG based in Amsterdam, Netherlands.

John Hindle is managing partner of Knowledge Capital Partners. He has an extensive international business background as a senior marketing executive and adviser to companies in the US and Europe. He is Vice Chair of the IEEE P2755 Intelligent Process Automation Working Group, a multilateral standards initiative for the growing Intelligent Process Automation industry. He holds a doctoral degree from Vanderbilt University and has held Adjunct Professorships in Human and Organisational Development with Vanderbilt, and International Marketing with New York University in London. He is a past Trustee of Vanderbilt University. He has published many papers on outsourcing, reengineering and automation and is co-author of *Becoming Strategic with Robotic Automation* (Stratford: SB Publishing).

Hrishi Hrishikesh is Partner and Director, Digital Transformation at BCG based in New Jersey, USA.

Julia Kotlarsky is a Professor of Information Systems at the University of Auckland Business School, New Zealand. Her research interests revolve around technology sourcing and innovation, digital transformation, digital sustainability and interface between artificial intelligence and humans. Her work was published in leading academic journals and books. Her publications are based on research conducted in companies such as IBM, Tata Consultancy Services, SAP, Infosys, Cognizant, Pactera and many others.

Oliver Krancher is an Associate Professor in the Business IT department of IT University of Copenhagen, Denmark. He holds a Ph.D. from University of Bern. His research interests revolve around knowledge processes in the development, use and management of information systems. He has published in outlets such as the Journal of Management Information Systems, the Journal of the Association of Information Systems, and the Proceedings of the International Conference on Information Systems. Prior to his academic career, he served as a consultant in enterprise software and outsourcing projects.

Mary C. Lacity is the David D. Glass Chair and Distinguished Professor of Information Systems in the Sam M. Walton College of Business at the University of Arkansas, USA. She was previously Curators' Distinguished Professor at the University of Missouri and has held visiting positions at MIT, the London School of Economics, Washington University, and Oxford University.

Eleni Lioliou is a Lecturer in International Business and Strategy at Queen Mary, University of London, UK. She has published her research in leading journals such as the Journal of World Business, Information Systems Journal, Journal of Information Technology and International Business Review. She is a core member of the Global Sourcing Research Interest Group at the University of Loughborough and an associate of the Outsourcing Research Unit at the London School of Economics. She also serves on the editorial board of the Journal of Information Technology.

Xiaohui Liu is a Professor in International Business at the University of Birmingham, UK. She has published widely in various journals, including Strategic Management Journal, the Journal of International Business Studies, Research Policy, Entrepreneurship Theory and Practice, Journal of World Business, Strategic Entrepreneurship Journal, Management International Review, International Business Review and Management and Organization Review. Her research has been funded by the ESRC, the Leverhulme Trust, the British Academy and the National

Natural Science Foundation of China. She has won Best Competitive Paper awards from the Academy of International Business (UK) and International Association for Chinese Management Research. She is Advisory Editor of *Research Policy* and serves on the editorial board of *Strategic Entrepreneurship Journal*, *International Business Review*, *Asian Business & Management* and the *Journal of Chinese Economic and Business Studies*. She is General Secretary of the Chinese Economic Association (UK) and a member of ESRC Peer Review College.

Dorit Nevo is a Professor of Management Information Systems at the Lally School of Management, USA. She joined RPI in 2012, and prior to that was an Associate Professor at the Schulich School of Business in Toronto. She obtained her B.A. and M.S. in Economics (Israel) and Ph.D. in Management Information Systems from the University of British Columbia (Canada). Since joining RPI, she held various administrative roles in addition to her teaching and research activities. Her research focuses on interactions between computers and their users within the business environment. Her work was published in leading academic and business journals including MIS Quarterly, Information Systems Research, Journal of Management Information Systems, Sloan Management Review and the Wall Street Journal.

Ilan Oshri is Professor of Information Systems and the Director of the Centre of Digital Enterprise at the University of Auckland Business School, New Zealand. His research interests revolve around sourcing, digital transformation, digital sustainability and emerging technologies. He conducted research and advisory with global firms such as IBM, Tata Consultancy Services, Boston Consulting Group, KPMG, Accenture and many others. His work was published in leading international journals. He has published 22 books and dozens of industry reports and teaching cases on global sourcing, digital transformation and emerging technologies.

Albert Plugge is a Senior Research Fellow at Nyenrode Business University, the Netherlands, and holds a Ph.D. in the field of Information Management. He lectures on information systems, information technology, strategic sourcing and digital business ecosystems. His research interests correspond to digital business ecosystems and IS governance in general and the impact of ESG on sourcing relationships in particular.

M. N. Ravishankar is Professor of Technology & Globalisation, and Dean & Head of Queen's Management School, UK. He works with a range of start-ups, multinational companies and public sector organisations globally. He has published peer-reviewed articles on the management of digital innovations, social entrepreneurship and global technology sourcing. His research has appeared in scholarly journals such as Information Systems Research, Journal of World Business, Information Systems Journal, European Journal of Information Systems and Journal of Strategic Information Systems.

Jatinder Sidhu is Professor of Management at Leeds University Business School, UK. Previously, he held various academic positions at the Rotterdam School of Management (RSM), Erasmus University, Netherlands, He earned his Ph.D. degree at the Tinbergen Institute, Erasmus School of Economics, Netherlands. His research has appeared in a variety of prestigious journals including Industrial and Corporate Change, Journal of Management, Journal of Management Studies, Journal of Product Innovation Management, Organization Science and Organization Studies. He serves on the Scientific Council of the European Academy of Management (EURAM) and as Editor for European Management Review, EURAM's peer-reviewed journal.

Jos van Hillegersberg is Professor Dr. and Academic Director of JADS.nl (Jheronimus Academy of Data Science) based in Den Bosch, the Netherlands. JADS is a 50/50 collaboration between TU/e Eindhoven and Tilburg University. He is also Professor of Design and Implementation of Information Systems at the University of Twente (0.2). He conducts research into innovative ICT for supply chain systems.

Anthony Vlasic is Partner and Associate Director, Technology Sourcing, at BCG based in Sydney, Australia.

Leslie Willcocks is Professor Emeritus at the London School of Economics and Political Science, Associate Fellow of Green Templeton College, Oxford (UK), and Co-Editor of the Journal of Information

Technology and JIT Teaching Cases. He has an international reputation for his work on automation and the future of work; ITO/BPO outsourcing; cloud computing; digital business; strategy; automation; IT and innovation; organisational change; and global business management. He has published 75 books and over 200 refereed papers in journals such as *Harvard Business Review*, *California Management Review*, *Sloan Management Review*, *Journal of Management Studies*, and *MIS Quarterly*. His recent books include: *Global Business: Strategy in Context* (SB Publishing, 2021); *Global Business: Management* (SB Publishing, 2021); and edited, with Nik Hassan, Advancing *Theories in Information Systems Volume 1: Rationale and Processes* (Palgrave Macmillan, 2021).

List of Figures

Fig. 2.1	Multisourcing arrangement: **a** dyadic and triadic relationships, **b** levels of analysis	21
Fig. 2.2	Research model	24
Fig. 2.3	**a–d**. Interaction plots (standardized variables, high [low] values are one standard deviation above [below] the mean)	46
Fig. 3.1	Direct and guardian models	68
Fig. 3.2	Research model	70
Fig. 3.3	Informal governance affecting joint performance under strong versus weak client's architectural knowledge	78
Fig. 3.4	Guardian model (versus direct model) affecting joint performance under strong versus weak governance	98
Fig. 3.5	Guardian model (versus direct model) affecting joint performance under strong versus weak client's architectural knowledge	99
Fig. 3.6	Governance affecting joint performance under direct versus guardian model and under client's weak architectural knowledge	99

Fig. 3.7	Governance affecting joint performance under direct versus guardian model and under client's strong architectural knowledge	100
Fig. 4.1	Guiding research framework	117
Fig. 4.2	Summary of findings	134
Fig. 5.1	Coding scheme	162
Fig. 5.2	Conflict resolution styles, conflict types, and outcomes	166
Fig. 5.3	Spillover effects of BSO conflict types	180
Fig. 5.4	BSO Conflict Resolution Styles and Outcomes Compared to Thomas and Kilmann (1974) (*Note*⁺Added to the Thomas and Kilmann framework (1974). *Inconsistent with prior theory)	181
Fig. 7.1	Conceptual model and hypotheses	255
Fig. 7.2	Moderation effect of expected financial loss	269
Fig. 7.3	Moderation effect of expected service quality decline	269
Fig. 7.4	Moderation effect of political climate favorable to backsourcing	270
Fig. 7.5	Moderation effect of available financial slack	270
Fig. 8.1	The globally distributed finance function	291
Fig. 9.1	Triple-Wins of service automation value are evident across multiple RPA and CA implementations	335
Fig. 9.2	Sourcing options for automation	337
Fig. 9.3	Intelligent automation action principles (*Source* Lacity et al. [2021])	342
Fig. 10.1	Governance of Artificial Intelligence and algorithms outsourcing research framework (interrelations between formal and relational governance and psychological contract are based on Lioliou et al. (2014 – Fig. 2, p. 520)	363
Fig. 10.2	Overview of core statements and findings	375
Fig. 11.1	Actors in the NIST cloud computing reference architecture	403
Fig. 12.1	A process perspective on emerging value in tournament-based and collaborative crowdsourcing	448
Fig. 13.1	The skills demand shift 2019–2030 (*Source* author)	463
Fig. 13.2	Automatable and human work skills 2019–2030	464
Fig. 13.3	Remote working—Four scenarios	467
Fig. 14.1	Digital transformation capabilities (*Source* Leslie Willcocks and John Hindle, 2023)	493

List of Tables

Table 2.1	Sample characteristics	34
Table 2.2	Control variables	35
Table 2.3	Validation results and construct correlations	37
Table 2.4	Descriptive statistics	39
Table 2.5	Regression results	40
Table 2.6	Summary of hypotheses testing results	42
Table 3.1	Sample characteristics	81
Table 3.2	Questionnaire items (CR = composite reliability, AVE = average variance extracted)	83
Table 3.3	Control variables	87
Table 3.4	Descriptive statistics and sample comparison	90
Table 3.5	Bivariate correlations	91
Table 3.6	Regression results	92
Table 4.1	Roles of research participants	121
Table 4.2	Codes and illustrative examples	139
Table 5.1	Research on inter-organizational conflicts in BSO relationships	152
Table 5.2	Sample codes for conflict outcomes	161
Table 5.3	Thirteen conflict case stories	163
Table 5.4	Data collected on 13 conflict stories	192

xxxvii

Table 6.1	Conflicting responsibilities and objectives of SSU and Bus	215
Table 6.2	Rounds of data collection and nature of data collected	216
Table 6.3	Paradoxical tensions in GDW	219
Table 6.4	Defensive behaviors and impact on tensions	225
Table 6.5	Interactive behaviors and impact on tensions	228
Table 6.6	Collaborative behaviors and impact on tensions	231
Table 6.7	Participant roles and data reference codes	242
Table 7.1	Sample information	262
Table 7.2	Descriptive statistics and correlations	266
Table 7.3	Structural equation model (SEM) results for inclination to backsource	267
Table 8.1	Status	293
Table 8.2	Actions and framings	303
Table 8.3	Neutralizing conflict through a second layer of interpretations	306
Table 9.1	Client adoption journeys	339
Table 10.1	Overview of interviewed experts in case organisations	365
Table 11.1	Cloud consumer and cloud provider activities	399
Table 11.2	Characteristics of online sourcing environments	416
Table 12.1	Data sources	430
Table 12.2	The list of interviewees	431
Table 12.3	Value of submission (illustrative quotes)	437
Table 12.4	Value dimensions over time: Firm and crowd perspectives	445
Table 12.5	Value-Related processes over Time	447

1

The Global Outsourcing Pivot: Advances and Challenges

Leslie Willcocks, Ilan Oshri, and Julia Kotlarsky

Introduction

Since 1989, organisations across the world's business, government and non-profit sectors have been increasingly choosing to rely on external service providers for IT hardware, software, telecommunications, cloud computing resources and automation tools, a practice known as information technology outsourcing (ITO). Meanwhile, especially since 1999 and several landmark human resource outsourcing deals, business process outsourcing (BPO) has also increasingly spread across fundamental back office functions like finance and accounting, procurement, legal,

L. Willcocks
LSE, London, UK

I. Oshri (✉) · J. Kotlarsky
University of Auckland, Auckland, New Zealand
e-mail: ilan.oshri@auckland.ac.nz

J. Kotlarsky
e-mail: j.kotlarsky@auckland.ac.nz

real estate, human resources, insurance claims and general administration. By early 2014, global outsourcing contracts for ITO and BPO services exceeded US$648 billion (ITO $344 billion; BPO $304 billion), according to HFS Research. By the beginning of 2015, the combined total exceeded US$700 billion. By the end of 2016, the global ITO and BPO services market was estimated to be US$1,007 billion (ITO $657 billion; BPO $322 billion) (Snowden & Fersht, 2016). Taking a conservative route through many estimates, we follow Snowden and Fersht (2016) in seeing the market experiencing a 2.2% ITO and a 4.0% BPO compound annual growth through 2016 to end of 2020, reflecting more activities being outsourced, and new service lines and delivery locations added.

More recently, as we argue in our *Handbook of Global Outsourcing and Offshoring* (4th edition), we need to be more circumspect about market data (Oshri et al., 2023). The last six years have seen many differently sourced, often wildly diverging, estimates of size and growth of the ITO and BPO markets. Name changes by interested parties from ITO/BPO to, for example, business services, business process management and/or managed services have only added further confusion. On market size, much depends on the assumptions made, the varying sources used—e.g. declared corporate expenditures, vendor revenues, national statistics—and the services specified—e.g. does some or all consultancy count as outsourcing, which online services count as outsourcing? Taking a more macro-approach, and consistent with the above figures, we estimate IT0 at the end of 2023 as $US 830 billion, and BPO as $US 483 billion. Looking across a range of forecasts, on conservative estimates IT outsourcing services could be expected to grow at 9.1% per annum and business services outsourcing at 9.6% per annum from 2023 to 2030.

But what has been particularly interesting, and we will deal with this in what follows, is how those figures conceal how radically those services have been changing in the period from 2016 to the mid-2020s, from traditional IT and business services, to online enabled and digital services, as a range of major digital technologies have been coming on stream. This amounts to what we call a global outsourcing pivot, which sees a steady transformation in the content of IT and business services, and how they are being delivered. In this chapter, we review major studies to establish a baseline for understanding IT and business services at the beginning of this transformation, in order to assess how far this transformation has progressed, and where it is heading.

IT and Business Services Sourcing Studies

The most comprehensive review of the global sourcing literature has been Lacity et al. (2016). It synthesised previous studies, including previous reviews by Lacity et al. (2010, 2011) and updated their findings to 2014. It indicated signs of the 'outsourcing pivot' from traditional IT and business services, towards more digital technologies supporting and requiring online enabled and digital services. The study provides a robust baseline for understanding global sourcing as practised at the beginning of the transformation of the global sourcing industry. The research and analysis was very comprehensive. We provide only selective findings here.

The authors found six sets of **major influences on sourcing decisions**:

- Client firm characteristics—an organisation experienced in outsourcing with a wide degree of internationalisation was more likely to outsource, while centralised organisation structures inhibited outsourcing decisions.
- Sourcing motivation—the main reasons were cost reduction, access to expertise and skills, quality improvement, enabling flexibility, refocus on core capabilities and access to global markets.
- Transaction attributes—outsourcing was attractive if service was standardised, knowledge formalised and where external production provided a cost advantage. However, high transaction costs and service complexity were inhibitors to the outsourcing decision.
- Client firm capabilities—having technical and methodological capabilities made outsourcing attractive.
- Provider firm capabilities—the big attractor here for clients was domain understanding.
- Country characteristics—the country of the service provider needed to be attractive financially and in terms of business environment.

On **determinants of positive sourcing outcomes**, the study found the following major influences:

- Client firm capabilities—the client needed to be ready for outsourcing, have absorptive capacity for the changes and new relationships, a strong transition management capability, and suitable technical and methodological capabilities.
- Provider firm capabilities—the provider needed to be strong in human resources management and technical and methodological capabilities.
- Service sourcing decisions—success was identified with offshoring and multisourcing decisions.
- Contractual governance—contracts needed to be detailed, with strong control mechanisms, and clear and applied key performance indicators.
- Relational governance—the strong success factors here were strong communication, effective knowledge sharing, trust, relational governance, commitment and cooperation by all parties, and good client-provider alignment and interface design.

There were inhibitors to success. Thus, on transaction attributes, where there were measurement difficulties, risk and/or complex transaction types, success was less certain. On country characteristics, cultural distance adversely affected success. Interestingly, provider and client firm characteristics, along with length of relationships between the client and provider, seemed to have little impact on success or otherwise.

The study came to several major conclusions about the state of global sourcing:

Levels of success. 48% of organisations studied reported beneficial outcomes from outsourcing business services, 30% reported unbeneficial outcomes, and 21% reported no significant changes in performance after outsourcing. The degree of outsourcing can also be used to calculate an overall 'batting average'. It revealed mixed results: 29% of the findings reported beneficial results from greater degrees of outsourcing, 36% reported unbeneficial outcomes, and 36% reported no significant changes in performance. Clearly much depends on the factors listed above as to whether outsourcing is successful or otherwise.

Contractual and relational governance. These are more complex than previously thought. Contractual governance and relational governance were substitutes that oscillated over time in that sometimes the partners relied more on contractual governance and sometimes they relied more on relational governance. Formal controls (i.e. contractual governance) and informal controls (i.e. relational governance) were simultaneously complements and substitutes. The relationship between contractual and relational governance oscillated between complements and substitutes based on goal fuzziness, goal conflict and goal misalignment.

Industry effects remained a mystery. Industry differences among client firms have been examined repeatedly with mixed and inconsistent results. Lacity et al. (2016) found that in ten studies a client's industry was not significant, meaning that clients from some industries were equally likely to outsource, offshore or erect a captive centre than clients from other industries. But in nine studies industry did matter for outsourcing or for the degree of outsourcing. It may well be that 'industry' is a research 'cul de sac', and not worth pursuing as a factor, and that client and provider capabilities are more influential, regardless of industry.

The Global Outsourcing Pivot

What do we know about the timing of this global outsourcing pivot? Telling evidence is provided by Snowden and Fersht (2016). Looking at global IT services in 2016, they found the following:

Applications Development and management services

- Rising demand to transition to more digital platforms
- More contracts moving to more output-centric models
- Expect proactive service providers attempting collaborative innovation models

- Apps importance sees increase in on-shore and internal teams—shifting to orchestrated development through DevOps.

IT Infrastructure market

- Demand 'in free-fall'—moves towards 'asset light' and cloud-based hybrid solutions
- Decline in traditional services across all regions
- 'Too many suppliers chasing too few deals'.

Professional IT Services

- Rising areas—digital transformation, governance, security, automation
- DevOps and Service Orchestration were helping to lead client transformation journeys.

The significant figures are that in 2016 the traditional IT services market was recorded at $US 550 billion, with a decline rate of 2.4% predicted for the 2016–2020 period, while the As-a-Service market was reported as $US 100 billion with a 21.7% compound annual growth rate for the same period. Here 'As-a-Service IT Services' includes infrastructure/application managed services delivered in a pay-per-use/ As-a-Service/via cloud platform and professional services revenues related to transformation to cloud/SaaS, digital engagement and move to IT-as-Service delivery models.

For the global BPO services market, Snowden and Fersht (2016) noted that:

- Pricing pressures were driving service providers to innovate further.
- 1 in 4 ITO and 1 in 7 BPO contracts were likely to switch provider.
- Clients changing provider were more likely to shift to As-a-Service (46% ITO, 37% BPO).

- CRM and customer care services would move from standard call centre work towards integrated and digital communication with end customers. More enterprises would pursue a technology-led omnichannel strategy with growth in social media, mobile apps, digital platforms and more consultancy opportunities.
- There would be increased bundling of finance and administration (F&A) and IT services, especially in retail and consumer goods, but the sourcing services industry was still dominated by legacy F&A BPO deals in need of better automation and analytics.
- There was a big trend towards shared service/global business service centres and consolidation/transformation. In 2016, 27% offshore work was global in-house centres.

According to Snowden and Fersht (2016), the traditional BPO market was $130 billion and set to grow at 2.6% per annum from 2016 to 2020, while As-a-Service BPO stood at $40 billion with a growth rate of 8.6% over the same period. Here 'As-a-Service BPO' includes BaPaaS and related platform-based business process services delivered in a pay-per-use / transactional / As-a-Service fashion. The study noted that there was a larger base of 'As-a-Service' in business process than in IT services, but it would register slower growth.

Willcocks et al. (2017) noted that cloud sourcing is potentially enormously disruptive of more traditional outsourcing models, and so it has proven (see below). One reason is that cloud computing enables and amplifies the effects of other emerging technologies, and in particular blockchain, mobile, social media, analytics, automation of knowledge work (robotic process automation, cognitive automation, AI), robotics, the Internet of Things, augmented reality and digital fabrication. Willcocks et al. (2017) speculated—correctly, it turns out—that the speed with which these emerging technologies and related services would eat into the traditional ITO and BPO models and markets was being overestimated, and that there would be a huge amount of legacy enterprise ITO and BPO in play for a decade or more, not least to enable organisations to move increasingly in the direction of more digital operations.

Lacity et al. (2016) noted previous studies recommending academic research progress on cloud sourcing, shared services, captive centres, bundled services, rural outsourcing, crowdsourcing and freelance sourcing. In practice, they found cloud services, including Infrastructure-As-a-Service (IaaS), Software-as-a-Service (SaaS) and Platform-as-a-Service (PaaS), had exploded in the 2010–2016 period. The size of the cloud services market was estimated by Forrester Research to be over US$100 million worldwide in 2015. Meanwhile, an ABI-Inform search revealed 1,203 articles on the subject published between 2011 and 2015. Before this date, there were only 269 articles. Lacity et al. (2016) believed that cloud sourcing represents such a paradigm shift in the provision of services that it warranted its own special review, so cloud services were excluded from their 2016 study.

The Move to Digital

According to HFS Research (2023), for 2024, organisations expected to increase their ITO services spending by 6.3%, their BPO services spending by 5.2% and their overall technology spending by 9.3%. The main enabling technologies these organisations were looking to work with were, in priority order: AI machine learning, generative AI, 5G, process automation, analytics, Internet of Things, cloud (public, private, hybrid, edge computing, conversational AI, Metaverse and IAops). This suggests that a lot of innovation was being planned, on top of the many technologies already adopted. Clearly, organisations were also looking to BPO/IT suppliers to help operationalise these technologies. This is more evidence in support of our argument for a major global sourcing and technology pivot from 2016 to 2017.

Our argument is consistent with Gupta and Fersht (2023) who also posit a transition from labour to technology (especially AI) arbitrage as a basis for BPO/ITO services. The potential to 2025, according to these researchers, is 30% more productivity, 5–10% improvements year on year and much better outcomes. From 2026 to 2030, they posit an additional 30–70% productivity on IT operations and business scope much more autonomous decision-making and exception processing, and more end-to-end enterprise working. But, of course all this depends on whether technology suppliers and organisations take the necessary strategic decisions and provide the necessary resources. What seems undebatable going forward is the central role of cloud sourcing.

As Lacity et al. (2016) posited, cloud sourcing has been fundamental to the subsequent outsourcing pivot to supporting digital technologies for clients and using digital technologies for delivering IT and business services.

Let us have a look here, then, at the past growth and future prospects for the IaaS, SaaS and PaaS markets. The main sources used here are Allied Market Research reports from April 2022, February 2022 and August 2021 because they use consistent data collection and analysis methods.

The IaaS Market

According to Allied Market Research (2022a), the global Infrastructure-As-A-Service (IaaS) market was valued at $US 51.3 billion in 2020 and projected to reach $US 481.8 billion by 2030, growing at a CAGR of 25.3% from 2021 to 2030.

The global IaaS market can be segmented on the basis of component type. By component, it is divided into storage, network, computer and several smaller types. IaaS is also deployed as private, public and hybrid models. IaaS is utilised by small and medium enterprises (SMEs) and large organisations. Major industries using IaaS are banking, financial services and insurance (BFSI), government and education, healthcare, telecommunication and IT, retail, manufacturing, and media and entertainment. The IaaS market spans North America, Europe, Asia–Pacific, and Latin America, Middle East and Africa (LAMEA).

The 'compute' segment has the largest market share, due to rising demand for consistent performance, on-demand Application Programming Interfaces (API) and network security. However, the Allied Market Research (2022a, b) expected the 'others' segment to grow at the highest rate across 2021–2030, due to '*increasing need to manage data throughout the lifespan, from conception and storage to archiving at the appropriate time*' all of which stimulates the need for managed IaaS.

A formative development that we highlight in Chapter 13 is that organisations globally are building mobile workforces, with employees accessing data from remote locations through Internet services. Virtualised IT components are needed such as servers, storage and networks. As a common IT infrastructure, IaaS gives faster data access regardless of data centre location. IaaS also has a low initial investment cost—it does not need an on-premise data centre, and the associated ongoing services and maintenance expenditures. By 2024 managed service providers such as Amazon Web Services, Inc., Microsoft Corporation and IBM Corporation were providing continuously available integrated cloud service 24 × 7x365. End customers can experience IaaS as a major cost saver, due to the scale and responsiveness characteristic of pooled cloud servers. Clients pay for use only. End users also can avoid the cost of getting individual servers up. All this will drive the IaaS Infrastructure-as-a-Service market growth across this decade.

The major business sectors mentioned above are rapidly adopting cloud services. A regulated industry like banking is motivated to adopt IaaS on a large scale, not least to achieve cost savings, data protection, regulatory coverage and disaster recovery capability.

The SaaS Market

Meanwhile, the global SaaS market size was valued at $US121.33 billion in 2020 and is projected to reach $702.19 billion by 2030, growing at a CAGR of 18.82% from 2021 to 2030 (Allied Market Research, 2022b). Major SaaS software suites are most typically provided for customer relationship management, enterprise resource planning (ERP), operations management, human resource management (HRM) and supply chain management.

SaaS uses the cloud delivery model. A software provider hosts programmer and associated data on its own network, servers, databases and computing resources. The provider distributes software and services to authorised end users via the Internet. Thus, clients have much less need to install and run software on their own PCs or data centres; they can also opt out of procuring installing and maintaining hardware, and looking after software licenses.

The COVID-19 crisis accelerated SaaS market growth because these platforms provided valuable features like remote access, digital data exchange, automated reporting and real-time work floor control. Also this resulted in a big uptake in more remote working. SaaS can also offer a single solution for many problems. It can integrate applications such as customer relationship management (CRM), business intelligence, supply chain management and e-commerce systems. It can also be customised for specific business needs and deployed across corporate networks on a variety of cloud platforms. Increasingly, businesses require SaaS platforms that build in corporate policies, rules, and processes and compliance with specific business requirements. These kind of apps can also help the rising number of mobile users perform better, improve communication and also corporate efficiency.

Large-scale enterprises are the major buyers and use SaaS for operational efficiencies and to gain strategic and a competitive advantage. The technologies also support discovering new insights on large-scale diverse data, including historical and recent data. SaaS is also suitable for running algorithms and analysis across a large set of data to find relevant relationships, entities and insights. Small and medium enterprises are shifting their business to digital platforms, so that segment is also expected to grow rapidly over the 2024–2030 period.

From early 2023, after the COVID-19 crisis, organisations were focusing on advanced technology such as artificial intelligence (AI), machine learning (ML), Internet of Things (IoT), cloud computing and analytics across industries such as BFSI, healthcare, and IT and telecoms. The driver of rising demand has been the need to perform contactless operation—other factors include increasing use of smart phones and app-based services, the rise in adoption of public and hybrid cloud, the growth of business outsourcing in the global economy as well as adoption of artificial intelligence (AI) and machine learning (ML) across industries such as BFSI, healthcare, and IT and telecoms. However, there are still inhibitors to uptake, for example fears over lack of security of data when using cloud-based platforms, and potential high costs associated with in-house implementation and maintenance of SaaS platform solutions.

The PaaS Market

The global Platform-as-a-Service (PaaS) market was projected to rise from $US56.2 billion in 2020 to $US 164.3 billion in 2026, with a CAGR of 19.6% in that period. It is projected to reach over $319 billion by 2030 (Allied Market Research, 2021).

Platform-as-a-Service (PaaS) provides a broad set of cloud-based application infrastructure and middleware (AIM) resources. A PaaS provider hosts hardware and software on its own infrastructure. As a result, PaaS frees up developers from having to install in-house hardware and software when developing or running a new application.

From 2019, the global Platform-as-a-Service market has been dominated by the application PaaS segment. Together with cloud services and PaaS technological developments, the growing capital investment into application development for mobile, web and enterprise is expected to fuel significant growth for this segment. Other fast growing segments include Business Analytics PaaS (BaPaaS) and API management PaaS (APImPaaS). BaPaaS offers analytical capabilities and tools as a service for visualisation data discovery and predictive modelling. As data management tools, business intelligence (BI) and analytics gather historical and present data, and use statistics and software to research raw information and deliver insights for decision-making.

Platform-as-a-Service (PaaS) offers cost and operational efficiencies for enterprises and developers. It can provide templates and app development tools on a utility basis. This supports easy and innovative application development and delivery. Increased enterprise interest in appliances, strongly backed by rising mobile adoption, will encourage PaaS growth. Indeed, the past few years have seen many major cloud providers enter the PaaS space. The COVID-19 pandemic was undoubtedly highly beneficial to the PaaS industry, with the substantial shift towards the use of online and cloud platforms and increase in the demand for online shopping. Many organisations are anticipating that, with growth in digitalisation, payments would create a cloud native environment and organisations would need to hire a third-party provider, which can use domestic, cross border and regional payment solutions via a single interface. Furthermore, many providers have been planning to manage down the complexities and difficulties associated with moving funds. Digitalisation and online payment product launches are expected to create multiple opportunities for the PaaS market.

Cloud computing offerings have been refined over the last eight years and by 2024 were much more productive, efficient, cheap and rapidly scalable. Compared to traditional methods and teams, at their best PaaS permits more rapid scaling, quicker maintenance and troubleshooting of applications. PaaS can now be accessed with minimum code experience, giving small and medium enterprises agility to plan and execute their operations without the need for an internal IT team or third-party service. Cloud solutions have also made it easier for businesses to cut down their time to market for their applications and services. PaaS also addresses the complexity challenges businesses face. PaaS helps to ease the load on organisations, enabling them to focus on the development and business tasks of the organisation. PaaS can also help extend the capabilities of development teams while eliminating the need to hire additional trained staff for certain operations. Such advantages, and many others, explain the increasing take-up of PaaS, though, of course, no technology new to an organisation comes without its challenges.

Conclusion

By 2017, one of the interesting speculations was whether we were witnessing the death throes of outsourcing. Many were claiming transformative powers for cloud computing (rent as a service over the Internet), digitisation (especially of sourcing and the supply chain), robotic process automation, cognitive automation and AI (move from a labour-centric to a machine-centric model, and the rise of global in-house centres (eliminating external service providers). It has not happened in quite that way. A transformation has been under way, but, as this chapter makes clear, in more complex, longer and less anticipated ways than imagined. In practice, all the indications are that outsourcing will continue to grow, though its content in terms of digital technologies and services will drastically change its character over time. One also needs to factor in that the imbeddedness of legacy systems, and of existing contracts signed for anything between three and ten years, will slow down the impacts of new trends and technologies.

That said, there are real disruptors in the overall growth pattern. As Willcocks et al. (2017) argued, outsourcing will increasingly change its character, as clients require service support for their digital transformations, and vendors themselves adopt new technologies, and build and offer services based on these (see Chapters 11 and 14). Cloud vendors and platform providers are now very large. 'Everything-as-a-Service' looks like a major, if long-term trend—not just data storage, applications, but infrastructure, business processes, and global human and virtual workforces as well, just to name some existing developments.

Globally, the COVID-19 crisis hit many firms hard, but as Oshri et al. (2023) note, it did not alter the need for businesses to prioritise smart sourcing strategies. In our view, global sourcing is undergoing hardly its death throes but a transformation, and we see eight future trends:

- Aggregate spending will continue to rise across global sourcing markets.
- The ITO and BPO markets will continue to grow through both smaller and mega deals.
- Digital resonance (the digital proficiency of a country) will become an important component of the service location decision.
- China's investment in ITO and BPO services is still signalling promise.
- Eco-systems and partnerships will pave the way to achieving innovations.
- The pandemic's impact has been to accelerate both digital transformation initiatives with vendors and deeper investment in internal capabilities.
- More sourcing services will emerge around the data-driven enterprise.
- The theme of sustainability will increasingly arise in sourcing strategies and outsourcing deals (see Chapter 14).

References

Allied Market Research. (2021, August). *Platform as a Service (PaaS) Market.* Allied Market Research, Wilmington.

Allied Market Research. (2022a, April). *Infrastructure as a Service (IaaS) Market.* Allied Market Research, Wilmington.

Allied Market Research. (2022b, February). *Software as a Service (SaaS) Market.* Allied Market Research, Wilmington.

HFS Research. (2023). Draft report, Personal Communication with CEO, Phil Fersht.

Gupta, S., & Fersht, P. (2023). *GBS (Global Business Services) Is Dead. Long Live GBS (Generative Business Services).* HFS Services website August 21.

Lacity, M., Khan, S., & Yan, A. (2016). Review of the Empirical Business Services Sourcing Literature: An Update and Future Directions. *Journal of Information Technology, 31,* 3. https://doi.org/10.1057/jit.2016.2

Lacity, M., Khan, S., Yan, A., & Willcocks, L. (2010). A Review of the IT Outsourcing Empirical Literature and Future Research Directions. *Journal of Information Technology, 25,* 395–433.

Lacity, M., Solomon, S., Yan, A., & Willcocks, L. (2011). Business Process Outsourcing Studies: A Critical Review and Research Directions. *Journal of Information Technology, 26,* 221–258.

Lacity, M., & Willcocks, L. P. (1998). An Empirical Investigation of Information Technology Sourcing Practices: Lessons from Experience. *MIS Quarterly, 22*(3), 363–408.

Oshri, I., Kotlarsky, J., & Willcocks, L. (2023). *A Handbook of Global Outsourcing and Offshoring* (4th ed.). Palgrave Macmillan.

Snowden, J., & Fersht, P. (2016). *The HFS Market Index—IT Services and BPO Market Size and Forecast 2016–2020.* HFS Research.

Willcocks, L., Lacity, M., & Sauer, C. (2017). *Outsourcing and Offshoring Business Services.* Palgrave Macmillan.

Part I
Governing Traditional Outsourcing Services

2

The Governing Mechanisms of Successful Multisourcing Projects

Oliver Krancher, Ilan Oshri, Julia Kotlarsky, and Jens Dibbern

Introduction

Information systems (IS) multisourcing—the practice of contracting *interdependent* IS services to two or more vendors (Bapna et al., 2010; Wiener & Saunders, 2014a)—has become an increasingly popular sourcing model. This chapter together with Chapters 3–6 focuses on multisourcing. Unlike traditional outsourcing arrangements characterized by a dyadic client-vendor relationship, *multisourcing* arrangements

---

Chapter 2 is a revised and updated version of Krancher, O., Oshri, I., Kotkarsky, J., & Dibbern, J. (2022). Bilateral, Collective, or Both? Formal Governance and Performance in Multisourcing. *Journal of the Association of Information Systems, 23*(5), 1211–1234.

O. Krancher
ITU, Copenhagen, Denmark

I. Oshri (✉) · J. Kotlarsky
University of Auckland, Auckland, New Zealand
e-mail: ilan.oshri@auckland.ac.nz

J. Dibbern
Bern University, Bern, Switzerland

© The Editor(s) (if applicable) and The Author(s), under exclusive licence to Springer Nature Switzerland AG 2024
L. Willcocks et al. (eds.), *Transformation in Global Outsourcing*, Technology, Work and Globalization, https://doi.org/10.1007/978-3-031-61022-6_2

require vendors to interact with each other due to interdependencies between the services they deliver as part of a larger integrated service to a client (Wiener & Saunders, 2014b). Therefore, clients embarking on a multisourcing journey not only need to ensure that each vendor, individually, delivers its respective service to the client's satisfaction (*individual performance*), but also that the overall service meets expectations so that interdependencies and conflicts between vendors are effectively addressed (*joint performance*). Moreover, given the complexity inherent to the management of interdependencies among multiple vendors, clients will aspire to achieve a high degree of *governance efficiency*. In this chapter, we examine the formal governance mechanisms clients can use to achieve these three facets of multisourcing success.

Although the existing outsourcing and control literatures provide useful foundations for investigating the relationship between formal governance and success in IS outsourcing, we note three important gaps in the context of IS multisourcing. First, the literature focuses on *success* in dyadic outsourcing relationships (Gopal & Gosain, 2010; Tiwana & Keil, 2009); however, multisourcing arrangements present a more complex setting in which both dyadic relationships (between the client and each vendor) and collective relationships (between the client and the set of vendors) exist (see also Fig. 2.1). In such settings, clients are likely to exercise governance mechanisms to ensure high levels of individual performance from each vendor, as well as high levels of joint performance, while also being mindful of the importance of governance efficiency. Although multisourcing settings call for the application of these three performance dimensions, there is little research and empirical observation that focuses on these three distinct dimensions of *multisourcing success*.

Second, while the existing literature emphasizes outcome control (i.e., the client's efforts to formally specify and monitor outcomes) as a key determinant of success (Choudhury & Sabherwal, 2003; Gopal & Gosain, 2010; Maruping et al., 2009), there are two types of outcome control in multisourcing: bilateral outcome control and collective outcome control. In *bilateral outcome control*, clients specify and monitor the outcomes to be achieved by each vendor individually. In contrast, in *collective outcome control*, the client specifies

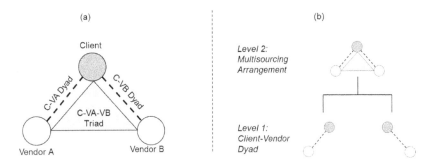

Fig. 2.1 Multisourcing arrangement: a dyadic and triadic relationships, b levels of analysis

and monitors the outcomes to be jointly achieved by the vendors. While bilateral outcome control can help establish accountability, collective outcome control potentially offers greater flexibility, gives vendors greater autonomy, and helps establish cooperative norms among vendors. Although existing research adumbrates the distinction between bilateral and collective approaches (Aubert et al., 2016; Bapna et al., 2010), there is little empirical evidence showing how these two types of formal governance affect multisourcing success. Moreover, the effects of combining both mechanisms in the same multisourcing arrangement are unclear.

Third, the interdependent nature of services in multisourcing potentially sets up a blame game between vendors (Bhattacharya et al., 2018). Conflict resolution *between vendors* is therefore imperative to achieving desired outcomes. Given the unique risk of between-vendor conflict in multisourcing, *conflict management procedures* (often specified through operational-level agreements) can help vendors resolve conflicts by themselves (Bapna et al., 2010; Barboza et al., 2011). However, empirical research on the effect of between-vendor conflict management procedures is lacking. It is also unclear how conflict management procedures affect multisourcing success if they are combined with outcome control-based mechanisms.

In light of these gaps, our research aimed to address the following question: *How does the interplay between bilateral outcome control, collective outcome control, and conflict management procedures affect success in multisourcing arrangements?*

To address this question, we developed a conceptual model that distinguishes between the two levels at which interactions take place in multisourcing settings: the dyadic client-vendor level and the triadic client-vendors level, as shown in Fig. 2.1. We then developed hypotheses and tested them using survey data from 189 multisourcing arrangements. The results provide novel insights into how formal governance mechanisms and the interactions between them affect different dimensions of success in multisourcing arrangements. A key implication from our results is that clients face a trade-off between focusing on individual performance through a bilateral governance approach versus focusing on a coherent, integrated service and governance efficiency through a collective governance approach.

Theoretical Background and Hypotheses

Multisourcing: Background

Multisourcing has become a common sourcing model. However, while multisourcing can help clients to access best-of-breed resources and reduce the risks associated with dependence on a single vendor, it also presents clients with considerable management challenges (Barboza et al., 2011; Krancher & Stürmer, 2018; Łoboda, 2013). At the heart of the management challenges is the need to cope with *interdependencies* between services provided by different vendors (Bapna et al., 2010; Wiener & Saunders, 2014a). As an example, a large European logistics service provider delegated the development of state-of-the-art software for the mobile devices used by its letter carriers to a team of six vendors. Each of the vendors developed a separate set of modules for the software, but it was essential that the modules fitted together to form an integrated, coherent software application. To deal with these interdependencies, the client urged the vendors to help each other, exchange information on a regular basis, and accommodate unforeseen changes (Hurni et al., 2015; Tomczak, 2015).

Although multisourcing arrangements, as in the above example, involve multiple vendors and rely on collaboration between vendors, the arrangements are based on a set of dyadic contracts between the client and each individual vendor (Barboza et al., 2011). Figure 2.1a illustrates a multisourcing arrangement involving two vendors. The arrangement encompasses two dyadic relationships, C-VA (i.e., Client-Vendor A) and C-VB, with each relationship based on a separate contract. However, reducing the arrangement to these two dyads creates an incomplete representation of multisourcing by overlooking the interdependencies between the services provided by vendor A and vendor B. These interdependencies come into the picture only if the arrangement is conceptualized as a triad involving the client, vendor A, and vendor B. As Fig. 2.1b illustrates, the dyadic and triadic relationships make a multisourcing arrangement a multilevel phenomenon (Klein & Kozlowski, 2000), where multiple client-vendor dyads (level 1) are nested within the multisourcing arrangement (level 2).

Acknowledging the multilevel nature of multisourcing is important as clients make formal governance decisions at both the level of the dyad and the level of the multisourcing arrangement. Further, success is measured on both these levels. We next elaborate on clients' formal governance choices and success dimensions at these two levels.

Formal Governance in Multisourcing

In line with the outsourcing and control literatures, we use the term *formal governance* to refer to the client's use of document-based mechanisms to regulate the behavior of vendors (Goo et al., 2009; Gulati et al., 2012; Poppo & Zenger, 2002). In contrast to formal governance, relational governance is based on shared beliefs that result from social processes (Poppo & Zenger, 2002). The single-sourcing research points to the relevance of both formal and relational governance (Huber et al., 2014; Lacity et al., 2009; Lioliou et al., 2014). However, the multisourcing research emphasizes the importance of formal governance (Bhattacharya et al., 2018) and the challenges of enacting relational governance in multisourcing relationships, which are characterized by competition between vendors (Bapna et al., 2010, p. 789). Our focus in this paper is therefore formal governance.

We distinguish three formal governance mechanisms in multisourcing: bilateral outcome control, collective outcome control, and conflict management procedures (see also the left-hand side of our research model in Fig. 2.2). In line with the control literature, we use the term *outcome control* to describe the extent to which a client attempts to regulate vendor behavior by specifying and monitoring outcomes (Keil et al., 2013; Kirsch, 1996; Rustagi et al., 2008). Outcome control can be of two different types in multisourcing: bilateral and collective. In bilateral outcome control, the client specifies and monitors outcomes to be achieved by each vendor individually. In contrast, in *collective outcome control*, the client specifies and monitors the outcomes to be jointly achieved by the vendors. This distinction echoes a suggested difference between individual and integrated service-level agreements identified by Bapna et al. (2010), although outcome control emphasizes not only the specification of outcomes (i.e., service-level agreements), but also their monitoring.

To illustrate the difference between bilateral and collective outcome control, consider the multisourcing project implemented by the logistics service provider mentioned above, which involved the development of several application modules by different vendors. In this project, the client could specify and monitor outcomes related to a single module, such as the output data the module should produce, the response times the module should adhere to, and the module development time. Since these criteria refer to outcomes to be met by a particular vendor, they

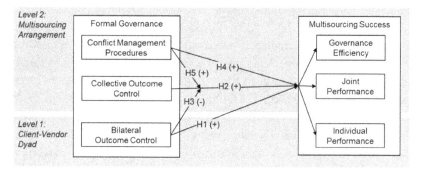

Fig. 2.2 Research model

reflect bilateral outcome control. The client could also specify and monitor the end-to-end business process enabled by all modules, or the response times resulting from the interaction of modules assigned to different vendors. These examples are instances of collective outcome control, as they refer to outcomes to be jointly produced by the vendors. The examples also illustrate that bilateral outcome control may vary for different dyads within a multisourcing arrangement, whereas collective outcome control does not. A client may tightly specify and monitor the outcomes of vendor A, but not vendor B (different levels of bilateral outcome control for each dyad), while the extent to which the client specifies and monitors joint outcomes is a property of the multisourcing arrangement.

The multisourcing literature also alludes to a third type of formal governance in multisourcing where clients specify conflict management procedures that define how vendors should resolve conflicts between themselves—a mechanism commonly known as operational-level agreements (OLAs) (Bapna et al., 2010; Barboza et al., 2011; Oshri et al., 2015). Although conflict management between client and vendor has been studied in the outsourcing literature (Goo et al., 2009; Kale et al., 2000; Lacity & Willcocks, 2017), conflict management procedures in multisourcing are unique in that they regulate the resolution of conflict between vendors without the client's involvement (Bapna et al., 2010; Barboza et al., 2011). Because conflict management procedures apply to the interactions between vendors, they are a property of the multisourcing arrangement rather than a particular client-vendor dyad.

Multisourcing Success

The vast majority of IS outsourcing studies have examined client success in a dyadic relationship with a single vendor. Examined from the client firm's perspective, indicators of success highlight the financial performance of the client firm (Wang et al., 1997), improved service levels (Dibbern et al., 2004), and the quality of the relationship with the vendor (Grover et al., 1996; Lee & Kim, 1999). These studies focus on what we term individual performance, i.e., the degree to which the services rendered by an individual vendor meet the client's expectations. Individual performance is thus a property of the client-vendor dyad.

Contrary to the dyadic setting, the multisourcing setting requires interactions between the different vendors in order to coordinate interdependencies between services outsourced to them (Wiener & Saunders, 2014b). To resolve interdependencies, client and vendors need to coordinate activities and information to ensure that the interdependent services are successfully integrated in a coherent whole IT service (Angst et al., 2017; Bapna et al., 2010). High levels of individual performance by each vendor are not sufficient to guarantee a high level of *joint performance*, i.e., the degree to which the combined performance of interdependent vendors meets the client's expectations, including cost savings. For instance, there can be two interdependent modules in a multi-module software development project. While vendor A may deliver software module A as per the contract (signifying high individual vendor performance), vendor A may fail to agree with vendor B on the interface required to ensure that module B and module A are easily integrated. Thus, although vendor B also fulfills its contractual obligations (again signifying high individual vendor performance), the client will be unable to perform the end-to-end business process because module B does not integrate well with module A (signifying low joint vendor performance). Achieving high joint vendor performance is particularly demanding for the client, because while outsourcing contracts are legally binding between the client and each vendor, they do not typically contain a legally binding statement covering joint vendor performance.

The third dimension of multisourcing success is governance efficiency, i.e., the degree to which coordinating, guiding, and monitoring interdependent vendors is free of effort for the client (Dibbern et al., 2012). Although the governance efforts required from the client can also be substantial in single-sourcing setting (Dibbern et al., 2008), they can increase even further in multisourcing arrangements due to the need to exchange information with multiple vendors, coordinate and integrate services from different vendors, and mitigate against opportunistic behaviors (Alchian & Demsetz, 1972; Bapna et al., 2010). Not surprisingly, management overhead is often cited as one of the most challenging aspects of multisourcing (Angst et al., 2017; Aubert et al.,

2016; Barboza et al., 2011; Wiener & Saunders, 2014b), suggesting that achieving governance efficiency should be a primary objective. Further, because governance efficiency includes efforts for inter-vendor coordination, it is a property of the multisourcing arrangement rather than the client-vendor dyads.

Development of Hypotheses

Figure 2.2 depicts our research model. The model includes five hypothesized relationships between the three types of formal governance (bilateral outcome control, collective outcome control, and conflict management procedures) and three dimensions of multisourcing success (individual performance, joint performance, governance efficiency). Two constructs, bilateral outcome control and individual performance, are relevant at the level of the client-vendor dyad (level 1), while the remaining four constructs are relevant at the level of the multisourcing arrangement (level 2).

Bilateral outcome control: Bilateral outcome control relies on legally binding agreements between the client and the vendor that capture the dyadic dimension of the multisourcing setting. The detailing of expected outcomes according to prespecified performance benchmarks provides clear guidance to the individual vendor on how the client firm will evaluate their performance (Henderson & Lee, 1992). Moreover, with its contractual grounding and explicit focus on deliverables by a particular vendor, bilateral outcome control is a particularly strong mechanism for discouraging opportunistic vendor behavior (Alchian & Demsetz, 1972; Dekker, 2004; Tiwana & Keil, 2009; Wiener & Saunders, 2014b), which may further improve individual performance levels.

High levels of bilateral control may also improve joint performance. Bilateral outcome control requires clients to anticipate interdependencies at the outset of projects and define the outcomes for each vendor in a way that effectively addresses interdependencies. For instance, clear specification of the inputs and outputs of individual software modules to be developed by individual vendors (a type of bilateral outcome control) may be critical for the later smooth integration of the modules into a coherent software system. This is in line with the control literature, which suggests that outcome control can help achieve coordination (Nidumolu & Subramani, 2003).

High levels of bilateral outcome control may also have positive effects on governance efficiency. As suggested by contingency theory (Van de Ven et al., 1976), prespecifying goals and procedures for each vendor, and ensuring adherence to them, is likely to require lower governance effort than the ongoing mutual adjustments across multiple organizational boundaries required in the absence of strong bilateral outcome control. The expectation that bilateral outcome control enhances governance efficiency also aligns with findings in the control literature on efficiency gains associated with the use of outcome control (Gopal & Gosain, 2010). We therefore posit:

H1: Higher levels of bilateral outcome control are associated with greater multisourcing success.

Collective outcome control: In addition to prescribing and monitoring expected outcomes for each individual vendor, clients may also exercise collective outcome control, i.e., they may specify and monitor the outcomes that vendors are expected to jointly achieve. Collective outcome control is likely to be particularly effective for achieving coordination among vendors, and thus, improving joint performance. First, when clients specify and monitor joint outcomes, this helps establish a common understanding of the overall goals to be achieved in the arrangement. A clear and common understanding of goals may allow vendors to mutually align their actions (Okhuysen & Bechky, 2009), even without further involvement from the client. For instance, vendors can refer to an overall expected outcome when they design their individual modules and the interaction between the involved modules. Further, collective outcome control emphasizes outcomes for which a team of vendors are jointly responsible, thus helping to establish cooperative norms between vendors (Johnson, 2003). Cooperative norms promote mutual support and improve coordination, both critical for joint performance. Last but not least, when multisourcing arrangements rely on collective outcome control, they retain the flexibility to change the nature and scope of the sub-tasks for which individual vendors are responsible (Aubert et al., 2016). This allows client and vendors to adjust their coordination approach in response to the learning that occurs over the course of the collaboration (Poston et al., 2009), leading to higher joint performance.

Although collective outcome control is likely to increase joint performance, it may also have beneficial effects on individual performance and governance efficiency. Collective outcome control grants vendors some discretion in the way they create their individual contributions, as long as these individual contributions integrate well with the contributions of other vendors. This will allow knowledgeable vendors to bring to bear their expertise (Tiwana & Keil, 2009), resulting in high individual performance. Collective control may also be a particularly efficient way for clients to manage multisourcing arrangements because it does not involve separate effort in relation to each individual vendor. We therefore argue:

H2: Higher levels of collective outcome control are associated with greater multisourcing success.

Interaction of bilateral and collective outcome control: A key tenet of the literatures on governance and control is that mechanisms often do not act in isolation, but rather complement or substitute each other (Huber et al., 2014; Poppo & Zenger, 2002). As Tiwana (2010) puts it: "Two things are complements if more of one increases the benefits of using the other. They are substitutes if more of one diminishes the benefits of using the other" (p. 88). We expect bilateral and collective outcome control to substitute each other because they undermine each other's strengths in the following ways. First, collective outcome control grants vendors discretion in defining their individual contributions. However, bilateral outcome control eliminates this discretion and thus prevents vendors from leveraging their own expertise for designing individual contributions. Second, collective outcome control may help promote cooperative norms by emphasizing shared responsibility among vendors, whereas bilateral outcome control promotes individualistic, competitive norms by setting the focus on the contributions of the individual vendors, which may undermine cooperative norms (Johnson, 2003).

Third, collective outcome control helps clients and vendors retain some flexibility in determining or changing the individual vendors' contributions at later stages of the collaboration, but bilateral outcome control eliminates this flexibility by requiring clients to specify individual responsibilities at the outset. Further, just as bilateral control may undermine the strength of collective outcome control, collective outcome control may undermine bilateral outcome control as well. Bilateral outcome control is relatively easily enforceable through dyadic contracts; however, its power may be reduced in situations where bilateral control and collective control contradict each other. In such situations, vendors may opportunistically choose to comply with the control that promises the greater gain for them, in the belief that the client's wishes cannot be enforced because of the ambiguities caused by the contradictory controls. We therefore anticipate:

H3: The positive association between collective outcome control and multisourcing success is weaker when bilateral outcome control is strong.

Conflict management procedures: Multisourcing settings may suffer from opportunistic behavior by vendors (Wiener & Saunders, 2014a). In particular, a high degree of performance ambiguity can encourage "blame games" between vendors (Bapna et al., 2010). It is therefore in the client's interest to go beyond the usual client-vendor management procedures used in outsourcing settings to clarify and govern conflict management between vendors. A common example of conflict management procedures is OLAs, which outline the principles for collaboration between vendors (Bapna et al., 2010; Barboza et al., 2011). We expect conflict management procedures to have positive effects on individual performance, joint performance, and governance efficiency for the following reasons.

First, conflict management procedures enhance individual performance and governance efficiency because they give vendors a tool to enforce particular behaviors or outcomes from other vendors without involving the client (Barboza et al., 2011). For instance, if vendor A does not deliver its individual service, vendor B, which depends on vendor A's contribution, may use the conflict management procedures to legitimize its efforts to put pressure on vendor A, leading to higher performance by vendor A without the client's involvement. Moreover, conflict management procedures promote interaction between vendors, which may help build stronger relationships between vendors and thus help reduce opportunistic behavior by individual vendors (Lioliou & Zimmermann, 2015). This can result in higher individual performance without the involvement of the client, which suggests high governance efficiency.

Conflict management procedures can also enhance joint performance. Formal systems for conflict resolution promote two-way communication, joint problem solving, and learning (Dant & Schul, 1992; Goo et al., 2009; Kale et al., 2000). In cases where cognitive conflicts prevent vendors from effectively addressing interdependencies (Conner & Prahalad, 1996; De Dreu & West, 2001), conflict management procedures may help provoke the interactions between vendors required to build common understanding in order to resolve cognitive conflicts. As such:

H4: Higher levels of conflict management procedures are associated with greater multisourcing success.

Collective outcome control and conflict management procedures: We argue that collective outcome control and conflict management procedures complement each other in two ways. First, although collective outcome control is a means to authoritatively communicate the overall goals of the multisourcing arrangement, collective outcome control does not establish accountability for individual contributions. Conflict management procedures, particularly in the form of OLAs, help compensate for this weakness by legitimizing inter-vendor management efforts, thereby supporting vendors in their endeavors to enforce the contributions needed from other vendors to achieve overall goals. Hence, individual accountability is established by the combination of authoritative overall goals through collective outcome control and inter-vendor management as legitimized through conflict management procedures. Second, conflict management procedures help vendors to negotiate common understanding at the more operational level of the cognitive conflicts that can arise in day-to-day work. While it is difficult to negotiate these conflicts without clarity about overall goals, it is also difficult to establish common understanding based only on the high-level understanding engendered through collective outcome control, thus indicating a complementary relationship. We therefore posit:

H5: The positive association between collective outcome control and multisourcing success is stronger when conflict management procedures are strong.

Methods

Sample and Procedure

In line with past IS outsourcing studies (e.g., Goo et al., 2009), we empirically tested our research model through a key informant survey (Pinsonneault & Kraemer, 1993). The questionnaire was administered to organizations spanning a variety of industries in the UK, Germany, France, Italy, Spain, and the US. In countries where English is not the first language, the original English version of the questionnaire was translated and checked by native speakers familiar with outsourcing. Responses were collected through telephone interviews and an online survey.

To gather informants, the questionnaire was distributed among middle- and top-level managers who were familiar with multisourcing arrangements in their firms. To ensure the targeted individuals' familiarity with multisourcing arrangements (thus qualifying them as "key informants"), the respondents needed to answer a set of screening questions and meet the following three criteria: (1) working for an organization with an outsourcing arrangement(s) in place, where a task or project has been consciously divided up and outsourced to different vendors; (2) working for an organization with at least 250 employees; and (3) familiar with the management of such a multisourcing arrangement(s) in their company. The respondents then had to select one particular multisourcing arrangement currently in place in their organization. Within this particular multisourcing arrangement, respondents were asked to select the two vendors contributing the most to the multisourcing arrangement (in terms of amount of work). The questions used to test our model pertained only to this particular multisourcing arrangement for the two chosen vendors, designated as vendor A and vendor B. Focusing on the two most important vendors rather than all vendors allowed us to keep the survey to a manageable size, and ensure the survey was identical for all arrangements. We worded the survey questions to make it clear to respondents whether questions referred to the multisourcing arrangement (level 2), or the relationship with individual vendors (level 1). Questions relating to level 1 were asked twice, once with regard to vendor A and once with regard to vendor B.

Before sending out the final questionnaire, the questionnaire items were pilot-tested with 15 international organizations to ensure that all questionnaire items were understandable and could be answered by the intended group of respondents. Each block of questions was followed by an open field for comments, where respondents pre-testing the survey were asked to note down any thoughts they had on the questions asked in the preceding section. These comments were considered during process of refining the questionnaire. In addition, we tested our model on the pilot data to assess the validity of the constructs. Items that loaded very low were removed from the questionnaire.

The finalized questionnaire was sent out to 2,000 organizations. Overall, 200 usable questionnaires were returned after several follow-ups with the panel of managers. From these 200 cases, 10 were excluded after a review of descriptions of the outsourced tasks. We excluded cases where the sub-tasks assigned to different vendors were not interdependent (e.g., outsourcing IT procurement to vendor A and sales advice to vendor B), or when the outsourced tasks did not match our target services, which were IT services and IT-supported business processes. We also excluded one outlier, which reported a joint performance four standard deviations below the sample mean but above-average individual performance, suggesting an erroneous measurement. Our final sample size was $n_2 = 189$ multisourcing arrangements, in which $n_1 = 378$ client-vendor dyads were embedded. Table 2.1 shows the sample characteristics.

Table 2.1 Sample characteristics

Characteristics of the sample		[Min; max]	Mean (std. dev.)
Respondent working experience	Number of years working in organization	[0.5; 35]	8.6 (6.5)
Age of multisourcing arrangement	Years that have passed since the start of the multisourcing arrangement	[1; 9]	3.7 (2.4)
		Number	Percentage (%)
Client size	250 to 1,000 employees	70	37
	1,001 to 5,000 employees	61	32
	5,001 to 50,000 employees	46	24
	More than 50,000 employees	12	6
Industry sector	Financial services	34	18
	Manufacturing	39	21
	Retail, distribution, and transport	25	13
	Public sector	35	19
	Other	56	30

Measures

Each construct was measured based on multiple items. Where possible, we used existing measures, which we adapted to the study context. All items were measured on a five-point Likert scale, ranging from "strongly disagree" (=1) to "strongly agree" (=5), with "neither agree nor disagree" (=3) as the mid-point. The items related to our focal constructs are shown in the Appendix. The items relating to *collective outcome control* were formulated so that they gathered efforts toward specifying and monitoring outcomes that involved *all vendors at the same time*. Conversely, the items relating to *bilateral outcome control* focused on efforts involving *single vendors*. To enable differential interpretation, we used highly similar items for both constructs, expecting the respondents to focus on all vendors versus one vendor at a time. Table 2.2 shows the operationalization of the control variables. As indicated in the table, we transformed some of the variables to reduce skew.

Table 2.2 Control variables

Country	Single-item question on the client's country (United Kingdom, France, Germany, Italy, Spain, USA); incorporated through five dichotomous dummy variables
Sector	Single-item question on the client's sector (financial services, manufacturing, retail, public sector, other); incorporated through four dichotomous dummy variables
Client size	The client's number of employees, as measured through a single-item question (transformation: natural logarithm)
Concentration one vendor	The fraction of the overall budget for the multisourcing arrangement that is allotted to this particular vendor, as measured through a single-item question (transformation: square root)
Concentration two vendors	The fraction of the overall budget for the multisourcing arrangement that is assigned to vendor A or B (transformation: square root)
Relationship age	Square root of the number of years since the start of the multisourcing arrangement, as measured through a single-item question
Guardian vendor	Where one of the vendors is responsible for managing all other vendors of the multisourcing arrangement, as measured through a single-item question (Bapna et al., 2010)
Architectural knowledge	Measured with three items (CR = 0.81) focusing on the client's knowledge of how the services provided by the vendors are related to each other (based on Henderson & Clark 1990; Takeishi, 2002)
Task interdependence	Measured with four items (CR = 0.77) focusing on the extent to which the tasks of vendor A and B are integrated, tightly coupled, and dependent on each other (based on Tiwana, 2008)

Instrument Validation

We validated our instrument through exploratory factor analysis in SPSS, and through confirmatory factor analysis in AMOS. The exploratory factor analysis identified items with low loadings on their focal construct, or high cross-loadings. As a result, we eliminated one item from bilateral outcome control, one item from conflict management procedures, and one item from governance efficiency (see Appendix). Moreover, to enable differential analysis of bilateral and collective outcome control, we eliminated the item from the collective outcome control construct analogous to the item eliminated from the bilateral outcome control construct.

We then conducted confirmatory factor analysis in AMOS to ascertain the validity of the resulting model. Table 2.3 shows the results for convergent and discriminant validity. The indicators for convergent validity are factor loadings, composite reliability, average variance extracted (AVE), and model fit (Straub et al., 2004). All factor loadings were above 0.6, with their average exceeding 0.7 for all constructs. Composite reliability was above the threshold of 0.7 for all constructs. AVE was above 0.5 for all constructs. Model fit indices were within recommended thresholds (MacKenzie et al., 2011), with an RMSEA of 0.06 (recommended threshold: 0.06), RMR of 0.03 (recommended threshold: 0.08), and CFI of 0.95 (recommended threshold: 0.95). Discriminant validity is indicated by model fit (Straub et al., 2004) and by comparing the square root of the AVE to the inter-construct correlations (Fornell & Larcker, 1981). The construct correlations were below the AVE square roots for all construct pairs, although the construct correlation between bilateral and collective outcome control (0.729) was only marginally below the AVE values (0.734 for collective outcome control and 0.736 for bilateral outcome control). Overall, the evidence supports convergent and discriminant validity. We also examined the threat of common-method bias by adding a latent method factor to our AMOS model (Podsakoff et al., 2003). The coefficient of the latent method factor was 0.00, indicating that common-method bias is unlikely to be a concern in our data.

Estimation Approach

Our regression approach reflects the multilevel nature of our research model, where the triadic multisourcing arrangement is at level 2 and the client-vendor dyad at level 1 (see also Fig. 2.1b). The models predicting

Table 2.3 Validation results and construct correlations

	Composite reliability	Average variance extracted	BOC	COC	CMP	IP	JP	GE
Bilateral outcome control	0.84	0.54	*0.74*					
Collective outcome control	0.84	0.54	*0.73*	*0.73*				
Conflict management procedures	0.85	0.74	*0.49*	0.52	*0.86*			
Individual performance	0.87	0.68	*0.66*	0.50	0.46	*0.83*		
Joint performance	0.87	0.53	*0.55*	0.68	0.52	0.71	*0.73*	
Governance efficiency	0.83	0.70	*0.25*	0.49	0.47	0.35	0.60	*0.84*

Note Figures in the fourth column to the right show construct correlations, with the exception of the diagonal (see figures in italics), which shows square roots of AVE

individual performance present a so-called *macro–micro multilevel situation* (Croon & van Veldhoven, 2007) because they include independent variables at level 2 ("macro", e.g., collective outcome control) that predict a dependent variable at level 1 ("micro", individual performance). Conversely, the models predicting joint performance and governance efficiency present a *micro–macro multilevel situation* because they include independent variables at level 1 ("micro", e.g., bilateral outcome control) that predict a dependent variable at level 2 ("macro", joint performance and governance efficiency) (Croon & van Veldhoven, 2007). In line with established practice in multilevel research, we relied on mixed models with random intercepts to estimate the macro–micro models (i.e., the models predicting individual performance) (Klein & Kozlowski, 2000; West et al., 2007). These models account for the fact that the observations for level-2 variables (e.g., collective outcome control) are not independent because they are identical within the same multisourcing arrangement. To estimate the micro–macro models (i.e., the models predicting joint performance and governance efficiency), we relied on a multilevel manifest covariate (MMC) approach (Lüdtke et al., 2008). This approach involves aggregating level-1 predictors (e.g., individual governance) to level 2 by taking the average of all level-1 observations (in our case: of both dyads) and then using ordinary least squares (OLS) regression. The MMC approach, which is more efficient than alternative approaches, is unbiased when data on all level-1 entities (i.e., on all dyads within the focal multisourcing arrangement) are available (Lüdtke et al., 2008). This condition was met in our analysis because we had data on all dyads that were part of the triadic multisourcing arrangements. As a check for robustness, we also estimated alternative specifications of the micro–macro models where we used the data from only one dyad (i.e., only vendor A or only vendor B) for level-1 variables. We preferred OLS regression to PLS or AMOS in these models because OLS regression is more similar to mixed models than either PLS or AMOS, and also has greater power in the analysis of interaction effects (Goodhue et al., 2007). We verified that the residuals followed a normal distribution and the variance inflation factors were below 10.

Results

Table 2.4 shows the descriptive statistics and 2.3 the bi-variate correlations. Table 2.5 shows the regression results. Models 1a–1c included controls only, where model 1a predicted individual performance, model 1b joint performance, and model 1c governance efficiency. Models 2a–2c included controls and main effects. We used models 2a–2c to test our main effect hypotheses: H1, H2, and H4. Models 3a-3c included controls, main effects, and interaction effects. We relied on models 3a–3c to test the interaction hypotheses: H3 and H5. Table 2.6 summarizes the results of the hypothesis testing.

H1 predicted a positive relationship between bilateral outcome control and multisourcing success. As the results for models 2a–2c show, the relationship was strong, positive, and significant for individual performance ($\beta = 0.40$, $p < 0.001$, model 2a), positive and insignificant for joint

Table 2.4 Descriptive statistics

	n	Minimum	Maximum	Mean	Standard deviation
Client size	189	250	3,000,000	27,494.00	218,903.84
Concentration one vendor	378	1	90	26.61	18.67
Concentration two vendors	189	3	100	53.21	30.81
Guardian vendor	189	0	1	0.30	0.46
Relationship age	189	1	9	3.66	2.39
Architectural knowledge	189	1	5	4.08	0.73
Task interdependence	189	1	5	3.47	0.94
Bilateral outcome control	378	1	5	4.02	0.78
Collective outcome control	189	1	5	4.02	0.75
Conflict management procedures	189	1	5	3.67	1.06
Individual performance	378	1	5	4.15	0.77
Joint performance	189	1.83	5	4.05	0.68
Governance efficiency	189	1	5	4.15	0.80

Note Descriptive statistics show values before transformation (e.g., before standardizing or before drawing square roots)

Table 2.5 Regression results

Predictor/dependent var	Models 1a–c: Controls only			Models 2a–c: Controls and main effects			Models 3a–c: Controls, main and interaction effects		
	a: Ind. Per	b: Jnt. Per	c: Gov. Eff	a: Ind. Per	b: Jnt. Per	c: Gov. Eff	a: Ind. Per	b: Jnt. Per	c: Gov. Eff
Intercept	0.39 (0.22)	0.23 (0.17)	0.41 (0.19)	0.40 (0.19)	0.19 (0.16)	0.41 (0.18)	0.32 (0.19)	0.16 (0.23)	0.26 (0.18)
Client size	0.03 (0.06)	−0.08 (0.07)	−0.01 (0.07)	0.01 (0.05)	−0.07 (0.06)	−0.01 (0.07)	0.03 (0.05)	−0.07 (0.06)	0.01 (0.07)
Concentration one vendor	0.04 (0.07)	−0.11 (0.16)	−0.19 (0.18)	−0.02 (0.07)	−0.11 (0.15)	−0.11 (0.17)	−0.03 (0.07)	−0.15 (0.15)	−0.15 (0.17)
Concentration two vendors	0.01 (0.08)	0.20 (0.16)	0.31† (0.18)	0.02 (0.07)	0.16 (0.15)	0.20 (0.17)	0.03 (0.07)	0.21 (0.15)	0.25 (0.17)
Relationship age	0.14* (0.06)	0.03 (0.07)	0.02 (0.07)	0.11* (0.05)	0.02 (0.06)	0.00 (0.07)	0.10† (0.05)	0.03 (0.06)	0.00 (0.07)
Guardian	−0.13 (0.13)	−0.21 (0.14)	−0.09 (0.15)	−0.09 (0.11)	−0.21 (0.13)	−0.09 (0.14)	−0.06 (0.11)	−0.18 (0.13)	−0.04 (0.14)
Client's architectural knowledge	0.42*** (0.06)	0.52*** (0.06)	0.35*** (0.07)	0.15* (0.06)	0.28*** (0.07)	0.17* (0.08)	0.13* (0.06)	0.25*** (0.08)	0.16* (0.08)
Task interdependence	0.01 (0.06)	0.02 (0.07)	−0.04 (0.07)	−0.05 (0.05)	−0.05 (0.06)	−0.06 (0.07)	−0.05 (0.05)	−0.04 (0.06)	−0.07 (0.07)
Bilateral outcome control	–	–	–	0.40*** (0.06)	0.12 (0.08)	−0.15 (0.09)	0.40*** (0.06)	0.13 (0.08)	−0.16† (0.09)
Collective outcome control	–	–	–	0.03 (0.07)	0.26** (0.08)	0.27** (0.09)	0.08 (0.07)	0.29*** (0.08)	0.36*** (0.10)
Conflict management procedures	–	–	–	0.19** (0.06)	0.16* (0.07)	0.27** (0.08)	0.18** (0.06)	0.13† (0.07)	0.26*** (0.08)

Predictor/ dependent var	Models 1a–c: Controls only			Models 2a–c: Controls and main effects			Models 3a–c: Controls, main and interaction effects		
	a: Ind. Per	b: Jnt. Per	c: Gov. Eff	a: Ind. Per	b: Jnt. Per	c: Gov. Eff	a: Ind. Per	b: Jnt. Per	c: Gov. Eff
Bilateral outcome control × collective outcome control	–	–	–	–	–	–	0.02 (0.05)	−0.15* (0.07)	0.10 (0.08)
Bilateral outcome control × conflict management procedures	–	–	–	–	–	–	−0.02 (0.06)	−0.08 (0.08)	−0.11 (0.08)
Collective outcome control × conflict management procedures	–	–	–	–	–	–	0.12† (0.07)	0.26** (0.08)	0.21* (0.09)
Random intercept variance	0.32	–	–	0.19	–	–	0.21	–	–
Sample size	$n_1 = 378, n_2 = 189$	$n = 189$	$n = 189$	$n_1 = 378, n_2 = 189$	$n = 189$	$n = 189$	$n_1 = 378, n_2 = 189$	$n = 189$	$n = 189$
AIC	973.7	–	–	901.1	–	–	907.7	–	–
ΔF	–	6.20***	3.65***	–	11.72***	7.97***	–	3.97**	3.86*
Adjusted R²	–	0.31	0.18	–	0.42	0.27	–	0.45	0.31

†$p < 0.1$, *$p < 0.05$, **$p < 0.01$, ***$p < 0.001$, standard errors in parentheses, significant numbers in bold, dummy control variables for country and sector not shown

Table 2.6 Summary of hypotheses testing results

Hypothesis/dependent variable	Individual performance	Joint performance	Governance efficiency
H1: Positive effect of bilateral outcome control	√		
H2: Positive effect of collective outcome control		√	√
H3: Negative interaction effect of bilateral and collective outcome control		√	
H4: Positive effect of conflict management procedures	√	√	√
H5: Positive interaction effect of collective outcome control and conflict management procedures	(√)	√	√

Note √: Support, (√): Marginal support

performance ($\beta = 0.17$, $p > 0.1$, model 2b) and negative and insignificant for governance efficiency ($\beta = -0.15$, $p > 0.1$, model 2c). Thus, H1 is supported for individual performance only.

H2 predicted a positive relationship between collective outcome control and multisourcing success. The relationship was positive and significant for joint performance ($\beta = 0.26$, $p < 0.01$, model 2b) and for governance efficiency ($\beta = 0.27$, $p < 0.01$, model 2c), while it was insignificant for individual performance ($\beta = 0.12$, $p > 0.1$, model 2a). Hence, H2 is supported for joint performance and governance efficiency.

H3 predicted a negative interaction effect between bilateral and collective outcome control. In line with this hypothesis, model 3b showed a significant negative interaction effect for joint performance ($\beta = -0.15$, $p < 0.05$, model 3b). Conversely, the interaction effect was insignificant and positive for governance efficiency ($\beta = 0.10$, $p > 0.1$, model 3c) and insignificant and close to 0 for individual performance ($\beta = 0.02$, $p > 1$, model 3a). Hence, H3 is supported for joint performance.

H4 predicted positive associations for conflict management procedures with multisourcing success. The results of models 2a–2c support this hypothesis. Conflict management procedures had positive and significant relationships with individual performance ($\beta = 0.19$, $p < 0.01$. model 2a), joint performance ($\beta = 0.16$, $p < 0.05$, model 2b), and governance efficiency ($\beta = 0.27$, $p < 0.01$, model 2c).

H5 predicted positive interaction effects between collective outcome control and conflict management procedures. Models 3b and 3c showed significant positive interaction effects for joint performance ($\beta = 0.26$, $p < 0.01$) and for governance efficiency ($\beta = 0.21$, $p < 0.05$). Moreover, Model 3a showed a marginally significant positive interaction effect for individual performance ($\beta = 0.12$, $p < 0.1$). Thus, H5 is supported, although with only marginal significance for individual performance.

To examine the robustness of these results, we estimated alternative specifications for the models predicting joint performance and governance efficiency, where we used the data from only one dyad (either vendor A or vendor B) for the level-1 variables instead of averaging data from both dyads. The results of these models were identical, in terms of statistical significance, to those reported above. This suggests that our findings are unlikely to be a statistical artifact of our aggregation approach.

Discussion

This study was motivated by the lack of research examining how formal governance mechanisms specific to multisourcing (bilateral outcome control, collective outcome control, conflict management procedures between vendors) affect success dimensions relevant for multisourcing (individual performance, joint performance, governance efficiency). In this section, we discuss and illustrate our findings for each success dimension, before discussing the contributions and limitations of the research.

Individual Performance

Although coordination between vendors is a challenge in multisourcing, clients will likely also strive to obtain high individual performance from each vendor (i.e., the services delivered individually by the vendor fully meet the client's objectives). Our findings show that bilateral outcome control is a key mechanism for ensuring high individual performance, as it was the strongest predictor of individual performance in our data. It appears that the dyadic specification and monitoring of outcomes inherent to bilateral outcome control are most likely to motivate vendors to deliver their individual contributions according to the client's expectations, and deter them from opportunistic behavior. The use of conflict management procedures is also positively related to individual performance. This finding is in line with our argument that conflict management procedures help deter vendors from "blame-game" attitudes and encourage them to enforce each other's individual contributions, leading to higher individual performance. However, in contrast to expectations, we did not find a significant relationship between collective outcome control and individual performance. Although we argued when developing our hypotheses that collective outcome control grants vendors autonomy and enables them to leverage their expertise, these benefits do not appear to translate into higher individual performance in all circumstances. However, the marginally significant positive interaction effect found between collective outcome control and conflict management procedures suggests the benefits from collective outcome control can translate into higher individual performance if collective outcome control is accompanied by conflict management procedures.

The interaction plot shown in Fig. 2.3a illustrates the interaction between collective outcome control and conflict management procedures. When weak conflict management procedures were in place, collective outcome control did not contribute to individual performance (see the flat, slightly negative slope of the dashed line). Conversely, when strong conflict management procedures were in place, collective outcome control contributed to higher individual performance (see the positive slope of the solid line), supporting a complementary effect. This finding implies that objectives specified through collective outcome control can cascade down to the level of individual performance, but only if conflict management procedures provide the infrastructure through which vendors can break down objectives to the individual level, and then legitimately enforce these contributions from the other vendors.

Joint Performance

While clients will strive to ensure high individual performance from each vendor, a key challenge in multisourcing lies in achieving high joint performance, which implies that interdependencies are effectively addressed. The governance mechanism that most strongly predicted joint performance in our data was collective outcome control. Indeed, collective outcome control aids coordination in multisourcing arrangements by providing vendors with "the big picture", promoting cooperative norms between vendors, and allowing some level of autonomy and flexibility in determining and adjusting individual contributions. Conflict management procedures were also positively and significantly related to joint performance. This finding is in line with our argument that conflict management procedures promote inter-vendor interaction, joint problem solving, and thus the resolution of cognitive conflicts (Dant &

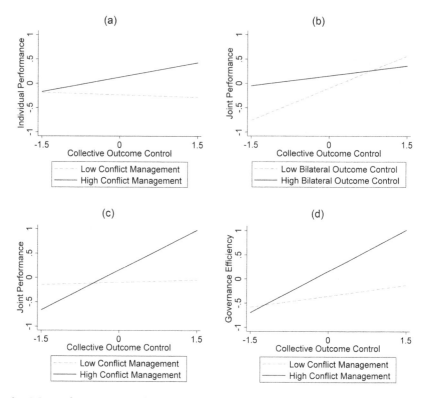

Fig. 2.3 a–d. Interaction plots (standardized variables, high [low] values are one standard deviation above [below] the mean)

Schul, 1992; De Dreu & West, 2001; Kale et al., 2000). The association between bilateral outcome control and joint performance was also positive but not significant. We have argued that bilateral outcome control may support coordination by inviting clients to anticipate interdependencies a priori and define the outcomes for each vendor in a way that effectively addresses interdependencies. However, it may be that such a-priori specification of individual contributions is too static to allow for smooth coordination over the course of multisourcing arrangements, which are typically several years long.

Our analysis also revealed two interactive effects of formal governance mechanisms on joint performance. Figure 2.3b illustrates the negative interaction between bilateral and collective outcome control, showing a steeper line for low than for high bilateral outcome control. This indicates that the benefits from collective outcome control diminish when bilateral outcome control is high, supporting a substitutional effect. It is interesting to compare multisourcing arrangements that relied on high versus low levels of collective outcome control, as also shown in Fig. 2.3b. Multisourcing arrangements reliant on high levels of collective outcome control achieved similar joint performance irrespective of whether they relied on high or low levels of bilateral outcome control (see the relatively close plotted lines at the right-hand side of Fig. 2.3b). In these arrangements, it appears that the benefits from the use of bilateral outcome control (i.e., the anticipated interdependencies are translated into individual goals) are offset by the substitutional effect of bilateral and collective outcome control (i.e., undermining autonomy, flexibility, cooperative norms, and unambiguousness). Conversely, multisourcing arrangements that relied on low levels of collective outcome control achieved higher performance when they exercised high levels of bilateral outcome control (see the distance between the plotted lines at the left-hand side of Fig. 2.3b). In such situations, it seems that bilateral outcome control does not interfere with the low level of collective outcome control and therefore bilateral outcome control supports coordination in the multisourcing arrangement, as indicated by higher joint performance.

Our analysis also revealed a positive interaction effect between collective outcome control and conflict management procedures on joint performance. The relationship is visualized in Fig. 2.3c. The figure shows that collective outcome control barely contributes to joint performance when conflict management procedures are lacking (see the relatively flat dashed line). On the other hand, collective outcome control has a strong effect on joint performance when conflict management procedures are present (see the steep solid line). These findings are consistent with the idea that conflict management procedures complement collective outcome control by mitigating the weak enforceability associated with collective outcome control, and by helping the vendors to resolve cognitive conflicts when they negotiate the individual contributions each vendor needs to make to achieve the collective goals.

Governance Efficiency

The preceding discussion suggests that clients may need to rely on bilateral outcome control and conflict management procedures to achieve high individual performance, and on collective outcome control and conflict management procedures to achieve high joint performance. However, relying on all three formal governance mechanisms may be costly. The findings for our third dependent variable, governance efficiency, provide some perspective on this trade-off. We found that collective outcome control and conflict management procedures are strongly positively related to governance efficiency, while bilateral outcome control has a negative, albeit insignificant, relationship to governance efficiency. Our findings highlight that it is quite effortful for clients to set up and maintain tight control relationships with individual vendors. Similarly to joint performance, we found support for a positive interactive effect of collective outcome control and conflict management procedures on governance efficiency. The interaction plot in Fig. 2.3d further illustrates this relationship. The figure demonstrates that collective outcome control contributes more strongly to governance efficiency when accompanied by high levels of conflict management, thus indicating a complementary effect. Hence, combining collective outcome control with conflict management procedures appears to yield superior governance efficiency, presumably because it allows a good portion of the coordination and conflict resolution effort to be delegated to the vendors.

Contributions

Our research makes three important contributions to the IS outsourcing literature by advancing our understanding of: (1) formal governance mechanisms specific to multisourcing; (2) complementary and substitutional relationships between formal governance mechanisms; and (3) success dimensions specific to multisourcing.

Distinguishing Three Formal Governance Mechanisms in Multisourcing

Understanding the governance mechanisms that lead to better multisourcing performance is imperative for both client firms and vendors. Indeed, although the multisourcing literature broadly discusses three key formal governance mechanisms, theoretical arguments and empirical evidence for how these mechanisms contribute to success have been limited. Against this backdrop, we show that the distinction between three formal governance mechanisms—bilateral outcome control, collective outcome control, and between-vendor conflict management procedures—is empirically valid. While bilateral outcome control is similar to outcome control in single-sourcing settings (e.g., Gopal & Gosain, 2010), collective outcome control and between-vendor conflict management are unique to multisourcing arrangements because of the need to influence interactions between vendors. Although the distinction we make between bilateral and collective outcome control echoes Bapna and colleagues' (2010) differentiation of individual and integrated SLAs, our paper goes beyond current understandings of these mechanisms by showing that bilateral and collective outcome control are empirically distinguishable and differentially related to different outcomes. Our findings on conflict management procedures are also novel. While conceptual ideas (Bapna et al., 2010) and qualitative evidence (Barboza et al., 2011) hint at the relevance of conflict management procedures, we show that the use of conflict management procedures is positively related to all dimensions of multisourcing success. Conflict management procedures thus play a key role in multisourcing. Our study demonstrates that conflict management procedures are the only formal governance mechanism that contributes to performance at both the dyadic level (such as by enabling vendors to enforce each other's individual contributions) and the collective level (such as by helping address cognitive conflicts between vendors).

Explaining Interactions: Complementary and Substitutional Relationships Between Formal Governance Mechanisms in Multisourcing

We also develop theoretical arguments and provide empirical evidence for the interactions between formal governance mechanisms in multisourcing. While the broader governance and outsourcing literature suggests that governance mechanisms often do not act in isolation (Huber et al., 2014; Poppo & Zenger, 2002), the research so far sheds little light on whether formal governance mechanisms in multisourcing are compatible with each other. We hypothesized that bilateral outcome control and collective outcome control are substitutes because they undermine each other's strength in four major ways (autonomy, flexibility, cooperative norms, and unambiguousness). In line with these claims, our findings indeed demonstrate a substitution effect in relation to joint performance. As such, bilateral outcome control weakens the potential of collective outcome control to coordinate the vendors toward a smooth joint performance. Accordingly, multisourcing arrangements that wish to advance the cooperative, flexible nature of collective outcome control cannot fully harness this potential if they, at the same time, rely on strong bilateral outcome control because it promotes individualistic norms and hinders adjustments in the design of individual contributions. Moreover, we find strong empirical support for the idea that collective outcome control and conflict management procedures act as complements to each other, as indicated by positive interaction effects in the models predicting individual performance, joint performance, and governance efficiency.

Establishing the Multidimensional and Multilevel Nature of Success in Multisourcing

Our third contribution lies in the development of the multisourcing success construct. Our conceptualization of multisourcing success offers a departure from the existing understanding of success as a predominantly dyadic construct by considering both the dyadic (individual performance) and collective (joint performance, governance efficiency) dimensions of multisourcing success. As with the assertion that "team members may perform well as individuals, but nevertheless function poorly as a united team" (Klein & Kozlowski, 2000, p. 214), vendors may perform well individually but nevertheless fail to provide a coherent service when required to collaborate in a multisourcing arrangement. As such, we find that control leading to high individual performance (e.g., bilateral outcome control) does not necessarily lead to high joint performance. This highlights the importance of researchers conceptualizing multisourcing success as a multilevel phenomenon to avoid falling prey to the atomistic fallacy (Hannan, 1971), that is, reducing success in multisourcing to the sum of success at the dyadic level.

A key practical implication from our results for different success measures is that clients should choose their governance mechanisms based on the performance dimension they value most. Clients who value individual performance (e.g., because interdependencies between vendors are easily manageable) should emphasize strong bilateral outcome control, supplemented by conflict management procedures. In essence, such a bilateral approach relies strongly on modularizing individual contributions (Aubert et al., 2016) by reducing the multisourcing arrangements to a number of dyadic relationships that are managed as a collection of single-sourcing relationships. However, Aubert and colleagues warn that an approach relying on "modularity makes it very difficult to modify the overall architecture since each module has to remain compatible with the other modules, and no party has control over all the components" (Aubert et al., 2016, p. 181). In line with this warning, we find that clients relying strongly on a bilateral approach are unlikely to obtain a highly coherent, integrated service (see the predicted values for joint performance in Fig. 2.3b).

In contrast, clients who value joint performance and governance efficiency should consider a collective approach that combines strong collective outcome control with conflict management procedures. This governance configuration grants some autonomy and flexibility to vendors, promotes cooperative norms among vendors, and enables vendors to enforce the contributions needed from other vendors in order to meet overall goals, while also helping the client to limit its governance effort.

Although this collective approach is at odds with the strong emphasis in single-sourcing relationships on contractually-anchored, bilateral service agreements (Goo et al., 2009), our results show that a collective approach can indeed yield a coherent, well-integrated service with relatively low governance effort. Admittedly, such an approach may not result in superior individual performance.

Conclusion

There are several limitations to this study that may encourage future research. First, although we have unpacked the effects of different formal governance mechanisms on various success dimensions, our focus did not include contingency factors that may moderate these effects. This is an exciting avenue for future research. Second, although we have argued for the different ways in which formal governance mechanisms complement or undermine each other, our data do not allow us to disentangle these effects. Future research could focus on potential mediators (e.g., flexibility, relational norms, opportunistic behavior) to give deeper insights into these interactions. Third, as we are among the first to examine governance in multisourcing, we have focused on formal governance, which is emphasized in the multisourcing literature (Bapna et al., 2010; Barboza et al., 2011). Future research could examine how various informal governance mechanisms contribute to different dimensions of multisourcing success (see also Chapter 4). Fourth, while we have focused on conflict management procedures, there may be a variety of ways in which conflict is managed in multisourcing relationships. Future work could draw on the existing work on conflict management (Lacity & Willcocks, 2017) to develop a richer perspective on conflict management in multisourcing (see also Chapter 5). Fifth, our chapter relies on survey data collected from a single source, which presents the potential threat of common-method bias. However, our latent factor test did not ascribe any variance to a common factor. Moreover, interaction effects, which play a key role in our paper, are unlikely to be artifacts of common-method bias (Siemsen et al., 2010). Sixth, our use of cross-sectional data and OLS regression sets some limits to the confidence at which causal effects can be inferred from our analysis. While very large sample sizes (e.g., 2,400) are required to overcome these limitations by using instrumental variables (Boef et al., 2014), such sample sizes are difficult to achieve in a survey about multisourcing arrangements. However, a large-scale empirical investigation could expand our research to further ascertain causal effects.

Appendix: Survey Instrument

Bilateral Outcome Control (Based on Kirsch et al. [2002])

To ensure that the vendor meets our expected service-level targets/quality we ... (separate columns to be answered for vendor A and vendor B).

BOC1: ... evaluate the extent to which services were delivered as defined in the contract regardless of how this goal was accomplished.
BOC2: ... test intermediary and/or final outcomes/deliverables against criteria defined in the contract, regardless of how these outcomes were achieved.
BOC3: ... have several sources of objective data we can rely on.*
BOC4: ... have defined quantifiable measures in place.
BOC5: ...have defined accurate and reliable measures.

Collective Outcome Control (Based on Kirsch et al. [2002])

To ensure that not the individual performance of vendor A and B, but rather their combined performance (i.e., solutions by vendor A and B in combination as part of the multisourcing arrangement) meet our objectives, we ...

COC1: … evaluate the extent to which combined services are delivered as defined in the contract regardless of how this goal is accomplished.
COC2: … test intermediary and/or final joint outcomes/deliverables against criteria defined in the contract, regardless of how this goal is achieved.
COC3: … have several sources of objective data we can rely on.*
COC4: … have defined quantifiable measures depicting the extent to which combined objectives are achieved.
COC5: … have defined accurate and reliable measures that indicate the extent to which the delivered services jointly meet our objectives.

Conflict Management Procedures (Based on Kale et al. [2000])

When it comes to disagreement between vendors A and B …

CMP1: … we have procedures in place for how to resolve them.
CMP2: … we have process descriptions to determine how the parties should resolve the conflict.
CMP3: … there are operational-level agreements between the vendors that determine how to resolve the conflict, without our involvement.*

Individual Performance (Based on Grover et al. [1996])

How would you characterize your satisfaction with the performance of each vendor so far? (separate columns to be answered for vendor A and vendor B)

INDPERF1: …the products/services delivered by the vendor meet our expectations.
INDPERF2: …we have met our goals with the vendor.

INDPERF3: …overall, we are satisfied with our relationship with the vendor.

Governance Efficiency (Based on Dibbern et al. [2012])

With regard to vendor A and vendor B …

GOVEFF1: … our overall cost and effort for managing the relationship with them is higher than expected.*
GOVEFF2: … our overall cost and effort for coordinating and monitoring them are within our expectations.
GOVEFF3: … our overall cost and effort for guiding their performance and service delivery are within our expectations.

Joint Performance (Based on Grover et al. [1996], Lee and Kim [1999], and Tiwana [2008])

With regard to the combined performance of vendor A and vendor B as part of the multisourcing arrangement so far …

JNTPERF1: … the products/services delivered meet our expectations.
JNTPERF2: … we have met our goals.
JNTPERF3: … we have completed key milestones in accordance with our objectives.
JNTPERF4: … we have achieved our desired cost savings.
JNTPERF5: … we are satisfied with our overall benefits from outsourcing.
JNTPERF6: … we have so far met project/service requirements.
(*Items with asterisk were removed during analysis)

References

Alchian, A. A., & Demsetz, H. (1972). Production, Information Costs, and Economic Organization. *The American Economic Review, 62*(5), 777–795.

Angst, C. M., Wowak, K. D., Handley, S. M., & Kelley, K. (2017). Antecedents of Information Systems Sourcing Strategies in U.S. Hospitals: A Longitudinal Study. *MIS Quarterly, 41*(4), 1129–1152. https://doi.org/10.25300/MISQ/2017/41.4.06

Aubert, B. A., Saunders, C., Wiener, M., Denk, R., & Wolfermann, T. (2016). How Adidas Realized Benefits from a Contrary IT Multisourcing Strategy. *MIS Quarterly Executive, 15*(3).

Bapna, R., Barua, A., Mani, D., & Mehra, A. (2010). Research Commentary-Cooperation, Coordination, and Governance in Multisourcing: An Agenda for Analytical and Empirical Research. *Information Systems Research, 21*(4), 785–795.

Barboza, M., Myers, M., & Gardner, L. (2011). *Information Technology Multisourcing at Fonterra: A Case Study of the World's Largest Exporter of Dairy Ingredients*. Presented at the Nineteenth European Conference on Information Systems, Helsinki, Finland.

Bhattacharya, S., Gupta, A., & Hasija, S. (2018). Single-Sourcing Versus Multisourcing: The Roles of Output Verifiability on Task Modularity. *MIS Quarterly, 42*(4), 1171–1186.

Boef, A. G., Dekkers, O. M., Vandenbroucke, J. P., & le Cessie, S. (2014). Sample Size Importantly Limits the Usefulness of Instrumental Variable Methods, Depending on Instrument Strength and Level of Confounding. *Journal of Clinical Epidemiology, 67*(11), 1258–1264.

Choudhury, V., & Sabherwal, R. (2003). Portfolios of Control in Outsourced Software Development Projects. *Information Systems Research, 14*(3), 291–314.

Conner, K., & Prahalad, C. (1996). A Resource-Based Theory of the Firm: Knowledge Versus Opportunism. *Organization Science, 7*(5), 477–501.

Croon, M. A., & van Veldhoven, M. J. (2007). Predicting Group-Level Outcome Variables from Variables Measured at the Individual Level: A Latent Variable Multilevel Model. *Psychological Methods, 12*(1), 45.

Dant, R. P., & Schul, P. L. (1992). Conflict Resolution Processes in Contractual Channels of Distribution. *The Journal of Marketing*, 38–54.

De Dreu, C. K., & West, M. A. (2001). Minority Dissent and Team Innovation: The Importance of Participation in Decision Making. *Journal of Applied Psychology, 86*(6), 1191.

Dekker, H. C. (2004). Control of Inter-Organizational Relationships: Evidence on Appropriation Concerns and Coordination Requirements. *Accounting, Organizations and Society, 29*(1), 27–49.

Dibbern, J., Chin, W. W., & Heinzl, A. (2012). Systemic Determinants of the Information Systems Outsourcing Decision: A Comparative Study of German and United States Firms. *Journal of the Association for Information Systems, 13*(6), 466.

Dibbern, J., Goles, T., Hirschheim, R., & Jayatilaka, B. (2004). Information Systems Outsourcing: A Survey and Analysis of the Literature. *ACM SIGMIS Database, 35*(4), 6–102.

Dibbern, J., Winkler, J., & Heinzl, A. (2008). Explaining Variations in Client Extra Costs Between Software Projects Offshored to India. *MIS Quarterly, 32*(2), 333–366.

Fornell, C., & Larcker, D. F. (1981). Evaluating Structural Equation Models with Unobservable Variables and Measurement Error. *Journal of Marketing Research, 18*, 39–50.

Goo, J., Kishore, R., Rao, H., & Nam, K. (2009). The Role of Service Level Agreements in Relational Management of Information Technology Outsourcing: An Empirical Study. *MIS Quarterly, 33*(1), 119–146.

Goodhue, D., Lewis, W., & Thompson, R. (2007). Research Note-Statistical Power in Analyzing Interaction Effects: Questioning the Advantage of PLS with Product Indicators. *Information Systems Research, 18*(2), 211–227.

Gopal, A., & Gosain, S. (2010). The Role of Organizational Controls and Boundary Spanning in Software Development Outsourcing: Implications for Project Performance. *Information Systems Research, 21*(4), 1–23.

Grover, V., Cheon, M., & Teng, J. (1996). The Effect of Service Quality and Partnership on the Outsourcing of Information Systems Functions. *Journal of Management Information Systems, 12*(4), 89–116.

Gulati, R., Wohlgezogen, F., & Zhelyazkov, P. (2012). The Two Facets of Collaboration: Cooperation and Coordination in Strategic Alliances. *The Academy of Management Annals, 6*(1), 531–583.

Hannan, M. T. (1971). *Aggregation and Disaggregation in Sociology*. Lexington Books.

Henderson, J. C., & Lee, S. (1992). Managing I/S Design Teams: A Control Theories Perspective. *Management Science, 38*(6), 757–777. https://doi.org/10.1287/mnsc.38.6.757

Huber, T., Fischer, T., Dibbern, J., & Hirschheim, R. (2014). A Process Model of Complementarity and Substitution of Contractual and Relational Governance in IS Outsourcing. *Journal of Management Information Systems, 30*(3), 81–114.

Hurni, T., Huber, T., & Dibbern, J. (2015). *Coordinating Platform-Based Multi-Sourcing: Introducing the Theory of Conventions*. Presented at the 36rd International Conference on Information Systems.

Johnson, D. W. (2003). Social Interdependence: Interrelationships Among Theory, Research, and Practice. *American Psychologist, 58*(11), 934.

Kale, P., Singh, H., & Perlmutter, H. (2000). Learning and Protection of Proprietary Assets in Strategic Alliances: Building Relational Capital. *Strategic Management Journal, 21*(3), 217–237. Retrieved from JSTOR.

Keil, M., Rai, A., & Liu, S. (2013). How User Risk and Requirements Risk Moderate the Effects of Formal and Informal Control on the Process Performance of IT Projects. *European Journal of Information Systems, 22*(6), 650–672.

Kirsch, L. J. (1996). The Management of Complex Tasks in Organizations: Controlling the Systems Development Process. *Organization Science, 7*(1), 1–21.

Kirsch, L. J., Sambamurthy, V., Ko, D. G., & Purvis, R. L. (2002). Controlling Information Systems Development Projects: The View from the Client. *Management Science, 48*(4), 484–498.

Klein, K. J., & Kozlowski, S. W. (2000). From Micro to Meso: Critical Steps in Conceptualizing and Conducting Multilevel Research. *Organizational Research Methods, 3*(3), 211–236.

Krancher, O., & Stürmer, M. (2018). *Explaining Multisourcing Decisions in Application Outsourcing*. Presented at the Twenty-Sixth European Conference on Information Systems.

Lacity, M. C., Khan, S. A., & Willcocks, L. P. (2009). A Review of the IT Outsourcing Literature: Insights for Practice. *The Journal of Strategic Information Systems, 18*(3), 130–146.

Lacity, M. C., & Willcocks, L. (2017). Conflict Resolution in Business Services Outsourcing Relationships. *The Journal of Strategic Information Systems, 26*(2), 80–100.

Lee, J., & Kim, Y. (1999). Effect of Partnership Quality on IS Outsourcing Success: Conceptual Framework and Empirical Validation. *Journal of Management Information Systems, 15*(4), 29–61.

Lioliou, E., & Zimmermann, A. (2015). Vendor Opportunism in IT Outsourcing: A TCE and Social Capital Perspective. *Journal of Information Technology, 30*(4), 307–324.

Lioliou, E., Zimmermann, A., Willcocks, L., & Gao, L. (2014). Formal and Relational Governance in IT Outsourcing: Substitution, Complementarity and the Role of the Psychological Contract. *Information Systems Journal, 24*(6), 503–535.

Łoboda, B. (2013). Motives for Multisourcing in the IT Sector. *International Journal of Management and Economics, 38*(1), 46–66.

Lüdtke, O., Marsh, H. W., Robitzsch, A., Trautwein, U., Asparouhov, T., & Muthén, B. (2008). The Multilevel Latent Covariate Model: A New, More Reliable Approach to Group-Level Effects in Contextual Studies. *Psychological Methods, 13*(3), 203.

MacKenzie, S. B., Podsakoff, P. M., & Podsakoff, N. P. (2011). Construct Measurement and Validation Procedures in MIS and Behavioral Research: Integrating New and Existing Techniques. *MIS Quarterly, 35*(2), 293–334.

Maruping, L. M., Venkatesh, V., & Agarwal, R. (2009). A Control Theory Perspective on Agile Methodology Use and Changing User Requirements. *Information Systems Research, 20*(3), 377–399.

Nidumolu, S. R., & Subramani, M. R. (2003). The Matrix of Control: Combining Process and Structure Approaches to Managing Software Development. *Journal of Management Information Systems, 20*(3), 159–196. https://doi.org/10.2307/40398644

Okhuysen, G. A., & Bechky, B. A. (2009). Coordination in Organizations: An Integrative Perspective. *The Academy of Management Annals, 3*(1), 463–502. https://doi.org/10.1080/19416520903047533

Oshri, I., Kotlarsky, J., & Gerbasi, A. (2015). Strategic Innovation Through Outsourcing: The Role of Relational and Contractual Governance. *The Journal of Strategic Information Systems, 24*(3), 203–216.

Pinsonneault, A., & Kraemer, K. (1993). Survey Research Methodology in Management Information Systems: An Assessment. *Journal of Management Information Systems, 10*(2), 75–105.

Podsakoff, P. M., MacKenzie, S. B., Lee, J.-Y., & Podsakoff, N. P. (2003). Common Method Biases in Behavioral Research: A Critical Review of the Literature and Recommended Remedies. *Journal of Applied Psychology, 88*(5), 879–903.

Poppo, L., & Zenger, T. (2002). Do Formal Contracts and Relational Governance Function as Substitutes or Complements? *Strategic Management Journal, 23*(8), 707–725.

Poston, R. S., Kettinger, W. J., & Simon, J. C. (2009). Managing the Vendor Set: Achieving Best Pricing and Quality Service in IT Outsourcing. *MIS Quarterly Executive, 8*(2), 45–58.

Rustagi, S., King, W. R., & Kirsch, L. J. (2008). Predictors of Formal Control Usage in IT Outsourcing Partnerships. *Information Systems Research, 19*(2), 126–143.

Siemsen, E., Roth, A., & Oliveira, P. (2010). Common Method Bias in Regression Models with Linear, Quadratic, and Interaction Effects. *Organizational Research Methods, 13*(3), 456–476.

Straub, D., Boudreau, M.-C., & Gefen, D. (2004). Validation Guidelines for IS Positivist Research. *The Communications of the Association for Information Systems, 13*(1), 63.

Tiwana, A. (2010). Systems Development Ambidexterity: Explaining the Complementary and Substitutive Roles of Formal and Informal Controls. *Journal of Management Information Systems, 27*(2), 87–126.

Tiwana, A., & Keil, M. (2009). Control in Internal and Outsourced Software Projects. *Journal of Management Information Systems, 26*(3), 9–44.

Tomczak, A. (2015). *WTO-Ausschreibung für App-Entwicklung, "Agile Beschaffung", Mini-tender, agiles Umfeld.* http://www.swissict.ch/fileadmin/customer/Fachgruppen/Lean_Agile_Scrum/20150828_A_Tomzcak_ScrumBeschaffung.pdf

Van de Ven, A. H., Delbecq, A. L., & Koenig, R. (1976). Determinants of Coordination Modes within Organizations. *American Sociological Review, 41*(2), 322–338.

Wang, E. T., Barron, T., & Seidmann, A. (1997). Contracting Structures for Custom Software Development: The Impacts of Informational Rents and Uncertainty on Internal Development and Outsourcing. *Management Science, 43*(12), 1726–1744.

West, B. T., Welch, K. B., & Galecki, A. T. (2007). *Linear Mixed Models: A Practical Guide Using Statistical Software.* CRC Press.

Wiener, M., & Saunders, C. (2014a). Forced Coopetition in IT Multi-Sourcing. *The Journal of Strategic Information Systems, 23*(3), 210–225.

Wiener, M., & Saunders, C. (2014b). Who Is the Favored Bride? Challenges in Switching to a Multi-Vendor Offshoring Strategy. In *Information Systems Outsourcing* (pp. 289–312). Springer.

3

What the Guardian Does in Multisourcing Projects

Ilan Oshri, Jens Dibbern, Julia Kotlarsky, and Oliver Krancher

Introduction

As detailed in Chapter 2, in the information systems (IS) domain, multisourcing is viewed as the practice of procuring interdependent information technology (IT) and business services from external vendors to achieve optimal business goals (Bapna et al., 2010). Such a definition brings to the fore the interdependencies between outsourced tasks

---

Chapter 3 is a revised and updated version of Oshri, I., Dibbern, J., Kotlarsky, J., & Krancher, O. (2019). An Information Processing View on Joint-Vendor Performance in Multi-sourcing: The Role of the Guardian. *Journal of Management of Information Systems*, 36(4), 1248–1283.

I. Oshri (✉) · J. Kotlarsky
University of Auckland, Auckland, New Zealand
e-mail: ilan.oshri@auckland.ac.nz

J. Dibbern
Bern University, Bern, Switzerland

O. Krancher
ITU, Copenhagen, Denmark

delivered by various vendors, thus implying the need for interactions between the vendors in order to jointly deliver an overall service (Bapna et al., 2010; Wiener & Saunders, 2014). In assessing the success of a multisourcing arrangement, it is not the performance of the individual vendors that matters most, but their joint performance, i.e., the degree to which the combined services delivered by the vendors meet the client's expectations. An example[1] of such a multisourcing arrangement is British Airways' (BA's) "Know Me Programme", which was initiated in 2013 and involved three vendors, Tata Consultancy Services (TCS), Opera Solutions, and e-Dialog (now Zeta Interactive).[2] Together, these three vendors formed a new personalized customer contact system. Although each vendor has its own responsibilities, i.e., TCS for collecting, integrating, and managing customer data, Opera Solutions for providing business analytics services, and e-Dialog for creating email-based marketing services, the success of the project relied on all three services working together. Accordingly, the vendors had to manage the interdependencies between their services, which required them to cooperate and coordinate their actions. This example resonates with Bapna et al.'s (2010) claim that: *"In contrast to dyadic client-vendor relationships that have been the subject of extant global sourcing research, multi-sourcing necessitates individual and collaborative efforts of multiple vendors at the back-end to come together to create a seamless, integrated service at the front end for the client"* (p. 786). While facets associated with governance of dyadic relationships, such as putting in place Service Level Agreements (SLAs) (Goo et al., 2009) and using various organizational controls to motivate vendors to achieve desirable results (Tiwana & Keil, 2009), are also relevant, the client firm needs to put greater effort into governing the vendor network in IT multisourcing (Levina & Su, 2008) as well as incentivizing and monitoring both individual and joint vendor performance (Bapna et al., 2010). On this account, the use of a guardian vendor to assist the client firm in governing the vendor network (Bapna

---

[1] For more examples, see Wiener and Saunders (2014): on p. 214 they provide several examples of multi-sourcing arrangements in the professional media, including ABN AMRO, General Motors, British Petroleum and Eastman Kodak.

[2] e-Dialog was part of GSI Commerce (which was acquired by eBay and renamed eBay Enterprise in 2013), and sold to Zeta Interactive in 2015 (http://zetaglobal.com/clients).

3 What the Guardian Does in Multisourcing Projects 63

et al., 2010; Wiener & Saunders, 2014) has been portrayed as one of the unique features of the IS multisourcing setting.[3]

While a few studies have examined multisourcing in the IS context (Bapna et al., 2010; Cohen & Young, 2006; Levina & Su, 2008; Su & Levina, 2011; Wiener & Saunders, 2014), we still know little about interactions and collaboration between multiple vendors and the effects on joint performance (but see also Chapters 2, 4, and 5). In this regard, research has shed light on the importance of appropriate task design (e.g., modularization) and task distribution among vendors (e.g., choosing specialized vendors while ensuring sufficient knowledge overlaps between them) (Wiener & Saunders, 2014). However, little is known about how the client can facilitate and support vendors to achieve successful joint performance. Moreover, it is not clear how the client's support role is affected if the client assigns one of the vendors the position of guardian, i.e., the responsibility for managing the other vendors. Currently, the literature suggests that the guardian vendor acts as a mediator, thus standing between the client and the other vendors (Wiener & Saunders, 2014). This implies that the guardian *substitutes* the client in facilitating and supporting coordination and cooperation activities among the vendors (Bapna et al., 2010; Wiener & Saunders, 2014). Alternatively, we propose that the guardian may improve joint performance by providing capacities that *complement* those of the client. It is within these areas of interest that this chapter seeks to advance our understanding of multisourcing settings by addressing the following questions: (i) *How does the client facilitate joint vendor performance in a multisourcing arrangement?* and (ii) *What role does the guardian vendor play in achieving joint performance?*

We frame the challenge of achieving joint vendor performance (hereafter, joint performance) as an information processing (IP) issue. Hence,

---

[3] It is important to note that the IS outsourcing literature has so far conceptually discussed the role of the guardian and suggested that it corresponds with the notion of a mediator. More specifically, two key studies have explored the guardian role: Bapna et al. (2010) are a research commentary and largely conceptual; second, while Wiener and Saunders (2014) report a case study that follows a direct rather than a guardian model, with some suggestions made regarding the guardian.

the challenge of achieving joint performance in a multisourcing arrangement is essentially one of effective IP to manage interdependencies between the vendors and between the client and the vendors, thus imposing considerable IP requirements. For instance, in the above example regarding British Airways, IP is needed to understand the functional and technical system requirements of the client (BA), and also to understand the interdependencies that exist between the TCS customer data management systems and processes, Opera Solutions data analytics processes, and E-dialog email platform. While such IP requirements may vary between multisourcing arrangements, subject to the degree of modularization (Tanriverdi et al., 2007) and task complexity (Bai et al., 2010), the involvement of numerous vendors and the interdependencies between them will pose challenges to the client in achieving joint performance if the client does not ensure sufficient and relevant IP capacity. In this regard, governance (formal and informal) and architectural knowledge have repeatedly been suggested as key factors affecting IP capacities (Brusoni et al., 2001; Galbraith, 1977; Mani et al., 2012).

Consequently, we examined how clients can ensure joint performance by assuming sufficient IP capacities in multisourcing arrangements (Galbraith, 1973, 1977), to support our claim that such IP capacities may be brought in by the client (i.e., as an internal IP capacity) or by the guardian vendor (i.e., as an external IP capacity) (Bapna et al., 2010; Wiener & Saunders, 2014). We also aimed to clarify whether the guardian vendor will have a substitutional or a complementary effect on the client's IP capacities.

Using an international data set of 189 IT multisourcing arrangements, we found that the two internal IP capacities complement each other. Indeed, the client's formal inter-vendor governance and the client's architectural knowledge positively affect joint performance, while informal inter-vendor governance has a significant effect on joint performance only when interacting with high architectural knowledge. With regard to the external source of IP capacity, we found that a guardian vendor complements the client's formal and informal inter-vendor governance while substituting the client's architectural knowledge. Thus, the guardian model is beneficial in settings where the client provides the formal framework for the guardian vendor to interact with the other vendors, where the client remains involved in this interaction, and where the client lacks architectural knowledge. This implies that, contrary to what has been suggested in the existing literature (i.e., Bapna et al., 2010; Wiener & Saunders, 2014), the role of the guardian vendor may be more fruitfully understood as one of architect rather than a mediator. The guardian compensates for the client's knowledge gaps, while the client still needs to engage in formal and informal governance of all vendors.

Next, we provide theoretical foundations and develop hypotheses. We then explain the method and findings, followed by a discussion of the results and their implications for research and practice.

Theoretical Background

The Information Processing View and Multisourcing

The Information Processing View (IPV) is a broad theoretical perspective that views entities (e.g., people, teams, organizations, and inter-organizational relationships) as information processing (IP) systems, and explains the structures and behaviors of these systems and their limitations (Hinsz et al., 1997; Huber, 1991; Galbraith, 1977; Simon, 1978). An important property of IP systems is their *IP capacity*, broadly defined as their ability to interpret, integrate, store, and transmit information (Daft & Macintosh, 1981, p. 210; Mani et al., 2010,p. 42). One prominent stream of IPV research (Galbraith, 1977) focuses on the IP capacity that is generated by *governance mechanisms*, namely "mechanisms for coordination and control" (Tushman & Nadler, 1978, p. 618). Governance mechanisms, such as goal setting, planning, and direct interaction, generate IP capacity because they provide the information infrastructure through which the constituent elements of IP systems align actions (i.e., achieve coordination) and interests (i.e., achieve cooperation) (Andres & Zmud, 2001/2002; Bensaou & Venkatraman, 1995; Premkumar et al., 2005). A second stream of IPV research focuses on IP capacity generated by *knowledge*. It draws on a cognitive IP perspective to argue that IP capacity depends on existing knowledge, because existing knowledge provides the infrastructure that enables humans to assimilate and integrate new information (Chase & Simon, 1973; Cohen & Levinthal, 1990; Grant, 1996). Building on these two streams, we seek to examine how IP capacity within the multisourcing environment affects joint performance.

Indeed, the use of the IPV appears particularly suited to the context of multisourcing in light of the following four gaps. First, multisourcing research lacks an overarching theory that fits with the idiosyncrasies of multisourcing as opposed to single sourcing. In our view, what makes multisourcing unique is its inherent complexity, which is based on interdependencies between vendors—as opposed to the client-vendor interdependencies of dyadic outsourcing. While IPV has been applied to studying dyadic relationships (e.g., Bensaou & Venkatraman, 1995; Mani et al., 2010), where IP requirements may substantially vary from case to case, we argue that triadic settings, such as multisourcing, add a layer of complexity that warrants focus on the composition of IP capacities. The interdependencies that exist between tasks allocated to multiple vendors pose significant IP requirements for the client. In particular, in comparison with single sourcing, the need to integrate sub-services or tasks outsourced to different vendors into a coherent whole creates additional IP requirements in multisourcing. Therefore, it is imperative to understand joint performance by modeling and testing the effects of certain IP capacities available within the multisourcing arrangement.

Second, with the exceptions of studies of an internal software development (Grant, 1996) and a single-sourcing setting (Goodhue et al., 2007), the two streams of IPV research, one focusing on governance and the other on knowledge as sources of IP capacity, have mostly been developed in isolation. Consequently, understanding the relationship between architectural knowledge and governance in multisourcing and how these two IP capacities interact is imperative for both IS outsourcing and IPV research knowledge.

Third, the IS outsourcing literature (Schwarz, 2014) and the literature on multisourcing have, so far, mostly treated performance as an aggregate of the performances of the individual vendors (e.g., Gopal et al., 2002). In this chapter, however, we emphasize that what makes multisourcing unique is that performance consists of more than the sum of the contributions of individual vendors. As such, it is imperative to develop an understanding of the combined or joint performance, rather than the individual contributions of the vendors.

Last but not least, the few references in the extant academic and professional[4] literature to the role that the guardian vendor plays in multisourcing settings (Bapna et al., 2010; Wiener & Saunders, 2014) raise questions about the contribution of this actor to joint performance. We argue that the guardian brings its own unique set of IP capacities that can either complement or substitute the IP capacities provided by the client.[5]

The Client's Challenge: With or Without a Guardian Vendor

IP capacity can be provided by either the client or the guardian vendor, if the client has appointed one vendor to act as guardian (see Fig. 3.1b).[6] In the direct model (see Fig. 3.1a), the client takes full responsibility for managing the vendors. In the guardian model, the client transfers some responsibilities to the guardian vendor. We argue that each model has important implications for the IP capacities needed to achieve a high joint performance.

---

[4] http://www.computerweekly.com/blog/Investigating-Outsourcing/IT-sourcing-models-are-shifting-A-Deloitte-perspective.

[5] As put by Tiwana (2010), "Two things are complements if more of one increases the benefits of using the other. They are substitutes if more of one diminishes the benefits of using the other" (p. 88).

[6] This is different from situations where the prime contractor is used, because in such a scenario the prime contractor is the only vendor contracted by the client and thus responsible for delivering the service. In the academic and professional literature, the prime contractor model "consists of a network with several vendors that operate under the control of the head contractor. The head contractor is accountable for the delivery of the service and liable for this under the terms of the contract" (Oshri et al., 2009, p. 134). For example, Koo et al. (2017) refer to the prime contractor outsourcing configuration as the "single-vendor-dominant model" where "a client directly contracts with one dominant vendor and indirectly contracts with other vendors through the dominant vendor" (p. 3). Such contracting should not be confused with a true multi-sourcing scenario, where each vendor is contracted directly by the client firm, as depicted in Fig. 3.1a.

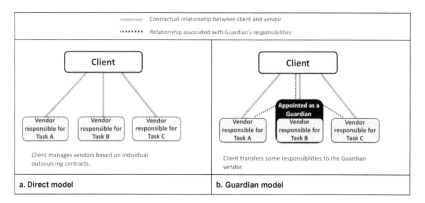

Fig. 3.1 Direct and guardian models

In the direct model, the client relies on two sources of IP capacity, namely governance and architectural knowledge. Governance in dyadic outsourcing relationships often manifests as formal and informal governance between a client and a vendor (Poppo & Zenger, 2002). However, in multisourcing, informal governance and formal governance are likely to be required to support the coordination of actions *between* multiple vendors, thus suggesting a need for *inter-vendor governance*, i.e., joint governance structures between the multiple vendors and the client firm. In line with the psychological IPV research stream, we argue that information processing requires appropriate knowledge to guide governance, in particular the client's architectural knowledge (Hobday et al., 2005; Prencipe, 2005; Takeishi, 2002).

While the conditions for achieving joint performance by utilizing the client's IP capacities are clear, it is still unclear how the choice of a guardian model affects these conditions. Currently, the few IS outsourcing studies that have discussed the guardian role suggest the guardian acts as a mediator, i.e., as an actor standing between the client and the rest of the vendors, thus relieving the client from facilitating coordination and cooperation between vendors (Bapna et al., 2010; Wiener & Saunders, 2014). To perform such a role, the guardian brings in its own IP capacity. From the client's perspective, therefore, the guardian acts as an external source of IP capacity, applying its own inter-vendor governance as well as its own architectural knowledge.

However, the view of guardian vendor as a mediator can be challenged. As reported in numerous sources,[7] the client maintains an individual contractual agreement with each vendor in the multisourcing setting, while the guardian vendor does not have legally binding contractual agreements with any of the vendors. Consequently, the guardian vendor's ability to enforce inter-vendor governance is in fact rather limited, particularly as the guardian vendor is restricted in the range of penalties and incentives it can use when governing the other vendors. Hence, it is unclear whether the guardian vendor does indeed assume a mediating role, as proposed in the literature (e.g., Bapna et al., 2010; Wiener & Saunders, 2014). Evidence from similar settings in manufacturing and construction predominantly suggests that the guardian vendor brings in superior knowledge about integrating the various contributions of individual vendors (Brusoni et al., 2001). As such, an alternative view to the role of the guardian-as-a-mediator is the guardian-as-an-*architect*. This describes the guardian vendor as assisting the client in managing the multisourcing arrangement by complementing the client's IP capacities, rather than substituting them.

Thus there are two views of the guardian vendor's role in multisourcing. In one, the guardian substitutes the client's inter-vendor governance (guardian-as-a-mediator) and, in the other, the guardian vendor complements the client's inter-vendor governance (guardian-as-an-architect).

With this in mind, we now turn to theorizing the effect of internal and external sources of IP capacity on joint performance.

Hypotheses

In this section, we use the IPV lens to derive hypotheses aimed at examining the effect of internal and external sources of IP capacity on joint performance. Figure 3.2 depicts our conceptual model.

---

[7] https://www.slaughterandmay.com/media/2535633/multi-sourcing-A-different-way-of-contra cting.pdf.

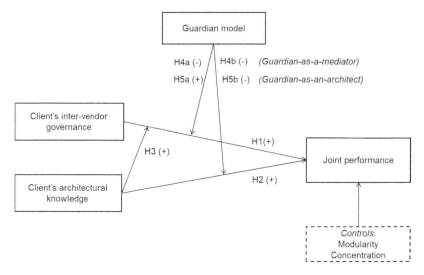

Fig. 3.2 Research model

The Client's Sources of Internal IP Capacity

The Client's Inter-vendor Governance

According to the IPV, governance is considered an important source of IP capacity (Galbraith, 1977). In the context of multisourcing, it is manifested in inter-vendor governance efforts directed at achieving coordination and cooperation among multiple vendors. The literature distinguishes between formal and informal governance mechanisms (Bharadwaj et al., 2010). Formal, or mechanistic, governance relies on pre-specified plans (or programs, procedures, and behaviors) and goals (or outcomes), and includes efforts toward specifying, monitoring, and enforcing these plans and goals. Thus, formal inter-vendor governance includes procedures that specify how vendors shall collaborate to achieve joint performance. As an example of a joint procedural mechanism, Wiener and Saunders (2014) described how a client firm set up a support team made up of representatives from each vendor for the duration of the contract. In this type of formal arrangement, vendors' representatives are able to communicate with each other in order to coordinate work on interdependent tasks, while the client firm maintains communications with all vendors to ensure compliance with the contract requirements.[8]

In contrast to such formal governance, informal or organic governance relies on ad hoc communication between people (Poppo & Zenger, 2002). The IPV literature refers to informal governance as the "creation of lateral relationships" that allow for "joint decision processes, which cut across levels of authority" (Galbraith, 1984, p. 24). In the context of multisourcing, this means communication is facilitated across different hierarchical levels between the client and all vendors. Hence, we conceptualize informal inter-vendor governance as more or less frequently undertaken efforts for joint communication, i.e., communication involving the client and all vendors that cuts across different hierarchical levels. For example, client representatives may meet with corresponding staff from all vendors in order to resolve accountability issues (Wiener & Saunders, 2014). In line with prior IPV studies, we anticipate that both formal and informal inter-vendor governance generate IP capacity and so help to improve joint performance (Mani et al., 2010). Accordingly, we hypothesize:

H1: The stronger the client's formal and informal inter-vendor governance, the higher the joint performance.

The Client's Architectural Knowledge

While the client can generate IP capacity through governance efforts to support coordination and cooperation between vendors, the cognitive stream of the IPV literature suggests that effective IP also depends on underlying knowledge. In this regard, in order to improve joint performance, it is imperative that the client brings in relevant knowledge on how the different services outsourced to different vendors should work together. Indeed, past research in the related domain of product development has shown that firms engaging in multisourcing have invested in developing abilities to integrate components delivered from various vendors (Brusoni et al., 2001; Hobday et al., 2005; Takeishi, 2002). Specifically, architectural knowledge is seen as a crucial

---

[8] https://www.information-age.com/how-to-make-multi-sourcing-work-123457348/.

resource that firms should retain or develop if choosing to source from multiple vendors (Brusoni et al., 2001; Takeishi, 2002) For example, in their analysis of specialization in knowledge production, Brusoni et al. (2001) reported that although one manufacturer had fully outsourced the development of aircraft engine control systems to multiple vendors, the manufacturer still made significant efforts to develop and retain its architectural knowledge, i.e., "knowledge about the ways in which the components are integrated and linked together into a coherent whole" (Gopal & Gosain, 2010, p. 11). Possessing such architectural knowledge improves the clients' ability to ensure joint performance in multisourcing arrangements (Brusoni et al., 2001, p. 614).

Thus, we argue that in addition to the governance efforts discussed above, a major factor determining a client's IP capacity for managing a multisourcing arrangement is the client's architectural knowledge. With the benefit of architectural knowledge, the client is then able to cope with the interdependencies between the outsourced sub-tasks and manage interfaces between services delivered by individual vendors. Therefore, we posit:

H2: The higher the degree of a client's architectural knowledge, the higher the joint performance.

The two sources of IP capacity discussed above—the client's inter-vendor governance and architectural knowledge—are likely to have complementary effects on joint performance. It is in inter-vendor governance efforts that the client can bring its knowledge to bear to improve the management of interdependencies. Knowledgeable clients are able to anticipate dependencies when they are specifying formal plans for joint action (Gopal & Gosain, 2010; Poppo & Zenger, 2002). They may also have a greater ability to interpret information about actual behaviors or outcomes than less knowledgeable clients (Brusoni et al., 2001). For example, they may be able to determine which vendor is accountable for a faulty delivery and leverage this information during formal and informal governance to avoid finger pointing (Bapna et al., 2010). Indeed Wiener and Saunders (2014) illustrated such a case, arguing that *"consistent with the competitive paradigm, when vendors are part of a sourcing arrangement involving multiple, interdependent vendors, they act in ways to make their performance look better than their competitors' and try* to develop advantages over them (e.g., a vendor may seek to blame the other vendors for project or service delivery problems)" (p. 212). Resolving such conflict requires both governance and architectural knowledge (Kirsch et al., 2002). A knowledgeable client, who well understands the nature of the interdependencies between the vendors, is likely to be able to apply appropriate informal and formal inter-vendor governance mechanisms that address the core of such conflict within the multisourcing arrangement. Clearly, lacking the required understanding of interdependencies would prevent the client firm from enacting appropriate inter-vendor governance mechanisms to resolve the problem. In sum, both formal and informal inter-vendor governing efforts are likely to be more effective for joint performance when the client has a strong architectural knowledge. Therefore, we hypothesize:

H3: A higher degree of architectural knowledge held by the client strengthens the positive association between inter-vendor governance and joint performance.

A Guardian Vendor as a Source of External IP Capacity

Our earlier examination of the guardian vendor's role suggests that the guardian may serve alternative purposes as *a mediator* or as *an architect*. The guardian in either role has differing implications for the client firm. For the guardian-as-a-mediator, it is expected that the client firm would retreat from governance efforts now to be carried out by the guardian vendor. For the guardian-as-an-architect, the client firm would retain governance effort while benefiting from the guardian's architectural knowledge. As the literature has so far only considered the guardian's mediator role, here we propose a competing explanation and seek to theorize the effect of each role on joint performance.

The Guardian-as-a-Mediator Perspective

Viewing the guardian vendor as a mediator suggests that the guardian vendor is positioned between the client and the other vendor(s) in the multisourcing arrangement. Seen through an IPV lens, the guardian-as-a-mediator receives and interprets information from the client (such as information about the overall service expected from all the vendors working together), conveys the information to the other vendors, and receives, interprets, and conveys information from the vendors back to the client. In line with this perspective, Wiener and Saunders (2014) argue that "the guardian vendor [...] coordinates the other vendors on the client's behalf" (p. 213). This assertion implies that the *client retreats from inter-vendor governance*, handing over this responsibility to the guardian vendor. The two internal sources of IP capacity, inter-vendor governance and the client's architectural knowledge, are then likely to become less important or even detrimental for joint performance.

Regarding the first, high amounts of inter-vendor governance by the client could even be detrimental to joint performance because confusion may arise if the guardian vendor believes it is to exercise inter-vendor governance, but the client continues to do so as well. A client who actively exercises inter-vendor governance would be at odds with the "single point of contact" (Wiener & Saunders, 2014, p. 213) principle inherent to the guardian-as-a-mediator perspective. Such parallel governance efforts are likely to result in coordination failures and accountability challenges.

The *client's architectural knowledge* is also likely to become less important with a guardian model based on the guardian-as-a-mediator perspective. Since the client retreats from inter-vendor governance, it is likely to have far fewer occasions to bring to bear its own knowledge. The occasions in which the client does bring to bear its own knowledge are then largely limited to interactions with the guardian vendor. So, although architectural knowledge may still be beneficial in helping to govern the guardian vendor more effectively, it is likely to be less critical than in the case of a direct model.

In sum, we argue that should the guardian assume the role of a mediator, it is plausible to suggest that the IP capacities of the client will be substituted by the IP capacity generated through the guardian model. We therefore assert that:

H4a/b: The choice of the guardian model weakens the positive effects (a) of the client's inter-vendor governance and (b) of the client's architectural knowledge on joint performance.

The Guardian-as-an-Architect Perspective

An alternative perspective to the guardian-as-a-mediator is the guardian-as-an-architect. This suggests that the guardian vendor contributes to joint performance by bringing in architectural knowledge that supports the client's governance efforts, rather than relieving the client from engaging in inter-vendor governance. In this perspective, the guardian vendor has a complementary relationship with the client regarding inter-vendor governance and a substitutive relationship with the client regarding architectural knowledge, as we will argue next.

According to the guardian-as-an-architect perspective, we expect a complementary relationship with the client's inter-vendor governance for two reasons. First, the guardian vendor brings in valuable knowledge, such as knowledge of governance structures effective for multisourcing relationships (Levina & Su, 2008), and of the service architecture that underlies the multisourcing arrangement. As we argued earlier, knowledge is likely to make governance more effective (Brusoni et al., 2001; Kirschet et al., 2002), as the client managers are able to leverage this knowledge to improve their inter-vendor governance. Second, while the guardian vendor may lack the formal authority and thus legitimacy to enact effective governance, the client maintains a high level of involvement in this capacity. Indeed, the client is the only party with legally binding contractual agreements with all the vendors (Bapna et al., 2010; Cohen & Young, 2006). High levels of inter-vendor governance by the client paired with a guardian model allow multisourcing arrangements to leverage the client's authority and the guardian vendor's knowledge at the same time. In sum, we expect that the external IP capacity generated through the knowledge brought in by the guardian will complement the internal IP capacity generated through the client's inter-vendor governance. These ideas echo Bapna et al.'s (2010) view of the governance efforts of the client in the presence of a guardian vendor, in that: "[...]

not only does the client still engage in multilateral contracts with multiple vendors but also has to consider the guardian's ability to ensure cooperation and coordination in determining its overall relationship structure" (p. 794).

In the guardian-as-an-architect perspective, while the guardian vendor complements the client's inter-vendor governance, it substitutes the *client's architectural knowledge*. Without the presence of a guardian vendor, the client requires strong architectural knowledge in order to exercise effective governance (e.g., to tackle accountability problems and to design effective plans for coordination). Conversely, the client's architectural knowledge is likely to be less critical (although still beneficial) in the presence of a guardian vendor. If a client lacks architectural knowledge, the guardian vendor can compensate by providing guidance on how to set up and exercise effective inter-vendor governance. Thus, the positive effect of the client's architectural knowledge on joint performance is likely to be weaker in the guardian model than in the direct model. This corresponds to a substitutive relationship (Tiwana, 2010, p. 88), whereby the benefits from the architectural knowledge held by the client decrease with the choice of the guardian model. Seen through the IPV, the external IP capacity generated through the guardian vendor's knowledge partially substitutes the internal IP capacity generated through the client's architectural knowledge.

In conclusion, the guardian-as-an-architect perspective leads us to the following hypothesis:

H5a/b: The choice of the guardian model (a) strengthens the positive effect of the client's governance on joint performance, while (b) weakening the positive effect of the client's architectural knowledge on joint performance.

Control Variables

While our research model focuses on sources of IP capacity and their interactions, we have also controlled for a number of other relationships established in the outsourcing and IPV literature. First, we controlled for modularity. Modularity refers to the degree to which the outsourced sub-tasks can be easily combined into a coherent whole (Sanchez & Mahoney, 1996; Tanriverdi et al., 2007). Outsourcing arrangements of high modularity rely on well-defined, standardized interfaces that facilitate the integration of the sub-tasks performed by the different parties (Baldwin & Clark, 2006; Mithas & Whitaker, 2007; Tanriverdi et al., 2007). From an IPV perspective, such modularity is a key determinant of IP requirements (Tanriverdi et al., 2007). Modular arrangements may ease the composition and integration of sub-tasks outsourced to different vendors and, so, lower IP requirements. Accordingly, modularity may increase joint performance independent of the IP capacity available in a multisourcing arrangement. Second, in line with the existing IPV research, we controlled for interactions of IP requirements with sources of IP capacity (Andres & Zmud, 2001/2002; Mani et al., 2010). Specifically, it can be argued that high modularity lowers the need for IP capacities to satisfy the client's expectations of joint vendor performance. We therefore controlled for interactions between modularity and formal and informal governance, the client's architectural knowledge, and the choice of the guardian model. Moreover, we controlled for concentration (i.e., the degree to which a large fraction of the project work is allocated to a few vendors) (Galbraith, 1977, p. 39), age of the arrangement (i.e., the number of years since the creation of the multisourcing arrangement), client size (as indicated by the number of employees), client country, client industry, and tasks included in the arrangement (business process outsourcing, application development). We also controlled for the interaction between concentration and choice of the guardian model. Low concentration indicates that many vendors are involved in the multisourcing arrangement. The lower the concentration, the more difficult may it be for the guardian vendor to manage the large number of other vendors, suggesting a possible interaction effect between concentration and the choice of the guardian model.

Methods

Data

We empirically tested the theoretical framework (Fig. 3.3) using a survey questionnaire and "key informants"[9] methodology for data collection (Pinsonneault & Kraemer, 1993), in line with past IS outsourcing studies (e.g., Goo et al., 2008). The data were collected in 2012 and 2013 with the help of a UK-based market research firm.

The questionnaire was administered to organizations across different countries, including the UK, Germany, France, Italy, Spain, and the US, and spanning a variety of industries. For this purpose, the original English version of the questionnaire was translated by the market research firm and checked by native speakers (chosen by the authors) who were familiar with the study context to ensure the correctness of

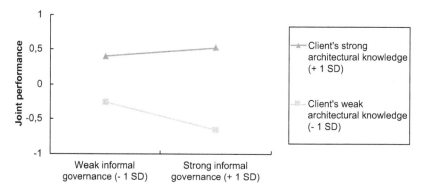

Fig. 3.3 Informal governance affecting joint performance under strong versus weak client's architectural knowledge

---

[9] Goo et al. explained why a "key informant" methodology was relevant for their study of outsourcing: "In survey research, targeted respondents assume the role of a key informant and provide information on a particular unit of analysis (a single outsourcing contract in this study) by reporting on group or organizational properties rather than personal attitudes and perception. This method relies on selecting members to provide information about an outsourcing setting. Informants were not chosen at random; rather, they are selected because they possess specific qualifications such as status, experience, or specialized knowledge" (p.485).

the translation. Responses were collected using both telephone interviews and an online survey.

The questionnaire was distributed among potential middle and top-level informants who were familiar with multisourcing arrangements within their firms. To ensure the targeted individuals' familiarity with multisourcing arrangements (so qualifying them as a "key informant"), the respondents needed to answer a set of screening questions and meet the following criteria[10]:

- Being employed by an organization with at least 250 employees,
- Having an outsourcing arrangement(s) in place where the organization had consciously divided a task or project into particular sub-tasks or sub-projects that were outsourced to different vendors, and
- Having familiarity with the management of such a multisourcing arrangement in her or his company.

The respondent then had to select one particular multisourcing arrangement currently in place in their company and with which they were familiar. Within this particular multisourcing arrangement, the respondent was asked to select the two vendors contributing the most to the multisourcing arrangement (in terms of amount of work). The questions relevant for testing our model pertained only to this particular multisourcing arrangement with the two chosen vendors, subsequently called vendor A and B throughout the questionnaire. Our study and empirical testing thus focused on one particular "triad" within the multisourcing arrangement (Choi & Wu, 2009), each triad consisting of the client and two key vendors. Focusing on triads ensured that the unit of analysis was the same for all respondents.

Before sending out the final questionnaire, the questionnaire items were pilot-tested with 15 international organizations to ensure that all items could be understood and answered by the intended group of respondents. Each block of questions was followed by an open field for comments, where respondents were asked to note down any

---

[10] The market research firm used these criteria to select key informants from a panel of individuals that had agreed to participate in surveys.

thoughts they had on the questions asked in the preceding section. The comments were considered in the refinement of the questionnaire and some amendments were introduced to improve the clarity of questions. In addition, we tested our model on the pilot data to assess the validity of the constructs. Items that loaded very low were removed from the questionnaire.

The finalized questionnaire was sent out to 2000 organizations. Overall, 200 usable questionnaires were made available after several follow-ups with the sample organizations. From these 200 cases, we excluded 10 after reviewing the descriptions of outsourced tasks. We excluded cases when the sub-tasks assigned to different vendors were not interdependent (e.g., outsourcing IT procurement to vendor A and sales advice to vendor B), or when the outsourced tasks did not match our target services, which comprised IT services and IT-supported business processes. For example, in one case the services were "providing a camera crew" (vendor A) and "providing special equipment for camera crew services" (vendor B). We also excluded one outlier, which reported a joint performance of four standard deviations below the sample mean although the same firm reported above-average satisfaction[11] with the outsourcing arrangement, suggesting an erroneous measurement. Our final sample size was $n = 189$. Table 3.1 shows the sample characteristics.

Measures

Each construct was measured with a block of indicators (questionnaire items). Where possible, we used existing measures that we adapted to the study context (Galbraith, 1977; Takeishi, 2002; Tanriverdi et al., 2007). All items were measured on a five-point Likert scale, ranging from "strongly disagree" (=1) to "strongly agree" (=5) with "neither agree nor disagree" (=3) as the mid-point. An overview of the constructs and measurement items is provided in Table 3.2. Joint performance was measured by six items (developed in IS outsourcing research) that focused on the degree to which the joint performance of the two vendors

---

[11] The survey included three items measuring satisfaction (composite reliability .87), which were not used for this study.

3 What the Guardian Does in Multisourcing Projects

Table 3.1 Sample characteristics

Characteristics of the sample		[Min; max]	Mean (std. dev.)
Respondent work experience	Number of years working in organization	[0.5; 35]	8.6 (6.5)
Age of multisourcing arrangement	Years that have passed since the start of the multisourcing arrangement	[1; 9]	3.7 (2.4)
		Number	Percentage (%)
Client size	Up to 1,000 employees	70	37
	1,001 to 5,000 employees	61	32
	5,001 to 50,000 employees	46	24
	More than 50,000 employees	12	6
Country	United Kingdom	33	17
	France	31	16
	Germany	33	17
	Italy	32	17
	Spain	30	16
	USA	30	16
Industry sector	Financial services	34	18
	Manufacturing	39	21
	Retail, distribution, and transport	25	13
	Public sector	35	19
	Other	56	30
Respondent's area of work within client firm	Owner/executive	22	12
	Finance	18	10
	IT	103	54
	Facilities	5	3
	Marketing	7	4
	Customer services	15	8
	Human resources	10	5
	Logistics	9	5

met the client's expectations. Architectural knowledge was measured by three items that focused on the client's knowledge in relation to the integration of the services delivered by the two vendors. Our measures of formal governance referred to the use of two key formal governance strategies in the IPV, i.e., procedures and goals (Galbraith, 1977). The measures focused on the client's efforts for specifying joint procedures and goals and for evaluating the vendors' adherence to the procedures and goals. Our measures of informal governance focused on what IPV researchers call lateral relations, i.e., "direct contact between two people who share a problem" at the same hierarchical level (Galbraith, 1977, p. 53). These measures, adapted from Takeishi (2002), assessed the amount of direct contact at three levels: IT staff, middle management, and top management. To assess whether a guardian vendor model was chosen, we asked whether one of the two vendors was responsible for managing other vendors. The measures for our control variable modularity were taken from Tanriverdi et al. (2007). Table 3.3 provides an overview of the measures for control variables.

Instrument Validation

To validate our survey instrument, we assessed convergent and discriminant validity through factor analysis procedures. To examine convergent validity, we first performed an exploratory factor analysis in SPSS (DeVellis, 2012, p. 153). This analysis reproduced the five latent factors of our research model with eigenvalues greater than 1.6. Eigenvalues greater than 1 suggest convergent validity (Campbell & Fiske, 1959). To further corroborate convergent validity, we calculated composite reliability (CR), average variance extracted (AVE), and standardized factor loadings, using confirmatory factor analysis procedures in SmartPLS (Gefen & Straub, 2005). CR was well above the threshold of 0.7 for all constructs (see Table 3.2). AVE was well above the threshold of 0.5 for all constructs (see Table 3.2). The standardized factor loadings were greater than 0.7 with the exceptions of FG1 (0.66) and FG4 (0.65), which were close to the threshold. These two slightly lower values could be due to our attempt to capture formal governance as broadly and comprehensively as possible. By and large, the measurement evidence supports convergent validity.

We then examined discriminant validity. We examined whether each item loaded higher on its construct than on any other construct (Gefen & Straub, 2005). For each item, the difference between the loading of the item on its construct and the cross-loading of the item on any other construct was above 0.2. Moreover, we examined whether the square roots of the AVE values exceeded correlations between latent

Table 3.2 Questionnaire items (CR = composite reliability, AVE = average variance extracted)

Construct	Item	Wording	Reference
Joint performance (CR = 0.90, AVE = 0.61)		With regard to combined performance of vendor A and vendor B as part of the multisourcing arrangement so far...	Grover et al. (1996)
	JP1	... the products/services delivered meet our expectations	
	JP2	... we have met our goals	
	JP3	... we have completed key milestones in accordance with our objectives	
	JP4	... we have achieved our desired cost savings	
	JP5	... we are satisfied with our overall benefits from outsourcing	Lee and Kim (1999)
	JP6	... we have so far met project/service requirements	Tiwana (2008)
Architectural knowledge (CR = 0.88, AVE = 0.72)		The following questions are related to the level of knowledge of you and your in-house colleagues. We have knowledge about	Takeishi (2002)
	AK1	... the design of the overall product and service architecture to which vendors A and B contribute	

(continued)

Table 3.2 (continued)

Construct	Item	Wording	Reference
	AK2	... how to structurally coordinate the products and services delivered by vendors A and B with all other related products and services of our organization	Henderson and Clark (1990)
	AK3	... the ways in which the products and services delivered by vendors A and B are integrated and linked together in a coherent whole	
Formal governance (CR = 0.90, AVE = 0.63)		To ensure that it is not the individual performance of vendor A and B, but rather their combined performance (i.e., solutions by vendor A and B in combination as part of the multisourcing arrangement) that meets our objectives, we	Kirsch et al. (2002)
	FG1	... expect both vendors to follow an understandable written sequence of steps that defines interactions between these two vendors	

Construct	Item	Wording	Reference
	FG2	... assess the extent to which both vendors interact in accordance to existing written procedures and practices when delivering the outsourced service	
	FG3	... evaluate the extent to which combined services are delivered as defined in the contract regardless of how this goal is accomplished	
	FG4	... test intermediary and/or final joint outcomes/deliverables against criteria defined in the contract, regardless of how this goal is achieved	
	FG5	... have several sources of objective data we can rely on	
	FG6	... have defined quantifiable measures depicting the extent to which combined objectives are achieved	
	FG7	... have defined accurate and reliable measures that indicate the extent to which the delivered services jointly meet our objectives	

(continued)

Table 3.2 (continued)

Construct	Item	Wording	Reference
Informal governance (CR = 0.86, AVE = 0.66)	IG1	Our IT staff interact jointly with both vendors' IT personnel	Takeishi (2002)
	IG2	Our middle managers interact jointly with both vendors' middle managers	
	IG3	Our top managers/executives interact jointly with both vendors' top managers/executives	
Guardian versus Direct (single item)	GU	Are either of the two vendors responsible for managing all other vendors in the multisourcing arrangement? • Yes, vendor A → Guardian • Yes, vendor B → Guardian • No, this is our responsibility → Non-guardian • Other (please explain) → Manually coded[12]	Self-developed
Modularity (CR = 0.81, AVE = 0.68)	MO1	Regarding the two tasks/projects outsourced to vendor A and B, … … it is very easy to combine their particular outcomes into a coherent whole	Tanriverdi et al. (2007)
	MO2	… they have well-defined interfaces with each other	

[12] Only one respondent selected the "Other" category. The comment suggested than a third vendor (not vendor A or B) was responsible for managing the other vendors. We therefore coded this response as a guardian model.

Table 3.3 Control variables

Variable	Measurement
Concentration	The fraction of the overall budget of the multisourcing arrangement that is assigned to vendors A and B; measured through a single-item question
Modularity	Measured through two questionnaire items (see Table 3.2)
Age of the multisourcing arrangement	The number of years since the start of the multisourcing arrangement; measured through a single-item question
Client size	The client's number of employees; measured through a single-item question (transformation: natural logarithm)
Country	Single-item question on the client's country (United Kingdom, Germany, Italy, Spain, USA, France); incorporated through five dichotomous dummy variables (reference category: France)
Industry	Single-item question on the client's sector (financial services, manufacturing, retail, public sector, other); incorporated through four dichotomous dummy variables (reference category: Other)
Business Process Outsourcing (BPO)	Indicates whether business processes (other than IT) were part of the outsourced tasks; coded based on task descriptions
Application Development	Indicates whether the development of application software was part of the outsourced tasks; coded based on task descriptions

constructs (Gefen & Straub, 2005). The square root of the lowest AVE value (0.75 for formal governance) was well above the highest correlation between two latent constructs (0.60 for the correlation between joint performance and formal governance). These results, and the fact that exploratory factor analysis reproduced the five latent factors, strongly support discriminant validity.

Regression Analysis

We used ordinary least squares (OLS) regression to test our hypotheses. Given our focus on interaction effects, we chose OLS regression over alternative approaches, such as partial least squares (PLS) and covariance-based structural equation modeling (SEM). OLS regression offers higher statistical power for detecting interaction effects than PLS or covariance-based SEM (Goodhue et al., 2007; Kline, 2023). The advantage gained in statistical power is particularly pronounced in models such as ours, in which many items are subject to interaction effects (Goodhue et al., 2007, p. 222). We relied on standardized mean scores to transform sets of items into regression variables.

We used a four-step hierarchical regression strategy. In the first step (Model 1), we included the main effects of control variables. In the second step (Model 2), we added the main effects of the hypothesized predictors. In the third step (Model 3), we added the interactions of IP requirements (i.e., modularity) with sources of IP capacity (i.e., formal and informal governance, architectural knowledge, guardian model) to control for interaction effects established in the IPV research. In the fourth step (Model 4), we added the hypothesized interaction effects.

We examined whether the assumptions of OLS were met (Wooldridge, 2009). The histograms and q-q plots showed that the residuals of all the models followed normal distributions, indicating that the assumption of normally distributed error terms was met. Variance inflation factors were below 3, suggesting that multicollinearity problems were not salient in the data. Plotting residuals and joint performance in a scatter plot diagram showed no departure from the assumption of homoscedastic error terms.

Although our study focused on interaction effects and interaction effects cannot be artifacts of common-method variance (e.g., Siemsen et al., 2010), we performed Harman's single factor test to appreciate whether item responses varied due to one single factor. We found that a single factor was able to explain 26% of the variance and that five factors were needed to explain half of the variance. Given these results and our focus on interaction effects, it is unlikely that the findings reported in this study are artifacts of common-method variance.

To examine nonresponse bias, we compared the means of eight key variables (joint performance, modularity, concentration, age of the arrangement, formal governance, informal governance, architectural knowledge, guardian) between multisourcing arrangements that were in our sample and multisourcing arrangements not included in the sample (most frequently due to the respondents' lack of willingness to provide descriptions of the outsourced tasks). Comparisons revealed no significant differences with the exception of formal governance, which was somewhat higher in the arrangements included in final sample than in those excluded (3.99 vs. 3.82; t test; $n = 369$; $p < 0.05$). With only one of out of eight comparisons yielding a significant difference, we inferred that nonresponse bias was unlikely to be a serious threat to the validity of our analysis.

Results

Table 3.4. shows descriptive statistics, separated by guardian versus direct subsamples. The only significant differences referred to business process outsourcing, which was more frequent in the guardian sample, and informal governance, which was stronger in the guardian sample. Table 3.5 presents bivariate correlations.

The results of our four-step OLS regression are presented in Table 3.6. The first column (Model 1) presents results related to our control variables. Modularity ($\beta = 0.44$; $p < 0.001$) and the country dummy variable for the US ($\beta = 0.50$; $p < 0.05$) had significant positive associations with joint performance while all other control variables were insignificant.

Table 3.4 Descriptive statistics and sample comparison

	Direct sample: mean (standard deviation)	Guardian sample: mean (standard deviation)	Difference statistically significant
Joint performance	4.06 (0.65)	4.02 (0.75)	No
Concentration	52.17 (31.49)	55.63 (29.28)	No
Modularity	3.72 (0.83)	3.96 (0.88)	No
Age of arrangement	3.76 (2.44)	3.44 (2.29)	No
Client size	7.88 (1.80)	8.03 (1.56)	No
Business process outsourcing	0.56 (50)	0.82 (0.38)	Yes ($p < 0.05$)
Application development	0.20 (0.40)	0.11 (0.31)	No
Formal governance	3.93 (0.74)	4.12 (0.56)	No
Informal governance	2.73 (1.06)	3.12 (0.96)	Yes ($p < .05$)
Architectural knowledge	4.03 (0.76)	4.19 (0.66)	No
Sub-sample size (n)	132	57	–

3 What the Guardian Does in Multisourcing Projects   91

Table 3.5 Bivariate correlations

	Joint perf	Con	Mo	Age	Cl. size	BPO	App. dev	Grd	Form. gov	Inf. gov	Arch. knowl
Joint performance	1										
Concentration	0.03	1									
Modularity	0.44*	0.13*	1								
Age of arrangement	0.07	−0.09	0.07	1							
Client size	−0.05	0.08	0.05	0.20*	1						
BPO	0.12	0.10	0.15*	0.14*	−0.10	1					
Appl. development	−0.12	−0.10	−0.12	−0.03	0.05	−0.38*	1				
Guardian	−0.02	0.05	0.13	−0.06	0.04	0.25*	−0.12	1			
Formal governance	0.58*	0.03	0.40*	0.01	−0.07	0.13	−0.14	0.12	1		
Informal governance	0.12	0.09	0.09	0.11	0.04	0.12	0.00	0.17*	0.15*	1	
Architectural knowledge	0.52*	−0.10	0.29*	0.04	0.07	0.03	−0.01	0.10	0.57*	0.16*	1

*$p < 0.05$

Table 3.6 Regression results

	Model 1	Model 2	Model 3	Model 4
(Constant)	−0.29 (0.23)	−0.13 (0.19)	−0.03 (0.19)	−0.13 (0.19)
Concentration	−0.03 (0.07)	0.02 (0.06)	0.15* (0.07)	**0.17*** (0.07)
Modularity	**0.43***** (0.07)	**0.23***** (0.06)	**0.25**** (0.08)	**0.24**** (0.08)
Age of arrangement	−0.02 (0.07)	−0.01 (0.06)	0.01 (0.06)	0.01 (0.06)
Client Size	−0.06 (0.07)	−0.04 (0.06)	−0.06 (0.06)	−0.04 (0.06)
County: Germany	−0.03 (0.23)	−0.15 (0.20)	−0.21 (0.19)	−0.06 (0.19)
Country: Italy	−0.06 (0.24)	0.04 (0.20)	0.09 (0.20)	0.16 (0.20)
Country: Spain	0.48 (0.25)	0.25 (0.21)	0.31 (0.21)	0.37 (0.21)
Country: UK	0.04 (0.23)	−0.07 (0.20)	−0.02 (0.20)	0.04 (0.20)
Country: US	**0.50*** (0.23)	0.25 (0.20)	0.22 (0.20)	0.29 (0.19)
Industry: Financial services	0.26 (0.20)	0.10 (0.17)	0.03 (0.17)	0.07 (0.16)
Industry: Public sector	0.03 (0.20)	0.10 (0.17)	0.02 (0.16)	0.05 (0.16)
Industry: Manufacturing	0.29 (0.19)	0.29 (0.16)	0.15 (0.16)	0.21 (0.16)
Industry: Retail	0.10 (0.22)	0.21 (0.19)	0.21 (0.19)	0.23 (0.18)
Business Process Outsourcing	0.06 (0.16)	0.10 (0.14)	0.08 (0.14)	0.06 (0.13)
Application Development	−0.11 (0.19)	−0.08 (0.16)	−0.08 (0.16)	−0.07 (0.15)
−0.31* (0.13)−0.32* (0.13)−0.37** (0.13)Guardian		**−0.31*** (0.13)	**−0.32*** (0.13)	**−0.37**** (0.13)
Formal governance		**0.31***** (0.07)	**0.26***** (0.07)	**0.18*** (0.08)
Informal governance		0.00 (0.06)	0.02 (0.06)	−0.07 (0.06)

	Model 1	Model 2	Model 3	Model 4
Architectural knowledge		0.29*** (0.07)	0.34*** (0.07)	0.46*** (0.08)
Modularity × Guardian			0 (0.13)	−0.04 (0.14)
Modularity × Formal governance			−0.11 (0.07)	−0.12 (0.07)
Modularity × Informal governance			0.06 (0.05)	−0.02 (0.06)
Modularity × Client's architectural knowledge			0.02 (0.07)	0.03 (0.07)
Concentration × Guardian			−0.42** (0.13)	−0.46*** (0.13)
Formal governance × Client's architectural knowledge				−0.01 (0.06)
Informal governance × Client's architectural knowledge				0.13* (0.06)
Guardian × Formal governance				0.42* (0.19)
Guardian × Informal governance				0.38** (0.14)
Guardian × Client's architectural knowledge				−0.52** (0.17)
Adjusted R^2	0.21	0.44	0.47	0.51
R^2	0.27	0.49	0.54	0.59
ΔR^2	0.27	0.22	0.05	0.05
F Change (d.f.)	4.34*** (15, 173)	18.33 (4,169)***	3.20*** (5, 164)	3.63** (5, 159)

*$p < 0.05$, **$p < 0.01$, ***$p < 0.001$

The second column in Table 3.4 (Model 2) shows the main effects of our four predictors (i.e., the sources of IP capacity), allowing us to test H1 and H2. H1 predicted positive main effects for formal and informal governance on joint performance. We found a significant positive effect for formal governance ($\beta = 0.31$; $p < 0.001$) but not for informal governance. Hence, H1 is partially supported. H2 predicted a positive main effect of architectural knowledge on joint performance. We found a significant positive effect ($\beta = 0.29$; $p < 0.001$), supporting H2. Although we did not hypothesize a main effect of the presence of the guardian vendor on joint performance, we obtained a significant negative main effect ($\beta = -0.31$; $p < 0.05$).

Before adding the hypothesized interaction effects, we controlled for possible interactions of our hypothesized sources of IP capacity with modularity (as to reflect IP requirements), and for the interaction of concentration with the choice of the guardian model. As the third column (Model 3) shows, none of interactions of sources of IP capacity with modularity was significant. Conversely, we found a significant negative interaction effect of concentration with the choice of the guardian model ($\beta = -0.42$; $p < 0.01$).

The fourth column (Model 4) presents the results of our full model, which include the interaction effects hypothesized in H3 to H5. H3 predicted positive interaction effects of formal/informal inter-vendor governance and the client's architectural knowledge. As can be seen, only the interaction between informal inter-vendor governance and the client's architectural knowledge was significant and positive ($\beta = 0.13$; $p < 0.05$), thus partially supporting H3. Following the guardian-as-a-mediator perspective, H4 predicted negative interaction effects between the choice of the guardian model and the client's formal/informal inter-vendor governance (H4a), and with the client's architectural knowledge (H4b). As Model 4 shows, we found positive rather than negative interaction effects of the guardian model with formal ($\beta = 0.42$; $p < 0.05$) and informal ($\beta = 0.38$; $p < 0.01$) inter-vendor governance. H4a is thus rejected. In line with H4b, the interaction effects between the guardian model and architectural knowledge were significant ($\beta = -0.52$; $p < 0.01$). While the results do not fully align with the predictions derived from the guardian-as-a-mediator perspective, they do align with the predictions derived from the guardian-as-an-architect perspective. In line with H5a, we found significant positive interaction effects of the guardian model with formal ($\beta = 0.42$; $p < 0.05$) and informal ($\beta = 0.38$; $p < 0.01$) inter-vendor governance. Moreover, in line with H5b, we found significant negative interaction effects of the guardian model and architectural knowledge ($\beta = -0.52$; $p < 0.01$).

Our full model (Model 4) showed the strongest explanatory power (adjusted $R^2 = 0.51$) of all the tested models (see the bottom of Table 3.4). The hypothesized interaction effects between sources of IP capacity (from Model 3 to Model 4) added statistically significant amounts of explained variance ($\Delta R^2 = 0.05$; $\Delta F = 3.63$; $p < 0.01$), supporting the relevancy of interaction effects expressed in H3 and H5. Next, we discuss our results.

Discussion

The purpose of this study was to examine joint performance in multisourcing arrangements in light of the interdependencies between multiple vendors. Indeed, multisourcing has become a dominant sourcing model, attracting growing attention in the IS community (Levina & Su, 2008; Wiener & Saunders, 2014). While multisourcing offers client firms numerous advantages through a competitive and yet cooperative regime, it also poses new challenges, mainly in the form of interdependencies that require the client firm to increase its efforts to achieve coordination and cooperation. Building on key IPV concepts, we framed these efforts as greater IP requirements. Given these IP requirements, a critical challenge in multisourcing arrangements is to generate sufficient IP capacity. In this regard, we proposed two possible sources of IP capacity. The first, the direct model (see Fig. 3.1a), relies on internal sources of IP capacity only, seeking to leverage the client's formal and informal governance and architectural knowledge. The second, the guardian model (see Fig. 3.1b), relies both on internal sources and on the use of a guardian vendor as a means of providing additional IP capacity.

Direct Model

Our results regarding the direct model (i.e., the client alone managing the multisourcing arrangement) suggest that both *formal inter-vendor governance* and *architectural knowledge* lead to higher joint performance. In particular, individually, each of these two sources of IP capacity (as captured in H1 and H2) equips the client firm with the IP capacity needed to manage interdependencies in the multisourcing arrangement. The results for the direct model highlight the importance of formal inter-vendor governance based on written procedures and the contractual agreement structure (e.g., objective and quantifiable measures) as a means of coping with coordination and integration efforts between vendors, manifested here as an IP challenge. Interestingly, formal inter-vendor governance seems to be an effective strategy irrespective of the client's level of architectural knowledge (see the insignificant interaction effect of formal inter-vendor governance and client's architectural knowledge).

On the other hand, *informal inter-vendor governance* seems to be effective only when the client has strong architectural knowledge (see the insignificant main effect of informal inter-vendor governance and the significant positive interaction effect of informal inter-vendor governance and client's architectural knowledge). The interaction plot depicted in Fig. 3.3 further illustrates the relationships. When a client possesses strong architectural knowledge (i.e., one standard deviation above the mean), greater informal inter-vendor governance is associated with higher joint performance. Conversely, when a client possesses weak architectural knowledge (i.e., one standard deviation below the mean), greater informal inter-vendor governance is associated with lower joint performance. The lack of a positive main effect of informal inter-vendor governance is rather surprising, given that the IS outsourcing literature has persistently found a positive effect of informal governance (often viewed as relational governance) on outsourcing performance in dyadic settings (e.g., Lacity et al., 2010; Poppo & Zenger, 2002). One possible explanation for the surprising result in our study is that informal inter-vendor governance in triadic relationships is different from informal governance in dyadic relationships. Having more than two parties involved may erode the sense of being "informal" and make all parties involved feel part of a "formal" relationship. The sense of competition (Wiener & Saunders, 2014) between the vendors is also likely to contribute to such a "formal" attitude. The relational benefits seen in dyadic settings, therefore, may be less pronounced in multisourcing settings.

Guardian Model

We found joint performance in arrangements using a guardian model to be very similar to arrangements using a direct model (4.06 versus 4.02 in a five-point scale, see the first row in Table 3.3). Nonetheless, we also found two significant interaction effects, suggesting that the effectiveness of the guardian model is contingent on the two internal sources of IP capacity.

Our results support the perspective that the guardian can best be utilized as an architect rather than as a mediator. Indeed, we found a complementary effect between the guardian vendor and the client's governance and a substitutive effect between the guardian vendor and the client's architectural knowledge, supporting our hypotheses derived from the guardian-as-an-architect perspective.

The interaction plot depicted in Fig. 3.4 illustrates the complementary effect of the guardian model and inter-vendor governance. A guardian model is likely to diminish joint performance when the client firm exercises weak formal and informal inter-vendor governance (see Fig. 3.4). Yet, the negative effect of the guardian model is reversed to positive when the client firm has strong formal and informal inter-vendor governance mechanisms in place. Therefore, in multisourcing settings, the internal IP capacity of governance (formal and informal) is required by the client in order to gain the benefits of the external IP capacity of architectural knowledge brought by the guardian vendor. This demonstrates the complementary effect of these two sources of IP capacity.

Our results also suggest a substitutive effect between the guardian's and the client's architectural knowledge, as illustrated by the interaction plot depicted in Fig. 3.5. The guardian model improves joint

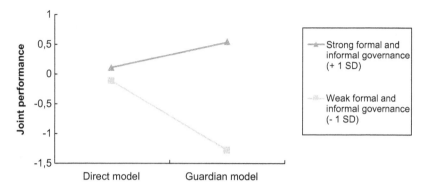

Fig. 3.4 Guardian model (versus direct model) affecting joint performance under strong versus weak governance

performance when clients have weak architectural knowledge, while it worsens performance when clients have strong architectural knowledge. Indeed, these results suggest a substitutive effect between the IP capacity brought forward by the guardian vendor and the client's architectural knowledge. In this regard, the guardian model compensates for the client's weak in-house architectural knowledge and, therefore, a client with weak architectural knowledge may benefit from the guardian's ability to integrate interdependent sub-tasks in multisourcing arrangements. Conversely, clients who possess strong architectural knowledge may benefit to a much lesser extent from the guardian's integration ability.

We found additional support for the perspective of "guardian-as-an-architect." As depicted in Fig. 3.6, the joint performance of the multisourcing arrangement will be higher should a client with weak architectural knowledge choose a guardian model and exercise strong formal and informal governance. On the other hand, a client with strong architectural knowledge will benefit from using the direct model, as Fig. 3.7 depicts. Interestingly, both Fig. 3.6 and Fig. 3.7 show that joint performance is at its lowest when the client chooses a guardian model and exercises weak inter-vendor governance. This is precisely the configuration prescribed by the guardian-as-a-mediator perspective. Irrespective of whether the client's architectural knowledge is high or low, employing

3 What the Guardian Does in Multisourcing Projects   99

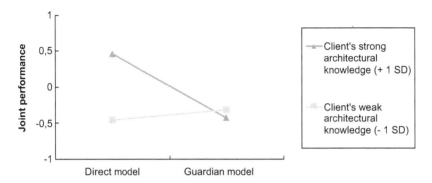

Fig. 3.5 Guardian model (versus direct model) affecting joint performance under strong versus weak client's architectural knowledge

a guardian-as-a-mediator model is likely to result in low levels of joint performance. These findings bear important implications for theory and practice, on which we elaborate next.

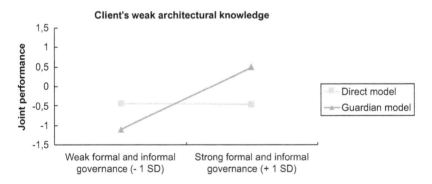

Fig. 3.6 Governance affecting joint performance under direct versus guardian model and under client's weak architectural knowledge

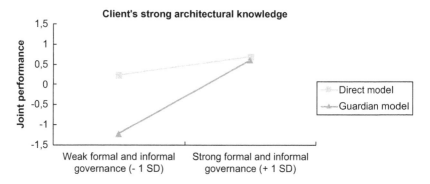

Fig. 3.7 Governance affecting joint performance under direct versus guardian model and under client's strong architectural knowledge

Implications

Theoretical Contributions

This chapter offers two main contributions to the IS outsourcing literature. First, to our best knowledge, this is the first study to model and test determinants of joint performance in IS multisourcing arrangements. While the IS outsourcing literature has, by and large, examined dyadic relationships as a basis for understanding the determinants of outsourcing success (Dibbern et al., 2004; Lacity et al., 2010), our study assumed interdependencies between multiple vendors, thus requiring an examination of triadic relationships at the minimum. As interdependencies may affect the likelihood of multisourcing success, formal and informal inter-vendor governance and architectural knowledge were examined as two key antecedents. Our study shows that while formal inter-vendor governance and the client's architectural knowledge are likely to improve multisourcing success, informal governance, often referred to as relational governance in the IS literature and considered key in achieving dyadic IS outsourcing success, shows no direct effect on joint performance. Our results show a positive effect of informal governance on joint performance only in conjunction with high levels of client's architectural knowledge, or with the choice of a guardian model. These results suggest that multisourcing does not simply mimic dyadic outsourcing at a larger scale. Its inherent independencies require unique governance mechanisms and associated abilities (i.e., architectural knowledge) directed toward the interface between vendors.

The second contribution of this study is in offering insights into the role that a guardian vendor plays in a multisourcing arrangement. Bapna et al. (2010) noted that, although the choice for or against a guardian model is one of the key design choices in multisourcing arrangements, "[t]here is little in the academic literature on the guardian vendor model" (p. 794). They called for research to examine "what aspects of the engagement should be handled by the guardian vendor and the client" (p794). Wiener and Saunders (2014) argue that the guardian model can be regarded as a "mediated model", wherein the guardian vendor acts as a "single point of contact" (p. 213), mediating the interaction between the client and the remaining vendors. This would imply that the only actor responsible for governing interdependencies between vendors is the guardian vendor. Our results, however, show that it can be perilous for the client to withdraw from governance efforts and mandate these to the guardian vendor. In fact, the least successful multisourcing arrangements in our sample were those where the client appointed a guardian vendor and then exercised weak joint formal and informal governance (see Fig. 3.7). In other words, the clients who practiced the guardian-as-a-mediator model were the least successful. We therefore theorized an alternative role in which the guardian acts as an architect.

Our results do indeed suggest that a guardian vendor may be better understood as an *architect* than as a mediator. Much like the architect of a building contributes knowledge of how the elements of a building fit with each other, the guardian-as-an-architect contributes knowledge as to how the sub-tasks of a multisourcing arrangement can be integrated. Two findings support the guardian-as-an-architect view. First, clients who lack architectural knowledge are particularly likely to benefit from the inclusion of a guardian vendor, suggesting that the guardian vendor compensates for the client's knowledge gaps. Second, much as the client's architectural knowledge enables more effective informal governance, so too does utilizing the guardian vendor as an architect. Informal inter-vendor governance involves complex ad hoc communication and decisions by the client, requiring considerable architectural knowledge in order to be exercised effectively. This knowledge may come either from the client, or from a guardian-as-an-architect to support the client in informal governance efforts. Thus, a guardian vendor complements the client's formal and informal inter-vendor governance while substituting the client's architectural knowledge. As such, the guardian model does not relieve clients from governance (as assumed in the guardian-as-mediator model), but it does help them compensate for knowledge gaps.

Another contribution of this study revolves around the body of research that explains the choice and effectiveness of governance mechanisms through an IPV lens. Indeed, the IPV-based literature stream on governance mostly argues that the choice of governance mechanisms determines the IP capacity of an organization, and that such IP capacity should fit IP requirements (Andres & Zmud, 2001/2002; Hui et al., 2008; Mani et al., 2010). Although another literature stream implicitly argues that architectural knowledge is an important source of IP capacity in inter-organizational relationships (Brusoni et al., 2001), these two literature streams have mostly developed in isolation. As a consequence, interactions between governance and knowledge have rarely been considered in IPV research. Conversely, a key argument of our study is that governance mechanisms, such as goal setting, planning, and direct interaction, enable effective IP to the extent that these mechanisms are enacted or assisted by a knowledgeable party.

Practical Implications

Our study offers specific recommendations for practice. Clients in multisourcing arrangements should consider their architectural knowledge when deciding for or against the guardian model. Clients with strong architectural knowledge (i.e., clients who understand well how the various sub-tasks outsourced to different vendors relate to each other) are advised to choose a direct model, whereas clients with weak architectural knowledge are better off with a guardian model. Although clients may believe that having a guardian model means they can economize on or relinquish governance efforts, this is not the case. Instead, clients are well advised to engage in extensive formal and informal governance efforts that involve all vendors. Specifically, clients should define and monitor the joint outcomes to be achieved and the joint procedures to be followed, and they should also put emphasis on informally interacting with all involved vendors at various levels. Importantly, extensive governance efforts are essential, both in a direct model, where the clients can leverage their own knowledge during informal governance in particular, and in a guardian model, where the guardian vendor should bring in additional knowledge to enable effective governance by the client.

Conclusion

There are several limitations to this study that may encourage future research. First, while this is one of the first studies to examine the effect of the guardian on a multisourcing arrangement, our study sheds little light on *what* exactly the guardian vendor does and what information capacities the guardian vendor brings to the multisourcing arrangement. Consequently, following on our guardian-as-an-architect perspective, our study provides a number of fruitful directions for future research. Future studies could take a practice-view and explicitly examine and document the IP requirements that multisourcing settings face. Consequently, future research could study the activities performed by the guardian vendor vis-à-vis the IP requirements, as well as in steering the relationships with the client and with other vendors in multisourcing arrangements. Building on this, future studies could also explore the relationship between the nature of the task (simple or complex) and the implications for the architectural knowledge and governance efforts that the guardian vendor contributes to multisourcing arrangements. Our study calls for a more in-depth examination of the practices and the knowledge contributions of the guardian vendor.

Second, we used OLS regression to examine the effect of governance choices on performance. Although the use of OLS regression is in line with prior research, it is unable to account for the potentially endogenous nature of governance choices. Future research could collect samples that are large enough to enable the use of instrumental variables-based techniques in order to address endogeneity issues.

Third, while our measures of formal and informal inter-vendor governance were closely linked to the IPV, they did not include some mechanisms of contractual governance, such as contract duration and contract type. Future research could integrate these mechanisms into IPV conceptualizations. Moreover, although we focused on the client's inter-vendor governance (i.e., governance involving all vendors at the same time), we did not contrast inter-vendor governance efforts to governance efforts that involve only one vendor at a time (such as an SLA applicable for a single vendor only).

We also see an opportunity for further research around the role of the client in a guardian vendor model. For example, drawing on our finding that informal governance—with the involvement of the client—complements the role of the guardian in achieving high levels of joint performance, a future study could zoom into such informal meetings and explore the activities performed by the client and the knowledge needed. Such a study could, in fact, explore the evolution of triadic relationships between client, guardian, and other vendors and how their actions and knowledge evolve over time (Cao et al., 2013).

Ultimately, such zooming into the client and guardian vendor roles would also further address our call for a more in-depth understanding of the interactions between IP capacities, by studying interactions not only between capacities, e.g., informal and formal governance, but also between the underlying knowledge and the practices needed to bring such capacities to fruition.

References

Andres, H. P., & Zmud, R. W. (2001/2002). A Contingency Approach to Software Project Coordination. *Journal of Management Information Systems*, *18*(3), 41–70.

Bai, G., Coronado, F., & Krishnan, R. (2010). The Role of Performance Measure Noise in Mediating the Relation Between Task Complexity and Outsourcing. *Journal of Management Accounting Research, 22*(1), 75–102.

Baldwin, C. Y., & Clark, K. B. (2006). The Architecture of Participation: Does Code Architecture Mitigate Free Riding in the Open Source Development Model? *Management Science, 52*(7), 1116–1127.

Bapna, R., Barua, A., Mani, D., & Mehra, A. (2010). Research Commentary—Cooperation, Coordination, and Governance in Multisourcing: An Agenda for Analytical and Empirical Research. *Information Systems Research, 21*(4), 785–795.

Bensaou, M., & Venkatraman, N. (1995). Configurations of Interorganizational Relationships: A Comparison Between US and Japanese Automakers. *Management Science, 41*(9), 1471–1492.

Bharadwaj, S. S., Saxena, K. B. C., & Halemane, M. D. (2010). Building a Successful Relationship in Business Process Outsourcing: An Exploratory Study. *European Journal of Information Systems, 19*(2), 168–180.

Brusoni, S., Prencipe, A., & Pavitt, K. (2001). Knowledge Specialization, Organizational Coupling, and the Boundaries of the Firm: Why Do Firms Know More Than They Make? *Administrative Science Quarterly, 46*(4), 597–621.

Campbell, D. T., & Fiske, D. W. (1959). Convergent and Discriminant Validation by the Multitrait-Multimethod Matrix. *Psychological Bulletin, 56*(2), 81.

Cao, L., Mohan, K., Ramesh, B., & Sarkar, S. (2013). Evolution of Governance: Achieving Ambidexterity in IT Outsourcing. *Journal of Management Information Systems, 30*(3), 115–140.

Chase, W. G., & Simon, H. A. (1973). Perception in Chess. *Cognitive Psychology, 4*(1), 55–81.

Cohen, L., & Young, A. (2006). *Multisourcing: Moving Beyond Outsourcing to Achieve Growth and Agility.* Harvard Business Press.

Cohen, W. M., & Levinthal, D. A. (1990). Absorptive Capacity: A New Perspective on Learning and Innovation. *Administrative Science Quarterly, 35,* 128–152.

Choi, T. Y., & Wu, Z. (2009). Taking the Leap from Dyads to Triads: Buyer-Supplier Relationships in Supply Networks. *Journal of Purchasing and Supply Management, 15*(4), 263–266.

Daft, R. L., & Macintosh, N. B. (1981). A Tentative Exploration into the Amount and Equivocality of Information Processing in Organizational Work Units. *Administrative Science Quarterly, 26*(2), 207–224.

DeVellis, R. F. (2012). *Scale Development: Theory and Applications.* Sage.

Dibbern, J., Goles, T., Hirschheim, R., & Jayatilaka, B. (2004). Information Systems Outsourcing: A Survey and Analysis of the Literature. *ACM SIGMIS Database: The DATABASE for Advances in Information Systems, 35*(4), 6–102.
Galbraith, J. R. (1973). *Designing Complex Organizations.* Addison-Wesley.
Galbraith, J. R. (1977). *Organization Design.* Addison-Wesley.
Galbraith, J. R. (1984). Organization Design: An Information Processing View. *Army Organizational Effectiveness Journal, 8*(1), 21–26.
Gefen, D., & Straub, D. (2005). A Practical Guide to Factorial Validity Using PLS-Graph: Tutorial and Annotated Example. *Communications of the Association for Information Systems, 16*(1), 91–109.
Goo, J., Huang, C. D., & Hart, P. (2008). A Path to Successful IT Outsourcing: Interaction Between Service-Level Agreements and Commitment. *Decision Sciences, 39*(3), 469–506.
Goo, J., Kishore, R., Rao, H. R., & Nam, K. (2009). The Role of Service Level Agreements in Relational Management of Information Technology Outsourcing: An Empirical Study. *MIS Quarterly, 33*(1), 119–145.
Goodhue, D., Lewis, W., & Thompson, R. (2007). Research Note—Statistical Power in Analyzing Interaction Effects: Questioning the Advantage of PLS with Product Indicators. *Information Systems Research, 18*(2), 211–227.
Gopal, A., & Gosain, S. (2010). Research Note—The Role of Organizational Controls and Boundary Spanning in Software Development Outsourcing: Implications for Project Performance. *Information Systems Research, 21*(4), 960–982.
Gopal, A., Mukhopadhyay, T., & Krishnan, M. S. (2002). The Role of Software Processes and Communication in Offshore Software Development. *Communications of the ACM, 45*(4), 193–200.
Grant, R. M. (1996). Prospering in Dynamically-Competitive Environments: Organizational Capability as Knowledge Integration. *Organization Science, 7*(4), 375–387.
Grover, V., Cheon, M. J., & Teng, J. T. (1996). The Effect of Service Quality and Partnership on the Outsourcing of Information Systems Functions. *Journal of Management Information Systems, 12*(4), 89–116.
Henderson, R. M., & Clark, K. B. (1990). Architectural Innovation: The Reconfiguration of Existing Product Technologies and the Failure of Established Firms. *Administrative Science Quarterly, 35*(1), 9–30.
Hinsz, V. B., Tindale, R. S., & Vollrath, D. A. (1997). The Emerging Conceptualization of Groups as Information Processors. *Psychological Bulletin, 121*(1), 43.

Hobday, M., Davies, A., & Prencipe, A. (2005). Systems Integration: A Core Capability of the Modern Corporation. *Industrial and Corporate Change, 14*(6), 1109–1143.

Huber, G. P. (1991). Organizational Learning: The Contributing Processes and the Literatures. *Organization Science, 2*(1), 88–115.

Hui, P. P., Davis-Blake, A., & Broschak, J. P. (2008). Managing Interdependence: The Effects of Outsourcing Structure on the Performance of Complex Projects. *Decision Sciences, 39*(1), 5–31.

Kirsch, L. J., Sambamurthy, V., Ko, D. G., & Purvis, R. L. (2002). Controlling Information Systems Development Projects: The View from the Client. *Management Science, 48*(4), 484–498.

Kline, R. B. (2023). *Principles and Practice of Structural Equations Modeling* (3rd ed.). Guilford Press.

Koo, Y., Lee, J. N., Heng, C. S., & Park, J. (2017). Effect of Multi-Vendor Outsourcing on Organizational Learning: A Social Relation Perspective. *Information & Management, 54*(3), 396–413.

Lacity, M. C., Khan, S., Yan, A., & Willcocks, L. P. (2010). A Review of the IT Outsourcing Empirical Literature and Future Research Directions. *Journal of Information Technology, 25*, 395–433.

Lee, J. N., & Kim, Y. G. (1999). Effect of Partnership Quality on IS Outsourcing Success: Conceptual Framework and Empirical Validation. *Journal of Management Information Systems, 15*(4), 29–61.

Levina, N., & Su, N. (2008). Global Multisourcing Strategy: The Emergence of a Supplier Portfolio in Services Offshoring. *Decision Sciences, 39*(3), 541–570.

Mani, D., Barua, A., & Whinston, A. (2010). An Empirical Analysis of the Impact of Information Capabilities Design on Business Process Outsourcing Performance. *Mis Quarterly, 34*(1), 39–62.

Mani, D., Barua, A., & Whinston, A. B. (2012). An Empirical Analysis of the Contractual and Information Structures of Business Process Outsourcing Relationships. *Information Systems Research, 23*(3-part-1), 618–634.

Oshri, I., Kotlarsky, J., & Willcocks, L. (2009). *The Handbook of Global Outsourcing and Offshoring* (4th ed., 2023). Macmillan.

Mithas, S., & Whitaker, J. (2007). Is the World Flat or Spiky? Information Intensity, Skills, and Global Service Disaggregation. *Information Systems Research, 18*(3), 237–259.

Pinsonneault, A., & Kraemer, K. (1993). Survey Research Methodology in Management Information Systems: An Assessment. *Journal of Management Information Systems, 10*(2), 75–105.

Poppo, L., & Zenger, T. (2002). Do Formal Contracts and Relational Governance Function as Substitutes or Complements? *Strategic Management Journal, 23*(8), 707–725.

Premkumar, G., Ramamurthy, K., & Saunders, C. S. (2005). Information Processing View of Organizations: An Exploratory Examination of Fit in the Context of Interorganizational Relationships. *Journal of Management Information Systems, 22*(1), 257–294.

Prencipe, A. (2005). Corporate Strategy and Systems Integration Capabilities: Managing Networks in Complex Systems Industries. In A. Prencipe, A. Davies, & M. Hobday (Eds.), *The Business of Systems Integration* (pp. 114–132). Oxford University Press.

Sanchez, R., & Mahoney, J. T. (1996). Modularity, Flexibility, and Knowledge Management in Product and Organization Design. *Strategic Management Journal, 17*(Winter), 77–91.

Schwarz, C. (2014). Toward an Understanding of the Nature and Conceptualization of Outsourcing Success. *Information & Management, 51*(1), 152–164.

Siemsen, E., Roth, A., & Oliveira, P. (2010). Common Method Bias in Regression Models with Linear, Quadratic, and Interaction Effects. *Organizational Research Methods, 13*(3), 456–476.

Simon, H. A. (1978). Information-Processing Theory of Human Problem Solving. *Handbook of Learning and Cognitive Processes, 5*, 271–295.

Su, N., & Levina, N. (2011). Global Multisourcing Strategy: Integrating Learning from Manufacturing into IT Service Outsourcing. *IEEE Transactions on Engineering Management, 58*(4), 717–729.

Takeishi, A. (2002). Knowledge Partitioning in the Interfirm Division of Labor: The Case of Automotive Product Development. *Organization Science, 13*(3), 321–338.

Tanriverdi, H., Konana, P., & Ge, L. (2007). The Choice of Sourcing Mechanisms for Business Processes. *Information Systems Research, 18*(3), 280–299.

Tiwana, A. (2008). Does Technological Modularity Substitute for Control? A Study of Alliance Performance in Software Outsourcing. *Strategic Management Journal, 29*(7), 769–780.

Tiwana, A. (2010). Systems Development Ambidexterity: Explaining the Complementary and Substitutive Roles of Formal and Informal Controls. *Journal of Management Information Systems, 27*(2), 87–126.

Tiwana, A., & Keil, M. (2009). Control in Internal and Outsourced Software Projects. *Journal of Management Information Systems, 26*(3), 9–44.

Tushman, M. L., & Nadler, D. A. (1978). Information Processing as an Integrating Concept in Organizational Design. *Academy of Management Review, 3*(3), 613–624.

Wiener, M., & Saunders, C. (2014). Forced Co-opetition in IT Multi-sourcing. *The Journal of Strategic Information Systems, 23*(3), 210–225.

Wooldridge, J. M. (2009). *Introductory Econometrics: A Modern Approach* (International Student Ed.). South-Western, Cengage Learning.

4

IT Multisourcing and Opportunistic Behavior in Conditions of Uncertainty

Eleni Lioliou, Leslie Willcocks, and Xiaohui Liu

Introduction

IT outsourcing has emerged as an important tool for enabling organizations to enhance their growth and competitiveness. Firms have become more mature in their outsourcing ventures and have progressed to externalizing more complex functions that often involve multiple vendors. Multisourcing, that is using multiple sources, to deliver service requirements has been a major trend in information technology outsourcing

---

Chapter 4 is a more developed and updated version of Lioliou, E., Willcocks, L., & Liu, X. (2019). Researching IT Multi-Sourcing and Opportunistic Behavior in Conditions of Uncertainty: A Case Approach. *Journal of Business Research, 103*, 387–396.

E. Lioliou
Queen Mary University London, London, UK

L. Willcocks (✉)
LSE, London, UK
e-mail: willcockslp@aol.com

X. Liu
Brunel University, Uxbridge, UK

(ITO) and business process outsourcing (BPO) for over 30 years (Cullen et al., 2014; Oshri et al., 2023). But ITO/BPO models have evolved even further in the past decade, and large outsourcing deals with a single supplier have been increasingly replaced by several selective contracts with a set of suppliers (Bapna et al., 2010; Lacity et al., 2016; Oshri et al., 2023; Snowden & Fersht, 2016).

In parallel with the massive growth of outsourcing and multisourcing arrangements, the existence of opportunistic behavior between the outsourcing partners has been widely acknowledged as of central concern in outsourcing activities (Aubert et al., 2004; Lacity et al., 2011). Opportunistic behavior can hinder collaborative activity, putting the effectiveness of outsourcing arrangements in danger. The risks and threats of such behavior become even more prominent in multisourcing arrangements (Poston et al., 2009).

Multisourcing arrangements constitute a distinctive context for the study of opportunistic behavior primarily for two reasons (see also chapters 2 and 3). First, multisourcing ventures are inherently more complex and therefore involve higher levels of uncertainty, as compared to dyadic outsourcing relationships. Clients need to manage a greater number of vendors at the same time, which inherently increases the uncertainty level they have to deal with.

Second, in contrast to earlier (and more traditional) outsourcing arrangements, contemporary multisourcing ventures are seeking to capitalize on the cooperation as well as the competition among outsourcing partners. This dual challenge of voluntary 'coopetition' (Nalebuff & Brandenburger, 1997; Osarenkhoe, 2010, p. 216) or forced-by-the-client 'coopetition' (Wiener & Saunders, 2014) represents a distinctive feature of multisourcing ventures that differs from traditional dyadic outsourcing arrangements.

Recent studies in the area of multisourcing make strong contributions but also suggest that much still needs to be done to fully reveal the challenges that these complex ventures present and the effective practices that might steer them (Wiener & Saunders, 2014; Bapna et al., 2010). More specifically, we currently have little understanding of how uncertainty challenges increase the risk for opportunistic behavior in a multisourcing context. There is also a scarcity of studies that investigate ways of reducing uncertainties, potentially facilitating therefore, as Wiener and Saunders (2014) suggest, the development of coopetition in a multisourcing context.

In this study, we aim to address these two issues and contribute to the literature on outsourcing by exploring opportunistic behavior in a multisourcing context, a theme that, to the best of our knowledge, has not been investigated in depth. Our primary research questions are going to be 'How does the existence of internal and behavioral uncertainties in a multisourcing arrangement increase the likelihood of opportunistic behavior? How do clients and their suppliers seek to reduce these uncertainties and their impact?'

We adopt a transaction cost economics (TCE) perspective to underpin our analysis since it has prevailed as a dominant (if criticized) theory in the explanation of phenomena related to opportunism. We aim to contribute to the outsourcing literature by providing a more thorough understanding of the role of uncertainty in the occurrence of opportunistic behavior in a multisourcing context. The findings from our study help to provide new insights on the conditions that reduce uncertainty and opportunistic behavior in multisourcing, and therefore enable the customer to develop coopetition between vendors.

Review of Literature

The growth of multisourcing arrangements has been attributed to using best-in-class vendors for specific work as well as the synergistic effects that collaboration between different vendors can bring. Clients are able to access the specialized expertise and capabilities of multiple vendors and receive agile and flexible services (Bapna et al., 2010; Lacity et al., 2016).

Multisourcing arrangements also may result in other benefits—for example, the spread of outsourcing risks among multiple vendors, the reduction of dependency by the client as well as improved adaptability to changing market conditions (Koo et al., 2016; Bapna et al., 2010). Multisourcing can also help clients source best-of-breed suppliers, reduce over-reliance on a single supplier, offer greater flexibility and control, promote competition and prevent complacency.

On the other hand, multisourcing brings very significant challenges and risks. Governance becomes more complex, and transaction costs rise with the increased management challenges (Cullen et al., 2014; Oshri et al., 2023). Research has revealed difficulties, including the design of interdependent contracts between independent providers, multi-party interfaces and handovers, end-to-end process management and governance challenges (Cullen et al., 2014; Lioliou et al., 2014; Parida et al., 2016).

Emerging risks include attracting the market for smaller slices of work, keeping providers interested and incentivized, integrating complexity and tracing accountability (Oshri et al., 2023). In practice, suppliers also incur more transaction costs due to shorter contract length, more competition for a greater number of small-sized deals and more frequent bidding for contracts (Cullen et al., 2014). In all this, the possibility for providers' opportunistic behavior may well rise.

Opportunistic behavior in a multisourcing context, while a major concern and challenge, has received relatively little academic investigation (Bapna et al., 2010; Wiener & Saunders, 2014). While this very significant theme has rarely been explicitly researched, there are a few rich cases in the literature where the issue and the counter-tactics can be identified. One such case, particularly thorough and holistic in illustrating the evolution of the multisourcing arrangement, is that of Adidas (Aubert et al., 2014). Since the Adidas case is representative of the issues, but takes a different path from our researched DUTCH case study, we will use it further for comparative purposes in our analysis section below.

The Adidas case is interesting because, while its authors in their comprehensive descriptions and overviews are clearly raising issues of opportunism, they do not address these issues conceptually or explicitly in their study. But, evidentially, the distinctive features of multisourcing create ample space for the existence of opportunism and can put at risk the effectiveness of an entire venture.

As will be illustrated, Adidas represents a multisourcing case that established a high degree of overlap in the work of the vendors and, relatedly, high supplier competition. In our own DUTCH case study, there were limited overlaps in the work of the vendors, and competition between them was relatively low. In both cases, however, (as happens in multisourcing), the clients aspired to exploit the benefits of vendor collaboration and synergistic endeavor. We therefore use the Adidas case study for its points of contrast to our own DUTCH case study, providing a fruitful avenue for comparative analysis.

Uncertainty, Opportunism and Transaction Cost Economics

The theory of transaction cost economics (TCE) has been widely used in the study of outsourcing. Transaction cost theorists have primarily focused on explaining governance choices (i.e., in-house, joint ventures, outsourcing, markets) in conjunction with the potential for vendor opportunistic behavior (Aubert et al., 2004; Tiwana & Bush, 2007).

Uncertainty is generated by phenomena that are hard to anticipate and, consequently, hard to specify in the contract. Taking into account the broadness of uncertainty as a concept, we observe that a number of TCE studies have operationalized uncertainty in a relatively constrained manner. TCE studies so far have taken into account certain facets of uncertainty while ignoring others or neglecting the role of uncertainty altogether (Thouin et al., 2009; De Vita et al., 2010).

Williamson (1985) did not provide a very detailed definition of uncertainty, but referred to the work of Koopmans (1957) and progressed to identify three classes of uncertainty. Firstly, the primary class of uncertainty which is 'state contingent.' The secondary class, which arises from a lack of timely and accurate communication which, however, is innocent and non-strategic in nature. Williamson further identified 'behavioral' uncertainty to refer to all those cases where there is strategic non-disclosure, disguise or distortion of information.

Williamson's conceptualization has not been sufficiently concrete to operationalize and further transaction cost economics studies distinguished between environmental, internal and behavioral types of uncertainty in the organizational context. Framed in this manner, environmental uncertainty tends to reflect Williamson's conceptualization of primary uncertainty; internal uncertainty resembles Williamson's conceptualization of secondary uncertainty; behavioral uncertainty corresponds to Williamson's third type of uncertainty.

The present study focuses on aspects of internal and behavioral uncertainty, as our research respondents did not bring forward any major issues of environmental uncertainty affecting their arrangements. In particular, regarding internal uncertainty, we will initially focus on the ability of a firm to define precisely its IT requirements and services. Furthermore, we follow Aubert et al. (2004) and examine the level of professionalization of the IT department. We also follow Lacity et al. (2011) as well as Karimi-Alaghehband et al. (2011) and pay particular consideration to measurement difficulties, which we also classify as elements of internal uncertainty.

Behavioral uncertainty stems from difficulties in predicting the actions of the exchange party, in the face of the possibility of opportunistic behavior. In practice, a number of TCE studies tend to relate behavioral uncertainty to the difficulty of measuring the performance of the vendor. We follow Lacity et al. (2011), as well as Karimi-Alaghehband et al. (2011), and argue that this link departs from the core of TCE, and therefore, we focus our assessment on possibilities for opportunistic behavior that the supplier may engage in.

With regard to his views on opportunism, Williamson defined opportunism as 'self-interest seeking with guile' (Williamson, 1985). On this basis, he suggested that opportunism combines (i) self-interest seeking with (ii) dishonest behavior, such as the 'incomplete or distorted disclosure of information, and calculated efforts to mislead, distort, disguise, obfuscate or otherwise confuse' (Williamson, 1985, p. 47).

Ghoshal and Moran (1996, p. 18) and later, Das and Rahman (2002), distinguished between the *attitude* of opportunism and its *behavioral* manifestation, that is, the occurrence of opportunistic behavior. The authors asserted that research should differentiate between these two facets of opportunism and referred to the attitudinal facet of opportunism as 'opportunistic propensity.' Opportunistic propensity therefore refers to a firm's willingness to engage in self-interested activity. Opportunistic behavior, on the other hand, refers to the actual engagement in such activity.

In our study, therefore, we examine opportunistic propensity by investigating whether the arrangement is based on relational, open-ended elements or on formal contracts and safeguards. We then examine the existence of opportunistic behavior, based on narratives around the evolution of the outsourcing relationship in the context of multisourcing arrangements. Our research aims to provide an exploratory understanding of how the existence of internal and behavioral uncertainties increases the risk of opportunistic behavior in a multisourcing context.

The following graph (Fig. 4.1) illustrates the guiding framework for our analysis.

Fig. 4.1 Guiding research framework

Research Strategy

The chosen research strategy is the case study method. The case study method is considered suitable because it enables the researcher to study contemporary phenomena over which he/she has little or no control and examine the context within which these phenomena take place (Yin, 2003). Benbasat et al. (1987) suggested that a single in-depth case study can be an appropriate method to test the boundaries of well-formed theory, which is exactly what we wanted to achieve with the theory of transaction cost economics. Along these lines, our intention was to conduct an in-depth case study that would enable us to examine and understand the predictive power of the theory of transaction costs on sourcing decisions, and the choice of governance in-depth and across time. The participant organization is a major financial services company from the Netherlands. We name the firm DUTCH for reasons of confidentiality. At the same time, we use a rich case study from the published literature—Adidas—to compare and contrast our findings and give analytical insight into the factors at play and how they shape events.

DUTCH offers a wide range of services including insurance, banking and mortgage products to consumers, businesses and institutions, and employs more than 22,000 employees in more than ten business and service units. The company initiated a major strategic multisourcing initiative in 2007 with three suppliers.

The entire deal represented a combined value of more than 415 million Euros. As mentioned, this deal represents a multi-vendor dominant model and the client created three different contracts with each of the suppliers, and was also exclusively responsible for their management. Our investigation was focused on all three strategic outsourcing contracts, which started at the same time in 2007, thus forming natural controls for the research process. All three contracts were medium term and would run for five years. The three suppliers will be named Supplier A, Supplier B and Supplier C, respectively.

Supplier A is an international IT services provider specializing in managing and transforming the IT operations of its customers. It is based in France and it offers a variety of services ranging from data centers and workplace solutions to infrastructure and information security solutions.

Supplier B is a leading telecommunications and ICT service provider in the Netherlands. It offers products including internet, wireless telephony and TV to consumers as well as integrated ICT services to business customers. Supplier C is a global supplier of information and communication technology services. It offers workspace management, security, communications as well as application and technology transformation services. It is headquartered in the Netherlands and employees about 25,000 people. As from October 2007, Supplier C became part of Supplier B.

We used multiple data collection methods in order to provide a stronger substantiation of our theoretical constructs (Eisenhardt, 1989). We conducted a total of twenty interviews from November 2009 to January 2010 and viewed the three outsourcing contracts under investigation. We sought to improve the reliability of our findings and triangulate our results by questioning interviewees on some common themes, from both the suppliers' and the client's side. Having the chance to view the three outsourcing contracts also enabled us to get a good understanding of the contractual apparatus of governance in place and get the reflections of our research participants on this. We had one interview with each of our thirteen research participants and an additional interview with seven of them. All interviews lasted approximately one hour. The interviews were cross-sectional and were based on participants' recollections. The interviews were then transcribed, coded and analyzed using Atlas software.

We followed an iterative process in our data analysis and compared emergent findings and pre-existing concepts (Eisenhardt, 1989). The DUTCH case study was a multisourcing arrangement characterized by high levels of modularity and low competition between the three suppliers. However, the evolution of the relationships and the performance of the three suppliers were different. We found these discrepancies intriguing and considered that a TCE theorization could illuminate various elements critical for the progress of the venture. Our subsequent data analysis enabled us to identify particular elements of uncertainty and provide insights on how opportunistic behavior can emerge in a multisourcing context.

We adopted a procedure of template analysis (King, 2004) while coding our data, which was informed by the TCE theorization. Our interviewees did not raise significant issues relating to environmental uncertainty, and we therefore focused our analysis on aspects of internal and behavioral types of uncertainty, opportunistic propensity and opportunistic behavior. On the basis of the responses of our participants, we created codes for each of these elements. The main codes and indicative quotes are provided in the Appendix. Using these codes, we followed an inductive approach in our data analysis.

To ensure a rigorous and valid interpretation of our data, we conducted many iterations of analysis, but we also re-visited our interview transcripts and other documents multiple times. Our intention while following this iterative process was to 'understand the whole' by constantly revising it in 'view of the reinterpretation of the parts' (Myers, 1995). Table 4.1 summarizes the roles of the research participants we interviewed.

In this study, we aim to provide an in-depth analysis by comparing and contrasting our observations against a complementary study mentioned in the literature review, namely the Adidas case study by Aubert et al. (2014). We set up this comparison and contrast in order to more systematically analyze the management and the coordination efforts of DUTCH and Adidas, as well as their actions to incentivize their vendors. Within this context, we compare and contrast a case study of low overlaps of work and low competition between the vendors (DUTCH) with a case study of high overlaps of work and high competition (Adidas). The following sections will present aspects of opportunistic propensity, internal and behavioral uncertainties for the two cases.

Case Study in Financial Services

Overview of the Arrangement

In 2004, DUTCH engaged in its first IT outsourcing venture with Supplier A on mainframe operations. The main reasons DUTCH decided to engage in this IT outsourcing venture were related to the

Table 4.1 Roles of research participants

Research participants from DUTCH	Role	Number of interviews
DUTCH case study		
RP1	IT director	One
RP2	Sector manager for sourcing arrangements	Two
RP3	Sector manager on IT operations	Two
RP4	IT demand manager	One
RP5	Consultant	One
RP6	Contract manager for Supplier A	Two
RP7	Contract manager for Supplier B	Two
RP8	Contract manager for Supplier C	Two
RP9	Outsourcing operations for Supplier B	Two
Research participants from Supplier A	**Role**	
RP10	Engagement manager	Two
Research participants from Supplier B	**Role**	
RP11	Engagement manager	One
Research participants from Supplier C	**Role**	
RP12	Client director	One
RP13	Contract manager	One

reduction of cost and the fact that the mainframe operations were not considered part of the company's core business. It was thus considered that outsourcing was a good strategy to utilize the technical expertise and competencies of a supplier specialized in this area. The outsourcing venture between DUTCH and Supplier A progressed successfully and resulted in significant cost reductions for DUTCH. The company thus decided to develop further its outsourcing scope, and at the end of 2007 signed a major multisourcing deal with three suppliers.

The entire 2007 deal with the three suppliers represented a combined value of more than 415 million Euros. All three contracts would run for five years. Supplier A would provide the datacenter services for DUTCH and focus on the availability, continuity and security of the service. The contract between DUTCH and Supplier A was worth 145 million Euros. Supplier B would provide communication services including land lines, mobile communications and data networks. The contract between DUTCH and Supplier B was worth 150 million Euros. Supplier C would be responsible for the management and further development of the workstation infrastructure. The company would be providing workstation systems for the entire DUTCH staff. The contract between DUTCH and Supplier C was worth 120 million Euros.

As an overview, across the 2007–2010 period, Supplier A performed well most of the time, and DUTCH did not appear to have serious issues with regard its performance. As illustrated later, there were some instances where DUTCH felt exploited by Supplier A, but there were no serious performance issues. Supplier B did not perform well during the initial phases of the arrangement, but its performance improved over time. There were many instances of mutual blame between DUTCH and Supplier B but, over time, and as the arrangement became more formalized, these instances became less frequent. The performance of supplier C, however, was disappointing throughout. Despite the advancement of DUTCH's governance capabilities and the noticeable performance improvements of the other suppliers (particularly Supplier B), Supplier C never managed to progress.

Aspects of Opportunistic Propensity

Having been engaged in only one outsourcing arrangement up to 2007, DUTCH was relatively inexperienced in outsourcing, and not at all experienced in multisourcing when it signed this major three supplier deal. Although they were about to enter a very big multisourcing arrangement, they did not perform a formal request for proposal (RFP) process that would have allowed them to compare different service delivery options. This was also the case in 2004 when DUTCH initiated its very first outsourcing engagement with Supplier A.

From our interviews, we established that DUTCH did not engage in a formal RFP process because it did not really have a good understanding of what the market could offer or what solution would fit them best. They were hoping that by outsourcing they could get the help of their partners to sort out their own IT requirements. Furthermore, DUTCH was in favor of informal ways of doing work and did not put much detail in the contracts with its three suppliers. The company preferred to rely on a spirit of partnership and RP3 (DUTCH sector manager on IT operations) reflected on this issue: *"We were convinced, seeing all the different outsourcing in the market at that moment, the only way to make it successful is when you try to establish a real partnership. That was our goal when we started."* Subsequently, the contracts that DUTCH signed were not sufficiently detailed, leaving room for ambiguity and differing interpretations.

According to our respondents, the choice by DUTCH to execute the deal primarily based on informal relationships was not a wise move and it increased the levels of opportunistic propensity for its three suppliers. The suppliers took advantage of the absence of a formal arrangement to charge more and justify (when needed) underperformance. DUTCH soon realized that the formalization of obligations and responsibilities around the arrangement was crucial to getting the project going and avoid losses. Our respondents expressed the concern that DUTCH was exploited for some time (primarily from Suppliers B and C, but to some extent by A too), and that more formalization was the only way to move things forward in a positive way.

In what follows, we will provide an overview of the various uncertainties prevailing in the internal operating environment within DUTCH, as well as the hazards of behavioral uncertainty the company faced. We will also illustrate the various ways in which DUTCH tried to reduce these uncertainties, and their impact.

Internal Uncertainty

Research participants within DUTCH indicated that their organization was not capable of clarifying their needs and requirements. This increased the likelihood of opportunistic behavior by the vendors, enabling them to blame DUTCH for lack of clarity and therefore justify time overruns or under performance. RP1 (DUTCH IT director) recognized that DUTCH had a very limited understanding of its own IT business needs and indicated: *"We should have been more accurate because if you outsource garbage, you get garbage back."*

DUTCH was also constantly making very specialized requests to its suppliers, which indicated some lack of discipline. RP7 (Contract manager for Supplier B) reflected on this issue: *"DUTCH wants everything as a specialty, really everything has a high priority and it's not standardized. We contracted PDC where all our products are designed, because we wanted to take standard products from Supplier B and Supplier C. The ink wasn't even dry and we had a specialty."* While Supplier B had trouble accommodating the non-standardized requirements of DUTCH, it did manage to finally take care of them, though with some time delays. RP7 (Contract manager for Supplier B) indicated that DUTCH was a very demanding customer and that some delays by Supplier B could be justified, but often these were too long. In the case of Supplier C, the situation was worse. The internal organization of Supplier C was not consistent, and consequently their ability to accommodate non-standard requests from DUTCH was limited. Sometimes Supplier C would blame DUTCH for making non-standardized requests in order to justify their own underperformance.

Furthermore, the internal organization within DUTCH at the time that these outsourcing contracts were signed appeared to be relatively weak. A major problem had to do with the diverse mindsets that existed within the company. DUTCH has been the product of a number of mergers and acquisitions, resulting in a diverse infrastructure and varying philosophies on how IT should be managed. Consequently, the complexity of the tasks was significant. RP13 (Contract manager from Supplier C) noted: *"You (have) got a kaleidoscopic IT world within DUTCH itself which is relatively unmanageable. If you want to outsource ... it really becomes a mess."* This situation increased the possibility that the suppliers would behave opportunistically.

DUTCH did not have a good command of the environment but, to make matters worse, it also did not have proper measurement and control mechanisms in place. By not establishing proper measurement and control mechanisms, the contracts were not effective in preventing vendors from behaving opportunistically. This was particularly the case with Supplier B and Supplier C which for a long time were claiming much better levels of performance than they were, in practice, putting in.

Furthermore, although DUTCH settled on making rough estimations about its IT needs, it was not capable of making valid assessments. As one example among many, when DUTCH calculated the storage capacity they would need from Supplier A their miscalculation was huge. DUTCH signed a deal worth EUR 120 million with Supplier A, but it turned out that the deal had to become much larger in order to accommodate the requirements of DUTCH. The final deal reached EUR 200 million (which represents a 66.7% deviation upward) and, according to DUTCH respondents, Supplier A took the opportunity to over-charge on additional services.

An over-reliance on a spirit of partnership, and the weak IT management capability of DUTCH, did not work well for any of the three arrangements. Respondents from DUTCH raised concerns that Supplier A, although reliable in terms of performance, took advantage of the weak IT management capability of DUTCH. Suppliers B and C also took many opportunities to offer excuses when their performance was poor. In essence, they were trying to escape responsibility for their variable performances.

In the case of Supplier C, while DUTCH tried to establish some measurement mechanisms, these were not effective. Some of the metrics were not disaggregated enough to challenge the supplier on exactly where they were failing. Furthermore, these metrics were averaged too much so that the supplier performance looked quite good at a general level, but failed to establish why there was such a level of disappointment about some parts of Supplier C's performance.

Behavioral Uncertainty

DUTCH chose to outsource to companies with which it already had some sort of business relationship. In a sense, prior history was assumed to be an indicator of the future prospects for cooperation. As mentioned,

DUTCH tended to be rather informal in its business relationships, therefore working with companies that they had already successfully collaborated with was significant for them. RP3 (DUTCH Sector manager on IT operations) noted: *"So we said, let's divide our infrastructure into three parts and have one supplier for data center, one for network and one for office automation… and in each of these parts we tried to see which supplier we had the best relationship with."*

DUTCH believed that working with organizations that they already had a business relationship with would enable them to have some expectations with regard to their way of doing business and their performance. What is interesting to note, however, is that not all the suppliers that were chosen for this multisourcing arrangement had had a successful record of business with DUTCH, or had a very positive reputation in the market. Respondents within DUTCH suggested that the choice of Suppliers A and B on the basis of their previous performance and reputation was reasonable. However, they were very skeptical about the choice of Supplier C. Firstly, although DUTCH had worked with Supplier C, they did not have any experience with them in the workspace environment. Additionally, in 2007, when the Supplier C contract was signed, Supplier C appeared to have a bad image in the market.

A number of research participants expressed their skepticism about whether Supplier C was chosen for good enough business reasons. RP3 (DUTCH Sector manager on IT operations) noted: *"For Supplier A, it is more or less understandable in terms of the fact that they already had a sourcing contract on the mainframe side and they were doing well on that contract. We were very satisfied with their performance and naturally they would be the first party you look at when you want to outsource platforms. Supplier B was of course already a very important business partner for us in terms of telecommunications. The selection process with regard to Supplier C… I do not have it on the table nor do I care too much because I am just managing the existing situation. But I have my suspicions this was not a very careful, scientific auditable process."* It turned out, however, that the former DUTCH IT director who signed the Supplier C contract in 2008 went to work for Supplier C a few months after the closing of the deal.

With regard to the overall orientation toward the arrangement, DUTCH was a big account for supplier A, and therefore a significant client. Supplier A also saw the potential for doing more business with DUTCH in the future, especially in the area of applications. Supplier A, therefore, appeared very interested and involved in this agreement and this increased the expectation of DUTCH that Supplier A would not behave opportunistically.

This was not so clearly the case with Supplier B. The development of the relationship between DUTCH and Supplier B had been rather patchy. An important reason for this appears to be that although the contract with Supplier B was big in terms of its value, DUTCH was not ranked among the top customers of Supplier B. RP7 (DUTCH Contract manager working with Supplier B) said: "*I believe that they see us as one of their customers… Just a customer because they have bigger customers. So we are just another one of their customers. That is how it feels.*" Therefore, because DUTCH was not a key customer for Supplier B, the possibility that Supplier B would not prioritize the needs of DUTCH was increased.

Supplier C was quite indifferent to the arrangement from the start. As already mentioned, the choice of Supplier C was perhaps influenced by political considerations, rather than based on rational business criteria. The former DUTCH IT director who signed the contract with Supplier C went to work for Supplier C, and therefore, it may well be that with this genesis, the venture was at risk from the start. However, from our respondent comments, it did not appear that Supplier C was particularly interested in keeping DUTCH satisfied as a customer.

Comparative Analysis

Overview of the Adidas case

It is useful at this point, for comparative purposes, to describe briefly the Adidas case, and the issues it raises. In 2009, Adidas, as a multinational wholesale and retail sporting goods company, had over 1000 IT employees and outsourced to an Indian IT supplier, as well as having a center in Hyderabad. A new CIO felt that the single vendor had become complacent, and that Adidas had become too dependent on one supplier. From 2011 to 2013, it adopted a multisourcing strategy. It brought in two new vendors—both medium sized, one a 'hungry' Indian supplier and the other from Eastern Europe (India 2 and Belarus). Their skill sets overlapped significantly with those of the incumbent large Indian single supplier; this was a deliberate Adidas policy. Each center of excellence in Adidas (e.g., Sales and Retail IT CofE, eCommerce, IT CofE) was instructed to work with at least two of the three vendors to deliver a full set of activities from development, testing through to integration and support. The relevant IT CofE was responsible for coordinating overall projects and programs. Thus, for any IT task Adidas could have all three suppliers bidding, creating both competition and a subsequent need for cooperation across the winning suppliers. The new suppliers learned much, including from the large supplier, while the amount of IT work at Adidas was increasing so none of the suppliers experienced a decline in revenues.

These arrangements had some drawbacks. They made it difficult for the vendors to achieve economies of scale and scope: higher transaction costs were incurred through increased interfaces and more bidding; Adidas had to take more final program management responsibility; a lot of skills replication was needed across the IT Centers of Excellence (CofEs). These drawbacks were addressed in the Phase 2 2013–2015 period. Having successfully brought on board the two new vendors, Adidas sought to 'industrialize' the IT organization by reorganizing to have development, testing, integration and support as separate processes across all CofEs. This new horizontal structure created fewer vendor overlaps but they were bigger in size, thus creating more volume bundling in the work bid for by the suppliers. The two new vendors would be assigned to each horizontal function (e.g., development) and subsequent functions had to be performed by different vendors. The aim was to create high levels of supplier competition and cooperation. The authors found that while all this reduced the number of interfaces considerably, the suppliers remained highly dependent on one another, had to learn from each other but also could bid for larger work blocks, thus leveraging economies of scale and scope, while Adidas reduced its coordination costs. Responsibilities also became more clearly demarcated. Overlapping suppliers also introduced a higher level of flexibility and agility than was possible using a more traditional multisourcing 'best-in-class' model with very few overlapping supplier activities.

In the following section, we compare and contrast the two cases on aspects of opportunistic propensity, internal uncertainty and behavioral uncertainty, as a basis for a more detailed discussion.

Aspects of Opportunistic Propensity

As already mentioned, DUTCH favored informal ways of working, and therefore did not put much detail in the contracts with its three suppliers. This choice, however—to rely on a spirit of partnership rather than concrete contractual safeguards—increased the propensity of its vendors to behave opportunistically. Right from the start of its multisourcing deal, DUTCH had to face issues of opportunistic behavior with all its vendors, even with Supplier A (with whom DUTCH had a long-standing relationship). Many respondents from DUTCH, including the IT director, recognized that relying on a spirit of partnership rather than a detailed formal contract worked against DUTCH when managing the behavior of its vendors.

Adidas, on the other hand, was very rigorous in creating a strong contractual regime with its suppliers. This attitude of Adidas decreased the opportunistic propensity of its vendors, and, right from the start, Adidas showed clear signs that it would keep tight control over the arrangement.

Internal Uncertainty

DUTCH had a relatively weak command of its IT environment and was less mature in its IT and outsourcing management compared to Adidas. As we saw, DUTCH was the product of many mergers and acquisitions and had to integrate diverse IT infrastructures. The company did not seem to have reached a robust state of IT integration at the time that it signed its multisourcing arrangement. For this reason—immature management capability which resulted to a lack of robust IT platforms—the company was unable to properly measure and control the work of its different vendors. As a result, internal uncertainties at DUTCH contributed to varieties and different levels of opportunistic behavior by the three suppliers.

Adidas, conversely, appeared to have a very good command of its internal IT operations. This was an important reason why the company was so effective in the reduction of internal uncertainties. Adidas was also competent in splitting IT projects among three vendors, without running into accountability issues; for example, which vendor was responsible for which aspect of the work, and who got paid for delivery? Adidas appeared to have strong retained capability and so emerged as very competent across both phases and regimes in how it divided its IT work and projects between the different vendors, and also in how it maintained effective ongoing control over vendor performance.

Behavioral Uncertainty

As mentioned, DUTCH chose to outsource to companies with which it already had some sort of business relationship. In particular, DUTCH had already had a successful outsourcing relationship with Supplier A and later on, it expanded the arrangement and included suppliers B and C. The details behind these arrangements but also the skepticism around the inclusion of Supplier C in the contract are mentioned earlier on.

With regard to Adidas, over the years of outsourcing to a single vendor, Adidas Global IT had begun to identify problems of over-dependency. Adidas had cooperated successfully with its largest supplier since 1998 and they had a good long-standing relationship, similarly to the DUTCH-Supplier A case. While in this case we did not find indications of opportunistic behavior by that supplier, Adidas itself certainly saw the need to reduce its dependency on a single vendor and mitigate behavioral uncertainties and opportunism. However, in their renewed outsourcing arrangement, they carried on their cooperation with India1 and brought in also India 2 and Belarus.

DUTCH was valued as a client by Supplier A, but not so much by Suppliers B and C. The fact that DUTCH was not seen as a particularly significant account for Suppliers B and C increased the likelihood of opportunistic behavior from these suppliers. The Adidas case does not present us with much information on how its suppliers valued it as a client; from the case study, however, it may be assumed that all suppliers were highly interested and highly involved in the arrangement and wanted to satisfy Adidas as a client. These elements reduced behavioral uncertainty risks for Adidas. India 1 had had a long-term relationship with Adidas, since 1998. The two additional vendors that were introduced in 2011 were tier-2 suppliers, that were most likely gaining a lot of reputational benefits from their collaboration to Adidas. In all three cases, Adidas was offering additional work, because IT was experiencing a rising workload across the research period. This, undoubtedly, reduced behavioral uncertainty risks and mitigated opportunistic behavior on the part of the suppliers.

Discussion

Comparison of the case studies has allowed us to develop insights into how opportunistic attitudes and behaviors on the part of vendors may arise in outsourcing and multisourcing arrangements. As previous studies also noted, we observed that multisourcing arrangements are much more complex by nature than single-sourcing arrangements, and require significant coordination efforts (Bapna et al., 2010—see also chapters 2 and 3). The division of roles, responsibilities and accountabilities in a multisourcing context is much more demanding and the ongoing governance much more challenging (Poston et al., 2009).

According to our findings, in the case of DUTCH, there was already high opportunistic propensity from the vendors as the arrangements were primarily dependent on relational elements and not a robust contractual regime. While previous literature has identified relational elements as key for successful outsourcing outcomes (Dibbern et al., 2008; Kishore et al., 2003), it seems that these elements cannot generate benefits unless there are adequate safeguards. Relational governance, therefore, does not always substitute for formal governance successfully (Huber et al., 2013; Lioliou et al., 2014). In contrast, for Adidas, the danger of vendors' opportunism was low because there were detailed contracts in place, which acted as safeguards from opportunistic behavior. Interestingly, having established a good formal framework for the arrangement, this encouraged the development of a better (i.e., more effective) relationship as compared to DUTCH.

We also found that the internal uncertainties within DUTCH shaped, in practice, an 'alignment of processes' problem. This problem indicated low governance maturity and low IT management capability. Without proper governance mechanisms in place, DUTCH was not able to effectively control or coordinate the work of its suppliers. Lack of 'alignment of processes' in this sense limited the space for effective collaboration. Previous literature has identified that the mechanisms setting communication lines, roles and responsibilities are key for effective collaboration (Kotlarsky et al., 2008). The absence of such mechanisms made collaboration very difficult indeed for DUTCH and its suppliers. Furthermore, DUTCH did not have a good command of its own IT environment and outsourcing this, therefore, exacerbated their problems. Conversely, Adidas demonstrated significant governance maturity and enhanced IT management capability. Internal uncertainties had been sorted and Adidas not only did not face significant issues related to opportunistic behavior, but went forward to build collaborative efficiencies in the work of its vendors.

We further found that behavioral uncertainties were also shaping in practice 'alignment of objectives' problems, increasing the likelihood for opportunistic behavior. Lack of alignment of objectives indicates an absence of common vision and orientation which hinders the effectiveness of the arrangement (Oshri et al., 2023). These problems further inhibited the proper incentivization of the suppliers. In the absence of aligned objectives, suppliers were not adequately motivated to perform and, as demonstrated in the DUTCH case, this situation led to instances of opportunistic behavior on the part of the vendors. On the other hand, Adidas not only managed to align its own objectives to each of its suppliers individually but went further to create harmonious roles and objectives between its suppliers.

The Adidas case shows how adept handling by the client can help to align and incentivize vendor attitudes and performance. While involving multiple vendors may reduce their motivation to make client-specific investments (Bapna et al., 2010), Adidas demonstrated that it was capable of maintaining the interest of all its vendors. Adidas successfully managed to generate competitive pressure among its different suppliers and keep them interested in winning more projects. Adidas also cleverly created mutual objectives between the suppliers because they became co-dependent on one another to perform effectively, and gain revenues. In DUTCH conversely, without the spur of organized competition across the multi-vendors, opportunistic behavior emerged.

The case analysis also reveals the actions clients may take to mitigate the vendors' propensity toward opportunism in specific circumstances. The cases are sufficiently rich and different to identify the major factors at work (for a summary of our results please see Fig. 4.2). DUTCH was deficient in its outsourcing experience, retained capability and application of the full gamut of effective management practices, let alone creating and applying new ones, and launched the agreement over-reliant on a partnering ethos which was not present in two of the vendors. Inside DUTCH there was increased internal uncertainty, which reduced its ability to align and coordinate its processes with the vendors. The essential finding here is that DUTCH faced significant 'alignment of processes' problems that hindered work and created the space for opportunistic behavior.

Adidas's greater experience with outsourcing and its more mature IT management and governance capabilities eliminated internal uncertainties and therefore 'alignment of processes' problems from the start. In this regard, Adidas did not have to work hard to mitigate issues related to opportunistic behavior (as happens in a lot of multisourcing arrangements). Therefore, Adidas was able to apply effective management practices identified in the academic literature (Cullen et al., 2014; Lacity et al., 2016), but also some novel ones, in particular that of using overlapping vendors to achieve keener competition, better cooperation and superior outsourcing performance.

While modularity and overlaps in work across multiple vendors can be seen in a negative manner, often because of the coordination issues they may create, the Adidas case shows that a firm that has good command of its internal processes (and therefore reduced internal uncertainty) can

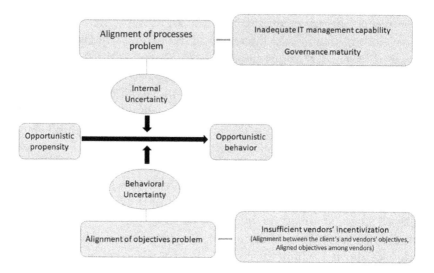

Fig. 4.2 Summary of findings

exploit more benefits from the simultaneous competition and cooperation between vendors, or 'coopetition' (Nalebuff & Brandenburger, 1997; Osarenkhoe, 2010, p. 216). Adidas was able to maintain constructive and effective relationships with all of its vendors. The climate of collaboration, but also constructive competition and learning that they created among the different vendors, appeared to work well.

More importantly however, it seems that Adidas had adroitly managed to make each of the vendors shadow the work of its peers. All vendors carried similar skill sets, and their work often overlapped. It could therefore be concluded that, in addition to the control exercised by Adidas, the vendors were set up to exercise control over between them, indicating the development of peer control, thus mitigating the possibilities for opportunistic behavior.

While 'alignment of processes' and 'alignment of objectives' problems are also evident in dyadic relationships, the challenge of managing these issues is exacerbated in a multisourcing context. In a multisourcing arrangement, as shown in the case of Adidas, the client needs to master its internal processes in such a way that it is able to fully control the work of each of the vendors individually, but also between them. The possibility for the exercise of peer control is another unique feature to multisourcing, as shown in the Adidas case. Conversely, DUTCH was not able to master its internal IT infrastructure well and entered its multisourcing arrangement in a very weak position to exploit multisourcing benefits. DUTCH hardly knew what sort of work it was handing and what it should expect. The outcome of the arrangement was consistently poor, until DUTCH managed to improve its internal retained management and governance capabilities.

Furthermore, 'alignment of processes' and 'alignment of objectives' issues in a traditional dyadic outsourcing relationship typically aim toward collaboration between the client and the supplier. In a multisourcing context, however, and in order to truly exploit the benefits of this model, 'alignment of processes' and 'alignment of objectives' should aim toward the cultivation of collaboration between clients and suppliers, but also the development of coopetition, as shown in the Adidas case study.

Conclusion

Focusing on the distinctive context of multisourcing arrangements, our research makes a number of contributions to the outsourcing literature. First, we investigate opportunistic behavior in a multisourcing context, which is a growing field in the industry, yet still lacks academic investigation (Bapna et al., 2010; Oshri et al., 2015a, 2015b; Oshri et al., 2023; Wiener & Saunders, 2014). More specifically, we explicitly examine how internal and behavioral uncertainties create the space for the occurrence of opportunistic behavior in a multisourcing context. Our investigation demonstrated that uncertainty elements play a key role in covering underperformance and blurring its boundaries with purposeful opportunistic activity. We illustrated that while uncertainty is an element that is often neglected from the analysis of many TCE studies, it is a dimension that deserves further consideration, particularly in the investigation of opportunistic behavior.

Secondly, we demonstrated that internal uncertainties shape an 'alignment of processes' problem and behavioral uncertainties create an 'alignment of objectives' problem which often result in opportunistic activity. We further illustrated that 'alignment of processes' problems are due to the lack of IT management capability and governance immaturity, while 'alignment of objectives' problems can be traced to an inability to appropriately incentivize vendors. Vendors' incentives should be aligned to the objectives of the client, but they should also create a harmonious relationship among vendors.

Thirdly, by comparing and contrasting the two cases, we were able to unpack the complexity associated with multisourcing arrangements and contribute to a more comprehensive account of the conditions under which coopetition between multiple vendors can be generated. In particular, we showed that the existence of internal and behavioral uncertainties acts as hindrances to the development of coopetition between the vendors. In other words, under conditions of internal and behavioral uncertainty, multiple vendors are highly likely going to behave opportunistically, therefore reducing the space for the development of coopetition.

In the case studies, one limitation is that we did not focus on environmental uncertainties. However, DUTCH vendor C showed that internal problems at a vendor due to external market conditions could lead to increased opportunistic behavior in relation to its outsourcing client DUTCH. One could also see that Adidas was experiencing rapid business growth in the global market during the research period. This contributed to creating more IT work for the multi-vendors, which certainly contributed to more cooperation and less opportunistic behavior than if the amount of IT work had been declining in the same period. Clearly, this aspect of external uncertainties and their possible correlation with opportunistic attitudes and behavior deserves more research attention, though it did not emerge as a major factor in the two case studies.

Future research could therefore explore this element and elicit how environmental uncertainties can affect the occurrence of opportunistic behavior. In a similar vein, a wide range of institutional factors, competition, markets, as well as wider industry practices and standards should be taken into account in the examination of the possibility for opportunistic behavior in a multisourcing arrangement.

Moreover, while our research has provided a point of departure, more research is needed in order to obtain a more profound understanding of how clients can create a regime of coopetition between their vendors. In particular, future research could explore how a good balance between the dimensions of cooperation and competition can be achieved. This theme of research is particularly topical, taking into account that a major driver for the growth of multisourcing is the actual exploitation of coopetitive benefits. It is also important to note that while the reduction of various types of uncertainties and opportunistic behavior enables coopetition (as shown in our findings), one could also argue that vendor coopetition can play a focal role in reducing opportunistic behaviors. The role of coopetition in the reduction of opportunistic behaviors can be further explored.

Furthermore, so far relatively limited research in multisourcing has taken into account the perspectives of the suppliers. Suppliers also need to carry the constant pressure of managing the interfaces between client and other suppliers in their multisourcing deals and they also face the danger of opportunistic behavior from the various parties involved. This is certainly a very significant and promising area for further research.

In addition, it needs to be recognized that while the development of coopetition in multisourcing arrangements is overall seen in a positive light, it may not be desirable for all types of multisourcing arrangements. Depending on the type of service that is outsourced (and the level of modularity) and the client's attitude toward outsourcing, clients can make different decisions on the levels of collaboration they seek to develop with and between their vendors, as well as the levels of competition among them. Future research could further explore these decisions.

Our findings are very relevant for practitioners, illuminating the fact that special attention has to be paid to the internal processes that coordinate work between the client and its multiple vendors. While the absence of effective internal processes can create risks and the facilitate the occurrence of opportunistic behavior even in dyadic outsourcing arrangements, these hazards are significantly more prominent in a multisourcing context. This context inherently is more complex, therefore creating more opportunities for the vendors to obscure their actions or mask performance problems.

Similarly, clients should be alert to the possibilities of creating more peer control among the different suppliers in multisourcing arrangements. As mentioned above, multisourcing can generate significant monitoring costs for the client; however, when vendors are set up to exercise control over themselves, the possibility for opportunistic behavior becomes more limited.

Our study further underlines the importance of incentivizing the different suppliers to perform as well as the alignment of objectives between the various parties involved. While multisourcing arrangements can be promising in terms of propagating benefits related to the joint collaborative effort of the suppliers, this potential may not materialize when appropriate incentives do not exist. In the absence of such incentives, the space for coopetition can become seriously constrained, and even more importantly, the threat for opportunistic behavior begins to rise.

Appendix

See Table 4.2

4 IT Multisourcing and Opportunistic Behavior ... 139

Table 4.2 Codes and illustrative examples

Constructs	Examples
Opportunistic propensity	
Level of formalization of the arrangement	"We were convinced, seeing all the different outsourcing in the market at that moment, the only way to make it successful is when you try to establish a real partnership. That was our goal when we started." RP3 (DUTCH sector manager on IT operations)
	"If we had contracted it differently and said, 'This is the date that you are responsible for migrating the services to the FMO and our prices are dropping at that moment', they would get pressured.... Now all the pressure and the issues are with DUTCH, not with our vendors.... They have all the reasons for some time to stay in the PMO (present mode of operation) or PMO Plus instead of moving to the Future Mode of Operations... So, basically, there is not a natural alignment of incentives.... From a contractual perspective, we did not establish the proper incentive to move to PMO Plus or FMO." RP1 (DUTCH IT Director)
Internal uncertainty	
Definition and stability of service requirements	"And when you are outsourcing, you should know what you need functionally and ask your provider to do it.... And we had a catalogue with services which was really far from complete... We should have been more accurate because if you outsource garbage, you get garbage back." RP1 (DUTCH IT Director)
	"DUTCH wants everything as a specialty, really everything has a high priority and it's not standardized. We contracted PDC where all our products are designed, because we wanted to take standard products from Supplier B and Supplier C. The ink wasn't even dry and we had a specialty." RP7 (Contract manager for Supplier B)
Level of professionalization	"When we outsourced our workspace management systems... we did this too fast and there were a lot of things that we did not know how they worked and we were asking the supplier to explain to us, while it should be the other way around... This meant that we were actually not in control..." RP1 (DUTCH IT Director)
	"We had not properly invested in the environment that we were moving to the vendors. We did not have the proper assessment levels, maintenance levels and we did not know what we were outsourcing to them. Consequently, in the first phase of the contract there was the verification phase. And what happened was 'We do not know what we have given to you, can you please tell us?" RP1 (DUTCH IT Director)
Ease of performance measurement	"If you are not capable of explaining your challenges as an IT business to the customers, you are always in reaction mode. This is a major challenge for DUTCH." RP4 (DUTCH IT demand manager)
	"You (have) got a very kaleidoscopic IT world within DUTCH itself which is relatively unmanageable. If you want to outsource that... it really becomes a mess." RP13 (Contract manager from Supplier C)
	"DUTCH is not one customer. DUTCH is a group of customers with their own history.... And these customers do not always concur with what one part of the company has thought and what DUTCH has contracted." RP8 (Contract manager for Supplier C)
	"They did not know how much hardware they had in their data centers. The contract was signed for 120 million over five years and it turns out to be 200 million... Storage is the bigger part of the contract and they miscalculated by an enormous percentage. DUTCH IT merged with Interpolis and because they were going to outsource they did not pay attention to the merger... They thought it is going to happen in the outsourcing and they did not look at the south of Holland. So they did not know their numbers." RP10 (Supplier A Engagement manager)
	"We saw an SLA performance of 50% and Supplier B was saying 'it looks like 50%, but there is this... and this... and they spoke it up to 80%, which is the minimum performance they should achieve." RP7 (Contract manager for Supplier B)
	"We said the performance had to be 80%. We show them the rating and it was 70%... They were always saying to us 70% is not correct... it is actually 85%.... So we are not talking about how we can get the performance to a higher level, but we are talking about the rating." RP9 (Outsourcing operations for Supplier B)

(continued)

Table 4.2 (continued)

Constructs	Examples
Behavioral uncertainty Predictability of behavior	"We did not want one single supplier. We wanted three suppliers because we did not want to lock in on one supplier... So we said 'Let's divide our infrastructure into three parts and have one supplier for data center, one for network and one for office automation.... and on each of these parts we tried to see which is our main supplier where we had the best relationship with." RP3 (DUTCH Sector manager on IT operations) "Supplier A was already in place because we had already outsourced our mainframe with them. We already had an experience with Supplier A in an outsourcing way of thinking... Supplier B was our connectivity partner... a large part of the network was already in the hands of Supplier B. Thus, we had a large understanding with Supplier B..... So Supplier A very logical, Supplier B logical -while also we did not have any outsourcing experience with them-... Supplier C really to be honest... a bit strange.... I am not sure where that came from... I know we did business with them but from my point of view, we did not do business with them on the workstations until then... So that was actually a rather strange decision afterwards... I am not sure who made that decision." RP3 (DUTCH Sector manager on IT operations) "I believe that they see us as one of their customers.... Just a customer because they have bigger customers. So we are one of their customers. That is how it feels." RP7 (DUTCH Contract manager for Supplier B)

References

Alaghehband, F. K., Rivard, S., Wu, S., & Goyette, S. (2011). An Assessment of the Use of Transaction Cost Theory in Information Technology Outsourcing. *The Journal of Strategic Information Systems, 20*(2), 125–138.

Aubert, B. A., Patry, M., & Rivard, S. (2004). A Transaction Cost Model of IT Outsourcing. *Information and Management, 41*(7), 921–932.

Aubert, B., Saunders, C., Wiener, M., Denk, R., & Wolfermann, T. (2014, February). Embracing Vendor Overlaps in IT Multi-sourcing: The Case of Adidas. *IAOP Research into Practice Workshop, Orlando.*

Bapna, R., Barua, A., Mani, D., & Mehra, A. (2010). Research Commentary—Cooperation, Coordination, and Governance in Multisourcing: An Agenda for Analytical and Empirical Research. *Information Systems Research, 21*(4), 785–795.

Benbasat, I., Goldstein, D., & Mead, M. (1987). The Case Research Strategy in Studies of Information Systems. *MIS Quarterly, 11*(3), 368–387.

Carson, S., Madhok, A., & Wu, T. (2006). Uncertainty, Opportunism, and Governance: The Effects of Volatility and Ambiguity on Formal and Relational Contracting. *Academy of Management Journal, 4*(5), 1058–1077.

Chen, A., & Bharadwaj, A. (2009). An Empirical Analysis of Contract Structures in IT Outsourcing. *Information Systems Research, 20*(4), 484–506.

Cullen, S., Lacity, M., & Willcocks, L. (2014). *Outsourcing—All You Need To Know.* White Plume.

Cullen, S., Seddon, P. B., & Willcocks, L. P. (2005). IT Outsourcing Configuration: Research into Defining and Designing Outsourcing Arrangements. *The Journal of Strategic Information Systems, 14*(4), 357–387.

Das, T. K., & Rahman, N. (2002). Opportunism Dynamics in Strategic Alliances. In F. J. Contractor & P. Lorange (Eds.), *Cooperative Strategies and Alliances* (pp. 89–118). Elsevier Science.

Das, T. K., & Teng, B. (1996). Risk Types and Inter-firm Alliance Structures. *Journal of Management Studies, 33*, 827–843.

De Vita, G., Tekaya, A., & Wang, C. (2010). Asset Specificity's Impact on Outsourcing Relationship Performance: A Disaggregated Analysis by Buyer-Supplier Asset Specificity Dimensions. *Journal of Business Research, 63*(7), 657–666.

Dibbern, J., Winkler, J., & Heinzl, A. (2008). Explaining Variations in Client Extra Costs Between Software Projects Offshored to India. *MIS Quarterly, 32*(2), 333–366.

Eisenhardt, K. (1989). Building Theories from Case Study Research. *The Academy of Management Review, 14*(4), 532–550.

Ghoshal, S., & Moran, P. (1996). Bad for Practice: A Critique of the Transaction Cost Theory. *Academy of Management Review, 21*, 13–47.

Goo, J., Nam, K., & Kishore, R. (2009). The Role of Service Level Agreements in Relational Management of Information Technology Outsourcing: An Empirical Study. *MIS Quarterly, 33*(1), 119–145.

Gopal, A., & Koka, B. (2012). The Asymmetric Benefits of Relational Flexibility: Evidence from Software Development Outsourcing. *MIS Quarterly, 36*(2), 553–576.

Granovetter, M. (1985). Economic Action and Social Structure: The Problem of Embeddedness. *American Journal of Sociology, 91*(3), 481–510.

Heiskanen, A., Newman, M., & Eklin, M. (2008). Control, Trust, Power, and the Dynamics of Information System Outsourcing Relationships: A Process Study of Contractual Software Development. *The Journal of Strategic Information Systems, 17*(4), 268–286.

Hoetker, G., & Mellewigt, T. (2009). Choice and Performance of Governance Mechanisms: Matching Alliance Governance to Asset Type. *Strategic Management Journal, 30*, 1025–1044.

Huber, T., Fischer, T., Dibbern, J., & Hirschheim, R. (2013). A Process Model of Complementarity and Substitution of Contractual and Relational Governance in IS Outsourcing. *Journal of Management Information Systems, 30*(3), 81–114.

Kern, T., & Willcocks, L. (2001). *The Relationship Advantage: Information Technologies, Sourcing and Management*. Oxford University Press.

King, N. (2004). Using Template Analysis in the Qualitative Analysis of text. In *Essential Guide to Qualitative Methods in Organisational Research*. Sage.

Kishore, R., Rao, H. R., Nam, K., Rajagopalan, S., & Chaudhury, A. (2003). A Relationship Perspective on IT Outsourcing. *Communications of the ACM, 46*(12), 86–92.

Koo, Y., Lee, J. N., Heng, C. S., & Park, J. (2016). *Effect of Multi-vendor Outsourcing on Organizational Learning: A Social Relation Perspective*. Information & Management.

Koopmans, T. (1957). *Three Essays on the State of Economic Science*. McGraw Hill.

Kotlarsky, J. V., Fenema, P., & Willcocks, L. P. (2008). Developing a Knowledge-Based Perspective on Coordination: The Case of Global Software Projects. *Information & Management, 45*(2), 96–108.

Lacity, M., Khan, S., Yan, A., & Willcocks, L. (2010). A Review of the IT Outsourcing Empirical Literature and Future Research Directions. *Journal of Information Technology, 25*(4), 395–433.

Lacity, M., Khan, S., & Yan, A. (2016). Review of the Empirical Business Services Sourcing Literature: An Update and Future Directions. *Journal of Information Technology, 31*, 3.

Lacity, M., & Willcocks, L. (2001). *Global Information Technology Outsourcing: In Search of Business Advantage*. Wiley.

Lacity, M., & Willcocks, L. (2014). Business Process Outsourcing and Dynamic Innovation. *Strategic Outsourcing: An International Journal, 7*(1), 66–92.

Lacity, M., Willcocks, L., & Khan, S. (2011). Beyond Transaction Cost Economics: Towards an Endogenous Theory of Information Technology Outsourcing. *Journal of Strategic Information Systems, 20*(2), 139–157.

Levina, N., & Su, N. (2008). Global Multisourcing Strategy: The Emergence of a Supplier Portfolio in Services Offshoring. *Decision Sciences, 39*(3), 541–570.

Lioliou, E., & Zimmermann, A. (2015). Opportunistic Behavior in IT Outsourcing: Insights from a TCE and a Social Capital Perspective. *Journal of Information Technology, 30*, 307–324.

Lioliou, E., Zimmermann, A., Willcocks, L. P., & Gao, L. (2014). Formal and Relational Governance in IT Outsourcing: Substitution, Complementarity and the Role of the Psychological Contract. *Information Systems Journal, 24*(6), 503–555.

Myers, M. D. (1995). Dialectical Hermeneutics: A Theoretical Framework for the Implementation of Information Systems. *Information Systems Journal, 5*(1), 51–70.

Nalebuff, B. J., & Brandenburger, A. M. (1997). Co-opetition: Competitive and Cooperative Business Strategies for the Digital Economy. *Strategy & Leadership, 25*(6), 28–33.

Ouchi, W. (1980). Markets, Bureaucracies, and Clans. *Administrative Science Quarterly, 25*(1), 129–141.

Osarenkhoe, A. (2010). A Study of Inter-firm Dynamics Between Competition and Cooperation—A Coopetition Strategy. *Journal of Database Marketing & Customer Strategy Management, 17*(3–4), 201–221.

Oshri, I., Dibbern, J., & Kotlarsky, J. (2015). Joint Vendor Performance in Multi-sourcing Arrangements: The Moderating Role of the Guardian. In *Academy of Management Proceedings* (Vol. 2015, No. 1, p. 17393). Academy of Management

Oshri, I., Kotlarsky, J., & Gerbasi, A. (2015b). Strategic Innovation Through Outsourcing: The Role of Relational and Contractual Governance. *The Journal of Strategic Information Systems, 24*(3), 203–216.

Oshri, I., Kotlarsky, J., & Willcocks, L. (2023). *The Handbook of Global Outsourcing and Offshoring* (4th ed.). Palgrave.

Parida, V., Wincent, J., & Oghazi, P. (2016). Transaction Costs Theory and Coordinated Safeguards Investment in R&D Offshoring. *Journal of Business Research, 69*(5), 1823–1828.

Parkhe, A. (1993). Strategic Alliances Structuring: A Game-Theoretic and Transaction Cost Examination of Interfirm Cooperation. *Academy of Management Journal, 36*(4), 794–829.

Pilling, B. K., Crosby, L. A., & Jackson, D. W. (1994). Relational Bond in Industrial Exchange: An Experimental Test of the Transaction Cost Economic Framework. *Journal of Business Research, 30*, 237–251.

Poppo, L., & Zenger, T. R. (2002). Do Formal Contracts and Relational Governance Function as Substitutes or Complements. *Strategic Management Journal, 23*(8), 707–725.

Poston, R., Kettinger, W., & Simon, J. (2009). Managing the Vendor Set: Best Pricing and Quality Service in IT Outsourcing. *MISQ Executive, 8*(21), 45–58.

Snowden, J., & Fersht, P. (2016). *HFS Market Index—The ITO and BPO Market Size and Forecast 2016–2020*. HFS Research.

Thouin, M., Hoffman, J., & Ford, E. (2009). IT Outsourcing and Firm-Level Performance: A Transaction Cost Perspective. *Information & Management, 46*(8), 463–469.

Tiwana, A., & Bush, A. (2007). A Comparison of Transaction Cost, Agency, and Knowledge-Based Predictors of IT Outsourcing Decisions: A US-Japan Cross-Cultural Field Study. *Journal of Management Information Systems, 24*(1), 259–300.

Uzzi, B. (1996). The Sources and Consequences of Embeddedness for the Economic Performance of Organizations: The Network Effect. *American Sociological Review, 61*(4), 674–698.

Wiener, M., & Saunders, C. (2014). Forced Coopetition in IT Multi-sourcing. *The Journal of Strategic Information Systems, 23*(3), 210–225.

Willcocks, L., Cullen, S., & Craig, A. (2011). *The Outsourcing Enterprise: From Cost Management to Collaborative Innovation*. Palgrave Macmillan.
Williamson, O. E. (1985). *The Economic Institutions of Capitalism*. Free Press.
Williamson, O. E. (1993a). Opportunism and its Critics. *Managerial and Decision Economics, 14*(2), 97–107.
Williamson, O. E. (1993). Calculativeness, Trust, and Economic Organization. *The Journal of Law and Economics, 36*(1, Part 2), 453–486.
Williamson, O. E. (1996). *The Mechanisms of Governance*. Oxford University Press.
Williamson, O. E. (1998). Transaction Cost Economics: How It Works; Where It Is Headed. *De Economist, 146*(1), 23–58.
Williamson, O. E. (2008). Outsourcing: Transaction Cost Economics and Supply Chain Management. *Journal of Supply Chain Management, 44*(2), 5–16.
Yin, R. (2009). *Case Study Research: Design and Methods*. Sage.
Zazac, E. J., & Olsen, C. P. (1993). From Transactional Cost to Transactional Value Analysis: Implications for the Study of Interorganizational Strategies. *Journal of Management Studies, 30*(1), 131–145.

5

Conflict Resolution in Business Services Outsourcing Relationships

Leslie Willcocks and Mary Lacity

Introduction

Business services outsourcing (BSO) is the sourcing of services—such as information technology, human resources, procurement, legal, logistics, financial, and accounting services—through external service providers. Estimates of the outsourcing market are many and varied, and dependent on how market size is measured. Chapter 1 provides details of the ITO and BPO markets that make up the BSO market. Some major recent trends in BSO are noticeable. Increasingly clients have been reducing external service provision to a small group of strategic suppliers. At the

---

Chapter 5 is updated from an earlier version of Lacity, M., & Willcocks, L. (2017). Conflict Resolution in Business Services Outsourcing Relationships. *Journal of Strategic Information Systems*, 26, 80–100.

L. Willcocks (✉)
LSE, London, UK
e-mail: willcockslp@aol.com

M. Lacity
University of Arkansas, Fayetteville, USA

same time, clients demand much more from these providers, expecting them to co-deliver innovation, impact on business outcomes, contribute to strategic direction, provide scarce skills, be closer to the business, and invest in their sourcing relationships (Cullen et al., 2015; Fersht & Snowden, 2016). The change is most noticeable with the issue of innovation (see also chapter 14). Lacity and Willcocks (2013) point to business innovation through outsourcing being rare until recently, but cite many cases where it has become a requirement that is delivered on. Aubert et al. (2015) suggest a similar development, as do Kotlarsky et al. (2015) and Oshri et al. (2023). Meanwhile, Cao et al. (2014) pointed to the rising strategic importance of contractual and relational governance. They found that conflicts between the two forms of governance can be addressed by ambidextrous ITO governance processes. On another issue, Jain and Thietart (2013) stressed the potentially strategic dimensions of knowledge-based transactions costs in IT outsourcing. Moreover, knowledge loss can lead to serious over-reliance on the service provider that can be grounds for subsequent conflicts with strategic implications. Outsourcing can also be part of strategic intent, as Sandeep and Ravishankar (2015) demonstrated in their work on impact sourcing companies in India.

In all this, it is easy to underestimate how all three forms of conflict we identify in this chapter—commercial, service, and relationship—can have strategic repercussions. Even operational conflicts that seem quite small—typically over contracts and service—can lead to underperformance, damage relationships, and in a highly connected business eco-system, disable strategy. As one example, bank cybersecurity issues and software failures in air transport systems seriously harmed corporate reputation and customer confidence in the organizations involved (Rayner, 2014; Shirbon, 2016). There is also now considerable evidence of large-scale outsourcing both enabling and also disabling the execution of business strategies (Lacity et al., 2016; Oshri et al., 2023; Willcocks et al., 2017).

BSO becomes concerning because—like all inter-organizational relationships—BSO has a mixed report card. Some sources estimate the failure rate for inter-organizational relationships to be as high as 70% (Barringer & Harrison, 2000; Hughes & Weiss, 2007). In the specific context of BSO relationships, a review of 1,304 empirical findings from 20 years of academic research found 30% of client-reported BSO outcomes were negative or not beneficial (such as poor service quality, significant hidden costs, and/or poor customer satisfaction) and 21% of client-reported findings resulted in no demonstrable impact on BSO outcomes as a consequence of outsourcing (Lacity et al., 2016). BSO failure rates as high as 50% have been reported (e.g., Gefen et al., 2008; Mani et al., 2012). The inability to resolve conflicts that arise in BSO relationships has been reported as a major cause of poor BSO outcomes (Goo et al., 2009; Lacity & Willcocks, 2015; Oshri et al., 2023; Rai et al., 2012).

The topic of **BSO conflicts,** defined as serious disputes between clients and service providers (e.g., Lee & Kim, 1999), remains an important yet under-researched issue. While prior research has examined the types of inter-organizational conflicts and conflict resolution styles in joint ventures, networks, consortia, alliances, and trade associations (Barringer & Harrison, 2000; Cropper et al., 2008) and in various inter-organizational contexts such as natural resource rights, labor relations, international relations, volunteering, and manufacturing alliance networks (e.g., Dyer & Nobeoka, 2000; Mandell & Keast, 2008; Molnar & Rogers, 1979; Renner, 2007), relatively little research has examined inter-organizational conflicts in the BSO context (Ndubisi, 2011), and this continues into the 2020s.

Concerning BSO conflict research, the review mentioned above of empirical business process outsourcing (BPO) studies revealed only six findings that examined conflicts or conflict resolution (Lacity et al., 2016). In general, prior studies found that the ability to resolve conflicts in BSO relationships was significantly correlated with BSO outcomes (Goo et al., 2009; Ndubisi, 2011, 2012; Rai et al., 2012; Swar et al., 2012; Winkler et al. 2008); Wüllenweber et al., 2008). Only two of these papers examined specifically how conflict resolution styles (integrating, accommodating and compromising) affected trust and commitment in human resource outsourcing (HRO) relationships using a survey of 122 Chinese and Indian providers (Ndubisi, 2011, 2012). The author found interesting cultural and gender differences: The compromising style had a significantly greater effect on commitment for the Chinese service providers than the Indian service providers (Ndubisi, 2011) and a "compromising conflict handling/trust relationship" had a significantly stronger effect for females than for males (Ndubisi, 2012, p. 26). Finally, from a qualitative study of 12 ITO relationships, Kern and Willcocks (2002) identified two types of BSO conflicts: (1) day-to-day problems and (2) operational, cultural, and contractual problems. They found that the conflicts were either resolved by the operational managers or escalated to senior managers as specified by contractual procedures. While these BSO-specific studies established a link between conflict resolution and better BPO outcomes, it is clear that more research is needed to better understand BSO conflict types and the most effective conflict resolution processes.

This chapter addresses this gap. It is based on research that initially asked a broad research question about the practices associated with top performing BSO relationships. During the process of inquiry, comprising interviews about 32 BSO relationships, it became evident that resolving conflicts to the satisfaction of both parties was an important process to realize the strategic benefits of outsourcing. In this sense we see the research as making an important contribution to the strategy as practice literature as represented in Jarzabkowski and Spee (2009), Golsorkhi et al. (2012), and Whittington (1996, 2014). Our research question and mode of research reflects our intent to contribute to our understanding of strategy as practice, and also how it can be researched.

Turning to the research, interviewees from 41% of the BSO relationships reported significant conflicts, yielding qualitative data on 13 conflict cases. As a result, we realized that we had enough interesting qualitative data to answer the question, "*What types of inter-organizational conflicts arise in BSO relationships and how do partners resolve them?*" We then reviewed the existing academic literature on inter-organizational conflicts and conflict resolution styles to see if we could make theoretical sense of the qualitative data. Using the literature as a guide, we initially developed a coding scheme for conflict resolution styles from Thomas and Kilmann (1974)—"competing," "avoiding", "accommodating," "compromising", and "collaborative" styles—and added a "switched" category as suggested by Khun and Poole (2000). Prior academic literature on inter-organizational *conflict types* was not as robust as the literature on *conflict resolution styles*, so we conceptualized a new typology of three conflict types specific to the BSO context: "commercial" conflicts, "service" conflicts, and "relationship" conflicts. We coded the 13 BSO conflict cases using the coding scheme and compared findings to theory.

The remainder of the chapter is structured as follows. We first provide a review of the findings from the literature. We next explain the codes we appropriated and extended from prior theory to categorize the BSO conflicts and conflict resolution styles. We then present the findings, discuss the contribution to theory and practice, and, lastly, recognize the limitations of the research. Details of the extensive data collection and analysis methods are relegated to the Appendix.

Literature Review

Table 5.1 summarizes the prior research on inter-organizational conflicts in BSO relationships. This body of research provides general insights on BSO conflicts. The research shows that conflicts directly harmed or moderated BSO outcomes (e.g., Cahill et al., 2010; Goo et al., 2009; Wickramasinghe & Nandula, 2015; Winkler et al., 2008). The research also shows that at a general level, resolving conflicts improved BSO outcomes (e.g., Ndubisi, 2011; Rai et al., 2012; Rhodes et al., 2016; Swar et al., 2012). These studies are valuable, but most did not aim to identify specific BSO conflict types or to assess specific conflict resolution styles, with the following exceptions:

There have been few studies of conflict resolution in outsourcing relationships since this review. Notable are Cho, D. (2020) which focuses on software development outsourcing projects, and Vijaykar et al. (2021) that analyses a single IT outsourcing case and applies what is called an structured solutions approach.

From an exploratory study of 12 ITO relationships, Kern and Willcocks (2002) identified two types of BSO conflicts: (1) day-to-day problems and (2) operational, cultural, and contractual problems. They found that the conflicts were either resolved by the operational managers or escalated to senior managers as specified by contractual procedures.

Table 5.1 Research on inter-organizational conflicts in BSO relationships

Authors	Study method	BSO conflict types	BSO conflict resolution styles	Details	General insights on BSO conflicts
Cahill et al. (2010)	Survey	Not investigated	Not investigated	Authors examined the moderating effect of "conflict frequency" on the relationship between outsourcing satisfaction (price satisfaction, relationship satisfaction, and service satisfaction) and customer loyalty. The authors surveyed 263 logistics professionals	Frequency of conflicts between BSO client and provider moderates "Customer Loyalty"
Chang and Chen (2016)	Case study	Not investigated	Not investigated	Authors used a case study of a Chinese manufacturer and its outsourcing provider to study how the parties resolved	Organizational structure affected conflict resolution effectiveness
Goo et al. (2009)	Survey	Not investigated	Not investigated	Authors argued that ITO relationships are characterized by uncertainty and information asymmetry which makes ITO relationships "rife with potential disputes and opportunism" (p. 126). The authors surveyed 92 South Korean IT executives	"Harmonious Conflict Resolution" positively and directly affects "Trust"

Authors	Study method	BSO conflict types	BSO conflict resolution styles	Details	General insights on BSO conflicts
Gregory et al. (2009)	Case study	Not investigated	Not investigated	Authors conducted 31 qualitative interviews in a single case study, focusing on interpersonal relationships between client-side team members and IT offshore supplier-side team members. "Conflict resolution" considered part of a negotiated culture	"Cultural intelligence" leads to a "negotiated culture" characterized by trust, shared understanding, and conflict resolution
Kern and Willcocks (2001)	Case studies	Identified two types of ITO conflicts: (1) day-to-day problems; (2) operational, cultural and contractual problems	Not investigated	Authors used 12 ITO cases to study relational governance	Conflicts were resolved by operational managers or escalated to senior management

(continued)

Table 5.1 (continued)

Authors	Study method	BSO conflict types	BSO conflict resolution styles	Details	General insights on BSO conflicts
Ndubisi (2011)	Survey	Not investigated	Integrating Accommodating Compromising	The author surveyed 122 Chinese and Indian service providers to examine the effects of three types of conflict handling styles (integrating, accommodating, and compromising) on trust and commitment in HRO relationships	Integrating, Accommodating, and Compromising approaches all positively and directly affected "Trust" and "Commitment"
Rai et al. (2012)	Survey	Not investigated	Not investigated	Authors viewed "conflict resolution" as a factor of relational governance. They hypothesized that conflict resolution would substitute for goal expectations in positively influencing BPO satisfaction. They surveyed 335 people from 215 German banks about four BPO services—settlement of securities, consumer credit, credit cards, and domestic payments	"Conflict Resolution" (and other relational governance factors) substitutes for contractually specified goal expectations

Authors	Study method	BSO conflict types	BSO conflict resolution styles	Details	General insights on BSO conflicts
Rhodes et al. (2016)	Survey	Not investigated	Not investigated	Authors surveyed 234 Singaporean managers to assess the associations among outsourcing motives, relationship interactions (which includes conflict resolution), and customer perceived value	"Relationship Interaction" (which included "conflict resolution") positively affected customer perceived outcomes
Swar et al. (2012)	Survey	Not investigated	Not investigated	Authors used a survey to examine the determinants of relationship factors (cooperation, trust, and mutual understanding) in South Korean public sector organizations. One of their independent variables was based on a construct called "conflict handling capabilities."	"Conflict Handling Capability" positively effected "Mutual Understanding," but it had no significant effect on "Cooperation" and only marginal effect on "Trust" (p < 0.10)
Winkler et al. (2008)	Five case studies	Not investigated	Not investigated	Authors conceptualized "conflict" as an aspect of relationship quality that affects outsourcing success. Based on case studies of ITO offshoring, the authors found that power distance can lead to conflicts which adversely affect success	"Conflict" adversely affects "Offshoring Success"

(continued)

Table 5.1 (continued)

Authors	Study method	BSO conflict types	BSO conflict resolution styles	Details	General insights on BSO conflicts
Wickramasinghe and Nandula (2015)	Survey	Not investigated	Not investigated	Authors collected surveys from 216 team members working in globally dispersed teams	Diversity in global teams leads to conflicts that adversely affected team performance
Wüllenweber et al. (2008)	Survey	Not investigated	Not investigated	Authors examined a construct they called "consensus" that was measured with three items related to conflict resolution. Based on a survey of 335 BPO projects in German banks, the authors found that consensus was related to BPO success	"Consensus" marginal effects "BPO Success" ($p < 0.10$)

Ndubisi (2011) surveyed 122 Chinese and Indian service providers to examine the effects of three types of conflict handling styles (integrating, accommodating and compromising) on trust and commitment in HRO relationships. All three conflict resolution styles positively, directly, and significantly affected trust and commitment. The author found an interesting cultural difference: The compromising style had a significantly greater effect on commitment for the Chinese service providers. Ndubisi (2012) used this same data set to see if the answers differed by gender and found that an "integrating conflict handling/trust relationship" is significantly stronger for males than for females. Furthermore, a "compromising conflict handling/trust relationship" is significantly stronger for females than for males.

Codes for BSO Conflict Types

To code the 13 conflict stories by conflict type, we initially searched the literature for existing conflict frameworks specific to BSO conflicts. Finding only the typology mentioned above (Ndubisi, 2011), we expanded the literature search to the general management literature. We found several typologies that differentiated between work conflicts and interpersonal conflicts (e.g., DeChurch & Marks, 2001; Molnar & Rogers, 1979; Yitshaki, 2008). DeChurch and Marks (2001) differentiated between *task-related* conflicts and *relationship* conflicts. They defined task-related conflicts as disagreements about work to be done or work performance. Relationship conflicts were defined as disagreements that arose from interpersonal relationships not directly related to the task. Using a similar dyad, Yitshaki (2008) differentiated between *cognitive* conflicts and *affective* conflicts. Cognitive conflicts are based on disagreements about achieving objectives whereas affective conflicts are based on interpersonal incompatibilities. DeChurch and Marks (2001) and Yitshaki (2008) illuminate an interesting distinction relevant to the BSO context because some of the BSO conflict stories seemed to be more about personalities (relationship; affective) than about the work (task-related/cognitive). However, the BSO work conflicts in our sample seemed to fall into two further types—conflicts over finances and conflicts over services. Therefore, we ultimately extended the conflict type coding scheme into three types: **commercial conflicts, service conflicts, and relationship conflicts:**

- **Commercial conflicts** are financial disputes that threaten economic outcomes for the client, provider, or both. For clients, higher than expected cost outlays can prompt a commercial conflict (e.g., Lacity & Willcocks, 1998; Saunders et al., 1997). For providers, failure to earn a profit on an account can lead to a commercial conflict (Kern et al., 2002).
- **Service conflicts** are disputes over service(s) that threaten the quality of the service(s) provided to a client. Many researchers have examined the importance of service delivery and performance in outsourcing relationships (e.g., Chakrabarty et al., 2008; Deng et al., 2013; Gopal & Koka, 2012; Gorla & Somers, 2014; Grover et al., 1996). Service conflicts over issues like slow service, error-prone service, or changing service requirements may be caused by many things and by many parties, even parties or factors external to the BSO relationship (Lacity & Willcocks, 2015).
- **Relationship conflicts** are people-related disputes that threaten the quality of the BSO relationship in which the parties disagree about how people should behave. For example, should the client direct provider employees or should the provider direct its own employees (Kern & Willcocks, 2002)?

Codes for Conflict Resolution Styles

In contrast to the sparse research on inter-organizational conflict types, many typologies of conflict resolution approaches have been proposed (Blake & Mouton, 1964; Deutsch, 1949, 1990; Gounaris et al., 2016; Hardy & Phillips, 1998; Khun & Poole 2000; McKenna & Richardson, 1995; Pruitt, 1983; Putnam & Wilson, 1982; Rahim, 2000, 2002; Thomas & Kilmann, 1974; Walton & McKersie, 1965; Yitshaki, 2008).

The early research on conflict resolution styles focused on dyads. Deutsch (1949) was one of the first authors to describe different individual approaches to conflict resolution. The author differentiated between only two styles: *cooperation* or *competition*. Simple dichotomies raised doubts about their ability to capture human complexity, so more complex typologies were created (Copley, 2008; Ruble & Thomas, 1976; Smith, 1987). Blake and Mouton (1964), Thomas and Kilmann (1974) and Rahim (2002) developed the richest typologies. All of these models were based on mapping two dimensions. Blake and Mouton (1964) initially proposed a five-style model of *leadership* (Country Club Leader, Team Leader, Impoverished Leader, Produce or Perish Leader and Middle of the Road Leader) that arose from two dimensions: concern for people and concern for production. Using the same dimensions, Nicotera (1993) adapted Blake and Mouton (1964)'s framework to identify five styles of conflict approaches: *Problem-solving, Smoothing, Withdrawal, Forcing,* and *Sharing*. Similarly, Thomas and Kilmann (1974) developed a five-style model (*avoiding, accommodating, compromising, collaborating* and *competing*) that arises from mapping two dimensions: degree of assertiveness and degree of cooperativeness. Rahim (2002) has yet another version of a five-style model (*integrating, obliging, dominating, avoiding,* and *compromising*) that emerges from mapping two dimensions: concern for self and concern for others. Although the dimensions are slightly different, one can see great overlap among the typologies proposed by Blake and Mouton (1964), Thomas and Kilmann (1974) and Rahim (2002). The authors also predict conflict resolution outcomes for each style:

1. **Avoiding/Withdrawal**: one side delays, postpones, or ignores the conflict, hoping it will just go away. Theory suggests the outcome will result in both parties losing because the conflict is never resolved (Friedman et al., 2000; Nicotera, 1993; Thomas & Kilmann, 1974).
2. **Accommodating/Smoothing/Obliging**: one side gives in to please the other side (Blake & Mouton, 1964; Rahim, 2002; Thomas & Kilmann, 1974). The reasons why one party accommodates another party are complex, including power differences, high desire to avoid stress caused by conflict, kindness, and strong focus on preserving the

relationship rather than "winning" the conflict (Pruitt, 1983). Theory suggests the outcome will result in a "winner" and a loser."

3. **Competing/Dominating/Forcing**: one or both sides aggressively defend(s) its own interests with little concern for the other side's interests. With a competing style, a party is "tough" by placing extreme initial demands, by having small concession rates and by being generally unyielding. This strategy can be effectively deployed by the more powerful party (Lewicki et al., 1992) and results, theory predicts, with a "winner" and a "loser."
4. **Collaborating/Problem-solving/Integrating**: both parties work together to develop a solution that benefits both sides. Theory suggests the outcome will result in both parties winning (Blake & Mouton, 1964; Rahim, 2002; Thomas & Kilmann, 1974).
5. **Compromising/Sharing**: each side seeks to balance wins and losses (Nicotera, 1993; Thomas & Kilmann, 1974).

Khun and Poole (2000) also included a "mixed" category because some conflicts started off with one conflict resolution style (e.g., avoiding, accommodating, or competing) and then the partners **switched** to another style.

6. **Switching:** one or both parties change from one conflict resolution style to another Khun and Poole (2000).

Thus, by considering prior literature and by reflecting on the conflict stories shared by participants, we decided to code five conflict resolution styles from Thomas and Kilmann (1974) and added the switched category from Khun and Poole (2000): competing, avoiding, accommodating, collaborative, compromising, and switching.

Coding conflict outcomes. Because each conflict story had a key informant from the client organization and a key informant from the provider organization, we were able to assess the conflict outcomes from each perspective. We coded "satisfied," "somewhat satisfied," or "dissatisfied" for client and provider views on a given BSO conflict outcome:

5 Conflict Resolution in Business Services Outsourcing ...

- Conflict outcomes were rated as "satisfied" when the participant was clearly pleased with the outcome.
- Conflict outcomes were rated as "somewhat satisfied" when participants said things like they could "accept" or "live with" the solutions.
- Conflict outcomes were rated as "dissatisfied" when participants were clearly annoyed, hostile, or hopeless about the outcomes.

Table 5.2 provides examples of how conflict outcomes were coded.
Figure 5.1 summarizes the coding scheme used to categorize the 13 BSO conflicts.

Table 5.2 Sample codes for conflict outcomes

	Satisfied	Somewhat Satisfied	Dissatisfied
Client view	"It created a far more collaborative environment and a far healthier environment for the account where we're happy to be straightforward and honest with each other."—Client Lead, Case 1	Not applicable—clients were either satisfied or dissatisfied	"So it was disappointing, it was embarrassing and it was probably the largest proof of the source of everything was for them, nothing was for us."—Client Lead, Case 5
Provider view	"We have a very good relationship with them now. They have the transparency and there's been good collaboration. There are good behaviors." Provider Lead, Case 4	"That was a bit of a constant battle we had because, philosophically, we were opposed. We couldn't really seem to resolve that. But in the end, we sort of came to a compromise...We sort of set up some guidelines we could live with and move forward from there."—Provider Lead, Case 10	"If we have a fault, we bend over backwards, sometimes a little too much for the client. Sometimes to our detriment, actually. We try and help them out and sometimes we can't."—Provider Lead, Case 6

Conflict Types:	Conflict Resolution Styles:	Conflict Outcomes:
1. Commercial 2. Service 3. Relationship	1. Avoiding 2. Accommodating 3. Competing 4. Collaborative 5. Compromising 6. Switch	1. Client Satisfied 2. Client Somewhat Satisfied 3. Client Dissatisfied 4. Provider Satisfied 5. Provider Somewhat Satisfied 6. Provider Dissatisfied

Fig. 5.1 Coding scheme

Findings: 13 BSO Conflicts

This section applies the theoretical codes to the 13 cases. In Table 5.3, we categorized the 13 BSO conflict cases into three types of conflicts (commercial conflicts, service conflicts, and relationship conflicts), five of the six types of conflict resolution styles (competing, avoiding, accommodating, collaborative and switching), and three types of outcomes (satisfied, somewhat satisfied, and dissatisfied).

Conflict Types

Commercial conflicts are disputes over financials, such as pricing and profit margins. Among the 13 conflict cases in our study, five were commercial conflict cases. Case 1 involved a pricing model that caused the provider to lose money on the deal. Case 2, also involving a pricing model, caused the client to spend more money than anticipated, thus eroding its business case to a negative return on investment. The third commercial conflict, Case 3, consisted of a client overestimating demand during contract negotiations, then giving the provider a much smaller piece of business than expected, resulting in a poor economic outcome for the provider. Case 4 entailed a client paying for bloated provider staffing because the provider lead kept his transition team in place too long after the transition. The last commercial conflict case, Case 5, involved partners fighting over a gainsharing clause that was designed to incentivize the provider to excel at performance. It backfired, resulting in a multi-million dollar dispute.

Table 5.3 Thirteen conflict case stories

Case story	Conflict type	Conflict resolution style	Conflict outcome (client view/ provider view)
1. A poor pricing model caused the provider to lose money on the deal	Commercial conflict	Switch to collaborative	Satisfied/ Satisfied
2. A poor pricing model caused the client to spend more money than anticipated	Commercial conflict	Collaborative	Satisfied/ Satisfied
3. A client overestimated demand	Commercial conflict	Collaborative	Satisfied/ Satisfied
4. A client paid for bloated provider staffing	Commercial conflict	Switch to collaborative	Satisfied/ Somewhat Satisfied
5. Partners fought over gainshare	Commercial conflict	Competing	Dissatisfied/ Dissatisfied
6. Provider overpromised and under-delivered on its foreign language capabilities	Service conflict	Avoiding	Dissatisfied/ Dissatisfied
7. A call center service had a rocky transition	Service conflict	Collaborative	Satisfied/ Satisfied
8. Third-party software caused service performance to plummet	Service conflict	Collaborative	Satisfied/ Satisfied
9. A client wanted a slicker tool	Service conflict	Switch to collaborative	Satisfied/ Somewhat Satisfied

(continued)

Table 5.3 (continued)

Case story	Conflict type	Conflict resolution style	Conflict outcome (client view/ provider view)
10. A client and provider clashed over the provider's work habits	Relationship conflict	Accommodating	Satisfied/ Somewhat Satisfied
11. A client and provider clashed over the provider's work habits	Relationship conflict	Accommodating	Satisfied/ Somewhat Satisfied
12. A client and provider clashed over the provider's work habits	Relationship conflict	Switch to collaborative	Satisfied/ Satisfied
13. A client lead made much ado about nothing	Relationship conflict	Switch to collaborative	Satisfied/ Satisfied

Service conflicts are disputes over services. Among our BSO cases, four service conflicts threatened service delivery. One service conflict case, Case 6, involved a provider telling its client it could support a foreign language service when it could not. Case 7 involved a rocky call center transition from the client to the provider, resulting in a surge in call volumes from users needing assistance. In Case 8, third-party software caused service performance to plummet. In the last service conflict case, Case 9, a client lead was not satisfied with one of the provider's tools used to deliver an HRO service.

Relationship conflicts are disputes in which the parties disagree about how people should behave. We have four cases of relationship conflicts. Case 10 involved the client lead escalating every small issue to the client's Chief Financial Officer (CFO), a storyline we call "much ado about nothing." Case 11, Case 12, and Case 13 were about clients and providers clashing over the providers' work habits. Clients from these last three stories wanted to dictate how provider employees should spend their time.

Conflict Resolution Styles

A **competing style** is characterized by a party's hard-lined defense of its own interests. We found only one example. In Case 5, both parties assumed a competing style and maintained this approach throughout.

An **avoiding style** is characterized by a party's hope that by delaying, postponing, or ignoring the conflict for a while, the conflict will be resolved without a confrontation. Case 6 exemplified this approach. As mentioned above, the case involved a provider telling its client it could support a foreign language service when it could not. The provider delayed telling the client it could not perform the foreign language service because it hoped to build up the capability.

An **accommodating style** is characterized by one party largely acquiescing to the demands or needs of the other party. In two BSO conflict cases—Case 10 and Case 11—the providers largely accommodated their clients' requests.

A **collaborative style** is characterized by partners who seek a solution that balances the needs of both parties. Four of the BSO cases adopted a collaborative style from the start to resolve conflicts—Case 2, Case 3, Case 7, and Case 8.

A **switch-to-collaborative style** starts off with one conflict resolution style and then the partners switch to another style. Five of the BSO cases switched from a competing or avoiding strategy to a collaborative style—Case 1, Case 4, Case 9, Case 12, and Case 13. This switching style is epitomized in the quote from a provider lead who said:

> I think all our conflicts tend to start off quite aggressive, where we're defending our position. And then in order to actually get any resolution, it has to become collaborative.

Conflict Resolution Outcomes

Among these 13 conflicts, seven cases—Case 1, Case 2, Case 3, Case 7, Case 8, Case 12, and Case 13—were resolved with both parties "satisfied." Four cases—Case 4, Case 9, Case 10, and Case 11—were resolved with the client "satisfied" and the provider "somewhat satisfied" and two (Case 5 and Case 6) resulted in both parties being dissatisfied (see Table 5.3).

Tying Conflict Types, Resolution Styles to BSO Outcomes

From the mapping of the 13 BSO conflicts in Table 5.3 to Fig. 5.2, the following patterns emerge regarding conflict types:

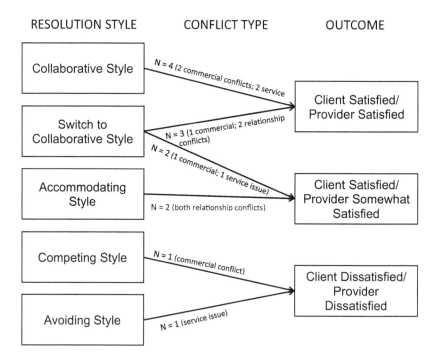

Fig. 5.2 Conflict resolution styles, conflict types, and outcomes

1. Commercial conflicts in our small sample clearly required a collaborative style to ensure both sides had fair economic outcomes. In contrast, the dogged adherence to a competing style to resolve a commercial conflict resulted in both parties being dissatisfied.
2. Service conflicts were also best resolved with a collaborative style.
3. As far as relationship conflicts, providers in two of our cases were willing to accommodate clients' wishes; parties in two other cases switched to a collaborative style. While both styles satisfactorily resolved relationship conflicts for clients, only the switch to a collaborative style fully satisfied providers

Concerning Resolution Styles:

1. Competing and avoiding conflict resolution styles resulted in both clients and providers being dissatisfied with the outcomes.
2. An accommodating conflict resolution style resulted in the accommodated party being satisfied and the accommodators being somewhat satisfied.
3. When adopted from the start, a collaborative conflict resolution style resulted in all parties being satisfied in all four cases.
4. A switch-to-collaborative conflict resolution style resulted in satisfied clients and either satisfied providers (three cases) or somewhat satisfied providers (two cases).

In the next sections, we describe each of the 13 BSO conflict cases. These rich stories were each given a name to capture the spirit of the narrative. The conflict stories themselves are interesting and valuable. These stories capture the myriad of BSO conflicts arising from pricing models, service volume predictions, incentivizing performance, culture clashes, and obstinate people, to name but a few. They also convey coding credibility by bringing the data closer to the reader (Lincoln & Guba, 1985).

BSO Commercial Conflict Stories

> The world fell apart [after the Global Financial crisis in 2008] and the foundation wasn't strong enough to withstand that because we did not have a lot of sophistication in our commercial arrangement... It's taken us awhile to come to terms with the fact that volume baselines were wrong, wildly wrong, because the forecast in growth on [the client's] part just wouldn't happen.—Provider Lead

Of all the problem types, commercial conflicts are the most serious because outsourcing relationships are firstly commercial transactions— a provider MUST earn a profit and a client MUST meet its economic business case to be viable (Kern et al., 2002). From our data, five BSO cases involved commercial conflicts, of which two were successfully resolved to the satisfaction of both parties by using a collaborative style. One BSO conflict was resolved to the satisfaction of both parties when they switched to a collaborative style. One conflict was resolved to the satisfaction of the client when both sides switched to a collaborative approach, but left the provider "somewhat satisfied." The last example of a commercial conflict involved parties using a competing style, which did not satisfactorily resolve the conflict for either party

Case 1: A poor pricing model caused the provider to lose money on the deal This case involved a shaky launch of an FAO deal. Part of the problem was a faulty pricing mechanism that prevented the provider from recovering its costs. Initially, the contract used unit-based pricing.[1] After about two years, according to the provider—"*Our unit pricing started to not look right anymore.*" The provider was losing money. From the client side, the relationship was not working for them either. The client lead said:

> Every time we had an idea, it was stopped in its tracks. We got to a point where we really weren't getting anywhere. They weren't bringing practical

---

[1] Unit-based pricing charges the client for each unit of service, such as paying per invoice processed or per laptop purchased by the provider on behalf of the client.

ideas to the table. The relationship was getting very, very strained between the two operational management groups.

The partners initially used avoiding and competing styles to resolve their problems and neither approach was working. Finally, the client lead demanded that the provider assign new leads. His request was granted. With new provider leads in place, both sides agreed to renegotiate the contract and *switched to a collaborative style* to find a solution that was economically viable for both parties. Both parties agreed to move to a different pricing model. The partners moved to FTE pricing. After the renegotiation, the BSO relationship operated effectively and *both sides were satisfied* with the solution.

Case 2: A poor pricing model caused the client to spend more money than anticipated On one account, the initial contract was priced using different rate cards for different skill levels. Soon after the contract went into effect, the client came to the provider and explained that the client's business case was not being met because the client underestimated the number and complexity of skills needed to perform the work. The client asked to renegotiate the pricing mechanism. The provider agreed because it understood that the relationship would fail in the long run if the client's return on investment was negative. In turn, the client understood it needed to give the provider something valuable in exchange for a different pricing model. Both assumed a *collaborative style* to conflict resolution. The provider agreed to a flat rate card in exchange for a longer contract and an increased scope of work. Both parties negotiated a better deal, *both sides were very satisfied*, and the relationship proved to be a high-performance one. Said the client:

> Our partner has performed very well. Put simply – they execute. We have found that if we set the bar high, they do all that they can to jump over it. In addition to providing transactional services that exceed service level agreements, they help us to think strategically about running our business.

Case 3: A client overestimated demand On this procurement deal, the provider's profits were tied to the size of the client's procurement spend.

During negotiations, the client estimated it would transfer £80 million worth of spend across seven categories to the provider. Six months into the deal, only £30 million in spend had been transferred to the provider. (For example, the partners initially thought that £25 million worth of learning and development spend was going to be transferred, but the actual number was only about 30% of the estimate.) This underestimation threatened the provider's ability to meet its projected profitability targets. Rather than simply say "too bad" to the provider, the client recognized the threat to the provider's financial position and the effect that it would ultimately have on its service levels and BSO relationship. The partners committed to resolving the conflict *collaboratively* and held many strategic planning sessions to address the shortfall. The partners agreed that it was in both of their interests to transfer over the intended critical mass of spend to the provider. This would be achieved by adding eight more categories of spend, bringing the provider's controlled spend to nearly £100 million by year end. **Both parties considered the solution a win–win.** The client saved money on the eight new categories it shifted to the provider, and the provider got a larger, more lucrative deal.

Case 4: A client pays for bloated provider staff On this FAO deal, a new client lead came on the account several years after it had been in effect. He repeatedly questioned the provider lead why he was paying for provider employees in a high cost area when most of the other work was already re-located in a low cost area. The client lead wanted the provider to move these resources to a low cost area. After taking seven months to respond, the provider lead said the client could not request staff relocation until next year and the client would have to pay for the severance packages, as the contract specified. The client lead was very annoyed at this answer because at the same time, the provider was trying to sell the client additional consulting services. The client said:

> I told them that they are not getting the message of strategic relationship and this is not the way to start things off. I had one of them calling me to meet with me about consulting work and I said, 'Why would I give you more business in consulting if you're basically giving us a hard time about correcting our account elsewhere?'

Eventually, the provider assigned a new provider lead and she immediately *switched to a collaborative style*. She investigated the work the onshore team was providing for her client. She determined that there was not enough work to occupy all the onshore resources anymore—they were imperative for the transition, but that was over long ago. She retained just half the staff to perform the client's work and she moved those roles offshore. Although no provider is happy to lose revenues, she was *somewhat satisfied* with the resolution because it paved the way for a revitalization of the relationship. *The client was thrilled with the resolution* and with the new provider lead. He said:

> [She] is fantastic. She's very action-oriented. She pushes back and can challenge things in the right way. That's the difference I think in terms of making it a more strategic approach.

Case 5: Partners fight over gainshare In this engagement for procurement services, the client and provider escalated the fight over gainshare allocations to a formal dispute.[2] The contract stipulated that the provider would get a percentage of any discount above a vendor's list price for any new products that the provider bought for the client. The provider renewed a hardware vendor contract on behalf of the client that was 55% lower than the hardware vendor's list price. The provider calculated a multi-million dollar gainshare, claiming the contract was for new products as evidenced by new material codes. The client refused to pay. The client claimed that its previous contract with the hardware vendor already had a 50% discount and the client was purchasing the same material, it was just that the vendor's newer models used different codes. The client allocated about 150 hours of in-house legal counsel to the dispute and brought back the advisory firm that helped negotiate the original contract into the deliberations. The client said: *"It went all the way to the dispute process, and it left an incredibly bitter taste with our executive team."* Eventually the provider's procurement services division was bought by another provider. The client thought, *"Good riddance!"* The

---

[2] Gainsharing is an incentive used by BSO clients to motivate providers to improve their performance by sharing financially in the gain (Lacity & Willcocks 2013).

style was *competing* throughout and *both sides were dissatisfied* with the process and outcome.

BSO Service Conflict Stories

> If the work we're getting back is not what we expect, that's as much our fault as the service provider's because we're not being clear in telling them what we want, and tooling them up to deliver it.—Client Lead

This section highlights service conflicts that disrupted service performance. The examples cover several contexts including LSO, FAO, and HRO. In the first service conflict example, the avoiding strategy resulted in an unsuccessful conflict resolution. In the next two examples, the service conflicts were successfully resolved using a collaborative style. The parties in the last service conflict case switched to a collaborative style, resulting in a satisfied client and a somewhat satisfied provider.

Case 6: A provider overpromised and under-delivered on its foreign language capabilities On one LSO account, the client asked the provider if it could support foreign languages. The provider indicated that it could support foreign languages from its Indian delivery center. After a trial period, it became apparent that the provider had never supported foreign languages from this location before, and the result—according to the client—was "*quite disastrous.*" The provider assumed an *avoid style* of conflict resolution by not telling the client it lacked French language capabilities. The client lead was more annoyed that the provider was not forthright about its capabilities than he was about the provider's lack of capabilities. From the provider lead's perspective, he thought a delay strategy would work because he intended to quickly build the capabilities in India to delight his prestigious client. *The client was not delighted* and took back foreign language support from the provider. *The provider was also disappointed* with the outcome (see Table 4 for quote).

Case 7: A call center service had a rocky transition Soon after one client transitioned its help line for its accounts payable function to a provider, the volume of calls surged. The client suspected the increase in volume was due to repeat callers, which would mean that the provider was not resolving the callers' issues during the first calls. Rather than just beat up the provider, the client took the calls back in-house to give the provider time to analyze the calls and to develop a plan on improving the service. The provider discovered that some of the "repeat callers" were the same people calling up with a completely different question, but the provider employee ticketed the new call as a repeat call. Thus, some of the repeat volumes were caused by insufficient training on how to tag calls. Some of the call volume issues were caused by the fact that it was year-end and people were scrambling to pay their invoices and complete expense reports. The client and provider agreed to an immediate plan and then developed a long-term plan to get service back on track. The provider praised the client's behavior:

"They absolutely pitched in to help… They stepped in when they didn't have to. They could have just said, 'Tough luck, you just missed your service level agreement.'" The client explained his collaborative approach: "Other clients might have said [to the provider]: 'This is your problem, don't bother me. It's your issue.' What I try and do is say: 'We are in this together.'" Both parties were clearly satisfied with the result.

Case 8: Third-party software caused service performance to plummet On one large account, the client implemented one software vendor's Enterprise Resource Planning (ERP) system and outsourced support of this system to another service provider. After the go-live day, user complaints skyrocketed. The users immediately blamed the service provider, not the ERP vendor. The provider lead recalled:

> So there was a lot of emails and a lot of yelling and screaming about, 'What the hell is going on?'

The client and provider leads worked together to investigate the problem. They each assigned senior level managers to oversee the resolution. The provider lead recalled:

We absolutely threw resources at it from consulting, from operations, from analytics to figure out what it is and lower the backlog and fix the root causes while, at the same time, putting Band-Aids on all the places that it was bleeding.

It took four months to get service issues completely resolved, but the *collaborative* style worked to the *satisfaction of both parties.*

Case 9: A client wanted a slicker tool A client from a consumer products company was very market-focused and valued slick user interfaces on all of its software products. One of the provider's tools did not have a glitzy interface. The provider was willing to customize the interface for an additional fee. The client did not think it should pay to improve the provider's tool. This debate went back and forth for quite a while without resolution. Finally, the provider agreed to find a cloud-based alternative that could replace its proprietary system. The provider lead said:

> We are looking at how we can make a swap out in a manner that commercially will work for each party with minimal to no investment on the part of [the client] and that isn't a huge margin eroding thing on our end. We are working very collaboratively on that.

This story demonstrates the value of *switching to a collaborative style.* Rather than focus on the tool at hand, the partners stepped back and focused on the features that the client wanted. The collaboration spawned "outside the box" thinking to find a solution that worked to *satisfy the client* and a solution with which the *provider could live (somewhat satisfied).*

1. BSO Relationship Conflict Stories

> The provider appointed a delivery account manager and through the initial period, the relationship did not work. I don't know whether it was chemistry or what; He may have been a very good person but I couldn't work with him.—Client Lead

5 Conflict Resolution in Business Services Outsourcing ...   175

This section presents four cases about relationship conflicts. The examples cover multiple contexts including HRO, call centers, ITO, and supply chain management outsourcing. The first three relationship conflicts all involve clients and providers clashing over the providers' work habits. The providers accommodated the clients' wishes in the first two cases, while the third case used a switch to collaborative style to renegotiate the terms. The fourth relationship conflict case was resolved when a client leader was replaced and the new leaders switched to a collaborative style.

Case 10: A client and provider clashed over the provider's work habits On this HRO deal, some of the provider's staff was located at the client site. Although the client was paying the provider based on outcomes, it still wanted to dictate how the provider's employees should behave. The client lead expected the provider's staff to maintain the same work hours as the client's staff. He constantly questioned how the provider's staff was spending its time. The client lead did not want the provider's staff in training or in meetings during "the client's time." The provider lead countered that his company was meeting its service levels, so the client lead should not be micromanaging the provider's staff. In the end, the provider acquiesced by *accommodating* the client's wishes so that the ***client was satisfied***. He said:

> We set up some guidelines that we wouldn't do team building activities until 4:00 in the afternoon. There would only be so many training days per year, per person. We sort of set up some guidelines **we could live with** and move forward from there.

Case 11: A client and provider clashed over the provider's work habits In this example, a client and provider disagreed on the role of middle managers. The context is an offshore customer care deal where the South African-based provider answers calls from the client's UK-based customers. The client felt that the provider's middle managers were too "hands off." The client was accustomed to middle managers who listen to calls daily and who coach call center agents. Conversely, in South Africa, middle managers are accustomed to delegating work to the teams. To resolve the conflict, the provider *accommodated* the client by doing what the client asked. *The client was very satisfied* and the *provider was somewhat satisfied* with the agreement.

Case 12: A client and provider clashed over the provider's work habits In a nearly identical storyline as Case 10, on an account halfway around the world, a client lead wanted a refund because the client claimed that the provider employees only worked six hours per day instead of eight. The provider lead felt the client should not be meddling with his staff. He said:

> I said it was my own responsibility to organize my team. If I'm able to meet service level agreements by having half of the staff that was expected, it's my decision. The same as if I have a problem and I have to duplicate the number of people, it's my problem.

Thus, the initial style was competing on both sides, but soon the parties realized that they needed a better approach and *switched to a collaborative style.* The parties recognized that both sides would be more comfortable with an outcome-based pricing mechanism. The provider lead concluded the story: *"We are now billing the client the proper price for the service, not related to the time the people are spending on the contract."* ***Both sides are satisfied*** with the solution.

Case 13: A client lead made much ado about nothing On one supply chain outsourcing account, the client lead escalated every small issue to the client's CFO. The provider lead tried working with the client lead, telling her: *"Let's work together to get this resolved."* She continued to escalate every small issue and made it a big problem at the client end. The client CFO finally intervened. He sent a scout to the provider's delivery center to investigate. When the scout returned with a good report on the provider's performance, the CFO replaced the original client lead. The new client lead reported that since the replacement, there had not been any major problems. The new leaders ***switched to a collaborative style*** to resolve problems and ***both sides are satisfied.*** He said: *"Both parties work hard at it to ensure there are no conflicts. We have had a few bumps on the road but those are normal in marriages as well."*

Discussion

In this section, we first recognize the research limitations then discuss the contributions this research makes to theory and practice.

Limitations

Although this study contributes to the theory and practice of conflict and conflict resolution in BSO relationships, it has several limitations. The sample of BSO relationships was small and opportunistic, restricting our ability to generalize (Kuhn & Poole, 2000). The BSO relationships do not represent a random sample, but rather a convenience sample facilitated by our research sponsors (see acknowledgements). The disadvantage of a convenience sample is that it includes sampling bias and findings may not necessarily represent the population of BSO relationships. In particular, the BSO relationships are likely to represent better than average performing relationships. In our sample, participants from 59% of the BSO relationships reported no significant conflicts. We conjecture that this under-represents conflict frequency in the larger BSO population given prior failure rates (Barringer & Harrison, 2000; Gefen et al., 2008; Hughes & Weiss, 2007; Lacity et al., 2016; Mani et al., 2012). On the other hand, a major advantage of this convenience sample was that we were able to obtain paired data that included both client and provider inputs, thus considering "multiple witness accounts" (Klein & Myers, 1999). Moreover, we were also able to get rich stories on a sensitive subject that is rarely studied (Ndubisi, 2011).

Interviewing by telephone introduces another limitation. Compared to face-to-face interviews, telephone interviews limit social cues and can result in the interviewee being interrupted at the workplace without the interviewer's knowledge (Opdenakker, 2006). These limitations were acceptable trade-offs given the advantages of telephone interviews: convenient access to people world-wide and lower cost of data collection compared to face-to-face (Mann & Stewart, 2000).

Contribution to Theory

ITO researchers (and more recently BPO researchers) have largely relied on reference disciplines to theoretically guide outsourcing research. Of late, researchers have questioned such theoretical appropriations (e.g., Karimi-Alaghehband et al., 2011; Schermann et al., 2016) and offered criteria for fair appropriations from other disciplines (Aubert & Rivard, 2016), such as juridical and structural–cultural frames of faithful theorical appropriations (Lee, 2016). Still other researchers have called for domain-specific, endogenous theories of IT (Lacity et al., 2011). One contribution to an endogenous theory is that we offer a richer typology of conflict types than the dyads previously used to study interorganizational conflicts that are specific to BSO (DeChurch & Marks, 2001; Kern & Willcocks, 2002; Molnar & Rogers, 1979; Yitshaki, 2008).

Prior literature distinguished between work conflicts (task/cognitive) and relationship conflicts (relationship/affective). We distinguished among **commercial conflicts, service conflicts**, and **relationship conflicts.**

Rather than just aggregate all the non-relationship conflicts under one type such as "task/cognitive," the BSO context can be more richly described by articulating two typical types of work conflicts—commercial and service. We observed that commercial conflicts threatened economic outcomes for the clients, providers, or both. For the clients in Case 2, Case 4, and Case 5, higher than expected cost outlays threatened their economic interests and prompted serious commercial conflicts. For the providers in Case 1, Case 3, and Case 5, failure to generate their expected profit margins caused commercial conflicts.

Service conflicts threatened service quality. In Case 5 and Case 6 service conflicts arose over the providers' lack of capabilities, resulting in poor service quality. In Case 7, a service conflict arose from a third-party provider's software, resulting in poor service quality. In Case 8, the client and provider argued over a tool used to provide a service.

The relationship conflicts threatened the relationship quality. Relationship quality is often used as an outcome measure of BSO relationships (e.g., Babin et al., 2011; Lioliou et al., 2014; Palvia et al., 2010). When people fight, the quality of the relationship suffered.

Do the three BSO conflict types apply more generally to other types of inter-organizational conflicts in joint ventures, networks, consortia, alliances, and trade associations (Barringer & Harrison, 2000; Cropper et al., 2008)? This is an empirical question that needs further investigation. While the three conflict types are distinctive, we do note that the consequences of one type of conflict can have ripple effects on economic outcomes, service quality, and relationship quality; Poor performance in one dimension can spill over to another dimension as depicted in Fig. 5.3.

A poor economic outcome can erode relationship quality (who likes a partner who is draining his or her wallet?) and service quality (who wants to invest in services on a losing account?). For example, in Case 1 (called "a poor pricing model caused the provider to lose money on the deal") the commercial conflict eroded economic performance but it also eroded the quality of the relationship (see arrow "a" in Fig. 5.3). The provider did not want to invest more time and resources into the account while it was losing money, so it stopped responding to the client, thus eroding service quality (see arrow "b" in Fig. 5.3). As the client lead said, "*The relationship was getting very, very strained.*" Once the commercial conflict was resolved, economic performance, service quality, and relationship quality improved.

Poor service quality can erode the provider's profit margins and/or escalate the client's costs when resources are diverted to fix service performance. In Case 9 (called "a client wanted a slicker tool") the main conflict was with the quality of the tool, but fixing it had economic consequences (see arrow "c" in Fig. 5.3). Poor service quality also eroded good feelings between the client and partner (see arrow "d" in Fig. 5.3).

In our data set, poor relationship quality seemed to have the weakest spillover effects. In our three cases involving clients and providers clashing over the providers' work habits, the service level agreements were being met (service quality was good) and the economic outcomes

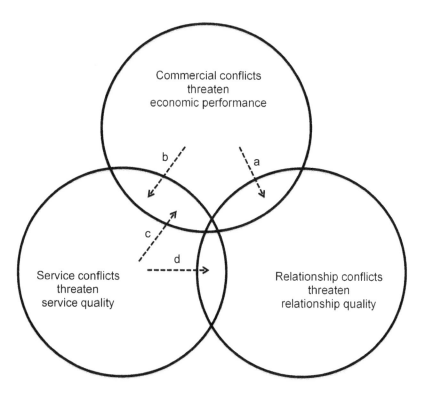

Fig. 5.3 Spillover effects of BSO conflict types

were not affected. As these spillover effects are novel to this study, more research is needed to understand them.

Theoretically, we found that five-factor frameworks like Thomas and Kilmann's typology of conflict resolution styles were robust enough to characterize the 13 BSO conflict cases, provided a switched category was added. Furthermore, most of the outcomes in the BSO case studies aligned with prior theory (e.g., Kuhn & Poole, 2000; Ndubisi, 2011; Thomas & Kilmann, 1974) on the following points:

1. Consistent with prior theory, the collaborative and switch-to-collaborative styles resulted in satisfied clients and satisfied or somewhat satisfied providers (see Fig. 5.4).

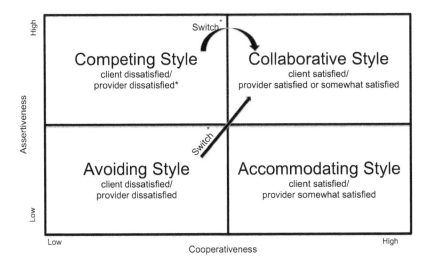

Fig. 5.4 BSO Conflict Resolution Styles and Outcomes Compared to Thomas and Kilmann (1974) (*Note*+Added to the Thomas and Kilmann framework (1974). *Inconsistent with prior theory)

2. Consistent with prior theory, an avoiding style resulted in dissatisfied clients and providers.
3. Theory suggests an accommodating style will result in one winner (i.e., satisfied) and one loser (i.e., dissatisfied). The BSO data had slightly better outcomes in that the clients (the accommodated) were satisfied and the providers (the accommodators) were somewhat satisfied. While not a perfect alignment, the fact that the accommodated was more satisfied than the accommodator is consistent with theory.

One conflict resolution style from Thomas and Kilmann (1974) is missing from Fig. 5.4, namely, a compromising strategy. None of the 13 BSO conflict cases used the "compromise" strategy. There is some anecdotal evidence among the 19 BSO cases that reported NO serious conflicts that a spirit of compromise may help to *prevent* a serious dispute (see Behavior 4 in Practitioner Contribution section below).

More research on BSO conflicts is needed to understand if this is a common phenomenon.

One finding, however, is inconsistent with prior theory. In Case 5, the partners both assumed a competing style throughout negotiations and both were dissatisfied with the outcome. In contrast, theory predicts a competing style will result in a winner (i.e., satisfied) and a loser (i.e., dissatisfied). While this finding is interesting, further investigation is needed to assess whether this is an isolated anomaly or something systematic and particular to BSO conflicts.

Contribution to Practice

Consistent with Markus (2014), we offer an important contribution to practice by identifying effective conflict resolution behaviors that managers can now adopt. In reading the transcripts of all 32 BSO relationships closely, five behaviors for avoiding conflicts or collaboratively solving BSO conflicts emerged. Although based on descriptive behaviors of what participants described as helpful behaviors as well as unhelpful behaviors, they are presented as normative behaviors of what clients and providers *should* do:

(1) never assign blame, but instead co-own all problems,
(2) be transparent about all relevant data,
(3) seek solutions that work for both partners,
(4) actively protect each other's commercial interests,
(5) ensure people behave appropriately or replace them.

These behaviors were reviewed and confirmed by research sponsors. Research participants reviewed and confirmed only the specific behaviors discussed by them during their interviews.

Behavior 1: Never assign blame, but instead co-own all problems We found this behavior evident in several of the BSO relationships. Case 8 (called "third-party software causes service performance to plummet") provides strong evidence of this behavior. The leaders in this story did not assign blame but instead co-owned the problem. During the ERP problem resolution process, the provider lead described the approach: *"We did a pretty good job of putting the right structure and the right resources in place to simultaneously mitigate the pain and fix the root cause. Both parties were pretty good at not blaming each other."* More impressive was the time, energy, and resources the provider allocated to a problem for which they were not the primary cause.

Evidence from some of the BSO relationships who claim they never experienced serious conflicts also mentioned this theme of not assigning blame. This quote from a provider lead illustrates this principle well: *"Throughout the process, we don't look at who performed the step that failed but what can we improve in the end-to-end processes so we can avoid that kind of problem in the future?"* One client lead from another BSO relationship described the behavior this way: *"Do not point your finger at the provider because when you do, four fingers point back to yourself."*

Behavior 2: Be transparent about all relevant data Transparency was frequently one of the top things interviewees talked about as a key to successfully resolving conflicts. One provider lead aptly captured this behavior in this quote: *"I'm committed to transparency with my counterpart. We try to be very open about what the interests are on each side so that when we're negotiating, we can negotiate commercial relationships that are good for the interests of both parties."* Transparency was evident on all the successfully resolved commercial and service conflicts. In contrast, Case 6 (called "a provider overpromised and under-delivered on its foreign language capabilities") illustrates the problems caused by a lack of transparency. The provider was quite reticent to expose its inabilities to clients, but the client eventually discovered them. This storyline is most common in offshore outsourcing, particularly when the provider is in a culture characterized by greater power distance and lower individualism compared to the client (Carmel & Tjia, 2005; Prikladnicki & Audy, 2012; Sakolnakorn, 2010).

Behavior 3: Seek solutions that work for both parties Ideally, a resolution will improve the circumstances for both parties, the so-called win–win solution. In several of the commercial conflict cases, solutions benefited both parties. In Case 3, (called "a client overestimated demand"), for example, the solution was to add more categories of procurement spend to the deal to make the volumes large enough for the provider to be satisfied. The client was satisfied because they were guaranteed cost savings on all the additional categories. In many cases, mutually acceptable solutions result from tough but fair negotiations and compromises. One provider lead who reported no serious BSO conflicts on his account captured the idea of tough but fair negotiations when he said: "*I'd like to say we follow a collaborative, win–win approach to conflict resolution. We do butt heads quite a lot on small things. We both want to win. So what I try and do, and what I counsel my managers to do, is to find a win–win and trade something off. We can get this and you can get that.*" This example provides some evidence that a **compromising strategy** may serve to prevent serious BSO conflicts.

Behavior 4: Actively protect each other's commercial interests Collaborative partners care about the other party's commercial interests. Caring about a partner's commercial well-being is not altruism; it is actually in the client's best interest to care about and protect the provider's commercial interests and vice-versa because client outcomes are tied to provider outcomes. If the provider fails to make a profit on an account, chances are the client will experience negative outcomes in terms of higher costs and lower service levels. Kern et al. (2002) have data on 85 outsourcing relationships that shows when a provider experiences a "winner's curse" (loss of profitability on an account), there is a high likelihood of it also affecting the client negatively. The aim is to create a new commercial deal that benefits both parties. This behavior was certainly true for both parties in Case 2, (called "a poor pricing model caused the client to spend more money than anticipated"), when the partners renegotiated the contract to, in effect, give the client lower prices and the provider a much larger volume of work.

Behavior 5: Ensure all people behave appropriately—or replace them! Prior research discussed the importance of the right leadership pair as a key to world-class performance and innovation (Davis & Eisenhardt, 2011; Lacity & Willcocks, 2013). In the cases, the right leadership pair resolved conflicts together and fairly. In several of the BSO conflict cases, the problem sometimes could not be resolved until a leader was changed, as evident in Cases 1, 4, and 13. Case 13, (called "a client lead made much ado about nothing") offers a great moral: Beware of the problem-solver who becomes the problem. In this story, the client lead was not acting appropriately, she blamed the provider for everything and she would not resolve problems with the provider. She became a bigger problem than the operational ones that needed to be solved. The CFO investigated the situation and then replaced her.

We also feel compelled to comment on the three cases where the clients and providers clashed over the providers' work habits (Cases 10, 11, and 12). Research finds that clients need to learn to manage the inputs and outputs to and from service providers rather than try to micromanage the provider's resources (Carmel & Tjia, 2005). If clients want complete control over the human resources that deliver a service, then perhaps they should bring the service back in-house (Bhagwatwar et al., 2011; Natasha et al., 2008). We understand the client's reasoning. Client's think: "*I am paying for the provider's dedicated staff so I better be sure they are productive.*" However, a better way to ensure that provider employees are productive is to require yearly mandatory productivity improvement clauses (Lacity & Willcocks, 2013). Turning to the providers' behaviors in these cases, they were diplomatic; they worked with their clients to develop compromises that both sides could accept.

Conclusion

Relationships and conflicts in inter-organizational types such as strategic alliances, joint ventures, and inter-firm collaborations for specific products and markets have been fertile ground for study in the strategic management literature. This has been less true in the Information Systems literature in general, and with the outsourcing phenomena in particular, despite the increasing size and strategic implications of much contemporary outsourcing practice. This chapter fills that research gap.

Here we used qualitative data to answer the research question, *What types of inter-organizational conflicts arise in BSO relationships and how do partners resolve them?* Consistent with prior research, we found that a collaborative style resulted in the best outcomes for both parties. Findings related to avoiding styles and accommodating styles were also consistent with prior research. Specifically, avoiding styles failed to resolve the conflicts in our cases satisfactorily. Accommodating styles were successful in resolving conflicts but led to the accommodators being less satisfied with the solution than the accommodated. However, we also found that a competing style resulted in both parties being dissatisfied with the outcome; this finding is counter to prior theory which predicts that competing styles lead to one satisfied party and one dissatisfied party. The 13 BSO conflicts mapped well to the new typology on BSO conflict types. In addition, findings suggest that there are spillover effects among commercial, service, and relationship conflicts. For example, one commercial conflict affected economic performance, service quality, and relationship quality.

In line with Jarzabkowski and Spee (2009), Golsorkhi et al. (2012), and Whittington (2014), this research aims to offer several important contributions to the development of strategy-as-practice research in Information Systems and other fields. The subject of conflict has been neglected but is a rich field for strategy-as-practice researchers to investigate. The 13 conflict stories in and of themselves are valuable (Barker & Gower, 2010; Sandelowski, 1991). Stories are a means to communicate experience, to help people make sense of complex situations, and to help build consensus during deliberations (Buttler & Lukosch, 2012). The subject of conflict in outsourcing relationships is often viewed as highly sensitive, indecorous, and secretive; consequently, clients may not have access to prior experiences. By sharing the positive and negative stories of the participants in our study, we provide a deeper understanding into the emotionally charged topic of conflicts that arise in business services outsourcing. For practitioners facing these problems or similar ones, the research offers guidance by identifying five effective conflict resolution behaviors. Our study has also shown how to develop theories of the problem and theories of the solution to address specific settings. We would argue that increasing adoption of such theories will make a valuable contribution to the toolbox for strategy-as-practice research. Our study may also be an indicator to other researchers that strategy cannot be a separate field of study isolated from its enactment, its execution. How strategy is executed by actors in organizations *becomes* the strategy. Examining what Jarzabkowski and Spee (2009) call *"micro-strategy making events, as they arise through the interaction between individual practitioners"* becomes, in our view, an important part of the ongoing research agenda. Our research also demonstrates to a degree the usefulness—reiterated by many strategy-as-practice commentators—of establishing much stronger connections between macro and micro phenomena, and the need to focus more strategy-as-practice research on substantiating outcomes. Finally, as suggested by Whitington (2014), we would argue that our study hopefully will encourage Information Systems researchers themselves to undertake more strategy-as-practice studies, not least because now and in the future, digital technologies have never had so much impact on strategy making and its execution.

Focusing on the findings on inter-organizational conflict, this study gives rise to some additional research questions. The generalizability of the three BSO conflict types to other inter-organizational conflicts is uncertain and needs examination. The novel findings about spillover effects, the finding that a compromising strategy may prevent serious BSO conflicts, and the finding that a competing conflict resolution style resulted in two losers (rather than a winner and loser as prior theory suggests) also all need further investigation. A comparison of findings on conflict, looking across different types of inter-organizational collaborations, including strategic outsourcing relationships, is also long overdue.

Appendix: Data Collection and Analysis Methods

Research Program Background

This research on BSO conflicts and conflict resolution emerged from a larger research program aimed to uncover the practices that distinguish outcomes. The research was sponsored by four organizations—Accenture, BPeSA, Everest Group, and The Source. The research program began in 2011 with an Everest survey of 263 BSO clients. The Everest survey found that eight practices were significantly correlated with BSO outcomes. These eight practices were:

1. Outsourcing Strategy: Focus on benefits beyond cost reduction.
2. Contractual Governance: Target strategic outcomes.
3. Relational Governance: Adopt a partnership-based approach to governance.
4. Transition of Work: Drive strong transition and change management capabilities.
5. Client Capabilities: Align the retained organization with the outsourced processes.
6. Client Capabilities: Take a holistic approach to the scope of the relationship.
7. Provider Capability: Contextualize data through domain expertise and analytics.
8. Provider Capability: Emphasize the benefits of technology in the relationship.

Data Collection Method

Key informant interview method. The Everest survey revealed *which* eight practices were associated with BSO outcomes in its sample, but the survey could not explain *how* practices influenced outcomes. Our initial research question, *How do practices associated with top performing BSO relationships influence outcomes?*, sought to elicit rich evidence that could corroborate, challenge, and/or extend the survey findings. To answer the initial research question, we selected a key informant interview method. Interviews with key informants were an appropriate method for understanding key stakeholder perspectives (Kvale, 1996; Klein & Myers, 1999), when seeking participation from busy or high-status respondents and when seeking answers to questions in which the subject matter is sensitive (like outsourcing) (Mahoney, 1997). Interviewees were "key" in that they provided particularly rich knowledge and insights of the BSO relationships through their seniority and through their specialist roles as client and provider leads in the setting (Bloor and Wood, 2013; Parsons, 2013).

Interview guide development. Based on the Everest survey results and on prior BSO literature, we designed two semi-structured interview guides, one for the client key informants and one for provider key informants. For client participants, the interview guide consisted of questions on outsourcing strategy, provider/partner selection, contractual governance, transition of work, ongoing delivery, relational governance, client and provider capabilities, decision outcomes, and overall lessons learned. The provider interview guide included a similar set of questions, but worded to assess the provider's perspective. The interview guides were four pages long. One specific set of questions about outsourcing conflicts generated the main data for this paper. These questions were:

- Please provide one detailed example of a significant conflict that arose in the relationship and how it was resolved.
- How would you characterize your organization's approach to resolving this conflict?
- How would you characterize the provider's approach to resolving this conflict? (client interviewees only)
- How would you characterize the client's approach to resolving this conflict? (provider interviewees only)

Research sponsors reviewed the interview guides for clarity, comprehensiveness, and understand-ability.

Key informant selection criteria. The main selection criterion was to target participants with full knowledge of the phenomenon under study to answer the questions on the interview guides (Creswell, 1998; Ponterotto & Casas, 1991; Seidler, 1974). To be sure we included both stakeholder perspectives, we interviewed the client and the provider leaders in charge of *established* BSO relationships. We needed *established* BSO relationships so that participants could assess BSO outcomes. We also sought a variety of BSO contexts.

Data collection. The research sponsors solicited participation from among their networks of clients and providers based on the targeted participants' knowledge of the issues and organizational positions

(Creswell, 1998; Elmendorf & Luloff, 2006; Fontana & Frey, 1994; Ponterotto & Casas, 1991; Seidler, 1974) as well as the client and provider leads' willingness to participate. The sample is opportunistic. The research sponsors provided us with client and provider names and contact information for 32 BSO relationships. We were in charge of contacting them and scheduling interviews. Participants were interviewed by phone because they were globally dispersed on four Continents. Among the 65 people from 32 BSO relationships we interviewed, 27 participants from 13 BSO relationships identified a conflict that they considered to be significant. This subset of data is the focus of this paper.

Table 5.4 describes in more detail the attributes of 13 BSO relationships that had experienced significant conflicts. The 27 participants were interviewed from October 2011 to first quarter 2014. For a given outsourcing relationship, we interviewed the client lead and the provider lead in charge of the account. Client interviewees were in charge of a BSO relationship in addition to their duties as shared service center, procurement, legal, operations, or human resource directors. The provider interviewees were the account delivery managers in charge of the BSO relationship. The interviews were conducted separately and confidentially. The interviews were typically 45 to 75 minutes in length. All interviews were tape recorded and transcribed.

We interviewed people in charge of different types of BSO relationships, including financial and accounting outsourcing (FAO), FAO/ITO, procurement outsourcing, legal services outsourcing (LSO), human resource outsourcing (HRO), customer care/call centers outsourcing, and supply chain outsourcing. The BSO contract start dates ranged from 1991 to 2011. Some of the older contracts have been renewed at least once. The 13 BSO relationships ranged in size from small (equal to 10 full time equivalents[3] for one procurement deal) to large (equal to 425 full time equivalents for one call center deal). The geographic scope of the deals ranged from a single country (Spain or Canada), to a Continent (like North America), to global delivery. As an example of global

---

[3] A full time equivalent (FTE) is a unit of measure that estimates how many provider employees are needed to perform the clients' services, assuming all employees work a full-time schedule. An FTE of 1.0 means that the person is equivalent to one full-time worker.

delivery, the provider from story #1 in Table 5.4 supports a client's operations located in 50 countries. The provider's 300 employees dedicated to this account primarily work out of the provider's delivery centers in the Philippines, China, the US, and Slovakia.

Data Analysis Methods

Data analysis: making practical sense of the data. The data analysis effort for the larger research program was immense, involving multiple iterations of reading the transcripts, coding the initial eight practices and outcomes, identifying emerging themes, debating ideas among coauthors, discussing findings with research sponsors and seeking input, review, and approval from research participants. We collapsed the initial eight practices identified on the Everest survey to six. We also identified three additional emergent practices that differentiated performance. One of those three emergent practices[4] was "resolving conflicts fairly." We identified five behaviors practitioners used to resolve conflicts to the satisfaction of both parties. These behaviors are presented in the discussion section. Based on positive feedback from research sponsors and participants, we were confident that we did a good job making *practical* sense of BSO conflicts and how to resolve them. However, we continued to reflect on those conflict stories and were inspired to make *theoretical* sense of the data.

Data analysis: making theoretical sense of the data. The remainder of this section describes the data analysis method used to make theoretical sense of the conflict stories. First, we wrote the 13 conflict examples as encapsulated stories. Storytelling provides the "content" of research (Klein et al., 2007) and is an effective method for understanding and communicating how an intervention like a conflict resolution strategy affects outcomes (Pidd, 1995). We gave each story a title to easily distinguish it among the 13 stories, such as "a poor pricing model caused the provider to lose money on the deal" or "a client overestimated demand." Second, we looked to understand the BSO stories from a theoretical

---

[4] The other two practices were "assign an effective leadership pair" and "prioritize and incentivize innovation.".

Table 5.4 Data collected on 13 conflict stories

Story #	BPO context					Interviewees		
	Business services outsourced	Contract start date	Contract size	Geographic scope	C = client P = provider	Interviewee title/role	Interviewee location
1	Financial and accounting services	2005 (renewed in 2008)	300 FTEs	Global	C	VP of Global Financial Shared Services	US
					P	Outsourcing Account Delivery Manager	US
2	Financial, accounting, and information technology services	2008 (7 years)	235 FTEs	Global	C	Client VP of Global Business Services	US
					P	Outsourcing Account Delivery Manager	US
3	Procurement services	2001 (10 years, renewed)	40 FTEs	Europe and US	C	Procurement Director	UK
					P	Category Director	UK
4	Financial and accounting services	1991 (renewed and extended many times)	330 FTEs	North America	C	Head of the Americas Business Shared Services	US

BPO context					Interviewees		
Story #	Business services outsourced	Contract start date	Contract size	Geographic scope	C = client P = provider	Interviewee title/role	Interviewee location
					C	Director, Americas Business Shared Services	US
					P	Outsourcing Account Delivery Manager	US
5	Procurement services	2006 (5 years, renewed in 2011)	10 FTEs	Western Europe and North America	C	VP of Operations	UK
					P	Senior VP for Sourcing	UK
6	Legal services	2010	18 FTEs	United Kingdom	C	General Counsel	UK
					P	Senior VP of Global Services	India
7	Financial and accounting services	2010	115 FTEs	Global	C	Senior VP of Global Business Services	US
					P	Outsourcing Account Delivery Manager	US
8	Financial and accounting services	2007 (7 years)	n/a	Global	C	Global Services Director	UK
					P	Outsourcing Account Delivery Manager	UK

(continued)

Table 5.4 (continued)

Story #	BPO context Business services outsourced	Contract start date	Contract size	Geographic scope	Interviewees C = client P = provider	Interviewee title/role	Interviewee location
9	Human resource services	2007 (7 years)	100 FTEs	Global	C	VP of Talent Management	US
					P	Outsourcing Account Delivery Manager	US
10	Human resource services	2006 (renewed in 2011)	200 FTEs	Australia	C	Director of Learning	Australia
					P	Senior Director for BPO Services	Australia
11	Customer care and call center	2011	425 FTEs	United Kingdom	C	General Manager	UK
					P	Managing Director	South Africa
12	Financial and accounting services	2006	35 FTEs	Spain	C	Operational Director	Spain
					P	Outsourcing Account Delivery Manager	Spain
13	Supply chain outsourcing	2007	240 FTEs	Canada	C	Manager of Global Workshare	Canada
					P	Outsourcing Account Delivery Manager	Canada

perspective. It was at this stage we took a deep dive into the academic literature; specifically, we were looking for a way to theoretically code BSO conflict types and conflict resolution styles (see chapter text).

References

Aubert, B., Kishore, R., & Iriyama, A. (2015). Exploring and Managing the Innovation Through Outsourcing Paradox. *Journal of Strategic Information Systems, 24*(4), 255–269.

Aubert, B., & Rivard, S. (2016). The Role of Transaction Cost Economics in Information Technology Outsourcing Research: A Meta-Analysis of the Choice of Contract Type. *Journal of Strategic Information Systems, 25*(1), 64–67.

Avasant. (2013). *Presentation Slides from the Service Provider Summit*, London, September 2013.

Babin, R., Briggs, S., & Nicholson, B. (2011). Emerging Markets Corporate Social Responsibility and Global IT Outsourcing. *Communications of the ACM, 54*(9), 28–30.

Barker, R., & Gower, K. (2010). Strategic Application of Storytelling in Organizations Toward Effective Communication in a Diverse World. *Journal of Business Communication, 47*, 295–312.

Barringer, B., & Harrison, J. (2000). Walking a Tightrope: Creating Value Through Interorganizational Relationships. *Journal of Management, 26*(3), 367–403.

Bhagwatwar, A., Hackney, R., & Desouza, K. (2011). Considerations for Information Systems "Backsourcing": A Framework for Knowledge Re-integration. *Information Systems Management, 28*(2), 165–173.

Blake, R., & Mouton, J. (1964). *The Managerial Grid*. Gulf Publishers.

Bloor, M., & Wood, F. (2013). 'Key Informant'. In *Keywords in Qualitative Methods*. Sage.

Buttler, T., & Lukosch, S. (2012, January 4–7). *Exploring the Uses of Stories in Patterns of Collaboration*. 45th Hawaii International Conference of System Sciences, 392–401, Maui, HI.

Cao, L., Mohan, K., Ramesh, B., & Sarkar, S. (2014). Evolution of Governance: Achieving Ambidexterity in IT Outsourcing. *Journal of Management Information Systems, 30*(3), 115–140.

Cahill, D., Goldsby, T., Knemeyer, A. M., & Wahenburg, C. (2010). Customer Loyalty in Logistics Outsourcing Relationships: An Examination of the Moderating Effects of Conflict Frequency. *Journal of Business Logistics, 31*(2), 253–277.

Carmel, E., & Tjia, P. (2005). *Offshoring Information Technology: Sourcing and Outsourcing to a Global Workforce*. Cambridge University Press.

Chakrabarty, S., Whitten, D., & Green, K. (2008). Understanding Service Quality and Relationship Quality in IS Outsourcing. *Journal of Computer Information Systems, 48*(2), 1–15.

Chang, K., & Chen, C. (2016). Innovative Resolution of Outsourcing Conflict: A Case Study of an Electrical Component Manufacturer in China. *International Journal of Organizational Innovation, 8*(3), 44–51.

Cho, D. (2020). A Contingent Approach to Facilitating Conflict Resolution in Software Development Outsourcing Projects. *Journal of Organizational and End User Computing, 32*(2), 20–42.

Copley, R. (2008). *Conflict Management Styles: A Predictor of Likability and Perceived Effectiveness among Subordinates* (Master of Arts Thesis). Department of Communication Studies, Indiana University.

Creswell, J. (1998). *Qualitative Inquiry and Research Design*. Sage.

Cropper, S., Huxham, C., Ebers, M., & Smith Ring, P. (2008). *The Oxford Handbook of Inter-Organizational Relations*. Oxford University Press.

Cullen, S., Lacity, M., & Willcocks, L. (2015). *Outsourcing—All You Need To Know*. White Plume Publishing.

Davis, J., & Eisenhardt, K. (2011). Rotating Leadership and Collaborative Innovation: Recombination Processes in Symbiotic Relationships. *Administrative Science Quarterly, 56*(2), 159–201.

DeChurch, L., & Marks, M. (2001). Maximizing the Benefits of Task Conflict: The Role of Conflict Management. *The International Journal of Conflict Management, 12*, 4–22.

Deng, C., Mao, J., & Wang, G. (2013). An Empirical Study on the Source of Vendors' Relational Performance in Offshore Information Systems Outsourcing. *International Journal of Information Management, 33*(1), 10–19.

Deutsch, M. (1949). A Theory of Cooperation and Competition. *Human Relations, 2*(1), 29–151.

Deutsch, M. (1990). Sixty Years of Conflict. *International Journal of Conflict Management, 1*(1), 237–263.

Dyer, J., & Nobeoka, K. (2000). Creating and Managing a High-Performance Knowledge-Sharing Network: The Toyota Case. *Strategic Management Journal, 21,* 345–367.

Elmendorf, W., & Luloff, A. (2006). Using Key Informant Interviews to Better Understand Open Space Conversation in a Developing Watershed. *Arboriculture & Urban Forestry, 32*(2), 54–61.

Fersht, P., & Snowden, J. (2016). *The HFS Market Index—IT Services and BPO Market Size and Forecast 2016–2020.* HFS Research.

Fontana, A., & Frey, J. (1994). Interviewing: The Art of Science. In Denzin & Lincoln (Eds.), *Handbook of Qualitative Research* (pp. 361–376). Sage.

Friedman, R., Tidd, S., Currall, S., & Tsai, J. (2000). What Goes Around Comes Around: The Impact of Personal Conflict Style on Work Conflict and Stress. *The International Journal of Conflict Management, 11*(1), 32–55.

Galliers, R., Markus, L. M., & Newell, S. (Eds.). (2007). *Exploring Information Systems Research Approaches: Readings and Reflections.* Routledge.

Gefen, D., Wyss, S., & Lichtenstein, Y. (2008). Business Familiarity as Risk Mitigation in Software Development Outsourcing Contracts. *MIS Quarterly, 32*(3), 531–551.

Golsorkhi, D., Rouleau, L. Seidle, D., & Vaara, E. (Eds.). (2012). Introduction: What is Strategy as Practice. In *Cambridge Handbook of Strategy as Practice.* Cambridge University Press.

Goo, J., Kishore, R., Rao, H. R., & Nam, K. (2009). The Role of Service Level Agreements in Relational Management of Information Technology Outsourcing: An Empirical Study. *MIS Quarterly, 33*(1), 119–145.

Gopal, A., & Koka, B. R. (2012). The Asymmetric Benefits of Relational Flexibility: Evidence from Software Development Outsourcing. *MIS Quarterly, 36*(2), 553–576.

Gorla, N., & Somers, T. (2014). The Impact of IT Outsourcing on Information Systems Success. *Information & Management, 51*(3), 320–335.

Gounaris, S., Chatzipanagiotou, K., Boukis, A., & Perks, H. (2016). Unfolding the Recipes for Conflict Resolution During the New Service Development Effort. *Journal of Business Research, 69,* 4042–4055.

Gregory, R., Prifling, M., & Beck, R. (2009). The Role of Cultural Intelligence for the Emergence of the Negotiated Culture in IT Offshore Outsourcing Projects. *Information Technology & People, 22*(3), 223–241.

Grover, V., Cheon, M., & Teng, J. (1996). The Effect of Service Quality and Partnership on the Outsourcing of Information Systems Functions. *Journal of Management Information Systems, 12*(4), 89–116.

Hardy, C., & Phillips, M. (1998). Strategies of Engagement: Lessons from the Critical Examination of Collaboration and Conflict in an Interorganizational Domain. *Organization Science, 9*(2), 217–223.

Hirschheim, R. (1985). *Office Automation: A Social and Organizational Analysis.* Wiley.

Hughes, J., & Weiss, J. (2007). Simple Rules for Making Alliances Work. *Harvard Business Review, 85*(11), 122–131.

Jain, A., & Thietart, R. (2013). Knowledge Based Transactions and Decision Framing in Information Technology Outsourcing. *Journal of Strategic Information Systems, 22*(4), 315–327.

Jarzabkowski, P., & Spee, A. (2009). Strategy-as-Practice: A Review and Future Directions for the Field. *International Journal of Management Reviews, 11*(1), 69–95.

Karimi-Alaghehband, F., Rivard, S., Wub, S., & Goyette, S. (2011). An Assessment of the Use of Transaction Cost Theory in Information Technology Outsourcing. *Journal of Strategic Information Systems, 20*(2), 125–138.

Kern, T., Willcocks, L., & Van Heck, E. (2002). The Winners Curse in IT Outsourcing: Strategies for Avoiding Relational Trauma. *California Management Review, 44*(2), 47–69.

Kern, T., & Willcocks, L. (2002). Exploring Relationships in Information Technology Outsourcing: The Interaction Approach. *European Journal of Information Systems, 11*, 3–19.

Klein, J., Connell, N., & Meyer, E. (2007). Operational Research Practice as Storytelling. *Journal of Operational Research Society, 58*, 1535–1542.

Klein, H., & Myers, M. (1999). A Set of Principles for Conducting and Evaluating Interpretive Field Studies. *MIS Quarterly, 23*(1), 67–88.

Kotlarsky, J., Oshri, I., Lee, J., & Jarvenpaa, S. (2015). Editorial: Understanding Strategic Innovation in IT and Business Process Outsourcing. *Journal of Strategic Information Systems, 24*(4), 251–254.

Kuhn, T., & Poole, M. (2000). Do Conflict Management Styles Affect Group Decision Making? *Human Communication Research, 26*, 558–590.

Kvale, S. (1996). *Interviews: An Introduction to Qualitative Research Interviewing.* Sage.

Lacity, M., Khan, S., & Yan, A. (2016). Review of the Empirical Business Services Sourcing Literature: An Update and Future Directions. *Journal of Information Technology, 31*(2), 1–60.

Lacity, M., Willcocks, L., & Khan, S. (2011). Beyond Transaction Cost Economics: Towards an Endogenous Theory of Information Technology Outsourcing. *Journal of Strategic Information Systems, 20*(2), 139–157.

Lacity, M., & Willcocks, L. (1998). An Empirical Investigation of Information Technology Sourcing Practices: Lessons from Experience. *MIS Quarterly, 22*(3), 363–408.
Lacity, M., & Willcocks, L. (2012). *Advanced Outsourcing Practice: Rethinking ITO, BPO, and Cloud Services*. Palgrave.
Lacity, M., & Willcocks, L. (2013). Beyond Cost Savings: Outsourcing Business Processes for Innovation. *Sloan Management Review, 54*(3), 63–69.
Lacity, M., & Willcocks, L. (2015). *Nine Keys to World-Class Business Process Outsourcing*. Bloomsbury Publishing.
Lee, A. (2016). Theory Appropriation and the Growth of Knowledge. *Journal of Strategic Information Systems, 25*(1), 68–71.
Lee, J., & Kim, Y. (1999). Effect of Partnership Quality on IS Outsourcing Success: Conceptual Framework and Empirical Validation. *Journal of Management Information Systems, 15*(4), 29–61.
Lewicki, R., Weiss, S., & Lewin, D. (1992). Models of Conflict, Negotiation, and Third Party Intervention: A Review and Synthesis. *Journal of Organizational Behavior, 13*, 209–252.
Lincoln, Y., & Guba, E. (1985). *Naturalistic Inquiry*. Sage.
Lioliou, E., Zimmermann, A., Willcocks, L., & Gao, L. (2014). Formal and Relational Governance in IT Outsourcing: Substitution, Complementarity and the Role of the Psychological Contract. *Information Systems Journal, 24*(6), 503–535.
Majchrzak, A., & Markus, M. L. (2013). *Methods for Policy Research: Taking Socially Responsible Action*. Sage.
Mahoney, C. (1997). Common Qualitative Techniques. In *User-Friendly Handbook for Mixed Method Evaluations* (pp. 1–17). Published by the Division of Research, Evaluation and Communication for the National Science Foundation, publication number NSF97-153.
Mandell, M., & Keast, R. (2008). *The Oxford Handbook of Inter-Organizational Relations*. Oxford University Press.
Mani, D., Barua, A., & Whinston, A. (2012). An Empirical Analysis of the Contractual and Information Structures of Business Process Outsourcing Relationships. *Information Systems Research, 23*(3), 618–634.
Mann, C., & Stewart, F. (2000). *Internet Communication and Qualitative Research*. Sage.
Markus, M. (2014). Maybe Not the King, But an Invaluable Subordinate: A Commentary on Avison and Malaurent's Advocacy of "Theory Light" IS Research. *Journal of Information Technology, 29*(4), 341–345.

McKenna, S., & Richardson, J. (1995). Business Values, Management and Conflict Handling: Issues in Contemporary Singapore. *Journal of Management Development, 14*(4), 56–70.

Molnar, J., & Rogers, D. (1979). A Comparative Model of Interorganizational Conflict. *Administrative Science Quarterly, 24*(3), 405–425.

Natasha, V., Saunders, C., & Kavan, B. (2008). Information Systems Backsourcing: Correcting Problems and Responding to Opportunities. *California Management Review, 51*(1), 50–76.

Ndubisi, N. (2011). Conflict Handling, Trust and Commitment in Outsourcing Relationship: A Chinese and Indian Study. *Industrial Marketing Management, 40*, 109–117.

Ndubisi, N. (2012). Role of Gender in Conflict Handling in the Context of Outsourcing Service Marketing. *Psychology and Marketing, 30*(1), 26–35.

Nicotera, A. (1993). Beyond Two Dimensions: A Grounded Theory Model of Conflict-Handling Behavior. *Management Communications Quarterly, 6*(3), 282–306.

Opdenakker, R. (2006). Advantages and Disadvantages of Four Interview Techniques in Qualitative Research. *Forum on Qualitative Social Research, 7*(4), Article 11.

Oshri, I., Kotlarsky, J., & Willcocks, L. (2023). *Handbook of Global Outsourcing and Offshoring* (4th ed.). Plagrave Macmillan.

Palvia, P., King, R., Xia, W., & Jain Palvia, S. (2010). Capability, Quality, and Performance of Offshore IS Vendors: A Theoretical Framework and Empirical Investigation. *Decision Sciences, 41*(2), 231–270.

Parsons, J. (2013). Key Informant. In P. Lavrakas (Ed.), *Encyclopedia of Survey Research Method*. Sage.

Pidd, M. (1995). Pictures from an Exhibition: Images of OR/MS. *European Journal of Operations Research, 81*, 479–488.

Ponterotto, J., & Casas, M. (1991). *Handbook of Racial/Ethnic Minority Counseling Research*. Charles C Thomas Press.

Prikladnicki, R., & Audy, J. (2012). Managing Global Software Engineering: A Comparative Analysis of Offshore Outsourcing and the Internal Offshoring of Software Development. *Information Systems Management, 29*(3), 216–232.

Pruitt, D. (1983). Strategic Choice in Negotiation. *The American Behavioral Scientist, 27*(1), 167–194.

Putnam, L., & Wilson, C. (1982). Communication Strategies in Organizational Conflicts: Reliability and Validity of a Measurement Scale. In M. Burgoon (Ed.), *Communication Yearbook* (Vol. 6, pp. 629–652). Sage.

Rahim, M. (2002). Toward a Theory of Managing Organizational Conflict. *The International Journal of Conflict Management, 13*, 206–235.
Rahim, M. (2000). *Managing Conflict in Organizations* (3rd ed.). Quorum Books.
Rai, A., Keil, M., Hornyak, R., & Wullenweber, K. (2012). Hybrid Relational-Contractual Governance for Business Process Outsourcing. *Journal of Management Information Systems, 29*(2), 213–256.
Rayner, G. (2014). UK Flights Chaos: Air Traffic Control Computers Using Software from the 1960s. *The Telegraph.* http://www.telegraph.co.uk/news/aviation/11291495/UK-flights-chaos-Air-traffic-control-computers-using-software-from-the-1960s.html
Renner, J. (2007). Coaching Abroad: Insights about Assets. *Consulting Psychology Journal, 59*, 271–285.
Rhodes, J., Lok, P., Loh, W., & Cheng, V. (2016). Critical Success Factors in Relationship Management for Services Outsourcing. *Service Business, 10*(1), 59–86.
Ruble, T. L., & Thomas, K. W. (1976). Support for a Two-Dimensional Model of Conflict Behavior. *Organizational Behavior and Human Performance, 16*, 143–155.
Sakolnakorn, T. (2010). The Good Aspects of Managing an Organization With an Outsourcing and Subcontracting Strategy. *International Journal of Management & Information Systems, 15*(3), 11–18.
Sandeep, M., & Ravishankar, M. (2015). Social Innovations in Outsourcing: An Empirical Investigation of Impact Sourcing Companies in India. *Journal of Strategic Information Systems, 24*(4), 270–288.
Sandelowski, M. (1991). Telling Stories: Narrative Approaches in Qualitative Research. *The Journal of Nursing Scholarship, 23*(3), 161–166.
Saunders, C., Gebelt, M., & Hu, Q. (1997). Achieving Success in Information Systems Outsourcing. *California Management Review, 39*(2), 63–80.
Seidler, J. (1974). On Using Informants: A Technique for Collecting Quantitative Data and Controlling for Measurement Error in Organizational Analysis. *American Sociological Review, 39*, 816–831.
Schermann, M., Dongus, K., Yetton, P., & Krcmar, H. (2016). The Role of Transaction Cost Economics in Information Technology Outsourcing Research: A Meta-analysis of the Choice of Contract Type. *Journal of Strategic Information Systems, 25*(1), 32–48.
Shirbon, E. (2016). Raid on 20,000 Tesco Bank Accounts Fuels Cybercrime Fears. *Reuters Technology News.* http://www.reuters.com/article/us-tesco-bank-idUSKBN1320SW

Smith, W. P. (1987). Conflict and Negotiation: Trends and Emerging Issues. *Journal of Applied Social Psychology, 17*, 641–677.

Swar, B., Moon, J., Oh, J., & Rhee, C. (2012). Determinants of Relationship Quality for IS/IT Outsourcing Success in Public Sector. *Information Systems Frontiers, 14*(2), 457–475.

Thomas, K., & Kilmann, R. (1974). *Thomas-Kilmann Conflict Mode Instrument*. Tuxedo.

Vijaykar, S., Gupta, M., & Bhaumik, P. (2021). Conflict Resolution in a Multi-level IT-enabled Outsourcing Network: A Structured Solution Approach. *Journal of International Technology and Information Management, 30*(1), 134–169.

Walton, R., & McKersie, R. (1965). *A Behavioral Theory of Labor Negotiations*. Sage.

Whittington, R. (1996). Strategy as Practice. *Long Range Planning, 29*(4), 731–735.

Whittington, R. (2007). Strategy Practice and Strategy Process: Family Differences and the Sociological Eye. *Organization Studies, 28*(10), 1575–1586.

Whittington, R. (2014). Information Systems Strategy-as-Practice: A Joint agenda. *The Journal of Strategic Information Systems, 23*(1), 87–91.

Willcocks, L., Lacity, M., & Sauer, C. (Eds.). (2017). *Outsourcing and Offshoring of Business Services*. Springer.

Wickramasinghe, V., & Nandula, S. (2015). Diversity in Team Composition, Relationship Conflict and Team Leader Support on Globally Distributed Virtual Software Development Team Performance. *Strategic Outsourcing: An International Journal, 8*(2/3), 13–155.

Winkler, J., Dibbern, J., & Heinzl, A. (2008). The Impact of Cultural Differences in Offshore Outsourcing—Case Study Results from German-Indian Application Development Projects. *Information Systems Frontiers, 10*, 243–258.

Wüllenweber, K., Beimborn, D., Weitzel, T., & König, W. (2008). The Impact of Process Standardization on Business Process Outsourcing Success. *Information Systems Frontiers, 10*(2), 211–224.

Yitshaki, R. (2008). Venture Capitalist-Entrepreneur Conflicts. *International Journal of Conflict Management, 19*(3), 262–292.

Zhang, J., Lawrence, B., & Anderson, C. (2015). An agency Perspective on Service Triads: Linking Operational and Financial Performance. *Journal of Operations Management, 35*, 56–66.

Part II
Advancing Sourcing Performance

6

Managing Tensions in Globally Distributed Work

Jade Brooks, M. N. Ravishankar, and Ilan Oshri

Introduction

Organizations rely on globally distributed work (GDW) to take advantage of complementary objectives. In typical arrangements, highly skilled onshore teams focus on strategy and customer interactions, while offshore teams focus on repetitive back-office activities, reducing costs and improving efficiencies. Individually, each side can operate within the scope of their own tasks, priorities and values. However, when they are required to collaborate on distributed processes, tensions stemming

---

Chapter 6 is an updated version of Brooks, J., Ravishankar, M. N., & Oshri, I. (2020). Paradox and the Negotiation of Tensions in Globally Distributed Work. *Journal of Information Technology*, 35(3), 232–250.

J. Brooks · I. Oshri (✉)
University of Auckland, Auckland, New Zealand
e-mail: ilan.oshri@auckland.ac.nz

M. N. Ravishankar
Loughborough University, Loughborough, UK

from inherent contradictions in the working relationship cause strain and discomfort to both sides (Barney et al., 2014).

The extant literature recognizes three main sources of tensions in GDW: knowledge asymmetries (Hahl et al., 2016; Vlaar et al., 2008); power asymmetries (Levina & Vaast, 2008; Ravishankar et al., 2013); and identity threats (Koppman et al., 2016; Petriglieri, 2011).[1] Collectively, these tensions can create communication problems (Hinds et al., 2014; Levina & Vaast, 2008), coordination issues (Kotlarsky et al., 2014; Oshri et al., 2008) and diminished opportunities for learning and innovation (Levina & Vaast, 2008; Tzabbar & Vestal, 2015). Tensions have also been found to reduce willingness to collaborate (Zimmerman and Ravishankar, 2014) and induce value-destroying conflict (Hinds & Mortensen, 2005; Ravishankar, 2015).

Much of the literature has focused on strategies for resolving and eliminating tensions. For instance, studies have found that codifying information helps reduce reliance on undocumented contextual knowledge (Leonardi & Bailey, 2008; Oshri et al., 2008), and that brokering helps reduce knowledge silos (Hahl et al., 2016; Leonardi & Bailey, 2008, 2013). Research has also found that contracts play an important role in clearer distribution of power and responsibility (Di Tullio & Staples, 2013), while training programs, reassignment of tasks, and joint selection and promotion systems help readdress status imbalances (Levina & Vaast, 2008; Ravishankar et al., 2013). Similarly, cultural intermediaries such as 'inpatriates' who transcend subgroup differences help ease identity threats (Eisenberg & Mattarelli, 2016).

Despite the strengths of this body of research, two important issues are yet to be addressed. First, there is an implicit assumption in extant research that tensions between parties engaged in collaborative GDW can always be permanently resolved. However, this assumption fails to account for the intrinsic and entrenched nature of tensions in GDW, given the inherently contradictory aspects of many onshore-offshore relationships. In contradictory and inherently paradoxical settings, notwithstanding efforts targeting them, tensions are known to persist (Smith &

---

[1] We use the terms knowledge tensions, power tensions and identity tensions to refer to the corresponding tensions.

Lewis, 2011). A key consequence of this preoccupation with permanent resolution is the limited focus on the process of generating meaningful collaborations within an entrenched system of onshore-offshore tensions. Second, prior research does not consider the interactions between different kinds of tensions and their implications for collaborative outcomes. Consequently, it remains unclear how successful collaborations are accomplished when multiple tensions are at play. In this chapter, we respond to these two gaps in scholarship by addressing two specific research questions:

- RQ1: How are tensions in GDW turned into collaborative opportunities?
- RQ2: How do knowledge, power and identity tensions relate to one another?

Drawing on an in-depth qualitative case study in a distributed finance organization, we apply ideas from paradox theory (Lewis, 2000; Smith & Lewis, 2011) and offer an alternative approach to understanding tensions in GDW. The notion of paradox suggests that tensions are not permanently resolved in the traditional sense because leaning toward one polarity (such as cost reduction and efficiency) puts increasing pressure on the other polarity (such as quality and innovation) (Lewis, 2000; Smith et al., 2017). Our findings show that in the wake of tensions, collaborating parties in GDW initially display defensive behaviors and attempt to force their own preferences. While such behaviors strain interactions and result in a period of conflict, our findings also suggest that in the process of negotiating tensions, teams can come to accommodate conflicting needs and develop new collaborative ways of working.

These findings make three contributions to research. First, we extend current debate in GDW, which sees conflict as either value destroying or value creating. Through the paradox lens, we move beyond seeing conflict in binary terms and propose understanding conflict as both disruptive and developmental. Second, we develop a phasal model which identifies specific team behaviors and explains how structural changes can trigger the evolution of tensions and the emergence of collaborative practices. Third, we complement existing research which identifies tensions specific to GDW (knowledge, power, identity) by illuminating the interactions between them. In doing so, we offer an extension to current understanding of tensions by drawing attention to the paradoxical complexities of team interactions. Our research demonstrates that tensions are persistent and interrelated, and demand more sophisticated solutions than prior research has presented. In the following sections, we review the literature on GDW with a specific focus on tensions and introduce paradox as an appropriate theoretical perspective. Next, we provide a detailed account of the methodology and case analysis. Finally, we discuss the chapter's main theoretical and practical implications.

Tensions in GDW

Globally distributed work (GDW) involves the demarcation and division of work into dispersed task-specific work units in order to enable innovative ideas (Eisenberg & Mattarelli, 2016; Levina & Vaast, 2008) as well as cost savings (Dibbern et al., 2008). The success of GDW mainly depends on the ability and willingness of onshore and offshore units to collaborate on distributed processes. It follows that variations in such ability and willingness create tensions between the two sides. The extant GDW literature finds there are three prominent sources of tensions at play: knowledge asymmetries, power asymmetries and identity threats. Knowledge asymmetries refer to the imbalance of knowledge and experience (Oshri et al., 2008; Vlaar et al., 2008) in performing specialized tasks (Leonardi & Bailey, 2013; Tiwana & Keil, 2007). Offshore units have been criticized for possessing only a limited knowledge of the onshore business and therefore contributing to poor organizational performance (Barney et al., 2014; Vlaar et al., 2008). For instance, Barney et al. (2014) found offshore Indian software engineers lacking in domain knowledge, leading to misunderstanding of requirements. On the other hand, onshore units have been criticized for information hiding (Connelly et al., 2011; Zimmerman and Ravishankar, 2014) and for not understanding offshore processes (Cha et al., 2008; Tiwana & Keil, 2007). Unmanaged knowledge asymmetries can hinder effective communication, reduce understanding (Levina & Vaast, 2008), limit positive knowledge spillover and reduce opportunities for joint problem solving (Jarvenpaa & Majchrzak, 2016). Firms invest in formal structures and systems to reduce knowledge tensions. Rules, standard operating procedures, codified directories and common lexicon are used to overcome gaps in knowledge (Oshri et al., 2008) and carefully designed structural arrangements help restrict the scope of collaborations, limit the need for knowledge sharing and mitigate the opportunity for conflict (Oxley & Sampson, 2004).

Power asymmetries in GDW stem from imbalanced access to resources and decision makers, allowing some parts of the organization to enjoy a higher status than others (Hahl et al., 2016; Levina & Vaast, 2008; Ravishankar et al., 2013). In general, research has found that power resides in onshore units that control structural resources (Levina & Kane, 2009; Ravishankar et al., 2013). Levina and Kane (2009) found that onshore teams are well connected to senior decision makers and have better access to budgets, training and technology. Onshore units also assume a higher status on account of their perceived advanced language skills and qualifications (Hinds et al., 2014), engagement with higher-value tasks and superior domain expertise (Levina & Vaast, 2008). More recent research suggests that in knowledge intensive collaborations, it is difficult to determine 'who owns the code', decipher where decision-making power should reside and evaluate how rewards should be distributed (Chen et al., 2017; Parker et al., 2017). Organizations draft unambiguous contracts (Dibbern et al., 2008; Parker et al., 2017), legalize ownership of intellectual property and formalize the distribution of power via clearer documentation of responsibilities (Parker et al., 2017) to mitigate and manage the harmful impact of power asymmetries. Studies also indicate that service-level agreements (SLAs) help formalize expectations and reduce power-related task conflicts (Deloitte, 2016; Goo et al., 2009).

Identity threats in the GDW context typically involve experiences that potentially violate an individual's or group's sense of professional self (Koppman et al., 2016; Petriglieri, 2011). Onshore identities are prone to threats as service offshoring matures, leading to migration of complex tasks (Zimmerman and Ravishankar, 2014, 2016) and increasing need for cross-cultural interactions to accomplish the said tasks (Petriglieri, 2011). On the other side, research has shown how offshore units' sense of identity and organizational membership are threatened when they are treated as subordinates by their onshore counterparts (Koppman et al., 2016; Leonardi & Rodriguez-Lluesma, 2013). In a study of German-Indian teams, Zimmerman and Ravishankar (2011) showed how offshore Indian engineers who considered themselves to be skilled professionals experienced significant identity threats when their onshore German colleagues assigned them repetitive and less interesting tasks.

Identity threats can give rise to a plethora of undesirable effects, including poor performance (Ravishankar, 2015), resistance to change (Zimmerman & Ravishankar, 2011), stigmatization and reluctance to share knowledge (Eisenberg & Mattarelli, 2016; Zimmerman & Ravishankar, 2011). Organizations have sought to resolve identity threats using cultural training (David et al., 2008; Newell et al., 2007) and intermediaries (or 'inpatriates'), who transcend cultural differences between subgroups and work to create a strong sense of identification with the larger organization (Eisenberg & Mattarelli, 2016). Other studies also show how more informal approaches such as framing narratives can be used strategically to resolve identity threats and temporarily reduce conflict in GDW (Petriglieri, 2011; Ravishankar, 2015).

A Paradox Perspective

Often described as 'two sides of the same coin', paradox is a condition where two individual elements are interrelated and necessary to each other's existence (Smith & Lewis, 2011), and yet seem to be opposing or contradictory (Poole & Van de Ven, 1989; Smith & Lewis, 2011). The tensions created by the pull of two paradoxical elements are not easily resolved since leaning toward one puts increasing pressure on the other (Lewis, 2000; Smith et al., 2017). In business and management research, the notion of paradox has been used to examine contradictory elements such as *competition* and *cooperation* in organizational alliances (Rai, 2016), *exploitation* of existing resources and *exploration* of new ideas in innovative projects (Andriopoulos & Lewis, 2009), and *novelty* and *usefulness* in creative endeavors (Miron-Spektor &

Beenen, 2015). Within the IS literature, studies have considered paradoxical contradictions between *control* and *autonomy* in self-managing teams (Druskat & Wheeler, 2003), *control* and *empowerment* in hybrid teams (Cousins et al., 2007), *flexibility* and *structure* in client-supplier innovation projects (Kotlarsky et al., 2016) and *trust* and *mistrust* in distributed teams (Zolin et al., 2004). Paradox brings into sharp focus the role of behaviors in heightening or relieving tensions created by the opposing elements. Paradox posits that defensive behaviors such as avoiding differences or forcing one-sided solutions may only provide temporary relief (Smith & Lewis, 2011). In fact, they can create vicious reinforcing cycles that perpetuate and intensify tensions (Lewis, 2000; Smith & Lewis, 2011). For example, individuals may defensively retreat to their own divisions and stop engaging with partners, worsening the tensions in collaborative-competitive relationships (Jarzabkowski et al., 2013); offshore teams may defend contradictory elements in offshoring as 'cultural differences', further amplifying tensions (Ravishankar, 2015).

The literature suggests two broad strategies for managing paradoxes (Poole & Van de Ven, 1989; Lewis, 2000). The first, separation-based strategy, involves demarcating and honoring conflicting elements. For instance, distinctive formal structures can create much needed physical and temporal separation between tension-elevating elements (Bengtsson & Kock, 2000; Stadtler & Wassenhove, 2016). Bengtsson and Kock's (2000) study of 'co-opetition' illustrates the creation of departments that focus on either competitive or cooperative strategies. Further, information technologies make it possible to minimize communication and task interdependence between separated teams while at the same time connecting them and supporting task integration (Dubé & Robey, 2009). Other studies suggest 'time-bound' separations—teams focusing on one strategy for a period before returning to attend to the other (Poole & Van de Ven, 1989). Although separation strategies may avoid conflict and instability, they sometimes ignore the potential of blending for turning disagreements into value creation (Johansen, 2018; Stadtler & Wassenhove, 2016).

The second, integration-based strategy, involves purposefully juxtaposing contradictory elements (Lewis, 2000; Lewis & Smith, 2011), thus seemingly intensifying tensions. However, if managed effectively, such tensions can be turned into good collaborative outcomes. For instance, Dubé and Robey (2009) found how employing individuals with experience of handling ambiguous situations, maintaining shared calendars for transparency and establishing a common focus while acknowledging differences helped overcome structure-flexibility tensions. In well-managed integration scenarios, actors break out of vicious cycles and move away from defensive responses by acknowledging tensions and reframing them as necessary or accepting them as natural conditions of work. The process of recognizing and accepting inherent contradictions can provide actors with a sense of 'freedom' in "learning to live with" the opposing elements (Lewis, 2000: 764). They may embrace tensions, making small cognitive and behavioral adjustments to find benefits within the otherwise tense environment (Jarzabkowski et al., 2013; Jarzabkowski & Le, 2017). Integration-based strategies can encourage critical self-reflection, stimulate more ambivalent interpretations of surroundings (Lewis, 2000; Smith et al., 2017) and avoid oversimplification of problems (Plambeck & Weber, 2010).

In summary, our synthesis of the literature suggests a paradoxical mind-set (i.e., a readiness to embrace inherent contradictions) can help organizations find more accommodating solutions (Bengtsson et al., 2016; Smith, 2014), improve organizational learning (Lewis, 2000; Sundaramurthy & Lewis, 2003), innovate more (Andriopoulos & Lewis, 2009), have higher problem solving capabilities and adapt better to change (Schuman et al., 2010), have successful inter-firm alliances and achieve overall superior performance (Rai, 2016). In terms of current research, we know a lot more about 'why' organizations strive for a paradoxical mind-set than 'how' it is achieved (Stadtler & Wassenhove, 2016). In the specific context of GDW, there is limited understanding of how tensions can be turned into collaborative ways of working. Further, there is scarce research on the implications of interactions between different tensions for collaborative outcomes. In the following sections, we present the case of a distributed finance function, where work has been demarcated and distributed between two sides—onshore business units and an offshore shared service center. Using this case, we explain how the two sides negotiate collaborative tensions.

Design and Methods

Research Approach

We wanted our research approach to allow us to explore the potentially complex challenges onshore-offshore unit members face as they collaborate. In line with past research, we adopted the qualitative case study method (Walsham, 2006) which generates rich data and helps advance understanding of under-researched phenomenon (Eisenhardt, 1989; Kotlarsky et al., 2014). We drew predominantly on interview data from both onshore and offshore units to gain an in-depth understanding of the structural, as well as the social context of collaborative GDW. The findings report data that emerged organically from our interpretivist approach to data analysis.

Research Setting

Our research is set in the finance function of a large global logistics firm made up of four business divisions. The research focuses on the paradox emerging from the migration of financial tasks from several onshore country-level business units (BUs) within the firm's largest business division to an offshore shared service unit (SSU). Our empirical material provides retrospective accounts, triangulated with several data sources, to capture tensions across significant changes in organizational structure. Throughout the chapter, we refer to employees working in the SSU as 'SSU members' and employees working in BUs as 'BU members'.

A centralization strategy, which began in 2008, aimed to consolidate resources from across the multiple country-level business units (BUs). Tasks were transferred out of the BUs into a dedicated financial shared services unit (SSU), which sat within a wider corporate center called Global Business Services (GBS). In addition to finance, GBS provided a range of support services to the BUs including procurement, legal, HR and IT support. The idea of centralizing finance was to help BUs improve financial reporting, better manage financial risk and improve customer focused activities. For instance, it was anticipated that moving a range of activities into the SSU would give BU members more time to visit customers, better understand their financial and shipment needs, offer more tailored customer service and increase sales by generating larger shipping orders. The SSU focused on standardizing and delivering a range of financial operations to the BUs such as the purchasing and paying for goods and services. The BUs paid for the SSU's services, which were governed via SLAs and performance was measured through key performance indicators (KPIs). During this period, BU members became increasingly dissatisfied with the service provided by the SSU. BU members were focused on being more responsive to customer queries and offering flexibility through shipment discounts and differentiated payment plans. SSU members, on the other hand, were focused on reducing the cost of finance and standardizing processes to gain efficiencies. In 2011, to achieve further cost savings, some transactional activities related to the invoicing provision were outsourced to a third-party provider. BU members saw this outsourcing arrangement as being at odds with their priorities and this view led to several BU-SSU disagreements. SSU members were also tasked with the long-term improvement of financial processes through standardization, integration of existing information systems and the implementation of new IT tools across multiple BUs. However, the BUs did not always have the funds to support these SSU objectives. Projects deemed to not have an immediate impact on BUs were often rejected by BU members who were more focused on their annual sales targets.

Finance Organization Restructuring: SSU Integration into Business Division

In late 2014, the SSU was structurally separated from the GBS. The SSU did not physically change location, and tasks remained centralized, but SSU members now reported to the business division rather than to GBS. As the SSU became integrated into the business division, BU and SSU members were expected to collaborate more closely to perform and improve distributed processes. Our data describes the tensions between the BUs (onshore units) and the SSU (offshore unit),

Table 6.1 Conflicting responsibilities and objectives of SSU and BUs

	Shared Service Unit (SSU)	Business Units (BUs)
Objectives	Reduce the cost of financial operations Long-term improvement of finance operations	Improve financial position and customer service
Tasks	−Delivery of financial operations: purchase-to-pay, record-to-report, order-to-cash −Standardize processes −Integrate and standardize information systems and information technology −Manage third-party provider	−Meet internal and external audit requirements −Support regional and global finance organizations −Improve customer experience of financial processes −Improve the financial position of BU: projects to speed up processing of invoices −Support sales team to increase revenue: e.g., work out discounts for customers to encourage them to commit to larger shipments or move from other logistics providers

given their conflicting objectives (see Table 6.1), and explains the process of accommodating contradictory needs and creating collaborative opportunities.

Data Sources

Data was collected in three rounds (see Table 6.2) in 2015–2016, mainly through in-depth interviews. Interviews focused on capturing retrospective accounts of the challenges participants faced as work was migrated into the SSU (focusing on 2008–2015), as well as accounts of the tensions participants faced as the finance function matured and transformed (2014–2016). The first round of interviews was conducted with SSU members at the offshore SSU head office in March 2015. With the help of an SSU manager, we selected participants from a range of management positions. (see Appendix for a complete list of positions and participant codes). The interviews were semi-structured and focused on 'change' and 'challenges' participants faced in their work. They were asked to elaborate and give examples of 'how' and 'why' they thought situations or events occurred. The intention was to let interesting themes emerge from this first round of data collection, while developing a good understanding of the organizational structure and its evolution, and the distribution of work and challenges of GDW. The second round of interviews in January 2016 also took place at the SSU head office. Interviewees included managers from the SSU and the firm's finance organization (FO) headquarters. The third round of interviews was conducted in June 2016 with BU participants from four different onshore countries.

The interviews lasted between 60 and 140 minutes, averaging 77 minutes and amounting to about 33 hours of interview data. All but three (teleconference) interviews were conducted face to face. We collected several other documents, including annual reports, internal communications, performance dashboards, employee opinion surveys

Table 6.2 Rounds of data collection and nature of data collected

	Round	Interviewees	Interviews	Focus
1	March 2015	SSU members	9	To understand the global organization of functions, the changes in the role of the SSU and challenges they face
2	January 2016	SSU and finance organization (FO) headquarters' members	8	To understand the tensions the SSU members face in their own work, and in collaborative projects To understand how SSU members cope with tensions
3	June 2016	BU members	9	To understand how BU members experience and cope with tensions in their own work, and in collaborative projects

and employee development initiatives. These documents helped understand the chronology of structural and organizational changes and offered additional insights into the behaviors of onshore-offshore members. We also spent time in the offices, spoke informally with several participants, took photographs of the working environment and produced field notes.

Data Analysis

We took the opportunity to organize and analyze data at each round of data collection. First, we transcribed all interviews from round one, studied the data and made extensive notes to identify emerging themes of each interview individually. Second, we combined the interview data with documentation and field notes. This helped us to map the organizational structure, reporting lines, workflow and responsibilities, objectives and performance metrics. Third, we set about identifying common themes across the complete round one dataset. To this end, we wrote short guiding narratives and constructed a table of themes. The presence of opposing objectives, the underlying power and knowledge asymmetries, and accounts of conflict between onshore (BUs) and offshore (SSU) units emerged organically from this round of interview data. We repeated this process for the second and third rounds of data collection. Data from the second round revealed in greater depth the conflicting objectives between the SSU and BUs and the apparent threats to participants' sense of professional self. FO informants discussed the application of formal tools and ICT to resolve issues, and the process of integrating the SSU into the business division. Data from the third round, consisting of BU interviews, also referred to different work, objectives, and highlighted the differences in the perceived value of work performed onshore—in the BUs and offshore—in the SSU. At the completion of three rounds of interviews, we made extensive notes and created a thematic table of onshore-offshore conflicts and tensions (e.g., Corley & Gioia, 2004) and their ongoing management by the FO headquarters. We then went back to the literature and iterated between theoretical explanations and the data until we were confident that our interpretation reached a reasonable level of theory-data alignment.

Case Analysis

Table 6.3 juxtaposes the perceptions of members from four onshore BUs with those from the offshore SSU to illuminate the specific paradoxical tensions in the relationship. In the analysis below, we show how members moved from defensive behaviors, which intensified tensions, to collaborative behaviors which attenuated them. We follow the analysis with a detailed discussion section.

Tensions and Defensive Behaviors

As summarized in Table 6.3, contrasting objectives, differing levels of knowledge and access to key decision makers, and issues of identity created tensions between the SSU and the BUs. SSU members noted that they struggled to coordinate and control information because of the BUs' reluctance to share business knowledge. This restricted access meant that the SSU was not able to fully understand the BUs' requirements. SSU members also explained that they did know enough about the activities performed by the third-party provider, which further limited their ability to support the BUs. When explaining their weak knowledge position, SSU members noted that they were seen as a 'cost-center' (i.e., the SSU did not directly generate revenue or make a profit and was instead perceived to cost the firm money). They reported that their position within the GBS, which was widely seen as a support service, had created a kind of status asymmetry between BU and SSU members. SSU members said that because they were support services, they were perceived as less capable, of less value, and as having different objectives to their BU counterparts. SSU members suggested they received limited financial investment and were unable to allocate resources needed to fully understand the activities performed in the BU, or to manage the third-party provider. In addition, despite being tasked with 'process

6 Managing Tensions in Globally Distributed Work 219

Table 6.3 Paradoxical tensions in GDW

Source of tensions	SSU's perceived tensions	SSU supporting data	BUs' perceived tensions	BU supporting data
Knowledge Asymmetries in process, domain and business knowledge	Need to coordinate activities but have limited understanding of customer business and third-party provider activities	The operations do not sit with us anymore, so it is difficult to have detailed conversations about an invoice that went totally belly up and why that was. (P1.9) There were specialities and local needs in BUs that we didn't know about. There were huge complexities in BUs in terms of systems, IT differences and processes. (P2.5) It's not that everybody's hiding information but to call 220 countries and representatives in a tight time frame is not easy. (P1.2)	Have a detailed understanding of own business and end customer needs but have limited understanding of wider processes Need to access information on an informal basis but are reliant on formal systems to improve processes and increase objectivity	When they (the customer) have an information need it's always urgent. (P3.9) There's a disconnect. First, there's a large gap between the SSU and the customer. Second, they don't just have one BU to manage. When it was in-house, we were in control. Now we are one of many the SSU serve. (P2.3)

(continued)

Table 6.3 (continued)

Source of tensions		SSU's perceived tensions	SSU supporting data	BUs' perceived tensions	BU supporting data
Power	Asymmetries in authority and status	Have limited access to decision makers and resources. Seen as a cost-center Need to reduce costs and produce efficiencies but do not have the authority or the financial resources to make changes	BUs wouldn't follow the standard processes. They had their own rules, their own ideas, and were continuously questioning us. They agree in principle but say "it's not possible for us" because of whatever reason. (P1.6) If a BU CFO said 'no I don't see that happening' then it didn't happen. We are a just a cost-centre. (P1.2) If we wanted to implement something it was seen as a huge one-off cost to the BUs. They always said that they only want to do projects that pay back in two years or less. There's not much we can do then. (P1.1)	Need to ensure the quality of outcomes but are expected to hand over control of processes	The decision power should always lie with us in the BU. Transactional work or data gathering can be with them. (P3.9) Control should sit with the person responsible for the end impact. Our CFO is responsible for his Profit and Loss (and not the SSU). (P3.3)

6 Managing Tensions in Globally Distributed Work

Source of tensions	SSU's perceived tensions	SSU supporting data	BUs' perceived tensions	BU supporting data
Identity Threats to sense of belonging	Identify strongly with the organization but feel that they (SSU) are treated like external suppliers Need to collaborate with BUs. But they (SSU) are focused solely on broad organizational objectives, which the BUs find hard to relate to	Us and them dynamic. (P2.6) The BUs were autonomous. As they were making profits, they could do what they wanted...they didn't appreciate us. (P1.1)	Acknowledge the SSU but feel that external units should not tell the BUs what to do Need to collaborate with the SSU, but struggle to accept the SSU as a same-status partner	The SSU was the poorer cousin who got the bad stuff. (P3.5) You (have to) end up with a supplier-vendor relationship. (P1.5) The SSU is seen more as a cost driving entity and the value driving entity, the business, is separate. By definition you are classifying a group of people as a cost. (P2.4)

improvement', they did not have the authority to implement new IT tools. Both BU and SSU members acknowledged the tensions as they transitioned toward a more centralized structure.

> The business was always run in a very entrepreneurial way. The BUs were very autonomous. Then suddenly you have this central support unit (GBS) that says the BU are going to do it totally differently. (P1.1)

Several members referred to the disparity between BU and SSU decision-making power. While the SSU was given the responsibility to centralize and improve financial processes, senior managers in the SSU suggested that they did not have the "stick" or "the backing" from the finance organization (FO) headquarters to force BU members to accept process changes and new IT tools. They highlighted problems of knowledge and control, referring to the relationship as "artificial" (P2.1), with "virtual" (P1.2) and "psychological barriers" (P2.3; P2.7). They also felt they were treated like "suppliers" (P2.4) despite being internal to the firm. A senior SSU manager recalled a humiliating experience where the BU had dismissed plans to develop a financial process and suggested that they "needed to have somebody from the business division looking into it" (P2.4).

From the BUs' perspective, they were legally accountable to external auditors for financial documents produced by SSU members. They were also accountable to the business division for the quality of financial reporting and to their customers for service quality. BU members felt this accountability was at odds with handing over control of related activities to the SSU. They did not have enough understanding of the SSU's activities to be able to generate the necessary reports or rectify mistakes. BU members also felt that the SSU's emphasis on IT standardization was in sharp contrast to the BUs' focus on flexibility. For instance, a BU member explained that their team's daily plan, which they referred to as a "living thing", was devised on a whiteboard and adapted throughout the day. Others noted that they frequently had to respond to urgent calls from customers and requests for information from senior managers. BU members saw the SSU as a "middleman" between themselves and the third-party provider who processed invoices. They felt this arrangement made accessing information and responding to customers more complex and time consuming. In addition, they questioned the SSU's ability to control and manage information and to improve financial processes. They highlighted the strategic importance of their own work and saw the SSU as the "poorer cousin…who got the bad stuff" (P3.5). On the other hand, SSU members felt unhappy at being perceived as merely a "cost saving entity" (P2.4) created to perform "transactional", "repetitive" and "back-office" work. They argued that such a view was not a true reflection of their ability to perform and improve processes. Many of them held master's degrees and formal accounting qualifications and argued that their low status in the relationship was unjustified.

Defensive Behaviors

SSU members claimed that the BUs actively resisted their (SSU's) efforts to standardize IT processes. BU members explained their resistance in terms of the rigidity the SSU initiatives could impose on the BUs' everyday work and on the BUs' freedom to make local adaptations. SSU members explained that BUs invoked the contractual nature of their relationship with the SSU to reject initiatives which aimed at further standardizing financial processes. These projects tended to be rejected because of the perceived cost.

> The first question was always "What is it going to cost and what is going to be the impact on my SLA? They were saying 'I only want to do projects that pay back in two years or faster'. There's not much you can do… it just doesn't work. (P1.1)

Some SSU members explained that BU resistance was often supported by the business division, which did not enforce centralized process changes.

> In the past if we challenged a process, we had nobody we could go to. If the BU didn't want to change, then they didn't change. The business division did not support our projects. We were there to deliver a service and that service could only be what the local BU 'needed'. We've never had that backing. (P2.1)

To access information quickly, BUs often avoided standardized formal processes and contacted the third-party provider directly. Although this meant that issues were resolved locally, deeper and more fundamental issues with the process were not flagged or fixed.

> I jump the gun and go to the [provider] to get a quick answer so I can quickly feedback to my manager. When it's to do with you, you're willing to jump any hoops to quickly resolve your issue. (P3.5)

From the SSU's perspective, these BU behaviors restricted their ability to perform their own roles effectively. One SSU member explained:

> We were under continuous pressure to drive costs down. At the same time BUs were not allowing us to change and to optimise the process which would allow us to decrease costs! It's an interesting 'spagaat' [translation: splits] - cost reductions on one side and on the other side not being allowed to change the process. (P1.9)

The SSU responded by trying to limit communication exchanges between the BUs and the third-party provider. For instance, SSU members improved formal documentation to reduce the need for direct communication. They kept 'log books' to record all mistakes and process delays and complaints from BU members. SSU members also tried to force BUs to use formal protocol and communication channels by boycotting deviations and not completing work that did not align with the standard format.

> Someone will phone up or send an email saying 'can you add this' and we say 'no you're not going to do that. You are going to send the form'. Often, we have implemented an IT tool they need and we make it stricter - and god that's something we want. We want to improve the controls. (P1.5)

The SSU also focused on the formal terms of their contracts with BUs in order to emphasize the obligations of all parties. SSU members invoked SLAs and statement of work documents, to reiterate the specific roles and objectives of the BUs, the third-party provider and the SSU.

6 Managing Tensions in Globally Distributed Work   225

Table 6.4 Defensive behaviors and impact on tensions

SSU defensive behaviors	BU defensive behaviors	Tensions
Emphasized the separation of responsibilities Enforced IT standardization Focused rigidly on contracts and SLAs	Worked around formal channels to access information Resisted IT standardization Monitored and escalated even extremely minor violations of contractual obligations	**Amplified** Tensions made more severe as both sides reach a "stalemate"

However, both BU and SSU members referred to SLAs (and the focus on contractual obligations) as one of the biggest collaborative challenges. BU members pointed out that SLAs codified the misaligned objectives between themselves and the SSU—cost reduction for the SSU and service quality for the BUs. They noted that the SSU, BUs and the third-party provider were rewarded through financial bonuses for meeting conflicting objectives. The SSU's bonuses were linked to cost savings and efficiencies, the BUs' to improving financial outcomes for the unit, and the third-party provider's bonuses were based on the number of invoices processed. They used the terms set out in the SLAs to defend their own objectives and bonuses. BUs showed their discontent with the SSU's inflexibility by issuing 'red SLAs' to signal that obligations had not been met. SSU members countered with 'blue SLAs' to justify their own actions, noting that the BUs had not provided the information needed for the SSU to fulfill its obligations. BU members felt that the SSU had developed a "fighter's mentality" (P2.6) and that the two sides became stuck in blaming contests and "stalemate" conversations about SLAs (see Table 6.4). At the same time, some BU members admitted that they found it challenging to hand over control of tasks they had earlier performed themselves.

Negotiating Tensions

In order to better align SSU's service provision with the needs of the BUs, the finance organization (FO) headquarters altered the organizational structure. The SSU was structurally removed from GBS and integrated into the business division. Beyond the structural change, there was a conscious effort to break "psychological barriers" and integrate the SSU into the division. Senior managers overseeing the transition made it clear that they did not want the structural change to be seen as a "hostile takeover" of the SSU by the division, but only as a means for the BUs and the SSU to "come together". They actively emphasized "togetherness" in their communications and referred to "putting pieces of the puzzle back together" and "working as one" (P2.6; P2.1; P2.5). The business division held a "welcome" event as a starting point for their new unity. One BU member said:

> We held a small celebration with them (the SSU). You feel that people are more engaged to deliver the best they can, not just because we gave them a glass of prosecco and a couple of candies, but because we tell them: "Look, what you guys are doing is really important". We show them the value in what they're doing, and they see their full contribution to the network. Through the network you're part of the family. (P.3.9)

Interactive Behaviors

The structural integration resulted in BU and SSU members being involved in more joint management meetings, joint service performance reviews (SPRs) and collaborative improvement projects. BU and SSU members reported that working together in this way was often more difficult than working independently. They found these meetings involved "uncomfortable" and "frank discussions". BUs also introduced a service 'health check' which rated service provision on a traffic light system (green—good; red—bad; and amber—requires improvement). Unlike formal performance indicators and SLAs, these health checks focused on more informal measures such as sentiment and feelings:

> Health checks gives a sense of how BU members are feeling about performance. For example, in November the UK BU felt there was just too much change. So it's not based on any poor performance - they just found the new IT tools overwhelming. The UK BU is big, so if there are

new tools then a lot of people have to be trained... Norway was red but now it has gone to amber. They were unhappy about duplicate entries coming from a new tool. That is now gone but they kept it amber just for monitoring. They had no issues but just didn't feel confident about it. (P2.1)

Some results were disputed, leading to heated discussions. A BU member described a difficult exchange with the SSU:

With this new focus on quality, and them being in the business division the standard wasn't okay anymore. We needed big improvements, so we introduced a traffic light system for reporting. I can tell that it's been contentious. It's important to the SSU and we suddenly made them red when it had always been green. I could really sense some negative emotion about that. The service hadn't got worse it's just that we hadn't set the target high enough before. At the end of a call with them they said: "Is it green as usual?" and we said, "No. It's red". It was the wrong way to do it, but we have to work together and clean it up. (P3.3)

However, BU and SSU members noted that while meetings led to uncomfortable discussions and blame passing, they also provided opportunities to better understand their counterpart's needs, confront them on issues and defend their own positions. As an SSU member explained:

They say how they feel and they usually give examples to explain issues. We give the
reasons and we give what actions we are taking. (P2.1)

A BU member explained that the increased interactions helped them empathize with the SSU:

I do see the problem for SSU. If they're not being included in the process, then they can't perform their job properly. Can you imagine if they were on a call with the BU CFO and they said, "No problems, everything's kosher, everything's running perfectly," but the CFO's got a long list of all the problems that have come to him directly? The SSU look bad but in reality they have not been given the visibility to do it! (P3.5)

Similarly, SSU members reported that they became more tolerant of the BUs' challenges:

> BUs do not want to get complaints from their suppliers about delayed payments. One BU in particular gets heat for that so we have to make sure that doesn't happen. (P2.1)

Several BU and SSU members explained that an important consequence of "coming together" was the easing of perceived "process boundaries". They acknowledged that collectively they would perform better if they integrated individual tasks and shared knowledge to develop new ideas (see Table 6.5). In the new collaborative environment, the BUs also felt that the SSU was ready to go beyond its formal obligations and work closely with the BU members to gain relevant business knowledge:

> Rather than just taking its narrow operational scope - working faster, harder, cheaper - the SSU actually had to collaborate with what's before and after them in the process. They're really making a difference now and it creates opportunity. The fences have gone down. It means that they now frequently cross borders and understand more about what happens in the other parts of the organization. (P2.6)

Table 6.5 Interactive behaviors and impact on tensions

SSU Interactive Behaviors	BU Interactive Behaviors	Tensions
Worked to develop knowledge of BU operations Attended management meetings with the BUs Empathized with BUs	Focused on less confrontational and informal indicators of performance Attended management meetings with the SSU Empathized with SSU teams	**Accommodated** Tensions were acknowledged and accommodated as both sides related better to each other's needs

Collaborative Behaviors

SSU members started to take a more collaborative view of their responsibilities and reflect on how their own actions impacted the larger organization. They spoke about picking their battles carefully and explained that they had become better aligned with the BUs' need for flexibility. As they increased their interactions, the focus on imposing rigid controls diminished significantly. One SSU member gave an example of a new online invoicing tool designed to require less manual input from the SSU when collecting payments. The idea was to speed up invoice processing times so that BUs received their customer payments quicker to improve cash flow. The implementation of the tool required the BUs to align their own systems and encourage their customers to adopt the online method of payment. The SSU's business plan aimed for 80% of invoices to be processed through the new invoice system. However, SSU members understood and empathized with the problems the BUs faced in adopting the tool. For instance, not all customers were able to access online payment systems. SSU members discussed the problems with their BU counterparts and agreed to aim for a more realistic 70%, which would allow for the local adaptations required by BUs to accommodate customers:

> When you have exceptions, escalations or urgent issues we can now work with SSU members to see how we can overcome them and what our options are. It is a much smoother process. Of course, the SSU has to comply with policy - so in the BUs we try to operate as much as possible within standard processes. But in emergencies we have some temporary flexibility. (P3.8)

BU members also engaged in more collaborative behaviors. They referred to an internal "change in attitude" and began to encourage their SSU counterparts to make their own decisions and propose "improvement projects":

> In the past they were treated as subordinates. I think they just kept their heads down because they were so scared of getting things wrong. No one

raised any issues, and no one ever came to me in case they'd have their heads bitten off. They now feel empowered to look for things. They'll talk to me and they'll suggest something. Nine times out of ten I'll say "What a brilliant idea. Let's do it". (P3.4)

SSU members noted that the BUs were more welcoming of new initiatives and were proactively approaching the SSU with ideas for improving their collaboration. SSU members explained they felt energized and put in more effort to share knowledge and ideas, and implement new IT tools. For instance, an SSU member, who managed the 'purchase-to-pay' area, implemented a set of global KPIs to align and reconcile the goals, objectives and expectations of the BUs, the SSU and the third-party provider:

> With the global KPIs there has been a shift from a pure processing focus (how many invoices have we processed?) to a real end-to-end view. Now, everybody needs to understand the tools [e.g. TradeShift and Basware]. In the SSU we need to see end-to-end if there are any issues and where they are coming from. This means going over the borders of our own unit, to the BU, and even towards procurement. (P2.4)

Several BU and SSU members explained that while the integration process had been challenging, it had led them to engage in more collaborative decision-making. The "psychological divide" between the SSU and the BUs had reduced, and the decision-making process had become faster. The SSU stopped complaining about the BUs' systematic resistance to change, and the BUs stopped opposing SSU initiatives. The confrontational approach was replaced by collaborative discussions and negotiations. The SSU continued to be responsible for cost reduction and process standardization. The BUs continued to be "customer-centric" in their financial decisions but worked collaboratively with the SSU. The BUs acknowledged that the SSU's work on cost reductions and process efficiencies was enabling them (the BUs) to focus squarely on improving their customers' experience:

> In the past a lot of the project change capacity was all focused on driving down cost. Now that capability is there for the BUs, but the CFO can

easily say "Hey guys, let's park the cost project or the standardization in Asia for a little bit, and focus on this commercial one that has a revenue and customer satisfaction impact". This is now possible! In the past there would be reiterations and reiterations on the SLA impact and the budget. All that stuff has gone. (P2.6)

While formal objectives did not change, the BU and SSU developed new ways of coping with tensions and working with one another to find collaborative solutions (see Table 6.6). In accommodating one another, both BU and SSU members made practical trade-offs. For example, the SSU decided to reduce focus on cost reduction projects and increase focus on customer experience projects. Similarly, the BUs volunteered to improve compliance with formal SSU processes. Both sides realized that not sharing knowledge was detrimental to achieving smooth distributed processes. Rather than prioritizing their own objectives, they worked on understanding one another's tasks as important components of a bigger picture. BUs empowered the SSU to make decisions in the larger interest of the organization even when such decisions made their own (BUs) work temporarily more challenging. SSU members engaged with BU members actively in the decision-making process. Overall, both sides explained that process performance had improved in terms of both efficiency (cost and speed) and quality (accuracy and customer service).

Table 6.6 Collaborative behaviors and impact on tensions

SSU Collaborative Behaviors	BU Collaborative Behaviors	Tensions
Reduced their demands for standardization Supported the creation of flexibility • Shared knowledge and ideas to support BUs Engaged in collaborative decision-making	Empowered SSU to propose new projects Engaged in collaborative decision-making Relinquished control of some processes	**Attenuated** Tensions were less salient as both sides learned to live with them. They worked to align goals and bridge misunderstanding

Discussion

The analysis above illustrates several inherent paradoxes in GDW. In particular, it shows how onshore-offshore collaborations involve opposing values and objectives and intense competition for resources and decision-making power. This analysis builds on extant literature which has identified three prominent sources of tensions in GDW—knowledge asymmetries (Hahl et al., 2016; Oshri et al., 2008), power asymmetries (Levina & Vaast, 2008; Ravishankar et al., 2013) and identity threats (Koppman et al., 2016; Petriglieri, 2011). In our case, the three tensions were most evident in the relationship between onshore BU units and the offshore SSU unit. While previous studies have acknowledged tensions and the conflict they create as a pertinent issue, thus far there has been very little understanding of how tensions can be turned into opportunities for effective collaborative practices. Further, only scant research has considered the interactions between tensions and how they play out in GDW. Drawing on our analysis and guided by ideas from paradox theory (Lewis, 2000; Smith & Lewis, 2011), we offer three contributions to the literature on GDW.

First, we illuminate how a sequential enactment of formal and informal solutions may help address tensions and generate more effective onshore-offshore collaborative practices in GDW.

In the literature, tensions and their manifestations have been viewed as being either value destroying or value creating. Symptoms of value-destroying tensions in GDW include a lack of ability and willingness to share knowledge (Zimmerman and Ravishankar, 2014), poor integration across distributed process (Levina & Vaast, 2008) and growth of 'in' and 'out' groups (Hinds et al., 2014). Symptoms of value-creating tensions include better integrated activities and acceptance and accommodation of ambivalent situations and contradictions (Lewis, 2000; Johansen, 2018; Sundaramurthy & Lewis, 2003). Our findings go beyond viewing tensions in binary terms. They help explain how instability-generating tensions (i.e., value destruction) in GDW can turn into an energizing catalyst and create opportunities for creativity and innovation (i.e., value creation). As we elaborate below, in our case formal structural integration that seemingly intensified paradoxical tensions also led the SSU and the BUs to confront paradoxes directly and move toward more effective collaborative practices.

The SSU had adopted defensive behaviors such as 'working to rule', hiding information and excessively emphasizing the need to follow processes. On the other side, the BUs leveraged their superior power position to resist change, access information directly from the third-party provider and force flexibility. These behaviors widened the relational gulfs, increased knowledge asymmetries and further reinforced the power imbalances and conflicting objectives. As prior research has shown, such defensive behaviors are frequently used to mute or disguise tensions and avoid 'paralyzing' conflict (Lewis, 2000; Ravishankar et al., 2013). They also ignore the practical effort required to make collaborations work and lead to diminished opportunities for better understanding the GDW partner (Levina & Vaast, 2008). Interestingly, the structural separation of the SSU and the BUs—with the SSUs reporting to the GBS and the BUs reporting to the business divisions—and the systems used to make this uncoupling work further exacerbated the paradoxical tensions. As our analysis shows, the two sides were unwilling to cooperate outside of formal obligations and share knowledge with one another and were prone to fiercely protecting their own positions. We would therefore suggest that simple formal solutions (e.g., structural separation of units) may not resolve the paradoxical tensions inherent in GDW. They can be too formulaic to tackle the inherent paradoxes and additionally, may fail to recognize opportunities to generate new collaborative practices from the paradoxical tensions. Equally, as the literature points out, standalone informal coping strategies such as arriving at blatantly stereotypical 'cultural' understandings of the GDW partner's actions may not resolve tensions either. They may in fact hinder collaboration and create bigger relational challenges in the long run (Ravishankar, 2015).

However, our case suggests that when actors are given the chance to confront paradoxical tensions directly through a careful sequential enactment of formal and informal solutions, it is very conceivable that this will help address tensions and develop more effective collaborative practices. As our analysis shows, structural integration of the SSU and BUs—a formal solution—created proximity and forced both sides to share time and space, triggering a series of informal positive interactive behaviors such as frank discussions, empathy for offshore (onshore) counterparts and demonstrations of better awareness of the paradoxical roots of their collaborative activities. In other words, both sides identified and negotiated relational challenges, and sought to address knowledge and power imbalances and align objectives. While these interactions were often described as uncomfortable, they energized both sides to develop new collaborative ways of working. For instance, our informants explained how 'new' joint meetings and frank discussions improved the speed of decision-making, led to greater knowledge sharing and empowered them to generate new IT tools for 'process improvement'. The key turning point for the emergence of collaborative behaviors was the actions taken by senior managers (i.e., BU CFOs) in overseeing the structural integration of the BUs and SSU. The integration retained the physical separation of the SSU and BUs but eliminated the structural separation. BU CFOs paid close attention to reducing the power and identity tensions, explaining to the SSU members that they were highly valued, and that the integration was an opportunity to work with the BUs as same-status partners. Thus, they provided both sides (esp. the SSU) a sense of psychological security to approach the integration with positive hope, and not worry and fear. This line of thought complements arguments in paradox theory which suggest that squarely facing up to opposing elements, albeit informally, within a safe and formally constructed space, helps mitigate tensions through better awareness and appreciation of mutual positions (Smith, 2014; Smith & Lewis, 2011). In this sense, confronting instead of avoiding may help turn potentially value-destroying tensions into opportunities for value creation (Johansen, 2018). There is a key insight here for the management of distributed teams, which often relies on distance to temper relationships and maintain stability: With an optimal combination of formal and informal solutions, tensions can be managed to improve relationships and encourage collaborate practices in GDW.

Second, based on our analysis we have developed a phasal model which helps explain the evolution and management of tensions in GDW.

Tensions evolve with onshore-offshore exchanges. Specifically, our empirical data shows how tensions are suppressed, amplified, accommodated or attenuated in globally distributed collaborations. Tensions evoke defensive behaviors and also evolve in response to the behaviors. For instance, SSU's enforcement of formal communication channels compelled BUs to find alternative flexible ways to access information, thus further amplifying tensions. The structural integration of the SSU into the business division meant that both sides had to squarely face the tensions and negotiate differences. The SSU and BUs moved from defensive behaviors, which suppressed and then amplified tensions, to more positive interactive behaviors through which they learned (at least temporarily) to 'live with' and accommodate tensions (Smith & Lewis, 2011). As explained earlier, this process of coming together enabled both sides to better understand the other's perspectives and empathize with the other's motives. Informal meetings led to workarounds, compromises and collaborative behaviors, thereby attenuating tensions.

Our data also suggests that given the inherent and entrenched nature of the paradoxical elements, any resolution or attenuation of tensions may only be temporary. Our informants noted that as situations changed, for example when new activities migrated to the SSU or new members joined the team, tensions re-emerged, requiring further renegotiation in search of an amicable solution. As both sides recognized the importance of dedicating time for honest and regular communication over thorny issues, monthly service performance review meetings and regular health checks were established. Thus, building on our phasal model, we suggest that at the heart of managing inherent tensions in GDW is the ongoing negotiation of amicable and 'best fit' solutions at that time.

Third, we extend prior research by empirically illustrating the interactions between tensions. Our analysis brought to light interactions between power, knowledge and identity tensions, which have been largely implicit in current debate. Only a small set of studies have hinted at interactions of power-knowledge-identity tensions in GDW. For instance, Hahl et al. (2016) imply such interactions in their study of knowledge asymmetries between teams and brokers when they highlight the 'esteem' of those brokering as an important influence on teams' willingness to share knowledge and reduce asymmetries. Similarly, Levina and Vaast (2008) refer to the status of teams as an important facet of knowledge sharing and innovation in GDW, while Zimmermann and Ravishankar (2011) argue that asymmetrical status positions influence the professional role identities of offshore-onshore units. Overall however, interactions between knowledge, power and identity tensions have not been explicitly considered or illustrated in prior GDW research. Our analyses point to such interactions and their importance for effective collaboration.

Defensive Behaviors and Interaction Between Tensions

In the suppression-amplification phases, the SSU tried to strengthen its weaker power-identity position in the relationship (being perceived as a 'transactional' 'poorer cousin' with limited access to decision makers, less investment and limited authority to enforce process changes) by asserting its stronger knowledge position and insisting that the BUs use formal systems for information exchanges. Such an emphasis on its knowledge position amplified the knowledge tensions between the two sides (Table 6.5). Thus, we would suggest that *against a background of defensive behaviors efforts to reduce power and identity tensions in GDW can further aggravate knowledge tensions.*

In turn, BUs attempted to maintain their stronger power-identity position and distract attention away from their weaker knowledge position. They emphasized their status as profit centers and their 'customer' proximity to ignore SSU mandates about the use of formal systems: *The decision power should always lie with us in the BU. Transactional work or data gathering can be with them* (P3.9). This behavior not only created further knowledge tensions by hiding important business information from the SSU team, but also reinforced the power and identity tensions. Extrapolating from these observations, we would suggest that *against a background of defensive behaviors efforts to maintain power and identity tensions in GDW can exacerbate knowledge tensions and worsen power and identity tensions.*

Interactive-Collaborative Behaviors and Interaction Between Tensions

The accommodation-attenuation phases involved a transition to interactive and collaborative behaviors. As the analysis shows, BUs empowered their SSU counterparts and in return, the SSU reduced knowledge tensions by better integrating distributed knowledge and by sharing their 'process' knowledge. Thus, we would suggest that *against a background of interactive-collaborative behaviors efforts to reduce power tensions in GDW can help reduce knowledge tensions.* Several informants noted this improvement in the knowledge tension situation: *The fences have gone down. It means that they now frequently cross borders and understand more about what happens in the other parts of the organisation (P2.6).*

The SSU also worked to improve their power position by offering more 'valued' services, which opened access to decision makers and financial resources. The SSU also started sharing knowledge with the BUs: *…there has been a shift from a pure processing focus (how many invoices have we processed?) to a real end-to-end view* (P2.4). The attenuation of power and knowledge tensions not only removed the hostility between teams, but (as described in the case analysis) also had a positive impact on reducing identity tensions (e.g., the 'us' and 'them' barriers). Thus, we would suggest that *against a background of interactive-collaborative behaviors efforts to reduce power and knowledge tensions in GDW can help reduce identity tensions.* From a theoretical standpoint, these preliminary insights about how addressing one tension can potentially impact others call for a greater focus on interactions between multiple tensions in distributed working environments. From a practical standpoint, it calls for more comprehensive and sophisticated strategies to manage tensions in GDW.

Implications for Paradox Research and GDW Practice

Thus far, studies of paradox have focused on a central actor who is challenged with accommodating two competing ideas (Lewis, 2000; Smith, 2014), such as novelty and usability, innovation and efficiency (Andriopoulos & Lewis, 2009), and competition and cooperation (Rai, 2016). In all these cases, the actor is positioned as the focal point, facing two opposing forces. As a point of departure, here we have elaborated on how one side of the paradox (BUs) is at odds with the other side (the SSU). This viewpoint extends the somewhat traditional focus in the paradox literature on one central actor (or group) who can comprehend each opposing element individually, to include actors (e.g., onshore-offshore units) that are often unfamiliar with the specifics of one another's tasks, objectives and values. Our analysis suggests that while formal strategies create a common lexicon and standardized rules for performing different parts of the distributed process, the inherently contradictory elements of the two GDW sides and the added complexity of distance mean that power, knowledge and identity tensions are harder to overcome. Our case suggests that organizations may need to take additional steps (e.g., structural realignments) to ensure that actors comprehend the inherently contradictory elements before attempting to engage in meaningful collaborative practices. Managers need to be sensitive, first and foremost, to the perceived power and identity tensions, which may amplify with the implementation of structural changes. They need to address the source of these tensions, by giving all sides the reassurance and confidence that their interests will be protected and by explaining the honest efforts being made to generate strategic value through the collaboration. The empirical material suggests that once individuals become better aware of, and empathize with, each other's positions, the perception of power asymmetries and identity threats is likely to subside. In such a relatively benign environment, as we saw in our data, conflicting teams are likely to take concrete measures on their own to reduce knowledge tensions.

The structural integration meant that the business division's CFO became responsible for the BU and SSU teams and in many respects acted as the arbitrator. The success of this simplified hierarchical arrangement has two implications for practice. First, it indicates that even when teams are physically separate, having a common leader can help mitigate tensions. Second, it suggests that it may be crucial for such a leader, in the aftermath of the structural integration, to engage with the conflicting sides on a 'human' and 'informal' level rather than escalating the dependence on formal IT tools and systems. It is possible that many managers leading GDW relationship rely on formal IT tools to ease coordination and communication challenges, and to minimize or overcome conflict. They may find this paper useful for designing or re-designing their management of distributed teams. Our study suggests that over-reliance on formal IT tools (e.g., the creation of a common lexicon and standardized processes) can be counterproductive. Instead, our findings suggest that organizations need to create opportunities for GDW teams to informally discuss, challenge and negotiate power, knowledge and identity tensions in an open and transparent manner. One way in which organizations can support this may be to invest in platforms (online or offline) which offer GDW partners a safe space to engage in informal, and potentially constructive, meetings. However, a big challenge organizations face (and one that is admittedly not fully explored in this study) is understanding whether defensive behaviors stem from attempts to overcome inadequacies in the work system, or whether they are driven by the self-interest of actors taking short-cuts, resisting change and protecting their jobs. If it is mostly the former, then the challenge for managers is to balance the inherent paradoxes in a stable and coherent work system that fosters constructive GDW partnerships. If it is the latter, managers need to re-empower teams by better communicating the value of new (or evolving roles) and helping actors develop positive evaluations of their professional selves.

Limitations and Future Research

The arguments in this chapter are based on a single in-depth case study. While this approach is consistent with the underlying principles and aims of qualitative research, care must be taken in transferring insights to other contexts. Another limitation of our study is that the data for phases 0 and 1 was captured retrospectively. We encourage scholars to adopt longitudinal methods to capture timely accounts of how multiple tensions evolve as GDW units collaborate over time. The collaborative behaviors we saw from both sides led to what some participants described as 'small wins'. There was a better handling of trade-offs as both sides began working with each other. However, we acknowledge that managing trade-offs is not the ultimate objective here. Collaborative behaviors and better appreciation of mutual positions lay a solid foundation for genuine value creation through the offshore (SSU)–onshore (BUs) relationship. More research is needed to explicate the process of generating strategic value through collaborative behaviors in paradoxical GDW relationships. Our case focuses on inherent contradictions in the relationship between onshore BUs and an offshore SSU. However, it is likely that the corresponding tensions could play out differently in different outsourcing and offshoring arrangements. Further research is needed to explore such variations. More work is also needed to understand how collaborative practices emerge as outsourcing/offshoring arrangements become more complex with the application of automation and artificial intelligence technologies.

We have shown how even when they cannot entirely resolve the inherent contradictions in GDW, a sequence of formal and informal solutions can address the corresponding tensions and improve collaborative practices. However, it is possible that in some cases, a sequence of similar formal and informal solutions may worsen rather than improving opportunities for collaboration. Future research needs to closely investigate the range of conditions in GDW that invariably lead to negative manifestations of tensions and poor relationships. Our case featured a relationship between onshore BUs and an offshore SSU. However, we have not investigated in detail the extent to which geographic distance influenced the tensions. Indeed, some of the tensions may also appear in co-located and proximally located teams although distance obviously introduces a new dimension to the relationship. More research is needed to compare and contrast the influence of the wide array of possible geographic distances from onshore units (e.g., offshore—in the same continent; offshore—in a different continent) on the evolution of tensions in GDW. Finally, given that empirical research on paradox has so far largely restricted itself to contexts of equal power relations, there is a need for a more explicit focus on management of paradoxes in settings riddled with significant power asymmetries (Hargrave & Van de Ven, 2017; Smith et al., 2017).

Conclusion

In this chapter, we have drawn on paradox theory in considering the intrinsic and entrenched nature of power, knowledge and identity tensions in GDW. While it may be hard to completely and conclusively reconcile the paradoxical elements underpinning GDW tensions, our study suggests that a sequential enactment of formal and informal solutions can help situated actors move toward better collaborative working practices with their GDW counterparts. Tensions in GDW evolve in phases and require a careful ongoing negotiation between diverse groups of stakeholders. Crucially, improvements in collaborative practices cannot be taken for granted since new demands, on say, an offshore unit may trigger new interactions between tensions and significantly harm the offshore unit's relationship with its corresponding onshore unit. Thus, effective management of paradox is a difficult and often fragile achievement in GDW settings. Given the increasing proliferation of GDW projects and initiatives, we would encourage scholars to build on our study and look closely into how specific interactions between tensions may be exploited to generate value for organizations engaged in GDW.

Appendix

See Table 6.7

Table 6.7 Participant roles and data reference codes

Round	Participant job role	Interview length (hours)	Team	Data reference
1	Transition and Transformation Manager for Europe	1:19	SSU	P1.1
1	Global Process Owner	1:31	SSU	P1.2
1	General / Site Manager and Global Process Owner	0:53	SSU	P1.3
1	Process Expert for Europe, the Middle East and Africa / Control Tower Lead	1:05	SSU	P1.4
1	Head of Transition and Transformation	1:12	SSU	P1.5
1	Transition and Transformation Project Manager	1:19	SSU	P1.6
1	Head of Learning and Development	1:27	SSU	P1.7
1	Global Deployment Manager	0:53	SSU	P1.8
1	Head of BPO	0:57	SSU	P1.9
2	Financial Accounting Manager	2:29	SSU	P2.1
2	Head of Performance Management Europe & Global Coordinator for Performance Management	1:09	SSU	P2.2
2	Acting Service Delivery Expert	1:18	SSU	P2.3
2	Global Process Owner	0:48	SSU	P2.4

(continued)

6 Managing Tensions in Globally Distributed Work 243

Table 6.7 (continued)

Round	Participant job role	Interview length (hours)	Team	Data reference
2	Global Head of Financial Accounting	0:57	FO	P2.5
2	VP, HR for Finance	1:46	FO	P2.6
2	Communications & Employee Engagement Manager	1:29	SSU	P2.7
2	Vice President, Provider Management	1:11	FO	P2.8
3	Chief Financial Officer: Country Level	0:52	BU	P3.1
3	Chief Financial Officer: Country Level	1:04	BU	P3.2
3	Head of Controlling: Country Level	1:34	BU	P3.3
3	Head of Governance: Country Level	1:10	BU	P3.4
3	Risk, Finance, and Reconciliation Controller: Country Level	1:03	BU	P3.5
3	Risk, Finance, and Reconciliation Controller: Country Level	1:11	BU	P3.6
3	Chief Financial Officer: Country Level	1:03	BU	P3.7
3	Chief Financial Officer: Country Level	1:33	BU	P3.8
3	Head of Commercial Controlling and OTC: Country Level	2:00	BU	P3.9

References

Andriopoulos, C., & Lewis, M. W. (2009). Exploitation-Exploration Tensions and Organizational Ambidexterity: Managing Paradoxes of Innovation. *Organization Science, 20*(4), 696–717.

Barney, S., Mohankumar, V., Chatzipetrou, P., Aurum, A., Wohlin, C., & Angelis, L. (2014). Software Quality Across Borders: Three Case Studies on Company Internal Alignment. *Information and Software Technology, 56*(1), 20–38.

Bengtsson, M., & Kock, S. (2000). "Co-opetition" in Business Networks—To Cooperate and Compete Simultaneously. *Industrial Marketing Management, 29*(5), 411–426.

Bengtsson, M., Raza-Ullah, T., & Vanyushyn, V. (2016). The Coopetition Paradox and Tension: The Moderating Role of Coopetition Capability. *Industrial Marketing Management, 53*, 19–30.

Cha, H. S., Pingry, D. E., & Thatcher, M. E. (2008). Managing the Knowledge Supply Chain: An Organizational Learning Model of Information Technology Offshore Outsourcing. *MIS Quarterly, 32*(2), 281–306.

Chen, Y., Bharadwaj, A., & Goh, K.-Y. (2017). An Empirical Analysis of Intellectual Property Rights Sharing in Software Development Outsourcing. *MIS Quarterly, 41*(1), 131–161.

Connelly, C. E., Zweig, D., Webster, J., & Trougakos, J. P. (2011). Knowledge Hiding in Organizations. *Journal of Organizational Behavior, 33*(1), 64–88.

Corley, K., & Gioia, D. (2004). Identity Ambiguity and Change in the Wake of a Corporate Spin-off. *Administrative Science Quarterly, 49*(2), 173–208.

Cousins, K. C., Robey, D., & Zigurs, L. (2007). Managing Strategic Contradictions in Hybrid Teams. *European Journal of Information Systems, 16*(4), 460–478.

David, G. C., Chand, D., Newell, S., & Resende-Santos, J. (2008). Integrated Collaboration Across Distributed Sites: The Perils of Process and the Promise of Practice. *Journal of Information Technology, 23*(1), 44–54.

Deloitte (2016). *Global Business Services: Performance Improvement.* https://www2.deloitte.com/content/dam/Deloitte/us/Documents/process-and-operations/us-operations-global-business-services.pdf

Di Tullio, D., & Staples, D. (2013). The Governance and Control of Open Source Software Projects. *Journal of Management Information Systems, 30*(3), 49–80.

Dibbern, J., Winkler, J., & Heinzl, A. (2008). Explaining Variations in Client Extra Costs Between Software Projects Offshored to India. *MIS Quarterly, 32*(2), 333–366.

Druskat, V. U., & Wheeler, J. V. (2003). Managing from the Boundary: The Effective Leadership of Self-Managing Work Teams. *Academy of Management Journal, 46*(4), 435–457.

Dubé, L., & Robey, D. (2009). Surviving the Paradoxes of Virtual Teamwork. *Information Systems Journal, 19*(1), 3–30.

Eisenberg, J., & Mattarelli, E. (2016). Building Bridges in Global Virtual Teams: The Role of Multicultural Brokers in Overcoming the Negative Effects of Identity Threats on Knowledge Sharing Across Subgroups. *Journal of International Management, 23*(4), 399–411.

Eisenhardt, K. M. (1989). Building Theories from Case Study Research. *Academy of Management Review, 14*(4), 532–550.

Goo, J., Nam, K., & Kishore, R. (2009). The Role of Service Level Agreements in Relational Management of Information Technology Outsourcing: An Empirical Study. *MIS Quarterly, 33*(1), 119–145.

Hahl, O., Kacperczyk, A., & Davis, J. P. (2016). Knowledge Asymmetry and Brokerage: Linking Network Perception to Position in Structural Holes. *Strategic Organization, 14*(2), 118–143.

Hargrave, T. J., & Van de Ven, A. H. (2017). Integrating Dialectical and Paradox Perspectives on Managing Contradictions in Organizations. *Organization Studies, 38*(3–4), 319–339.

Hinds, P. J., & Mortensen, M. (2005). Understanding Conflict in Geographically Distributed Teams: The Moderating Effects of Shared Identity Shared Context, and Spontaneous Communication. *Organization Science, 16*(3), 290–307.

Hinds, P. J., Neeley, T. B., & Cramton, C. D. (2014). Language as a Lightning Rod: Power Contests, Emotion Regulation, and Subgroup Dynamics in Global Teams. *Journal of International Business Studies, 45*(5), 536–561.

Jarvenpaa, S. L., & Majchrzak, A. (2016). Interactive Self-Regulatory Theory for Sharing and Protecting in Interorganizational Collaborations. *Academy of Management Review, 41*(1), 9–27.

Jarzabkowski, P., Lê, J. K., & Van de Ven, A. H. (2013). Responding to Competing Strategic Demands: How Organizing, Belonging, and Performing Paradoxes Coevolve. *Strategic Organization, 11*(3), 245–280.

Jarzabkowski, P. A., & Lê, J. K. (2017). We Have to Do This and That? You Must be Joking: Constructing and Responding to Paradox Through Humor. *Organization Studies, 38*(3–4): 433–462.

Johansen, J. H. (2018). *Paradox Management: Contradictions and Tensions in Complex Organizations.* Palgrave Pivot.

Koppman, S., Mattarelli, E., & Gupta, A. (2016). Third-World "Sloggers" or Elite Global Professionals? Using Organizational Toolkits to Redefine Work Identity in Information Technology Offshore Outsourcing. *Organization Science, 27*(4), 825–845.

Kotlarsky, J., Scarbrough, H., & Oshri, I. (2014). Coordinating Expertise Across Knowledge Boundaries in Offshore-Outsourcing Projects: The Role of Codification. *MIS Quarterly, 38*(2), 607–627.

Kotlarsky, J., Rivard, S., & Oshri, I. (2016*). On a Supplier's Paradoxical Practices: The Case of Technological Innovations in Outsourcing Engagements.* Conference Proceedings, Thirty Seventh International Conference on Information Systems, Dublin 2016. https://aisel.aisnet.org/icis2016/ISStrategy/Presentations/2/#.XQPHRJNNPcU

Leonardi, P. M., & Bailey, D. E. (2008). Transformational Technologies and the Creation of New Work Practices: Making Implicit Knowledge Explicit in Task-Based Offshoring. *MIS Quarterly, 32*(2), 411–436.

Leonardi, P. M., & Bailey, D. E. (2013). Recognizing and Selling Good Ideas: How Brokers Mediate Knowledge Transfer. *Academy of Management Proceedings, 2013*(1), 10663.

Leonardi, P. M., & Rodriguez-Lluesma, C. (2013). Occupational Stereotypes, Perceived Status Differences, and Intercultural Communication in Global Organizations. *Communication Monographs, 80*(4), 478–502.

Levina, N., & Kane, A. (2009). "I Am Not One of Them Anymore": Onshore Immigrant Managers on Offshore Development Projects. *Academy of Management Proceedings, 2009*(1), 1–6.

Levina, N., & Vaast, E. (2008). Innovating or Doing as Told? Status Differences and Overlapping Boundaries in Offshore Collaboration. *MIS Quarterly, 32*(2), 307–332.

Lewis, M. W. (2000). Exploring Paradox: Toward a More Comprehensive Guide. *Academy of Management Review, 25*(4), 760–776.

Miron-Spektor, E., & Beenen, G. (2015). Motivating Creativity: The Effects of Sequential and Simultaneous Learning and Performance Achievement Goals on Product Novelty and Usefulness. *Organizational Behavior and Human Decision Processes, 127*, 53–65.

Newell, S., David, G., & Chand, D. (2007). An Analysis of Trust Among Globally Distributed Work Teams in an Organizational Setting. *Knowledge and Process Management, 14*(3), 158–168.

Oshri, I., Van Fenema, P., & Kotlarsky, J. (2008). Knowledge Transfer in Globally Distributed Teams: The Role of Transactive Memory. *Information Systems Journal, 18*(6), 593–616.

Oxley, J. E., & Sampson, R. C. (2004). The Scope and Governance of International R&D Alliances. *Strategic Management Journal, 25*(89), 723–749.

Parker, G., Van Alstyne, M., & Jiang, X. (2017). Platform Ecosystems: How Developers Invert the Firm. *MIS Quarterly, 41*(1), 255–266.

Petriglieri, J. L. (2011). Under Threat: Responses to and the Consequences of Threats to Individuals' Identities. *Academy of Management Review, 36*(4), 641–662.

Plambeck, N., & Weber, K. (2010). When the Glass is Half Full and Half Empty: CEOs' Ambivalent Interpretations of Strategic Issues. *Strategic Management Journal, 31*, 689–710.

Poole, M. S., & van de Ven, A. H. (1989). Using Paradox to Build Management and Organization Theories. *Academy of Management Review, 14*(4), 562–578.

Rai, R. K. (2016). A Co-opetition-Based Approach to Value Creation in Interfirm Alliances. *Journal of Management, 42*(6), 1663–1699.

Ravishankar, M. N. (2015). The Realignment of Offshoring Frame Disputes (OFD): An Ethnographic "Cultural" Analysis. *European Journal of Information Systems, 24*(3), 234–246.

Ravishankar, M. N., Pan, S. L., & Myers, M. D. (2013). Information Technology Offshoring in India: A Postcolonial Perspective. *European Journal of Information Systems, 22*(4), 387–402.

Schuman, S., Stutz, S., & Ward, J. (2010). *Family Business as Paradox*. Palgrave.

Smith, W. K. (2014). Dynamic Decision Making: A Model of Senior Leaders Managing Strategic Paradoxes. *Academy of Management Journal, 57*(6), 1592–1623.

Smith, W. K., Erez, M., Jarvenpaa, S., Lewis, M. W., & Tracey, P. (2017). Adding Complexity to Theories of Paradox, Tensions, and Dualities of Innovation and Change: Introduction to Organization Studies Special Issue on Paradox, Tensions, and Dualities of Innovation and Change. *Organization Studies, 38*(3–4), 303–317.

Smith, W. K., & Lewis, M. W. (2011). Toward a Theory of Paradox: A Dynamic Equilibrium Model of Organizing. *Academy of Management Review, 36*(2), 381–403.

Stadtler, L., & Van Wassenhove, L. N. (2016). Coopetition as a Paradox: Integrative Approaches in a Multi-Company Cross-Sector Partnership. *Organization Studies, 37*(5), 655–685.

Sundaramurthy, C., & Lewis, M. (2003). Control and Collaboration: Paradoxes of Governance. *Academy of Management Review, 28*(3), 397–415.

Tiwana, A., & Keil, M. (2007). Does Peripheral Knowledge Complement Control? An Empirical Test in Technology Outsourcing Alliances. *Strategic Management Journal, 28*(6), 623–634.

Tzabbar, D., & Vestal, A. (2015). Bridging the Social Chasm in Geographically Distributed R&D Teams: The Moderating Effects of Relational Strength and Status Asymmetry on the Novelty of Team Innovation. *Organization Science, 26*(3), 811–829.

Vlaar, P. W., Van Fenema, P. C., & Tiwari, V. (2008). Cocreating Understanding and Value in Distributed Work: How Members of Onsite and Offshore Vendor Teams Give. *Make, Demand, and Break Sense, MIS Quarterly, 32*(2), 227–255.

Walsham, G. (2006). Doing Interpretive Research. *European Journal of Information Systems, 15*(3), 320–330.

Zimmerman, A., & Ravishankar, M. N. (2011). Collaborative IT Offshoring Relationships and Professional Role Identities: Reflections from a Field Study. *Journal of Vocational Behavior, 78*(3), 351–360.

Zimmermann, A., & Ravishankar, M. N. (2014). Knowledge Transfer in IT Offshoring Relationships: The Roles of Social Capital, Efficacy and Outcome Expectations. *Information Systems Journal, 24*(2), 167–202.

Zimmermann, A., & Ravishankar, M. N. (2016). A Systems Perspective on Offshoring Strategy and Motivational Drivers Amongst Onshore and Offshore Employees. *Journal of World Business, 51*(4), 548–567.

Zolin, R., Hinds, P. J., Fruchter, R., & Levit, R. E. (2004). Interpersonal Trust in Cross-Functional, Geographically Distributed Work: A Longitudinal Study. *Information and Organization, 14*(1), 1–26.

7

On Dissatisfaction with Offshore-Outsourcing: Is Backsourcing the Right Response?

Ilan Oshri, Jatinder Sidhu, and Julia Kotlarsky

Introduction

There is tremendous interest in academic and professional circles for a better understanding of the drivers and outcomes of firms' sourcing decisions, such as, *what*, *where*, and *how* to outsource (Dibbern et al., 2012; DiRomualdo & Gurbaxani, 1998; Mudambi & Tallman, 2010; Mudambi & Venzin, 2010; Tanriverdi et al., 2007)[1] and offshore (Aron & Singh, 2005; Doh et al., 2009; Farrell, 2006; Musteen, 2016).

Chapter 7 is an updated version of Oshri, I., Sidhu, J., & Kotlarsky, J. (2019). East, West, Would Home Really Be Best? On Dissatisfaction with Offshore-Outsourcing and Firms' Inclination to Backsource. *Journal of Business Research*, 103, 644–653.

I. Oshri (✉) · J. Kotlarsky
University of Auckland, Auckland, New Zealand
e-mail: ilan.oshri@auckland.ac.nz

J. Sidhu
Leeds University, Leeds, UK

---

[1] Most articles cited here focus on both outsourcing and offshoring decisions. Here we use the terms offshoring and offshored as shorthand for, respectively, offshore-outsourcing and offshore-outsourced activities, functions, and processes.

© The Editor(s) (if applicable) and The Author(s), under exclusive licence to Springer Nature Switzerland AG 2024
L. Willcocks et al. (Eds.), *Transformation in Global Outsourcing*, Technology, Work and Globalization, https://doi.org/10.1007/978-3-031-61022-6_7

In relation to this interest, transaction-cost economics (TCE) and the resource-based view (RBV) have often been scholars' theoretical lenses of choice for modeling firms' sourcing decisions as rational choices that either capitalize on cost or resource advantages offshoring provides (Aubert et al., 1996; Lewin et al., 2009; Mudambi & Venzin, 2010; Vivek et al., 2008). Notably, despite an increasing trend to bring back offshored operations in-house (see, for example, Bhagwatwar et al., 2011; Ejodame & Oshri, 2017), there has so far been little scrutiny of firms' decision to backsource. A handful of studies that have focused on the phenomenon indicate that backsourcing seems to follow disenchantment with offshoring as firms fail to realize anticipated performance improvements and goals (Veltri et al., 2008; Whitten & Leidner, 2006). More recently, the suggestion has been that increased automation, together with adverse geo-political conditions, would accelerate backsourcing (Oshri et al., 2023).

Importantly, however, offshoring disenchantment has not always culminated in backsourcing, raising the intriguing question why disappointed firms differ in their inclination to backsource. In this chapter, we address the question by using the influential lens of the behavioral theory of the firm (e.g., Argote & Greve, 2007; Desai, 2016; Gavetti et al., 2012; Tyler & Caner, 2016). With roots in the work of scholars at the Carnegie School (Cyert & March, 1963), the behavioral theory of the firm (BTF) offers an account of the decision-making process in firms that, based on realistic assumptions about human cognition and relations, suggests that managerial decisions reflect the bounded rationality of decision makers and the politicized nature of decision making. As discussed in more detail later in the chapter, drawing on the core ideas of BTF, we articulate a model in which the variation in firms' inclination to backsource is ascribed to the level of dissatisfaction with offshoring and the problemistic search that follows. Furthermore, the model suggests that the effect of offshoring dissatisfaction on backsourcing behavior is likely to depend on decision makers' expectations regarding the technical difficulty of reintegrating offshored work, financial loss on account of discontinued offshoring, service quality decline due to termination of offshore contracts, on the political support that exists in a firm for backsourcing, and on the availability of financial slack to facilitate the re-aggregation of the firm's value chain.

Structural equation modeling of data from a cross-industry survey of firms located in the U.S.A. and the U.K. provides support for the theoretical model. Empirical results show that, while greater dissatisfaction with offshoring is indeed associated with a greater inclination to backsource, the relationship is conditional on both managerial perceptions and the political climate. In particular, the more the financial loss and service quality decline managers expect from discontinuing offshoring, the weaker the effect of dissatisfaction with offshoring on the inclination to backsource. Surprisingly though, decision makers' expectations regarding the technical difficulty of reintegration do not seem to influence the effect of offshoring dissatisfaction. As regards political climate, the effect of offshoring dissatisfaction indeed becomes stronger the more the political support in the firm for backsourcing. Quite interestingly, in defiance of our theoretical model, we find financial slack to weaken the effect of offshoring dissatisfaction. The result suggests that, by providing more buffer, greater financial slack discourages a switch from offshoring to backsourcing—rather than undertaking such a radical shift, firms seem to prefer the status quo, pinning their hopes on an offshoring strategy despite dissatisfaction with it.

This chapter makes several contributions. It presents one of the first theoretical and empirical inquiries into differences in firms' inclination to backsource. The chapter provides insight into why firms often appear reticent to backsource despite numerous accounts in the news and business press of dissatisfaction with offshoring. In particular, it casts light on the role that expectations of boundedly-rational decision makers and firm politics can play in inhibiting backsourcing, variables that have not received much attention in the literature. More generally, by employing the BTF lens, the chapter enriches the literature, complementing earlier research that has used TCE and RBV frameworks to suggest that sourcing decisions are guided by rational cost and resource considerations. Inasmuch as backsourcing and outsourcing are essentially two sides of the sourcing coin, we indicate that there may be value in examining the latter by also using a BTF lens—outsourcing choices may very well be a reflection of managerial perceptions and company politics. In this regard, the chapter speaks to a nascent stream of offshoring research that has started to draw on BTF to advance understanding of sourcing decisions (Massini et al., 2010; Musteen, 2016). Overall, we offer a behavioral explanation for why some firms may be more inclined to "re-make" rather than to "continue-to-buy", while others continue to outsource.

Research Background

Sourcing Decisions and the Incidence and Challenges of Backsourcing

Throughout this book, we see outsourcing, offshoring, and backsourcing forming a spectrum of sourcing options (Aron & Singh, 2005; Dedrick et al., 2011; Metters, 2008; Mudambi & Venzin, 2010). Whereas outsourcing refers to the contracting of external service providers for the execution of some of a client firm's value-chain functions, processes, and activities for a specified length of time and at an agreed-upon cost and service level, offshore-outsourcing refers specifically to the contracting of external service providers operating from an offshore location, usually a developing country separated from the client firm's country by an ocean (Oshri et al., 2015, 2023). Backsourcing, in contrast, is the practice of bringing back offshored operations in-house (Hirschheim & Lacity, 1998; Whitten & Leidner, 2006). The backsourcing process starts with a decision by a client firm to terminate existing offshore-outsourcing contracts, and it culminates with the reintegration of the previously offshored operations into the client firm's value chain.[2] (As a cautionary note, backsourcing is sometimes used as a phrase to include bringing

---

[2] As defined here, backsourcing can be distinguished from insourcing, which refers particularly to the termination of an outsourcing contract with a view to rebuild the IT infrastructure internally (e.g., Hirschheim and Lacity, 2000). Backsourcing can also be distinguished from reshoring, which describes the practice of bringing back to the home country or the home continent—and not in-house—an offshore-outsourced function (e.g., Gray et al., 2013; Musteen, 2016).

back in-house operations that have been offshored, e.g., repatriating parts or all of a captive center in India back to the U.S.A. The present study looks at only the decision to backsource, or not, offshore-outsourced activities.)

The last decade has witnessed a growth in the phenomenon of backsourcing across industries. For example, in the context of the retail sector, in 2006, Sainsbury backsourced its IT systems from Accenture largely ending a deal worth over $2 Billion. In the context of the banking sector, in 2011, the Spanish bank Santander brought back its contact centers from India to the U.K. In 2013, Maybank Singapore brought back its IT function in-house after ten years of a multi-million dollar contract with CSC Computer Services. In terms of sheer scale, the termination of a contract—centering on data-center, helpdesk, and data and voice networks outsourcing—between JP Morgan and IB stands out for the U.S.$ 5 billion sum of money involved (Bhagwatwar et al., 2011; Overby, 2005). These and other backsourcing cases (see, e.g., Kotlarsky & Bognar, 2012) seem to signal that firms may backsource even more frequently in the future as part of their overall sourcing strategy (Dibbern et al., 2004). The most common explanation for this growing trend toward backsourcing ascribes the phenomenon to disenchantment with offshoring because of non-realization of offshoring goals (e.g., Bhagwatwar et al., 2011; Veltri et al., 2008).

Despite the recurring trend, it is important to note that the successful backsourcing of offshored operations is not an easy, straightforward process. It represents a major change in sourcing strategy, and can be anticipated to produce substantial technical and financial challenges of the kind that usually accompany large system reintegration projects (Volkoff et al., 2005), and may additionally entail legal difficulties linked to the termination of contracts with service providers (Bhagwatwar et al., 2011). In relation to technical challenges, a prominent potential difficulty is that a firm's capabilities for performing offshored operations in-house may have atrophied and, thus, may need re-building through the commitment of time and monetary resources to allow effective incorporation of offshored operations into the firm's value chain (Bhagwatwar et al., 2011; Ejodame & Oshri, 2017). Below, we draw on the insights of BTF to submit that, among other factors, decision makers' expectations concerning the technical difficulty of reintegrating offshored operations, as well as expectations about financial loss and quality decline due to the termination of offshore contracts, will form a crucial element in determining how dissatisfaction with offshoring affects the inclination to backsource.

The Behavioral Theory of the Firm (BTF) and Firms' Inclination to Backsource

That decision makers in firms have bounded rationality and that firms are political entities made up of coalitions who may have shared as well as conflicting interests and goals are two salient premises of BTF (Cyert & March, 1963; Eisenhardt & Zbaracki, 1992; Gaba & Joseph, 2013; Gavetti et al., 2012). On the basis of these premises, BTF maintains that the decision-making process in firms tends to be inconsistent with the postulates of rational models of decision making, which portray managerial decisions as the selection of an optimal solution following a cost–benefit examination of all possible alternatives. BTF suggests that, typically, managerial decisions are in fact satisficing solutions which reflect the bounded rationality of those making the decisions and the need for compromise, given the varied interests and goals of different factions in a firm. According to BTF, a failure to achieve an aspirational level of performance triggers a problemistic or problem-driven search for a satisfactory rather than an optimal solution. As decision makers do not have complete knowledge of all alternative solutions and the payoffs from them, decision makers' coarse-grained expectations of the consequences of choosing a potential solution visible to them play a key role in decision making. Furthermore, political support for a solution is vital because the implementation of a mutually acceptable solution is essential for conflict avoidance in the firm. In addition, BTF accords attention to the slack available to a firm, because greater slack allows for the absorption of the costs and risk of switching to an acceptable alternative.

BTF thus identifies failure to achieve aspirations, problemistic search, managerial expectations, politics, and slack as key concepts having a bearing on decision making in firms, and thus on organizational behavior

7 On Dissatisfaction with Offshore-Outsourcing: Is ...

and outcomes. We draw on these core ideas of BTF to propose the model outlined in Fig. 7.1, in which the level of dissatisfaction with offshoring due to a failure to achieve performance goals predicts firms' inclination toward backsourcing as a satisfactory alternative. In keeping with BTF, the model suggests that managerial expectations about the technical difficulty of re-incorporating offshored operations into the firm's value chain and about the financial loss and service quality decline from discontinuing offshoring will moderate the extent to which offshoring dissatisfaction inclines firms to backsource. The model moreover holds that political backing for backsourcing and the amount of financial slack available for it will also moderate the effect of offshoring dissatisfaction on the inclination to backsource. We expand on these relationships next and present the study's formal hypotheses by weaving together BTF arguments with available accounts of offshoring and backsourcing.

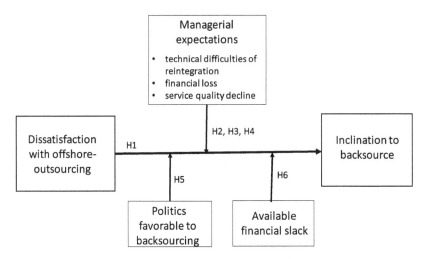

Fig. 7.1 Conceptual model and hypotheses

Hypotheses

Dissatisfaction with Offshoring and the Inclination to Backsource

By all accounts, the offshoring of parts of a firm's value chain is motivated by the hope that it will lead to performance improvements, because of either lower costs or higher quality of factor inputs such as expertise, knowledge, and skills by contracting with offshore providers (Carmel & Tjia, 2005; Manning et al., 2015; Oshri et al., 2015; Varadarajan, 2009). There is considerable evidence, however, that actual performance improvements vary greatly across firms that offshore (Lacity et al., 2016; Mani, 2006). Dibbern et al. (2008, p. 334) note in this regard that, *"while realized cost savings through offshore outsourcing may range between 20 and 50 percent, studies also show that in about 50 percent of the cases offshore projects fail to achieve cost savings or that costs actually increase"*. From BTF, one important implication of not achieving the aspired performance improvements is that it becomes more likely that a problemistic search will be triggered, such that decision makers begin to look for a way to raise performance (e.g., Desai, 2016; Greve, 2008). As backsourcing of offshored operations is an obvious alternative to offshoring that decision makers could choose (Whitten & Leidner, 2006; Whitten et al., 2010), all else being the same, an increase in dissatisfaction with offshoring should predict an increase in the inclination to backsource. Contrariwise, the more the satisfaction with offshoring, the lower should be the inclination to backsource. Formally:

> H1: The more the managerial dissatisfaction with offshoring, the greater the firm's inclination to backsource.

The Moderating Effect of Managerial Expectations

According to BTF, managerial expectations play a pivotal role in shaping decision making. In relation to backsourcing as a potential alternative to offshoring, managerial expectations about the difficulties of reintegrating offshored activities with home operations are likely to influence the effect of offshoring dissatisfaction on the inclination to backsource. It is instructive to note in this context that reintegration may entail a high or a low level of technical difficulties. While some of these difficulties may relate to the compatibility of systems, others may be linked to the inability of re-gaining expertise for executing backsourced activities in-house (Bhagwatwar et al., 2011; Ejodame & Oshri, 2017). Expertise may need to be re-developed, either because the client firm has lost domain and functional knowledge over the years as a result of the offshore-outsourcing or because attention in the client firm has shifted from a focus on technical aspects to the managing of relations with service providers (cf. Bhagwatwar et al., 2011; Cullen et al., 2005). Further, the level of difficulty may depend on the type of expertise needing re-development and the interdependencies between backsourced activities and a firm's other value-chain activities (Ejodame & Oshri, 2017). Vitally, in the absence of complete foresight as to whether it will be possible to fully resolve the technical difficulties down the road, decision making will depend on managerial expectations (Cyert & March, 1963; Gavetti et al., 2012). The more the belief that technical difficulties will thwart successful reintegration, the less likely it is that decision makers will regard backsourcing as a satisfactory solution, and thus the weaker the relationship between offshoring dissatisfaction and backsourcing inclination. Formally:

H2: The positive relationship between dissatisfaction with offshoring and the inclination to backsource will be weaker (stronger) when more (less) significant technical difficulties of reintegration are expected.

Managerial expectations concerning the financial and product/service quality consequences of discontinuing offshoring are also likely to have a bearing on firms' sourcing decisions, by either strengthening or weakening the influence of offshoring dissatisfaction on the inclination to backsource (Bromiley, 1991; Cyert & March, 1963). Regarding financial consequences in particular, backsourcing can involve financial loss in the form of non-capitalization of returns on capital and psychological investments in offshoring relationships (Whitten et al., 2010). Moreover, financial loss could result from the penalties and legal fees of terminating contracts. Bhagwatwar et al., (2011, p. 166) report, for example, that, *"JP Morgan paid IBM millions of dollars for terminating [their] outsourcing contract, which approximated to some 15% of the total cost. This approximated to JPMC spending somewhere between $14 million and $107 million in 2005 to bring its IT back in-house".* Similarly, Sainsbury incurred a substantial financial loss of U.S. $65 million due to early contract termination to allow backsourcing of IT systems and business processes (Bhagwatwar et al., 2011). As full information about financial losses due to the discontinuation of offshoring is normally not available to managers who are considering backsourcing, expectations about the level of financial loss will be key for decision making (Cyert & March, 1963). In line with earlier research (Bromiley, 1991; Shinkle, 2012), we surmise that the more financial loss is expected, the less that backsourcing is perceived as a satisfactory solution and, accordingly, the weaker the impact of offshoring dissatisfaction on the inclination to backsource. Formally:

H3: The positive relationship between dissatisfaction with offshoring and the inclination to backsource will be weaker (stronger) when more (less) financial loss is expected from discontinuing offshoring.

A similar causal logic can also be predicted in relation to the effect of expectations concerning decline in product/service quality. That backsourcing can entail a quality decline has been noted in the literature (e.g., Veltri et al., 2008). As an illustration, consider the case of backsourcing data-center operations—the backsourcing firm may simply not have the infrastructure and technical resources for using current platforms (e.g., cloud-based services) to ensure continuity in the speed and scale of service provision. JP Morgan's experience of backsourcing its data-center and helpdesk operations indicates that during the backsourcing process and, even up to one year later, the service quality was severely affected because people transferred back from the service provider, IBM, were *"not getting any work done [...] they did not want to commit to projects and they started slacking off"* (Bhagwatwar et al., 2011, p. 169). In addition, expectations of quality decline may be based on assessments of whether requisite knowledge is still there in the organization to enable provision of existing levels of quality; in the case of negative assessments, decision makers may wonder about the time that will be needed for quality improvement (see also, Ejodame & Oshri, 2017). In the light of the preceding and consistent with our earlier hypotheses, we postulate formally:

H4: The positive relationship between dissatisfaction with offshoring and the inclination to backsource will be weaker (stronger) when more (less) service quality decline is expected from discontinuing offshoring.

The Moderating Effect of Organizational Politics

As discussed, BTF underscores the significance of organizational politics for decision making. A firm consists of individuals and groups who may not always agree on means and ends, and so give and take are a hallmark of the decision-making process in firms. The decision choices that emerge from such a process are satisficing solutions for which there is broad approval in the firm (Cyert & March, 1963; Eisenhardt & Zbaracki, 1992). Consistent with this, several studies have noted the role that internal relations, the distribution of power, and politics play in outsourcing decisions (Bidwell, 2012; Chakrabarty & Whitten, 2011; Heiskanen et al., 2008). We expect political considerations to matter in the context of backsourcing decisions as well. Backsourcing can have serious implications for organizational structure and for work interdependencies. It can engender uncertainties and impact people's tasks, workflows and workload, and evaluation and rewards (Overby, 2005). As such, a decision to backsource can face considerable internal resistance. Indeed, companies such as Cable & Wireless, Sears, and Washington Mutual seem to have brought new people into key decision-making positions with a view to steer the firm toward a climate more open to backsourcing (Veltri et al., 2008). In the light of this, we anticipate that political support for backsourcing will affect the impact of offshoring dissatisfaction on the inclination to backsource. With less internal resistance to bringing back operations, and thus a political climate that is favorable to backsourcing, the impact of offshoring dissatisfaction on the inclination to backsource should be stronger. Formally:

H5: The positive relationship between dissatisfaction with offshoring and the inclination to backsource will be stronger (weaker) when there is a more (less) favorable political climate for backsourcing.

The Moderating Effect of Financial Slack

The notion of slack implies that there is more of a resource available to a firm than is strictly needed for carrying out operations. BTF emphasizes the important influence of financial slack on decision making in firms (Cyert & March, 1963; Singh, 1986). Since financial slack affords a buffer for the absorption of costs and risk taking, it is often suggested to be an encouragement to search for new solutions to problems (Iyer & Miller, 2008; Salge, 2011). In line with this, we expect greater financial slack to strengthen the effect of offshoring dissatisfaction on the inclination to backsource. As financial slack increases, backsourcing should become a more feasible alternative to offshoring, because slack gives greater wherewithal to deal with the numerous costs and expenses associated with backsourcing. For example, greater financial slack should make it easier for the firm to meet the substantial costs of terminating offshored operations and bringing them back in-house (Overby, 2005). Greater financial slack should also allow the easier absorption of costs of: the searching for, acquiring and setting-up physical assets for the backsourced activities; the re-hiring of experts; the training of personnel; and the additional workload on supporting functions, such as human resources, finance and accounting, and procurement. For example, Ejodame and Oshri (2017) describe how a bank earmarked a significant amount of money to hire and train personnel to facilitate backsourcing. In view of this discussion, we expect greater financial slack to strengthen the effect of dissatisfaction with offshoring on the inclination to backsource. Formally:

H6: The positive relationship between dissatisfaction with offshoring and the inclination to backsource will be stronger (weaker) when more (less) financial slack is available.

Methods

Sample and Data Collection

The sample for hypotheses testing was drawn from firms in the U.S.A. and the U.K. (the two largest markets worldwide in terms of spending on offshored operations). For the sake of generalizability of findings, we targeted firms in varied business sectors, including financial services, distribution and logistics, and manufacturing. Using panel data on consumers of offshore services, representatives of 36,038 firms in the U.S.A. and 13,804 firms in the U.K. were invited to complete a Web-based survey. Following the "key informant" approach to data collection, the invited representatives were the firms' senior-most executives (e.g., Goo et al., 2008). We used a set of screening questions to ensure that respondents were: (i) executives (i.e., CEOs, CIOs, CTOs, or COOs) who took offshoring and backsourcing decisions, (ii) had two or more years of offshoring experience in their firm, and (iii) whose firms were paying U.S. $50,000 or more annually to offshore service provider(s). Of the 1192 representatives who accepted our invitation, 849 were screened out. We received usable, fully completed responses from 196 invitees, implying a response rate of 16% among those who expressed interest in the survey. No evidence of non-response bias was found when comparing the industry affiliation of responding and non-responding firms. Further, a comparison of early and late respondents (i.e., those responding in the last three days of the one-week period for which the survey was open) did not reveal any significant difference with respect to any of the study's variables. Table 7.1 presents descriptive information about the sample.

To avoid bias in the measurement of variables, we followed closely the guidelines suggested for Web-based surveys (Dillman, 2000). As a precaution against bias on account of confusion, all questions and items

Table 7.1 Sample information

Descriptor		Frequency	Percentage
Country	U.S.A	99	51
	U.K	97	49
Total assets	Up to $ 50 million	37	18.8
	$ 50 million to $ 150 million	73	37.2
	More than $ 150 million	86	44.8
Business sector	Commercial	23	11.7
	Distribution & logistics	30	15.3
	Electronics	22	11.2
	Energy	15	7.6
	Financial services & insurance	39	19.8
	Manufacturing	30	15.3
	Media & telecommunications	20	10.2
	Pharmaceutical	17	8.6
Offshore-outsourced Activities (not mutually exclusive)	Business processes (customer related, engineering, finance & accounting, human resources, procurement, R&D)	277	
	IT development & maintenance (application development, application maintenance, data center, infrastructure)	333	

were worded unambiguously, and response options were clearly explained and presented. Moreover, a "don't know" response category was always included to avert inaccurate responses should a respondent not be able to answer a particular question or item. Furthermore, with a view to encourage factual answers, respondents were assured confidentiality and we underlined that the survey was linked to a scientific research project. Despite the steps we took, data from single informants can nevertheless contain common method bias or variance. To verify that this was not the case, we employed Harman's one-factor test (Podsakoff & Organ, 1986). As four factors having an eigenvalue of more than unity were necessary to account for the variance in the data, common method bias did not seem to be a problem in our dataset.

Measurement of Variables

The study's explanatory, moderating and dependent variables were measured using Likert-type items with seven-point response formats. All items were anchored at "strongly disagree" and "strongly agree" (see, e.g., Nunnally & Bernstein, 1994).

The study's explanatory variable, *dissatisfaction with offshoring*, was measured using three items: (i) offshore-outsourcing has been a disappointment for us; (ii) the net benefits from offshore-outsourcing have been minimal; (iii) we are satisfied with the performance levels of offshore-outsourced activities (reverse scored). Respondents were asked to keep in mind their firm's experience with offshoring in the last three years when rating the items. Cronbach's reliability coefficient for the three-item instrument was 0.78.

The five moderating variables were operationalized using single-item instruments. Specifically, we measured (i) *expected technical difficulties of reintegration* with the item "we would experience significant technical difficulties in reintegrating offshore-outsourced operations with in-house activities". To measure (ii) *expected financial loss* due to the discontinuation of existing offshore contracts, the item we used was "we would suffer considerable financial loss if contracts with offshore service providers were to be terminated". Further, to measure (iii) *expected service quality decline* should contracts with offshore service providers be terminated, we used the item "should we bring back offshore-outsourced operations, we can expect a decline in the quality of our product/service". As regards the measurement of (iv) *political climate favorable to backsourcing*, we employed the item "the political climate in our company is unfavorable to bringing back offshore-outsourced operations" (reverse scored). Lastly, for measuring (v) *available financial slack*, we relied on the item "we have enough financial slack in the company to facilitate reintegration of offshore-outsourced operations with in-house activities".

For measuring the study's dependent variable, *inclination to backsource*, we employed the following three items: (i) we are seriously considering bringing back offshore-outsourced activities; (ii) we are firm in our commitment to offshore-outsourcing (reverse scored); (iii) we are thinking of sourcing more from our offshore service providers (reverse scored). Respondents were asked to keep in mind their intentions regarding offshoring in the coming three years when rating the items. Cronbach's reliability coefficient for the three-item instrument was 0.76.

In addition to the above, we included several control variables in our analysis that may potentially affect the inclination to backsource. To control for the effect of the firms' home country on backsourcing, we included a dummy variable for firms located in the U.S.A.; firms in the U.K. served as the reference category. We similarly included dummy variables to control for industry effects on backsourcing. At the firm level, we controlled for firm size as indicated by firms' total assets. We additionally controlled for the global sales revenue of firms, and for firms' disbursements to offshore service providers. Moreover, based on respondents' "yes" or "no" answers to the question whether their company had brought back any offshored activity during the last three years, we included a dummy variable to control for firms' prior backsourcing experience (Gefen et al., 2008). Lastly, because the decision makers' experience may have a bearing on the inclination to backsource, we also controlled for the length of positional tenure of respondents.

Analysis and Results

We examined our data with SPSS Amos 22 software. We first did a confirmatory factor analysis (CFA) to estimate a measurement model of relationships between the study's constructs and the items used for measuring the constructs; we then estimated a structural equation model of cause-effect linkages. With regard to the former, we used maximum likelihood estimation to estimate parameters. The CFA results indicated a measurement model with a good fit ($\chi^2 = 44.30$, d.f. $= 28$, $p = 0.03$, CFI $= 0.98$, TLI $= 0.96$, RMSEA $= 0.05$). Furthermore, the composite reliability (CR) and the average variance extracted (AVE) for construct measures were respectively above 0.80 and 0.50. Whereas these CR and AVE values can be taken to indicate convergent validity (Fornell & Larcker, 1981), we also examined the size and the significance of the factor loadings of items on the underlying constructs. All factor loadings were above the recommended threshold of 0.50 (the lowest and the highest being respectively 0.63 and 0.82) and all were statistically significant at the one percent level, indicating convergent validity. Furthermore, as correlation coefficients for the construct measures were less than the square root of the AVE for the measures, the results also indicate discriminant validity. Taken together, the estimation results suggest that one can have confidence in the measurement properties of the instruments used to operationalize the study's constructs.

Table 7.2 shows the descriptive statistics and correlations between the study's variables. For estimating the structural equation model, we again used maximum likelihood estimation. The standardized values of the study's main and moderating variables were used to build interaction terms for hypotheses testing (Dawson, 2014). The results showed a structural model with an acceptable fit ($\chi^2 = 81.37$, d.f. $= 49$, $p = 0.00$, CFI $= 0.97$, TLI $= 0.91$, RMSEA $= 0.06$). Table 7.3 presents the parameter estimates, standard errors (S.E.), and the significance levels. As regards the study's control variables, Table 7.3 reveals several statistically significant relationships. It would appear that bigger firms (by assets) display a greater inclination to backsource offshored activities. On the other hand, firms with a larger sales revenue show a lesser inclination to backsource. Also, prior backsourcing experience has a negative effect on the inclination to backsource, plausibly due to the challenges and difficulties experienced previously when reintegrating offshored activities with in-house operations. Interestingly, decision makers' length of tenure has a negative influence on the inclination to backsource, indicating that decision makers with longer tenure are more likely to continue to offshore. And importantly, in support of Hypothesis 1, dissatisfaction with offshoring has a strong positive effect on the inclination to backsource ($\beta = 0.57$, $p < 0.001$).

As regards the hypothesized moderation effects, Table 7.3 indicates that, of the five interaction terms constructed to capture these effects,

Table 7.2 Descriptive statistics and correlations

Variable	Mean	SD	1	2	3	4	5	6	7	8	9	10	11	12	13
1. Firm location	0.51	0.50	1.00												
2. Firm size (assets)	6.69	1.84	−0.05	1.00											
3. Firm global revenue	6.37	2.35	0.01	0.79	1.00										
4. Offshored amount	6.32	1.86	0.05	0.50	0.51	1.00									
5. Backsourcing experience	0.42	0.49	−0.07	−0.03	−0.10	−0.02	1.00								
6. Tenure length	6.03	1.52	0.05	0.18	0.15	0.20	−0.00	1.00							
7. Dissatisfaction with offshoring	3.33	1.12	−0.23	0.14	0.07	0.09	0.01	−0.14	1.00						
8. Expec. tech. difficulties reintegration	4.38	1.42	0.23	−0.11	0.06	0.04	−0.18	0.05	−0.48	1.00					
9. Politics favorable to backsourcing	3.38	1.35	−0.24	0.05	−0.01	0.02	0.18	0.02	0.23	−0.41	1.00				
10. Available financial slack	4.73	1.43	0.24	0.05	0.06	0.01	0.18	0.03	0.23	0.34	−0.55	1.00			
11. Expec. financial loss	3.73	1.53	−0.18	0.03	−0.05	0.02	0.26	−0.13	0.36	−0.35	0.34	−0.43	1.00		
12. Expec. service quality decline	4.49	1.37	0.10	−0.16	−0.06	0.08	−0.07	0.07	0.61	0.50	0.11	0.13	−0.25	1.00	
13. Inclination to backsource	3.03	1.05	−0.24	0.08	0.06	0.16	−0.11	−0.17	0.62	−0.50	0.17	−0.26	0.19	−0.48	1.00

$N = 196$; correlation coefficients above 0.14 in absolute value are significant at the 5% level and those above 0.18 in absolute value are significant at the 1% level

Table 7.3 Structural equation model (SEM) results for inclination to backsource

Path		Estimate	S.E
Controls			
Firm location	→Inclination to backsource	−0.16	0.11
Firm size (assets)	→Inclination to backsource	0.11	0.05*
Firm global revenue	→Inclination to backsource	−0.10	0.04*
Offshored amount	→Inclination to backsource	−0.03	0.03
Backsourcing experience	→Inclination to backsource	−0.21	0.11*
Tenure length	→Inclination to backsource	−0.10	0.04**
Main effects			
Dissatisfaction with offshoring (DISO) [H 1]	→Inclination to backsource	0.57	0.08***
Expected technical difficulties of reintegration	→Inclination to backsource	−0.25	0.07***
Expected financial loss	→Inclination to backsource	−0.23	0.06***
Expected service quality decline	→Inclination to backsource	−0.02	0.07
Politics favorable to backsourcing	→Inclination to backsource	0.17	0.07*
Available financial slack	→Inclination to backsource	−0.20	0.07*
Moderation effects			
DISO * expec. tech. difficulties reintegration [H 2]	→Inclination to backsource	−0.08	0.06
DISO * expec. financial loss [H 3]	→Inclination to backsource	−0.19	0.06***
DISO * expec. service quality decline [H 4]	→Inclination to backsource	−0.14	0.06*
DISO * politics favorable to backsourcing [H 5]	→Inclination to backsource	0.14	0.07*
DISO * available financial slack [H 6]	→Inclination to backsource	−0.18	0.07*

$N = 196$; * $p \leq 0.05$; ** $p \leq 0.01$; *** $p \leq 0.001$

four are statistically significant. The significant linkages are shown visually in Fig. 7.2–7.5 to aid interpretation. Starting with the first moderation effect summarized in Hypothesis 2, there is no support for the idea that the expected level of technical reintegration difficulties will moderate the effect of offshoring dissatisfaction on the inclination to backsource. It should be noted though that the variable does have a significant direct impact on the inclination to backsource, such that the latter decreases as the former increases ($\beta = -0.25$, $p < 0.001$). Further, in support of Hypothesis 3, expected financial loss due to termination of offshore contracts moderates the effect of offshoring dissatisfaction ($\beta = -0.19$, $p < 0.001$); as captured in Fig. 7.2, there is lesser inclination to backsource in the event of higher expected financial loss. Further, Hypothesis 4 finds support as well. The relevant interaction term is negative ($-\beta = 0.14$, $p < 0.05$) and, as illustrated in Fig. 7.3, with growing levels of offshoring dissatisfaction, there is lesser inclination to backsource when there are higher levels of expected service quality decline. Further, Hypothesis 5 is also supported—political climate has a significant moderation effect ($\beta = 0.14$, $p < 0.05$). As shown in Fig. 7.4, as offshoring dissatisfaction increases, there is greater inclination to backsource if the political climate is more in favor of backsourcing. Surprisingly, Hypothesis 6 does not find support—the negative interaction term ($\beta = -0.18$, $p < 0.05$) in Table 7.3 and the plot in Fig. 7.5 indicate that as offshoring dissatisfaction increases, there is a lesser inclination to backsource when there is more financial slack. We discuss this unexpected result in the next section.

Discussion

Building on the core tenet of BTF that decision making in firms is guided by performance aspirations, a problemistic search, managerial expectations, politics, and slack availability, we propose a model suggesting that dissatisfaction on account of non-attainment of offshoring aspirations will fuel the inclination to backsource by instigating a problemistic search for a satisfactory alternative strategy. The model moreover suggests that the effect of offshoring dissatisfaction on the inclination to backsource

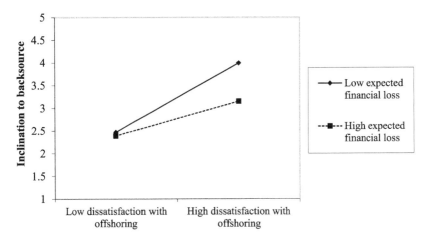

Fig. 7.2 Moderation effect of expected financial loss

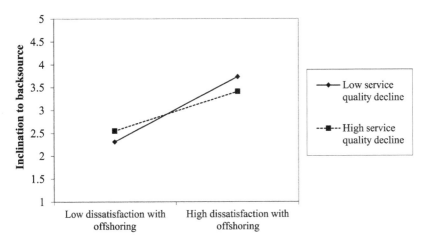

Fig. 7.3 Moderation effect of expected service quality decline

will be conditioned by managerial expectations regarding technical challenges, financial loss, and quality decline following backsourcing, as well as by internal political support and financial slack for backsourcing.

Analysis of data from firms located in diverse industries in the U.S.A. and U.K. provides partial support for the model. As theorized, unsatisfactory offshoring experience appears to have a strong positive effect

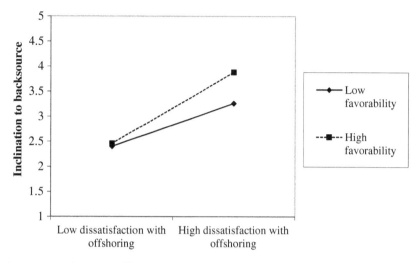

Fig. 7.4 Moderation effect of political climate favorable to backsourcing

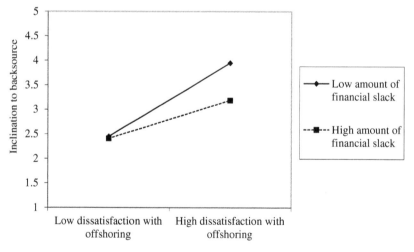

Fig. 7.5 Moderation effect of available financial slack

on the future inclination to backsource, a result wholly consistent with BTF's assertion that a failure to achieve performance aspirations triggers decision makers with bounded rationality to look for a satisfactory alternative strategy to improve performance (Cyert & March, 1963; Tyler & Caner, 2016). The result suggests the surge in backsourcing in recent years to be reflective of problem-driven search by managers, rather than rational planning based on the systematic evaluation of long-term threats and opportunities connected to different sourcing alternatives, such as greater investment in current offshoring relationships, switching vendors, or moving to a new offshore location (cf. Bhagwatwar et al., 2011; Veltri et al., 2008). Furthermore, as theorized, managerial expectations seem an important moderator of the effect of offshoring dissatisfaction on the inclination to backsource, which is in line with BTF's argument that limits to human rationality imply that the decision makers' preferred solution to a problem is based on subjective perceptions or interpretations of the environment rather than objective cost–benefit analysis.

Interestingly, while the level of expected difficulty of reintegrating offshored operations with those in-house was found to be inversely related to the inclination to backsource, it did not attenuate the positive relation between offshoring dissatisfaction and the inclination to backsource. The negative direct affect aligns with the identification of technical reintegration challenges as a major issue for firms engaged in backsourcing in case-study research (Bhagwatwar et al., 2011; Ejodame & Oshri, 2017). As theorized, we found that higher levels of expected financial loss and quality decline reduced the effect of offshoring dissatisfaction on the inclination to backsource. While at one level these results underscore the significance of financial costs and product/service quality in sourcing decisions, at another level they complement earlier work that has pointed to a link between factual costs and quality and the decision to continue offshoring (cf. Veltri et al., 2008; Whitten & Leidner, 2006). It would thus seem that not only actual investments to set up offshoring arrangements are relevant, but also decision makers' cost and quality expectations should there be a switch in sourcing strategy from offshoring to backsourcing. Thus, as emphasized by BTF, managerial expectations seem salient to the backsourcing decision (e.g., Gavetti et al., 2012).

We also found that political backing for backsourcing strengthens the effect of dissatisfaction with offshoring on the inclination to backsource. BTF deems politics to be important in the identification of a satisfactory solution, in that a course of action which enjoys broad support in the firm should keep conflict at bay, the potential for which is rife in companies (Cyert & March, 1963; Gaba & Joseph, 2013). As the received view of backsourcing directs attention primarily to the economic logic of costs and benefits as explanation for why firms do or do not backsource, the effect of politics we report brings to the literature a new element centering on subgroup processes and dealings. As organizational structure, resource allocation, distribution of power, and social relations more generally are likely to undergo change in the event of backsourcing (e.g., Overby, 2005), politics is a significant factor in sourcing decisions that should not be overlooked. Surprisingly, while our prediction was that financial slack would amplify the effect of dissatisfaction with offshoring by providing a buffer to facilitate backsourcing (Cyert & March, 1963; Salge, 2011), we found the opposite. As explanation, slack may engender a complacent mode of thinking, working against a sense of urgency to look for a sourcing alternative (cf. Desai, 2016). Relatedly, managers may believe that slack will allow them to resolve offshoring dissatisfaction through additional investments—for example, by implementing more controls (e.g., Kang et al., 2012).

On the whole, as compared to existing studies that limit attention to rational cost and quality considerations when discussing sourcing decisions, we contribute a more comprehensive model centered on offshoring firms' inclination to backsource. Drawing on BTF, the model goes beyond earlier accounts and complements them by bringing to light the significance of decision makers' expectations or beliefs about payoffs from a change in sourcing strategy. In doing so, the model captures an important point that is rarely touched upon in the literature, namely that managerial perceptions or cognitive biases could be influential in affecting the choice between sourcing alternatives. This is the case because expectations are likely to be shaped by subjective factors such as personality (e.g., optimism and sense of self-efficacy) and experiences (e.g., past successes and failures), and not just by objective facts and figures. The model also captures another under-appreciated point, namely that like other strategic (change) decisions (e.g., Desai, 2016; Gaba & Joseph, 2013), sourcing decisions are not arrived at in an a-contextual vacuum. Decision makers and decision making in companies are immersed in multi-level political and social relations and dynamics, and therefore sourcing decisions can be expected to embody this reality. By contributing a more comprehensive model, we push forward research on sourcing decisions and set the ground for further inquiry and dialogue to advance understanding.

At a practical level, for disappointed decision makers who must choose between continuation of offshoring and backsourcing, the article isolates the set of factors needing careful consideration for a sound decision. A reversal from offshoring to backsourcing implies a radical change in strategy, and the implementation of the strategy is likely to be a complex technical and social process that has important economic consequences (see, e.g., Kotlarsky & Bognar, 2012). Those in charge would do well to consider whether dissatisfaction with offshoring can be resolved—for example, through the re-setting of performance targets, re-negotiation of contracts, or dispute resolution and relationship building (see e.g., Herath & Kishore, 2009; Oshri et al., 2015). As regards the backsourcing option, decision makers could seek to supplement gut feelings and perceptions of technical, quality, and financial ramifications with fine-tuned assessments that draw on all the information and expertise that can be marshaled by engaging those who will be involved with and affected by backsourcing (cf. Veltri et al., 2008). A detailed feasibility study could, for example, provide more definitive insight into the extent of quality decline to be expected and the time needed to re-build quality to existing levels. In addition, the chapter points to the importance of managing internal politics. If intuition and data suggest backsourcing to be the better alternative, a more favorable climate for backsourcing should result if decision makers articulate a narrative and plan that anticipate and address credibly the concerns of those who will be affected. In this respect, decision makers need to think about how best to earmark available financial slack for absorbing the costs of backsourcing and alleviating concern.

Conclusion

Although backsourcing by firms is getting increasing attention in academic circles and the professional media, it is the least understood sourcing decision in the sourcing literature. One reason for this is that firms usually refrain from disclosing information about backsourcing to avoid jeopardizing relationships with suppliers and to avoid the admission of failure vis-à-vis their offshoring decisions and investments. Against this backdrop, while this research provides new insight into why firms that are dissatisfied with offshoring tend to differ with respect to backsourcing, the data we obtained from decision makers could not be supplemented with secondary data for greater confidence in the study's results. Future research that can overcome this limitation of the present study would therefore be of great value.

In addition to the above, this study only examined firms' inclination to backsource. To build a fuller understanding, however, it would be very useful to also examine the actual backsourcing of activities in future work. Furthermore, it is conceivable that firms dissatisfied with offshoring might attempt to deal with the situation by searching for and entering into contracts with new offshore service providers. This follows from our unexpected finding that firms with more financial slack are less inclined to backsource, despite their dissatisfaction with offshoring. Plausibly, given the challenges backsourcing entails, resource-rich firms may prefer to find new service providers rather than to backsource. Future work that investigates this would further improve our understanding.

This study's data was limited to firms located in the U.S.A. and in the U.K. While these two countries are the largest consumers of offshore-outsourcing services in the world, other countries and regions are beginning to spend more on offshoring—a case in point are the Nordic countries in Europe. In light of this, it would be useful to study the backsourcing decisions of firms that are located in other countries/regions but have accumulated significant offshoring experience. Clearly, much more research is needed to develop a better understanding of the backsourcing phenomenon, how it varies around the globe, and what factors allow firms to backsource successfully. In particular, we did not address the impact of more recent accelerating automation and an increasingly unpredictable, dynamic risky geo-political climate on propensity to backsource from offshore-outsourcing decisions. We hope that this inquiry will stimulate further work on backsourcing in today's ever-changing global business environment.

References

Argote, L., & Greve, H. R. (2007). A Behavioral Theory of the Firm—40 Years and Counting: Introduction and Impact. *Organization Science, 18*(3), 337–349.

Aron, R., & Singh, J. V. (2005). Getting Offshoring Right. *Harvard Business Review, 83*(12), 135–143.

Aubert, B. A., Rivard, S., & Patry, M. (1996). A Transaction Cost Approach to Outsourcing Behavior: Some Empirical Evidence. *Information & Management, 30*(2), 51–64.

Bhagwatwar, A., Hackney, R., & Desouza, K. C. (2011). Considerations for Information Systems "Backsourcing": A Framework for Knowledge Re-integration. *Information Systems Management, 28*, 165–173.

Bidwell, M. J. (2012). Politics and Firm Boundaries: How Organizational Structure, Group Interests, and Resources Affect Outsourcing. *Organization Science, 23*(6), 1622–1642.

Bromiley, P. (1991). Testing a Causal Model of Corporate Risk Taking and Performance. *Academy Management Journal, 34*(1), 37–59.

Carmel, E., & Tjia, P. (2005). *Offshoring Information Technology*. Cambridge University Press.

Chakrabarty, S., & Whitten, D. (2011). The Sidelining of Top IT Executives in the Governance of Outsourcing: Antecedents, Power Struggles, and Consequences. *IEEE Transactions on Engineering Management, 58*(4), 799–814.

Cullen, S., Seddon, P., & Willcocks, L. (2005). Managing Outsourcing: The Lifecycle Imperative. *MIS Quarterly Executive, 4*(1), 229–246.

Cyert, R. M., & March, J. G. (1963). *A Behavioral Theory of the Firm*. Prentice Hall.

Dawson, J. F. (2014). Moderation in Management Research: What, Why, When, and How. *Journal of Business and Psychology, 29*(1), 1–19.

Dedrick, J., Carmel, E., & Kraemer, K. L. (2011). A Dynamic Model of Offshore Software Development. *Journal of Information Technology, 26*, 1–15.

Desai, V. M. (2016). The Behavioral Theory of the (Governed) Firm: Corporate Board Influences on Organizations' Responses to Performance Shortfalls. *Academy of Management Journal, 59*(3), 860–879.

Dibbern, J., Chin, W., & Heinzl, A. (2012). Systemic Determinants of the Information Systems Outsourcing Decision: A Comparative Study of German and United States firms. *Journal of the Association for Information Systems, 13*(6), 466–497.

Dibbern, J., Goles, T., Hirschheim, R., & Jayatilaka, B. (2004). Information Systems Outsourcing: A Survey and Analysis of the Literature. *DATA BASE, 35*(4), 6–102.

Dibbern, J., Winkler, J., & Heinzl, A. (2008). Explaining Variations in Client Extra Costs Between Software Projects Offshored to India. *MIS Quarterly, 32*(2), 333–366.

Dillman, D. A. (2000). *Mail and Internet Surveys*. Wiley.

DiRomualdo, A., & Gurbaxani, V. (1998). Strategic Intent for IT Outsourcing. *Sloan Management Review, 39*(4), 67.

Doh, J. P., Bunyaratavej, K., & Hahn, E. (2009). Separable But Not Equal: The Location Determinants of Discrete Services Offshoring Activities. *Journal of International Business Studies, 40*, 926–943.

Eisenhardt, K. M., & Zbaracki, M. J. (1992). Strategic Decision Making. *Strategic Management Journal, 13*(2), 17–37.

Ejodame, K., & Oshri, I. (2017). Understanding Knowledge Re-integration in Backsourcing. *Journal of Information Technology, 33*(2), 136–150.

Farrell, D. (2006). Smarter Offshoring. *Harvard Business Review*, 85–92.

Fornell, C., & Larcker, D. F. (1981). Evaluating Structural Equation Models with Unobservable Variables and Measurement Error. *Journal of Marketing Research, 18*(1), 39–50.

Gaba, V., & Joseph, J. (2013). Corporate Structure and Performance Feedback: Aspirations and Adaptation in M-form Firms. *Organization Science, 24*, 1102–1119.

Gavetti, G., Greve, H. R., Levinthal, D. A., & Ocasio, W. (2012). The Behavioral Theory of the Firm: Assessment and Prospects. *The Academy of Management Annals, 6*(1), 1–40.

Gefen, D., Wyss, S., & Lichtenstein, Y. (2008). Business Familiarity as Risk Mitigation in Software Development Outsourcing Contracts. *MIS Quarterly, 32*(3), 531–551.

Goo, J., Huang, C. D., & Hart, P. (2008). A Path to Successful IT Outsourcing: Interaction Between Service-Level Agreements and Commitment. *Decision Sciences, 39*(3), 469–506.

Gray, J. V., Skowronski, K., Esenduran, G., & Rungtusanatham, J. M. M. (2013). The Reshoring Phenomenon: What Supply Chain Academics Ought to Know and Should Do. *Journal of Supply Chain Management, 49*(2), 27–33.

Greve, H. R. (2008). A Behavioral Theory of Firm Growth: Sequential Attention to Size and Performance Goals. *Academy of Management Journal, 51*(3), 476–494.

Heiskanen, A., Newman, M., & Eklin, M. (2008). Control, Trust, Power, and the Dynamics of Information System Outsourcing Relationships: A Process Study of Contractual Software Development. *The Journal of Strategic Information Systems, 17*(4), 268–286.

Herath, T., & Kishore, R. (2009). Offshore Outsourcing: Risks, Challenges, and Potential Solutions. *Information Systems Management, 26*(4), 312–326.

Hirschheim, R., & Lacity, M. C. (2000). The Myths and Realities of Information Technology Insourcing. *Communications of the ACM, 43*(2), 99–107.

Hirschheim, R. A., & Lacity, M. C. (1998). *Reducing Information Systems Costs through Insourcing: Experiences from the Field.* Paper presented at the 31st Annual Hawaii International Conference on System Sciences, Hawaii.

Iyer, D. N., & Miller, K. D. (2008). Performance Feedback, Slack, and the Timing of Acquisitions. *Academy of Management Journal, 51*(4), 808–822.

Kang, M., Wu, X., Hong, P., & Park, Y. (2012). Aligning Organizational Control Practices with Competitive Outsourcing Performance. *Journal of Business Research, 65*(8), 1195–1201.

Kotlarsky, J., & Bognar, L. (2012). Understanding the Process of Backsourcing: Two Cases of Process and Product Backsourcing in Europe. *Journal of Information Technology Teaching Cases, 2,* 79–86.

Lacity, M. C., Khan, S. A., & Yan, A. (2016). Review of the Empirical Business Process Sourcing Literature: An Update and Future Directions. *Journal of Information Technology, 31,* 269–328.

Lewin, A. Y., Massini, S., & Peeters, C. (2009). Why are Companies Offshoring Innovation? The Emerging Global Race for Talent. *Journal of International Business Studies, 40,* 901–925.

Mani, D. (2006). Successful Business Process Outsourcing. *Sloan Management Review, 47*(2), 5–6.

Manning, S., Larsen, M. M., & Bharati, P. (2015). Global Delivery Models: The Role of Talent, Speed and Time Zones in the Global Outsourcing Industry. *Journal of International Business Studies, 46*(7), 850–877.

Massini, S., Perm-Ajchariyawong, N., & Lewin, A. Y. (2010). Role of Corporate-Wide Offshoring Strategy on Offshoring Drivers, Risks, and Performance. *Industry and Innovation, 17*(4), 337–371.

Metters, R. (2008). A Typology of Offshoring and Outsourcing in Electronically Transmitted Services. *Journal of Operations Management, 26*, 198–211.

Mudambi, R., & Venzin, M. (2010). The Strategic Nexus of Offshoring and Outsourcing Decisions. *Journal of Management Studies, 47*(8), 1510–1533.

Mudambi, S. M., & Tallman, S. (2010). Make, Buy or Ally? Theoretical Perspectives on Knowledge Process Outsourcing Through Alliances. *Journal of Management Studies, 47*(8), 1434–1456.

Musteen, M. (2016). Behavioral Factors in Offshoring Decisions: A Qualitative Analysis. *Journal of Business Research, 69*, 3439–3446.

Nunnally, J. C., & Bernstein, I. H. (1994). *Psychometric Theory* (3rd ed.). McGraw Hill.

Oshri, I., Kotlarsky, J., & Willcocks, L. P. (2015). *The Handbook of Global Outsourcing and Offshoring* (3rd ed.). Macmillan.

Oshri, I., Kotlarsky, J., & Willcocks, L. P. (2023). *The Handbook of Global Outsourcing and Offshoring* (4th ed.). Macmillan.

Overby, S. (2005). Backsourcing Pain. *CIO Magazine, 18*(22), 64–72.

Podsakoff, P. M., & Organ, D. W. (1986). Self-reports in Organizational Research: Problems and Prospects. *Journal of Management, 12*(4), 531–544.

Salge, T. O. (2011). A Behavioral Model of Innovative Search: Evidence from Public Hospital Services. *Journal of Public Administration Research & Theory, 21*(1), 181–210.

Shinkle, G. A. (2012). Organizational Aspirations, Reference Points, and Goals: Building on the Past and Aiming for the Future. *Journal of Management, 38*(1), 415–455.

Singh, J. V. (1986). Performance, Slack, and Risk Taking in Organizational Decision Making. *Academy of Management Journal, 29*(3), 562–585.

Tanriverdi, H., Konana, P., & Ge, L. (2007). The Choice of Sourcing Mechanisms for Business Processes. *Information Systems Research, 18*(3), 280–299.

Tyler, B. B., & Caner, T. (2016). New Product Introductions Below Aspirations, Slack and R&D Alliances: A Behavioral Perspective. *Strategic Management Journal, 37*, 896–910.

Varadarajan, R. (2009). Outsourcing: Think more Expansively. *Journal of Business Research, 62*(11), 1165–1172.

Veltri, N. F., Saunders, C., & Kavan, C. B. (2008). Information Systems Backsourcing: Correcting Problems and Responding to Opportunities. *California Management Review, 51*(1), 83–102.

Vivek, S. D., Banwet, D. K., & Shankar, R. (2008). Analysis of Interactions Among Core, Transaction and Relationship-Specific Investments: The Case of Offshoring. *Journal of Operations Management, 26*, 180–197.

Volkoff, O., Strong, D. M., & Elmes, M. B. (2005). Understanding Enterprise Systems-Enabled Integration. *European Journal of Information Systems, 1*(42), 110–120.

Whitten, D., Chakrabarty, S., & Wakefield, R. (2010). The Strategic Choice to Continue Outsourcing, Switch Vendors, or Backsource: Do Switching Costs Matter? *Information & Management, 47*, 167–175.

Whitten, D., & Leidner, D. (2006). Bringing IT Back: An Analysis of the Decision to Backsource or Switch Vendors. *Decision Sciences, 37*(4), 605–621.

8

Status Differentials and Framing in the Implementation of Task Migration Strategies

Jade Brooks, M. N. Ravishankar, and Ilan Oshri

Introduction

Information Systems (IS) research has taken significant interest in the migration of tasks across firm and national boundaries. In particular, the IS sourcing literature has explored the migration of IT-enabled tasks to both internal support units (insourcing) and external providers (outsourcing) in different parts of the world (Gospel & Sako, 2010; Levina & Vaast, 2008; Mani et al., 2014). Strategic-level decisions around the migration of non-core tasks to support units are typically arrived at through compelling predictions of future cost savings and

---

Chapter 8 is a revised and updated version of Brooks, J., Ravishankar, M. N., & Oshri, I. (2021). Status Differentials and Framing in the Implementation of IT-enabled Task Migration Strategies. *Information Systems Journal, 32*(2), 414–439.

J. Brooks · I. Oshri (✉)
University of Auckland, Auckland, New Zealand
e-mail: ilan.oshri@auckland.ac.nz

M. N. Ravishankar
Loughborough University, Loughborough, UK

promise of efficiencies and flexibility (Lacity et al., 2016; Tiwana & Keil, 2007).

However, as research has shown, a strategic imperative call to migrate IT-enabled tasks does not always translate into smooth action. Despite the presence of strict contracts, rules and procedures, 'grey areas' and 'seam issues' can emerge at the interface of the 'client' business unit and the 'supplier' support unit, leading to ambiguities around what task migration responsibilities are 'in' and 'out' of scope (Gospel & Sako, 2010 p. 1378). Thus, a strategic organizational mandate to migrate IT-enabled tasks cannot be conflated with the actual execution of strategy since a high-level consensus does not always specify in detail the precise sequencing and pacing of task migration (i.e., when, what, how and how much). In the absence of clear and specific guidelines, situated actors are left to negotiate how the broad strategic mandate for task migration should be implemented in practice—a situation that opens spaces for status-led enactments of power (Ravishankar, 2015).

Through an in-depth qualitative case study of task migration in a distributed finance function, this chapter illuminates the unfolding of frame disputes between business units and a support unit, following a high-level strategic decision to migrate tasks. It addresses two questions: (1) How do high-status business units frame their task migration actions? and (2) How does a low-status support unit frame and account for the actions of the high-status business units? The paper critically examines the perspective of both high-status business units from where tasks are migrated and the low-status subsidiary unit that performs the migrated tasks. The findings show how high-status business units frame their own actions as a case of protecting, offering support and monitoring the migrated tasks while the low-status support unit frames the same set of actions as a sign of resistance, interference and hypercriticism. Theoretically, we draw on the notion of framing (Goffman, 1974), which helps explain the diverse, retrospective and often conflicting interpretations of actors occupying different status positions in an official hierarchy. The literature on framing also helps better understand how contrasting status-led enactments of power may lead to frequent disputes and hinder effective implementation of strategy in distributed work environments (Ravishankar, 2015).

The chapter contributes to a better understanding of IT-enabled task migration trajectories in globally distributed settings and illustrates high-status units' exercise of power in steering the implementation of strategy. It sheds new light on how status differentials influence dispute resolutions in task migration scenarios and suggests that low-status entities take reflexive account of their weaker power position in interpreting the actions of high-status entities. Thus, the chapter answers calls in IS research to unpack the dynamics of power and to elucidate the role of status in unit-level interactions (e.g., Marabelli & Galliers, 2017; Pinjani & Palvia, 2013). It also contributes to recent research on framing (e.g., Leonardi, 2011; Sandeep & Ravishankar, 2015; Su, 2015) and shows how low-status entities seek to avoid conflict by offering a set of softer attributions for the actions of high-status counterparts. From a practitioner perspective, the chapter's findings suggest that status differentials are an important power dynamic which needs to be accounted for when designing, as well as operationalizing IT-enabled task migration strategies in distributed work environments.

The chapter is structured as follows. First, we review the literature on framing and its potential to explicate how actors make sense of one-another's actions. We then describe the relevance and applicability of the notion of framing and frame disputes to task migration relationships. Next, we present our research methods and the findings from a qualitative case study of task migration from high-status business units to a low-status unit support in a globally distributed finance function. The in-depth discussion and conclusion sections offer implications for theory and practice.

Theoretical Background

Frames are socio-cognitive structures that create and attach meaning to objects, people and events (Cornelissen & Werner, 2014; Goffman, 1974). Frames, like windowpanes, offer a unique perspective of the world. In his seminal work Frame Analysis, Goffman (1974) suggests that perspectives are influenced by things "seen" in the past, which shape values and understandings, and which influence how actors continue to construct and find meanings in the world around them. An important part of the framing process involves actively figuring out which frames to apply (Benford & Snow, 2000) in response to a situation. Research has found that framing could be an inherently biased and subjective process (Fösterling, 2001; Litrico & David, 2017). Actors can be selective about the information they collect and the way in which they interpret it. Instead of simply accepting a set of easily available cues in the world around them, actors may instead draw inspiration from an alternative set of less obvious cues in their environment. When two entities openly frame the same activity, event or situation in mutually competing and contrasting ways a 'frame dispute' may occur (Ravishankar, 2015). Frame disputes are often resolved in framing contests whereby actors compete, challenge each other's framings and redefine collective meaning (Azad & Faraj, 2011; Litrico & David, 2017).

Some IS research has drawn on framing theory to explain how actors with different values, experiences, priorities and backgrounds 'frame' reality and interpret situations in a multitude of ways, leading to conflicting situations (Litrico & David, 2017; Ravishankar, 2015; Sandeep & Ravishankar, 2015). For instance, contrasting perspectives about specific technologies (i.e., 'technology frames') can result in resistance, social chasms and misunderstandings (Davidson, 2002; Ivaturi & Chua, 2019). Davidson (2002) showed how stakeholders' inability to align differing IT requirements' frames can lead to implementation failure. Similarly, framing misalignments could lead to problems and conflicts in IT offshoring settings, with offshore teams disputing the onshore unit's framing of their (offshore unit's) actions and instead deploying 'cultural' frames to interpret what they saw as unacceptable behaviour on the part of their onshore colleagues (Ravishankar, 2015). Research suggests that the challenging process of resolving frame disputes may involve collective action (Benford & Snow, 2000), institutional changes (Werner & Cornelissen, 2014) and integration of diverse groups (Sandeep & Ravishankar, 2015).

Task Migration, Status Differentials and Frame Disputes

Task migration, as conceptualized in IS research, covers both the internal transfer of IT-enabled activities from one part of an organization to another and external transfer to a different organization. Typically, tasks are moved 'as is', which is commonly referred to in practitioner-speak as 'lift and shift' (Deloitte, 2017; KPMG, 2016). Task migration is often associated with global sourcing, wherein activities are lifted from business units and shifted to support units, which are often based in a different location (Gospel & Sako, 2010). The idea is that post-migration, business units will be able to focus on activities that create strategic value, leaving the support unit to perform the shifted tasks with greater efficiency (Tiwana & Keil, 2007). There is also an underlying expectation that post-migration, the support unit will simplify processes and undertake transformative projects by adopting more advanced IT tools (Leonardi & Bailey, 2017). Task migration strategies in global sourcing settings are prone to frame disputes arising from status differentials-led enactments of power.

Hardy (1985, 1996) conceptualized power in terms of the superior or inferior influence stemming from a comparative advantage over resources (including money, time, technology, knowledge and ownership of information), processes (including networks, access to decision makers, organizational position, reporting lines and autonomy) and meaning (social influence and ability to direct construction of organizational realities) (Azad & Faraj, 2011; Hardy, 1996; Jasperson et al., 2002). Hardy (1996) argued that resources, processes and meaning are three central modes of power that confer high-status. They are used by influential groups to 'defeat' challenges and overcome resistance by legitimizing positions, justifying behaviour and persuading opponents to accept outcomes (Hardy, 1985; Pfeffer, 1981). Displays of power and political one-upmanship, although under-researched (Marabelli & Galliers, 2017; Smith et al., 2017), have been documented in the broader IS scholarship (Azad & Faraj, 2011; Brancheau & Wetherbe, 1987; Jasperson et al., 2002; Markus, 1983) and a keen awareness of status positions has been identified as a compelling cue for situated actors to act and make sense of their actions in ways that echo their social power (Levina & Vaast, 2008; Ravishankar, 2015).

Studies have explored the role of power plays and politics in IT implementation and use (Dhillon, 2004), software selection (Howcroft & Light, 2006), IT innovations (Swan & Scarborough, 2005) and IS strategizing (Marabelli & Galliers, 2017). In the specific context of global sourcing of IT-enabled processes, research has found that distances created by firm boundaries, as well as geographic and cultural distances can lead to status differentials and subsequent enactments of power in collaborative teams. In particular, prior work suggests that arbitrary and forceful displays of power weaken collaboration between global teams (Hinds et al., 2014; O'Leary & Mortenssen, 2010), reduce innovation (Levina & Vaast, 2008) and inhibit project success (Jain et al., 2011; Levina & Orlikowski, 2009).

During the implementation of task migration strategies, support units struggle to hold their own and are typically at the weaker end of status differentials and power displays. As identified in previous IT outsourcing research, they are known to possess an inferior power position in relation to business units (Leonardi & Bailey, 2017; Ravishankar, 2015). Typically, support units have limited access to resources, have lower levels of access to key decision makers (Leonardi & Bailey, 2017), stay marginalized from core membership (Tiwana & Keil, 2007) and are perceived as being low-value (Hahl et al., 2016). These restrictions place them in a relatively low-status position, and they are often unhappy with the domineering nature of high-status units. On the other hand, high-status units are known to be scornful and suspicious of the capabilities of low-status support units. Studies have also found that support units are not always treated respectfully by business units, with the use of derogatory terms such as "third-world sloggers" and "cheap Indians" reported in the IT offshoring context (Koppman et al., 2016; Leonardi & Rodriguez-Lluesma, 2013). Despite an organizational emphasis on migration of tasks (e.g., transfer of non-core tasks to a centralized support structure) (Barua & Mani, 2014; Gospel & Sako, 2010), business units are known to invoke status differentials, exercise their position of power and demonstrate a high level of reluctance to enact task migration in practice, leading to frame disputes (Zimmerman & Ravishankar, 2016). In other words, task migration settings are particularly liable to suffer from frame disputes arising from status differentials.

The following empirical sections show how in the wake of an organizational task migration strategy, the framings of high-status units reflect their position of higher power (cf. Kaplan, 2008; Maitlis & Christianson, 2014). On the other hand, the framings of a low-status unit and the accompanying attributions (i.e., diagnoses of the fundamental issues and the quest for a 'cause' or 'blame'), though not logical in an objective sense, serve as a useful tool to achieve preferable outcomes such as avoiding conflict and making sense of uncomfortable situations (cf. Försterling, 2001; Harvey et al., 2014). We advance these arguments through the case of a distributed finance function in a global logistics firm where high-status business units (BUs) and a low-status shared service unit (SSU) negotiated the implementation of an organizational task migration strategy.

Design and Methods

We wanted our research approach to allow us to explore the potentially complex challenges of implementing task migration. We adopted the qualitative case study method, which helps develop a deeper understanding of the everyday interactions through which participants construct and develop their social worlds. We were interested in the structural and constructed boundaries between distributed work units and how they influenced interactions and collaborative processes. We drew on participants' 'reported accounts' of task migration (Zimmermann & Ravishankar, 2016). Our research was based in the distributed finance function of a global logistics firm, where tasks have been migrated from multiple high-status onshore business units (BUs) to a low-status nearshore shared service unit (SSU), which provides a range of support services back to the BUs.

This case provided a good opportunity to understand task migration within a finance function, which enjoyed a high level of autonomy and decision-making authority to move to a shared service model. Thus, we focus on the distributed finance function as a bounded unit of analysis to capture the IT-enabled tasks' migration phenomenon. The case captures a typical issue for multinational organizations—when functions are given strategic direction but little operational guidance leading to ambiguous situations open to multiple meaning construction of situated actors. The case is set in the context of a superior power position enjoyed by one group of actors—they have superior access to resource, decision-making power and access to key political stakeholders within the organization—making implementation of IT-enabled task migration particularly susceptible to status differentials-led enactments of power. We took an interpretivist approach to data analysis and have reported data that emerged organically (Strauss & Corbin, 1998).

Fieldwork and Preliminary Analysis

In total we conducted 26 interviews (Appendix 8.1), which was our main source of data. All interviews were conducted face to face in English, except three, which were via teleconference. Each interview lasted between 60 and 140 minutes (average 77 minutes). They were audio-recorded and later transcribed verbatim. In addition, we collected and analysed documentation including internal communications, performance dashboards, employee opinion surveys and employee development plans. We used these documents to better understand the structural organization, the formal distribution of work (e.g., the hierarchical structure) and the formal mechanisms in place to manage migrated IT-enabled tasks (e.g., key performance indicators (KPIs), service-level agreements (SLAs) and performance metrics). We also spent time in the participants' offices chatting informally and took photographs of their working environment.

Data was collected and analysed in three rounds, between 2015 and 2016. The first round of interviews was conducted with SSU members in their Netherlands-based head office. We selected participants from a range of management positions to capture multiple perspectives. The interviews were semi-structured and focused on the challenges of performing migrated tasks and collaborating on related activities

(Appendix 8.2). Participants were asked to elaborate or give examples of 'how' and 'why' they think situations or events occurred, as well as how they overcame them. The intention was to let interesting themes emerge from this first round of data collection while beginning to understand interactions, workflow and the challenges of performing distributed work from the SSU perspective. We began in the SSU as the unit worked with multiple BUs. The idea was to identify which of the 23 European BUs would be most valuable to include in the case. We transcribed all interviews from the first round of interviews, studied the data and made extensive notes to identify emerging themes. We then combined the interview data with documentation and field notes, which helped us to map the organizational structure, reporting lines, control mechanisms and responsibilities. With this we began identifying common themes across the first round of interviews. Interviews referred to actions outside of formal protocol and contracts that made performing migrated tasks challenging. For example, SSU members described not being able to make changes to migrated tasks, not being able to implement new tools, and being criticized by the BUs despite meeting targets.

The second round of interviews also took place at the SSU head office. Participants included additional SSU members and senior management from the firm's global finance organization (GFO). The second round of semi-structured interviews were designed to confirm and further explore the challenges SSU members faced and better understand how they performed the migrated tasks. We asked SSU members about their interactions with BUs and how migrated tasks were controlled and monitored. While GFO data is less directly reported, these interviews were fundamental in identifying and understanding the broad strategic objectives which led to task migration, as well as the impact of conflicts on financial processes during task migration. Again, we transcribed all interviews from the second round, studied the data and made extensive notes to detail both evolving and new themes.

The third round of interviews was conducted with members of four country BUs: France, Netherlands, Belgium and UK. BUs were selected to capture a variety of perspectives. During the initial analysis (of Round 1 and Round 2 data), BUs involved specifically in IT-enabled task migration projects and known to have 'challenging' relationships (were often more resistant to task migration or difficult to work with) with the SSU were identified. They represented a variety of BU sizes (BUs were given size 'tiers' based on the overall number of full-time employees and number of retained finance employees after task migration) and income levels. The purpose of these interviews was to understand the challenges BU members experienced after the organizational mandate for IT-enabled task migration, how their work had changed, and how they managed the migrated tasks. BU members were very open in describing their relationship with the SSU and the nature of their interactions. Again, we transcribed all interviews, studied the data and made extensive notes to support emergent themes, and made extensive notes on new ones. Triangulation of the different data sources was used to identify and reconcile conflicting perspectives. For instance, in comparing individual accounts of task migration, and more objective corporate data, we found contradictory accounts, which helped us develop the theoretical arguments around status differentials and frame disputes.

Data Analysis

We analysed the complete data set through an iterative process of going back and forth between emergent findings and theory (Eisenhardt, 1989). We organized our empirical data by theme before returning to theory for further guidance. Data and broad themes were organized in Nvivo 10. We paid close attention to how the same events or issues were perceived by SSU and BU members. For instance, we made detailed notes on themes that were present in the SSU empirical material but not in BU material (e.g., resisting, interfering and hypercriticizing) and vice versa. Having tentatively selected our focal themes, we drew on an extensive review of the scholarly literature to create a theoretically grounded description, which could explain the fundamental structure of the emergent findings. Goffman's (1974) notion of framing and frame disputes aligned closely with the kind of differences at play in the SSU-BUs relationship. The notion of 'framing' and 'frame disputes' helped explain participants' different perceptions of reality and how they shaped interpretations of both the low-status SSU and the high-status BUs. We found that the interpretations of the SSU members specifically admitted and acknowledged the powerful position of the BUs. This process led to the inductive development of the paper's key arguments, which were supported both by the empirical data and by the theory on framing.

Case Background

Our research is set in a large multinational logistics firm. We focus on the firm's globally distributed finance function, which includes the Global Finance Organisation (GFO), finance teams within individual country-level business units (BUs) and the firm's internal financial shared service unit (SSU) (see Fig. 8.1).

Finance Organization and Status Differentials

The Global Finance Organisation (GFO) is a strategic team based in the firm's headquarters, which sets the firm's global finance strategy. In 2008, the GFO launched a centralization strategy. The aim was to lift many IT-enabled financial processes from across the firm's multiple country-level business units (BUs) and shift them to an internally owned shared

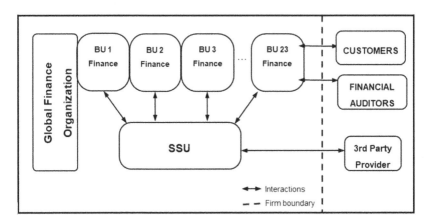

Fig. 8.1 The globally distributed finance function

service unit (SSU), where resources could be consolidated, and processes improved. The expectation was that the SSU would perform financial operations more efficiently and cheaply from its centralized location and the BUs would focus on more 'strategic' and 'customer-facing' financial activities.

The GFO provided strategic instruction for which tasks should be shifted from BUs to the SSU. However, the BUs were embedded in their own unique national and institutional contexts. For example, some of them faced specific national-level regulatory obligations for financial and data management and were therefore not in a position to migrate certain tasks. Therefore, the GFO left managers in the SSU to operationalize the migration of tasks by negotiating with each BU on an individual basis.

SSU—Low-Status Unit

The SSU is responsible for performing a range of IT-enabled financial operations (e.g., general ledger activities and end-to-end management of financial processes such as purchase-to-pay, record-to-report and order-to-cash) and providing them back to 23 BUs across Europe (on which this research focuses), as well as to BUs across North America, Africa and the Middle East. The SSU is tasked with improving financial processes through IT standardization (e.g., consolidating and implementing global standards), integration of the BUs different IT systems (e.g., those provided by Sun, Oracle and SAP) and implementation of new IT tools (e.g., e-billing tools) that can automate tasks.

The SSU is seen as generating costs for the business without bringing in any additional income. As a cost-centre, the SSU is expected to minimize expenditure where possible and has somewhat limited access to resources. It is held accountable for performing and delivering services to the BUs via service-level agreements (SLAs), which include instructions over what services are to be provided, as well as the required quality and regularity of services. The SSU's performance is measured through KPIs (e.g., number of electronic invoices processed per month). Structurally, the SSU's centralized position distances it from both the GFO management team (who set strategic objectives and regional mandates) and the

Table 8.1 Status

Status	SSU—Low-status	Bus—High-status
Role status	Operational, support, back-office	Core, strategic, customer facing
Commercial status	Cost centre	Profit centre
Structural position	GBS, Centralized	Divisional, localized
Decision-making authority	Operational, limited	Strategic, autonomous

BUs. In this sense, the SSU has limited decision-making authority. Some routine transactional activities are also performed offshore by a third-party provider in India. These activities are managed by the SSU who remain responsible for their delivery. Table 8.1 summarizes key features of the SSU's status in the official hierarchy.

BUs—High-Status Units

BUs are responsible for supporting the logistics business to improve its financial position and to enhance services provided to the business' customers. For instance, BUs work with customers to create personal payment plans and better manage cash flow positions. They also create special discounts to encourage customers to buy more space on the firm's planes, ships and lorries. BUs are also accountable for financial documentation (e.g., balance sheets and country-level financial reporting). The BUs are often referred to as 'strategic' or 'customer-centric' and the tasks they perform are highly valued within the organization. They are considered as profit-centres and often receive financial bonuses for their contributions. BUs enjoy decision-making authority and a degree of autonomy with the most influential BUs seen as pivotal to the firm meeting its sales targets. Structurally, as shown in Fig. 8.1, the BUs' proximity to the Global Finance Organisation (GFO) allows them superior access to resources and decision makers. Table 8.1 summarizes key features of the BUs' status in the official hierarchy.

Operationalizing Task Migration

Operationalizing task migration involved the SSU and BUs collectively identifying which tasks would be appropriate to shift to the SSU and negotiating how this would take place. SSU members began to shift some tasks into the SSU by working with BUs members to document processes. This was done through explicit instruction documents, task shadowing in the BU locations and expertise sharing. The SSU *stabilized* (i.e., the process of maintaining an acceptable task performance) the migrated tasks before they began 'transformation projects' to further improve efficiency and reduce costs.

BUs chose to migrate specific IT-enabled financial operations and paid the SSU for performing them. This arrangement gave the BUs the flexibility to manage specific requirements around language dependencies, process complexities and legislative obligations. However, it also meant there was little short-term incentive for BUs to migrate tasks or invest in task improvement through expensive new IT tools. Potential savings would accrue only over a two- to five-year period. Larger projects would take much longer to see a return. Following the initial set-up and migration of tasks to the SSU, an increasing number and variety of tasks have been identified as appropriate for migration by the organization. However, some BUs have not transferred tasks and continue to perform them internally. They have imposed strict restrictions about what tasks should be migrated, shifting only the simplest processes. A few BUs have migrated tasks involving some complex processes but have retained extensive intra-BU teams to closely coordinate and manage the SSU's performance.

Case Analysis

Our findings suggest that because clear and specific guidelines were not prescribed it was left to the BUs and SSU to operationalize the task migration strategy. Members had to decide which tasks would be migrated, as well as when and how. The high-status BUs engaged in the *retaining, fixing* and *detailing* of tasks. BU members framed these actions as necessary for 'protecting', 'supporting' and 'monitoring' the migrated tasks. However, the SSU members framed these same actions as a sign of the BUs 'resistance' 'interference' and 'hypercriticism', respectively (summarized in Table 8.2). In the following analysis, we show how status differentials were at the heart of these contrasting framings. We highlight a 'second layer' of SSU members' interpretations that worked to defuse an escalation of conflict.

Retaining Actions

Retaining actions refer to the continued performance of 'migratable' tasks within the BU and the holding back of task transfer in its entirety:

> I wasn't willing to move parts that I was controlling. P2.3

Often, tasks (or part of tasks) were migrated to the SSU but on the condition that the processes did not change. Both BU and SSU informants referred to a "lift and shift" style migration, meaning the SSU took on tasks and performed them but were not at liberty to make process changes. In other words, the SSU did not have the power or influence to force the BUs' hand:

> We want to simplify processes but we have so many BUs and every BU goes 'oh yeah but we can't change anything because we have to have this' [BU specific requirement]. And that's the challenge. P1.5
>
> The power of all the different BUs each saying they want to decide how the process looks resulted in real fragmentation. Processes were supposed to be moved here from one BU but they said 'Ah no that's too complex for you' and 'We don't trust you with this'. BU P1.2

SSU members framed these actions as symptomatic of a wider 'resistance' to change. They felt the BUs had a lot of autonomy to make their own decisions. They believed BUs were not "buying into the direction the company was moving into" because "they knew they would have to comply" with centrally driven decisions and standardize their existing IT-enabled processes which would threaten their autonomy (P1.1):

> The BUs usually had quite a lot to say. When BUs say 'No I don't see that task moving', then it didn't happen. We did not have the stick, or the backing to say 'We have to do it for you'. So we had to spend a lot of the time discussing and convincing BUs to migrate and hand over services. P1.2

The SSU members noted that BUs were possessive and unfairly so, with frequent references to "my files, my processes", and anyone working on those tasks as, "my people" (P1. 9). For the SSU not migrating a significant amount tasks in their entirety meant a constant struggle to achieve economies of scale and reduce operating costs.

On the other hand, BU members framed their retaining actions as 'protective' on three fronts. First, they believed they were protecting their need to make local alterations to processes in line with customers' requirements. They felt that migration of tasks leading to standardization would limit their ability to provide good service at the BU level. Second, they suggested they were protecting the BU profit margins and their own professional reputations. They were convinced the SSU would be unable to perform tasks to a high standard:

> I knew, looking at examples of how things had failed in the past, that I wasn't in the right mind-set to move tasks to the SSU. I would have needed to answer [to the BU and GFO] not just for the old processes, but the new processes as they made changes as well. I would rather have kept it in the BU. P2.3

Third, BUs believed they were protecting their time. In their view, the actual process of migrating tasks was time consuming and not really a high priority. There were many more pressing issues within the BUs which meant task migration was a distraction:

> So for example, we make financial entries, and at month end you post journals [detailed accounts of all the financial transactions] with those entries. One of my team posts between 80 and 120 journals [more than average]. I extracted all of those journals and did an analysis of which ones he could have handed over to the SSU. I worked out that probably half of them were standardized and could easily be handed over. But,

I haven't followed that through far enough. There would need to be a forced change for me to really make it happen. P3.3

Fixing Actions

Fixing actions refer to the amendments made to the work done by SSU on already migrated tasks:

> The SSU will provide the financial information for that month. It looks similar to last month but actually someone's added a new entry in the file…my team will bring it back here (to the BU) to be fixed. P3.3

BUs' fixing actions also featured the development of shadow systems, such as parallel spreadsheets. For instance, some BUs maintained a duplicated excel file to identify errors and fix 'fleet accrual expenses' tasks (i.e., allocation of expenses related to planes and delivery vans), which had already been migrated to the SSU in order to create standardized accrual process instructions. SSU members framed fixing actions as 'interference' from the BUs:

> BUs open every single invoice themselves and add the dates that it applies to into an Excel sheet (even though we have already recorded the invoice!). You can pick up from the description in the documents what it is. That should be enough of a check! They shouldn't have to go back, make an Excel sheet, and fill in all the details again. P2.1

From the SSU members' point of view, they were frequently asked to account for their contribution to the efficiency of financial processes, which they felt was being undermined by the BUs' interference:

> If it's going to be efficient it needs to be clear what each unit does and is responsible for. We benefit from performing and controlling tasks here in one centre and they (BUs) should focus on their core business. P2.1

SSU members attributed the interference to BU members' "personalities" (P1.1; P2.1), "their need for control" (P2.1), "being emotionally attached" and their "autonomy" over how activities are performed.

On the other hand, BU members framed their fixing actions as 'supporting' the SSU "to make sure failures don't happen":

> I went and sorted out the process for them and got the aging back in alignment. It took me a good few weeks, and I had to propose a loss of income from the profit and loss account, but they were back on track again. A year later things failed again because they didn't have the understanding of how to fix it. I was called back in again… I am there now to support. P3.5

The BUs felt it was necessary to support the SSU to 'stabilize' processes following migration of tasks. BU members explained that the SSU had made mistakes in the past that impacted some BUs' profitability and quality of financial reporting. During the migration of one simple process (much before the implementation of the current task migration strategy), the SSU team had failed to send invoices to customers for monies owed to a BU. By the time this was picked up, the SSU team were trying to collect invoices that were up to two years old—much of which could not be paid and had to be 'written off':

> The write-off was driven from the failed decisions that were made in the SSU when tasks were moved. Who is held liable for the financial repercussions? If H&M or Amazon did something like that you would probably stop shopping with them. But what would you do to the SSU? That's my perception - driven from my experience with them. P3.5

Despite acknowledging that some of the mistakes had occurred up to 10 years prior to data collection, BUs felt they could not trust the SSU and needed to support them to stabilize tasks during migration:

> If you stay involved you're covered to make sure failures don't happen. If a guy in the SSU is saying, "No, things should be done like this", you can challenge them. You have understanding of the task and don't just take their word for it… P2.3

8 Status Differentials and Framing ... 299

> If the external financial auditors deem that our accounts are not accurate or are not a true reflection of our financial position they will issue a legal statement that suggests accounts do not meet the necessary standards of general accounting. Even if this is because of something that wasn't managed properly in the SSU, the firm's CFO is not going to go to them. Yes, the SSU have their role to play but he will come to me. Ultimately, I'm responsible for the quality and integrity of the financial information for this BU. P3.2

BU members perceived the SSU as disconnected from the impact of failures and therefore needing support following task migration. They explained that it would be natural for the SSU to think "well no one is looking so I don't care" (P3.4). In addition, members were frustrated that "sexy service agreements" and formal job roles did not protect BUs from the SSU overlooking errors:

> If they do not believe they own the process they'll go – "It's your problem". Ownership is truly believing 'this is my problem and I need to sort it out'. At the moment, with the SSU, it's a bit grey. P3.4

The BUs expected the SSU to develop a track record of implementing high process standards during task migration before they (BUs) could stop offering extra support:

> When you know people are doing what you expect them to do and they can talk confidently about what they are doing, then you can let the leash off a little bit. P3.2

Detailing Actions

Detailing actions refer to steps taken by BUs to manage the performance of migrated tasks at a detailed level. These actions involved frequent conversations with the SSU and detailed checks about the performance of specific processes:

> We challenge them on what they have done and why they did it. During the month I also have bi-weekly meetings with them to check if there are any issues or if there are any customer complaints which need to be resolved or [challenged] by me or by the team. And of course, during the month it's constant traffic of emails and calls. P3.9
>
> They could turn around and say the reconciliations are done. They are all good. I could either say 'That's good' or I could say 'Let me check. Prove that it is reconciled properly. Prove it. That is part of my role. Checking up on what they are doing, making sure they are doing it correctly, and getting them to prove it to me. P3.4

SSU members framed BU detailing actions as the BUs being 'hypercritical'. Despite improving task performance, SSU members believed the BUs were finding small mistakes in their work. They felt their abilities were continuously under question and that they struggled to please the BUs who said results were either "not good enough" or "too good" to be believable:

> It's not that BUs now have more issues with invoices. They just focus on it. If one line is not coded right it will be a major issue and escalated. They wanted to open every single invoice to check if it has been recorded correctly. P2.1
>
> They keep monitoring you and they want to understand everything that is happening. BUs are usually still convinced that they know better than anybody else. P1.1

SSU members attributed the hypercriticism to unfair expectations. When tasks were migrated, the SSU were expected to perform tasks more quickly and efficiently than they had been performed by BUs. For instance, the SSU were expected to process more invoices per day for a cheaper cost. To achieve this, the SSU relied on standard operating procedures to perform activities more efficiently, and where possible had adopted new IT tools to automate processes. The SSU acknowledged that their targets for increasing process speed and reducing costs were sometimes at the expense of detailed invoice inspections—the quality expected by BUs. However, they felt the BUs did not acknowledge the process improvements and savings made. SSU members explained that

BUs were often hung-up on how processes had been performed earlier internally, and continued to inspect invoices in the same way:

> We have tried to enhance the process and improve it but BUs just compare it with three years ago when they did it. They always criticize because they think did a better job before. P1.2

SSU members also attributed the hypercriticism to the lack of trust between the BU and SSU teams. BUs had kept a team of people internally specifically to check details of the SSU's work, which SSU members saw as a signal that they were not trusted to perform them:

> They have never trusted us. Not after ten years! We have five people here working on the task for them and they still keep five people in the BU too, just because they still check every single bit we do. P1.1

Conversely, BU members framed detailing actions as an appropriate means of monitoring tasks, and part of their job:

> If something does go wrong then that's because we weren't monitoring it properly and closely enough. P3.2
>
> We have this relationship where we push, we drive, and we monitor to make sure they are doing what they should be doing. Hopefully they're not under any false impression - the quality of work expected from them is extremely high. P3.2

Specifically, BUs were concerned that important details were being missed by the SSU which was more focused on speed and efficiencies:

> The CFO for our billion-dollar business (referring to the BU's income) is a maniac, but he's brilliant! He'll say to the SSU "Why's that 50 Euros lost?". If each invoice is for a 25 Euros we have to do 50 million of them to get to that one billion of revenue. The point is, if we're doing something even a cent wrong on each of those 25 euros shipments it adds up to a huge figure. P3.3
>
> I have done it myself earlier. I have had exposure to how everything works. I understand every item in the balance sheet they produce. When

you understand the "ins and outs" of the task then you're in the perfect position to manage the SSU because you have a bottom level perspective of the entire process. P2.

Neutralizing Conflict Through a Second Layer of Interpretations

The SSU's 'resisting', 'interfering', and 'hypercriticizing' framings were the most logical and obvious interpretations of the BUs' actions. However, the tensions accompanying these framings did not play a dominant role in the SSU's interactions with the BUs during the implementation of task migration. Although the tensions were present at a cognitive level, they remained suppressed. We would highlight these framings as the SSU's first layer of interpretations of the BUs' actions. A second layer of SSU interpretations demonstrated a strong awareness of the status differentials and was more visible in how the SSU interacted with BUs' in practice. SSU members took meaning from what they perceived as unequal power relations and in particular, their own weaker position of power. SSU members referred to the "power of BUs", their "influence", relative "autonomy", and contrasted it with their own lower status position. They acknowledged their inability to stop the BUs' retaining, fixing and detailing actions. Paradoxically, this second layer attributed the perceived 'unfairness' of the BUs' actions to several reasonable underlying causes. In other words, we found that a keen sense of their relative (weaker) power position led SSU members, in a second layer of interpretations, to simultaneously activate a set of softer attributions for the BUs actions. These narratives were, by design, more accommodating of the BUs' approach to the relationship (summarized in Table 8.3).

SSU members constructed alternative, more neutral, explanations for the BUs' retaining, fixing and detailing actions. They admitted that migrating tasks to the SSU must be difficult for BUs. They described how BU members had actually "fought and lost a battle" over task migration, portraying them as "victims" of a "hostile takeover". SSU members

Table 8.2 Actions and framings

Actions	Low-status perspective (SSU)	High-status perspective (BUs)
RETAINING BUs did not transfer tasks	Resisting They think like - my files, my processes, my people It was very difficult to change processes. They wanted us to take over the work but keep it as it is You try to put in a tool and BUs are like "Why? We never used to do this" It was very difficult to change processes. They wanted us to take over the work but keep it exactly as it is	Protecting I wasn't willing to move parts that I was controlling. Looking at examples of how things had failed I wasn't in the right mind-set. I would have needed to answer not just for the new [tasks] but the new processes as well. I would rather keep it onshore Ultimately, I'm responsible for the quality and integrity of the financial information
FIXING BUs stepped in to amend work done by SSU on already migrated tasks	Interfering One person even took over and did the complete activity herself! It is already in the SSU but the (BU) guy is still so emotionally attached that everything happening in that project he is on top of it and has to go through him BUs open every single invoice themselves and add the dates that it applies to into an Excel sheet (even though we have already recorded the invoice!). You can pick up from the description in the documents what it is. That should be enough of a check. They shouldn't have to go back, make an Excel sheet, and fill in all the details again	Supporting We realized that we need to help sort problems out. For the last year or so we've been working really, really closely with the SSU trying to get them to a good level of quality We need to be looking for the failures, managing the root cause of those failures, fixing them over time...making sure we support the SSU to improve the quality of work The SSU have to come to when there's a problem

(continued)

Table 8.2 (continued)

Actions	Low-status perspective (SSU)	High-status perspective (BUs)
DETAILING BUs stepped into manage the performance of migrated tasks at a detailed level	Hypercriticizing We have tried to enhance the process, but BU controllers compare it with three years ago when they did it. They always criticize because they think did a better job before One BU in particular escalates even extremely minor items. They are really into every single little detail. If one line is not coded right, it will be a major escalation They keep five people in the BU to check every single bit we do	Monitoring When you know people are doing what you expect them to do and they can talk confidently about what they are doing, then you can let the leash off a little bit Ultimately responsibility rests with us so we can never turn away from it. If something goes wrong it's because we weren't monitoring it properly or closely enough They could turn around and say the processes are done. They are all good. I could either say 'That's good' or I could say 'Let me check. Prove that it is done properly. Prove it. That is part of my role. Checking up on what they are doing, making sure they are doing it correctly, and getting them to prove it to me We have this relationship where we push, we drive, and we monitor to make sure they are doing what they should be doing. Hopefully they're not under any false impression - the quality of work expected from them is extremely high

used emotive metaphors to describe the BUs' losses as a death that BU members needed to "mourn":

> If we change a process it's like a mourning process for them. They need to say goodbye to something that they've been doing before and it seems very difficult to get people over that first hill. People say "Yeah. Yeah. The task is moving" – But they still don't believe it is happening. It's like a real denial phase. Then afterwards they start to challenge everything. They say "How can we ever get to that target?" and "We can't move that - it's never going to work." So we come to the angry phase, right?... Eventually, people very slowly start the beginning of the acceptance. P2.4

Some SSU members even identified themselves as the aggressor in this narrative of "loss" and "victims". They described how "something was taken away from them [BUs] and we [The SSU] were the ones that took it" (P1.9). Rather than acting on their frustrations, SSU members found alternative meaning in BUs' actions and suggested that task migration should be handled "more sympathetically". Others identified the global finance organization (GFO) as the aggressor, referring to "direction from 'corporate' and suggesting that 'it changed our relationship with the BUs" (P1.9):

> The GFO went to the BUs and basically told them 'OK so as of next month your job is going to be cut in half'. From the start, this change cultivated the relationship of enemies. Many people must have felt bad over the way the split was made and so they really resented us for that. P2.6

SSU members also acknowledged the impact that their past mistakes had on BUs:

> We had to write-off a lot of invoice payments that we still had not collected from customers. That goes directly against the profit of the companies we were serving - which is of course not a very nice message. We just did not know what we were doing...you just have to learn from it. P1.1

Table 8.3 Neutralizing conflict through a second layer of interpretations

Status context	Attributions	Neutralizing Narratives
Status differentials limit opportunities to stop actions of high-status counterpart	BUs have suffered a loss because we have taken their team	BUs are: Victims of battle Mourning the death of their team
	BUs actions are justified because we made mistakes	It is normal for BUs to be frustrated with mistakes
	BUs have poor expectations because they have been influenced by external discourse	It is normal for BUs to be anxious about outsourcing

Many SSU members invoked the negative external discourse around 'outsourcing' and 'offshoring' to justify the BUs' controlling attitudes and reluctance to implement task migration. They suggested that all the negative 'press' and anxiety around outsourcing had amplified the BUs negative perception of task migration. SSU had been portrayed in the media as "low quality work units", "unreliable" due to "high staff turnover", useful only for repetitive, "low skilled" work, and as the cause of mass "redundancy" and falling national "employment". They felt it was only natural that the BUs questioned their skills, qualification and their professionalism, resulting in the SSU team being an "easy victim" when things went wrong (P1.9). Overall, in the second layer of interpretations, SSU members normalized the BUs' otherwise hostile responses, thus ensuring that the potential for escalation of conflict was reduced.

Discussion

The above analysis shows how a strategic imperative for IT-enabled task migration does not always translate into smooth action. It suggests that frame disputes can be triggered when situated actors are left to negotiate the implementation of a broad strategic mandate for IT-enabled task migration. The BUs' *retaining, fixing and detailing* of tasks was recognized by both sides as precisely that—i.e., the retaining, fixing and detailing of tasks respectively. In other words, there was no disagreement about the structure and substance of BUs' actions. However, there were clear frame disputes around the purpose and meaning of these actions. While the BUs framed these actions as essential—protecting, supporting and monitoring the implementation of the task migration strategy—the SSU framed the same actions as unnecessary and viewed them as a sign of the BUs' resistance, interference and hypercriticism, respectively.

High-Status Units and Power in the Implementation of Task Migration

The BUs' framing perspectives (protecting, supporting and monitoring) provide insights into the enactment of status differentials-led power in the implementation of task migration strategies. It shows how control over the three central modes of power—resources, processes and meaning (Hardy, 1996)—can have a significant impact on the unfolding of task migration in practice. The BUs had better access to resources and processes in their role as strategic customer-facing units maintaining a close relationship with the senior management of the finance function. In the broader organization, BUs were also in a better position to control the narrative about what they did and who they were. The internal organizational discourse about BUs always highlighted their 'profit-centre' status, in contrast to the 'cost-centre' language used to describe the SSU. Thus, exercising their position of superior status, the BUs were able to control (and in some cases, disrupt) the firm's strategic aspiration to migrate tasks and improve the efficiency of financial processes. By actively enforcing their framing positions, the BUs' made it difficult for the SSU to migrate, standardize and automate a range of tasks. From their position of high-status, what the BUs could mainly perceive was their own local requirements and the need for freedom to make adaptations to processes. The larger aspiration of collaborating with the SSU and achieving efficiencies and cost savings at the finance function level was not something they were willing to commit to. These actions of the BUs lead us to propose:

Proposition 1: In the implementation of task migration strategies, the framing perspectives of high-status units may exercise power to support immediate unit-level objectives rather than long-term firm-level objectives.

Underpinning BUs' framing perspectives was a clear sense of self-importance and superiority. The objectives of the task migration strategy were deemed to be secondary to the financial goals and quality considerations of the BUs themselves. BU members viewed the status differential between themselves and the SSU as an inviolable fact. They did not believe there was a need to explicitly articulate their position of higher power and authority in order to justify their actions. Their approach to the exercise of power was subtler, with frequent references to their important responsibilities *(e.g., "ultimately I am responsible for the quality and integrity of the financial information", "it's always us they come to when there's a problem", "we push, we drive, and we monitor to make sure they are doing what they should be doing"* etc.*)*. Thus, we propose:

Proposition 2: In the implementation of task migration strategies, the framing perspectives of high-status units may invoke their important responsibilities to justify the exercise of power over low-status units.

Low-status Units and Power in the Implementation of Task Migration

The SSU's framing perspectives (resisting, interfering and hypercriticizing) illustrate, first and foremost, an instinctive response to the exercise of power by the BUs. In this first layer of interpretations of the BUs' actions, we see a sense of frustration at the perceived unfairness (*"they always criticize because they think did a better job before"*), possessiveness (*"my files, my processes"*) and lack of trust in the relationship (*"taking over and doing the complete activity!"*). SSU's framing also shows how low-status units have the capability to respond to the behaviours of the high-status unit as they see it, as self-contained actions, without recourse to matters outside (e.g., the status differentials and power context) the immediate interactive environment. At this level of interpretation, the low-status unit may not read too much into the status differentials. Thus we propose:

Proposition 3: In the implementation of task migration strategies, the framing perspectives of low-status units can respond instinctively to perceived enactments of power, without reference to status differentials.

In the second layer of interpretations of the BUs' actions, the SSU both acknowledged the frame disputes and betrayed a deep sense of worry about their possible escalation into a full-blown conflict. This layer of interpretations is analytically insightful because it shows the limited effectiveness of low-status units' instinctive responses in settings of status differentials. As Maitlis and Christianson (2014) observe, different actors have different abilities—power, influence and opportunity—to frame effective discourses. SSU members knew that it was hard to stop the BUs' actions and cited the "power of BUs", at the same time pointing to their own relative powerlessness. Rather than entering into framing (or meaning construction) contests (Azad & Faraj, 2011; Kaplan, 2008) with BUs (which they felt they would not win), they deployed narratives that depicted the actions of the BUs in a softer light (Table 8.3, case analysis). These actions of the SSU suggest that low-status units in task migration relationships show a reflexive awareness of their weaker position and do not enter into potentially volatile frame negotiations with their high-status counterpart. The overarching objective is often self-preservation and the avoidance of conflict (Försterling, 2001; Ravishankar, 2015). This experience of the SSU indicates that in power-laden task migration settings, actors may not be able to deploy and sustain particular frames at will (cf. Kaplan, 2008). Rather, bigger equations of power may determine the opportunities available to advance initial framing positions. In our case, a deep awareness of status differentials (and a strong motivation to avoid conflict with high-status units) influenced the actions of the low-status unit. They did not feel they had too many opportunities within the system to confront the BUs. Thus, we propose:

Proposition 4: In the implementation of task migration strategies, taking full cognizance of the power of high-status units, framing perspectives of low-status units offer conflict-neutralizing narratives.

Theoretical Implications

This research has explored the contrast between the framings of several high-status units and one low-status unit during the implementation of a task migration strategy. The interpretations (protecting, supporting and monitoring) of the high-status units lend themselves to enactments of power while the interpretations (resisting, interfering and hypercriticizing) of the low-status unit have nuanced outcomes, demonstrating both an instinctive response to the exercise of power and the use of neutralizing narratives to avoid conflict. Building on the discussion above, several theoretical implications may be suggested.

First, the neutralizing narratives deployed during the implementation of task migration can be effective only because they have a certain commonsensical quality about them. For instance, in our case the anxieties surrounding outsourcing and the perceived losses of onshore business units have been well documented in the business press (Metiu, 2006; Ravishankar, 2015). Thus, the low-status SSU could readily access a range of 'reasonable' explanations for the BUs' enactments of power. It follows that, in task migration relationships where such justifications are not available in the wider institutional environment, frame disputes may lead to an escalation of conflict rather than an acceptance of status quo through multiple layers of interpretation. We would, therefore, suggest that the stability of task migration relationships could depend on the extent to which actors can access both local and global narratives that help them make logical sense of, and accept, enactments of power.

Second, the SSU experience suggests that the question of whether low-status actors in task migration relationships internalize the neutralizing narratives and believe in the softer attributions appears to be less important than the opportunities the narratives provide in making subjective sense of frame disputes. The value of these narratives seems to lie, then, not in their truth value, but in their potential to help make creative sense of status differentials-led power enactments. Thus, in many task migration relationships, given the self-awareness about their weak power position and the perceived consequences of antagonizing the high-status units, the true beliefs of low-status units may struggle to find honest expression over any sustained period.

Third, our study indicates that the potential for 'framing contests' (Azad & Faraj, 2011; Goffman, 1974; Jasperson et al., 2002; Litrico & David, 2017) to resolve frame disputes may be overstated. Framing contests wherein there is competition and challenge to each other's framing positions assume a degree of symmetrical relations of power. In contexts of significant status differentials on the other hand, framing contests can fizzle out even before they begin as the low-status unit becomes acutely conscious of its weaker position and works to maintain cordial relations with high-status units. Resolution of frame disputes may typically take the form of the low-status unit accepting the conditions of the high-status unit in order to stop the relationship from collapsing. It may, then be, left to key individuals to make special efforts to disrupt the status quo. Although we did not see such agentic work in our case, prior research suggests that both 'powerful' and 'ordinary' actors could enter the framing contests and instigate institutional-level changes (Reay et al., 2006; Zilber, 2009) to disrupt current arrangements of power.

Fourth, the BUs' framing perspectives highlight how power-laden environments may see an extended period of dominance by high-status units before a meaningful process of frame dispute resolution is activated. Prior research has found that frames are tools for motivating collective social action (Benford & Snow, 2000), instigating change (Werner & Cornelissen, 2014), influencing diverse groups (Sandeep & Ravishankar, 2015) and resolving issues (Leonardi, 2011; Su, 2015). However, this body of research is somewhat silent about the temporal dimension to the resolution of frame disputes. In asymmetrical power relationships, it may take much longer for a high-status (say) business unit to respond positively when faced with the prospect of losing control to (say) a support unit, even when such a loss of control may be in the overall interest of the larger organization.

Fifth, the SSU's softer attributions and focus on conflict avoidance suggest that some frame dispute resolution efforts in contexts of power may yield little more than what Argyris referred to as 'defensive routines' (1986, p. 75). Rather than advancing their initial framing perspectives, the SSU found it simpler to repeat neutralizing narratives that offered a justifiable defence of the BUs' actions. While this defensive retreat helped "manage the relationship" given the glaring power differential, their inability to confront the BUs meant that it was difficult for the SSU to initiate transformative IT-enabled projects post-task migration. Thus, we would argue that a conflict avoidance-based approach to framing comes with an excessive deferential attitude and may have a long-term negative impact on the strategic success of task migration strategies.

Lastly, our study exemplifies the disconnect between normative expectations and implementation of IT-enabled strategies in distributed environments. The expectations produced by a central discourse has for long been seen, in IS literature, as a powerful tool in uniting multiple groups within (and across) organizations, limiting disputes through goal framing cues (Barua & Mani, 2014; Lindenberg & Foss, 2011). For instance, prior IT offshoring literature has suggested that a central imperative helps to demonstrate corporate authority, align multiple stakeholders and communicate collective goals and objectives (Lindenberg & Foss, 2011). In contrast to these observations and expectations, our study implies that despite an organizational mandate for a strategy, different values, experiences, priorities and power-positions of groups lead to frame disputes that are not easily resolved. Individual and group-level frames are often detached from the organizational framing discourse (Cornelissen & Werner, 2014). High-status actors, in particular, utilize their power to either accept or redefine the normative expectations articulated in strategy documents (Azad & Faraj, 2011). Overall, instead of simply accepting a set of obvious (dominant) or directed organizational cues actors select social cues from their situated environment, making power differentials, a more salient and persuasive influence (Cornelissen & Werner, 2014; Goffman, 1974).

Implications for Practice

Our study emphasizes status differentials as an important power dynamic which needs to be accounted for when designing and operationalizing task migration. Although it may be impractical for a strategic imperative to be translated into clear operational instructions at a detailed level (Gospel & Sako, 2010), managers need to be proactive in assessing the impact of a planned task migration strategy on team dynamics (paying specific attention to power and status). In particular, they need to find ways of empowering low-status units and enhancing their ability to contribute meaningfully to distributed work. The possibility of conflicts arising from contrasting interpretations of a set of actions has important implications for senior managers. They may need to have a clear 'sequencing and pacing' approach to IT-enabled task migration. Initially, it might be better to migrate simple tasks that are loosely coupled (i.e., having a limited impact on the business unit), so the support unit can take them up 'safely', without worrying about retaliation from the business unit. An extended period of performance of such safe tasks might help develop mutual confidence and understanding, setting the stage for the migration of highly integrated and complex tasks that demand better coordination and collaboration.

Support units may need to adopt a proactive approach to get c-suite executives in the firm to commit and support the task migration strategy (Leonardi & Bailey, 2017). Rather than reacting to the *retaining, fixing* and *detailing* of tasks, support units could focus more on making a strong business case upfront to (say) the CFO, detailing the strategic advantages of task migration. The full and visible backing of senior executives might mitigate against displays of power by high-status units. In such a business case for task migration, support units may need to showcase their current IT capabilities, emphasizing the critical role they can play in transforming processes and improving efficiencies. Further, in task migration scenarios with significant status differentials all stakeholders need to critically evaluate the firm-level consequences of their framing positions. A greater respect and empathy for mutual positions can help both business units and support units not only reduce arbitrary enactments of power, but also achieve a smoother implementation of task migration strategies.

Conclusion

In this chapter, we have not explicitly considered the degree to which specific aspects of 'status' provide compelling cues for enactments of power during task migration. Both BU and SSU members had similar educational backgrounds—they were either qualified accountants or had undergraduate degrees in finance. We also found no evidence of status differentials linked to geographic distance as has been the case in earlier research (e.g., Zimmermann & Ravishankar, 2016). Status differentials seemed to stem instead from a complex combination of access to finance, prestige surrounding job roles and membership of organizational 'in-groups'. Further research is needed to evaluate the impact of individual status markers on task migration outcomes.

Despite the focus on both BUs and the SSU, our recounting of the case somewhat privileges the perspective of the SSU. We have suggested they were unable to migrate tasks to the fullest possible extent because of (a) their weaker status position in the official hierarchy and (b) the exercise of power by the high-status BUs. While all the empirical evidence we collected supports this claim, we acknowledge the possibility that in a small number of cases BUs' approach to task migration (e.g., retaining) may be linked to factors other than enactments of power (e.g., changes in the local regulatory environment). This possibility is an opportunity for future research to carefully disentangle elements of 'power' from other influencing factors. There is also an implicit assumption in our study that support units tend to possess a low-status. While this condition was certainly prevalent in our case, it is possible that an organizational strategy to migrate tasks to a central support unit might result in the support unit becoming extremely powerful at the cost of business units. More research is needed to explicate the processes through which political power gets transferred to specific types of organizational units. Our study has focused on an internal organizational support unit. It seems probable that a task migration relationship with an external unit will feature tighter controls and contractual obligations, leaving less room for status and power games. More research is needed to compare the experiences of an internal unit with that of an external unit. Similarly, studies could explore the implications of status differentials for implementation outcomes when in-depth instructions about the operational mechanics and the sequence and pacing of task migration are provided to actors on all sides. Finally, while our research has reported on events that unfolded during a particular timeframe, a more longitudinal approach will help explicate the processes of reconciliation and trajectories of future collaboration when senior management of the larger organization eventually intervene to resolve task migration tensions.

Appendix 8.1 Case Study Interviewees, Reference Codes and Interview Data

Round	Participant Job Role	Interview length (hours)	Team	Data Ref
1	Transition and Transformation Manager for Europe	1:19	SSU	P1.1
1	Global Process Owner	1:31	SSU	P1.2
1	General / Site Manager and Global Process Owner	0:53	SSU	P1.3
1	Process Expert for Europe, the Middle East and Africa / Control Tower Lead	1:05	SSU	P1.4
1	Head of Transition and Transformation	1:12	SSU	P1.5
1	Transition and Transformation Project Manger	1:19	SSU	P1.6
1	Head of Learning and Development	1:27	SSU	P1.7
1	Global Deployment Manager	0:53	SSU	P1.8
1	Head of BPO	0:57	SSU	P1.9
2	Financial Accounting Manager	2:29	SSU	P2.1
2	Head of Performance Management Europe & Global Coordinator for Performance Management	1:09	SSU	P2.2
2	Acting Service Delivery Expert	1:18	SSU	P2.3

(continued)

(continued)

Round	Participant Job Role	Interview length (hours)	Team	Data Ref
2	Global Process Owner	0:48	SSU	P2.4
2	Global Head of Financial Accounting	0:57	FO	P2.5
2	VP, HR for Finance	1:46	FO	P2.6
2	Communications & Employee Engagement Manager	1:29	SSU	P2.7
2	Vice President, Provider Management	1:11	FO	P2.8
3	Chief Financial Officer: Country Level	0:52	BU	P3.1
3	Chief Financial Officer: Country Level	1:04	BU	P3.2
3	Head of Controlling: Country Level	1:34	BU	P3.3
3	Head of Governance: Country Level	1:10	BU	P3.4
3	Risk, Finance, and Reconciliation Controller: Country Level	1:03	BU	P3.5
3	Risk, Finance, and Reconciliation Controller: Country Level	1:11	BU	P3.6
3	Chief Financial Officer: Country Level	1:03	BU	P3.7
3	Chief Financial Officer: Country Level	1:33	BU	P3.8
3	Head of Commercial Controlling and OTC: Country Level	2:00	BU	P3.9
	Total interview length (hours)	**33:22**		
	Average interview length (hours)	**1:17**		

Appendix 8.2 Interview Protocols

Global Finance Organization (GFO) Informant Protocol

The interview: The research project seeks to understand transformation of the finance function as a result of moving work to shared services. We are also keen to understand the motivations for task migration, as well as how this was achieved.
  Representative interview questions:

1. Introduction to yourself, your role and background.
2. Talk me through your current role in the global finance organization?
3. Talk me through your involvement and interactions with the European regional finance function.
4. What was the vision and the main motives for utilizing SSU to deliver finance operations?
5. Talk me through how the SSU was set up and how work was divided.
6. Since initial migrations, has the SSU model realized the value you hoped?
7. What have been the main challenges in getting there?
8. How do the BUs and SSU manage distributed processes?
9. How would you describe the relationship between BU and SSU?
10. From your knowledge, how would you describe the 'retained' finance team in the BUs?
11. From prior interviews, the SSU have suggested that some BUs are restrictive or resist task migration. Have you found this to be the case?

SSU Informant Protocol

The interview: The research project seeks to understand transformation of the finance function as a result of moving work to shared services. We are also keen to understand how you perform work, how this has changed, and understand the nature of the relationship between your team and the BUs you work with.

Representative interview questions:

1. Introduction to yourself, your role and background.
2. Talk me through your current role in the finance function?
3. How has your role emerged/changed as (more) work has moved to the SSU?
4. How has the above impacted your team and the work you do?
5. What are the biggest challenges you and your team face?
6. To what extent do you understand what the BUs do?
7. Describe your relationship with the BUs you work with?
8. How do you and your team manage, coordinate or govern the distributed work?
9. What are the biggest challenges you face in your role now?

BU Informant Protocol

The interview: It would be really helpful to understand from you, and your team's perspective, how the work you do in the BU has changed as a result of moving work to the firm's shared services centre. We are also interested in understanding where task migration has created value for you, as well as understanding some of the challenges.

Representative interview questions:

1. Introduction to yourself, your role and background.
2. Talk me through your current role in the finance function?
3. How has your role changed since work began to move to SSU?
4. How has the above impacted your team?
5. What are the advantages for you and your team in having a SSU?
6. What are the biggest challenges you and your team face as a result?
7. Describe your relationship with the SSU team.
8. How do you and your team manage, coordinate or govern the distributed work?
9. What are the biggest challenges you face in your role now?

References

Argyris, C. (1986). Skilled Incompetence. *Harvard Business Review, 64*(5), 74–79.
Azad, B., & Faraj, S. (2011). Social Power and Information Technology Implementation: A Contentious Framing Lens. *Information Systems Journal, 21*(1), 33–61. https://doi.org/10.1111/j.1365-2575.2010.00349.x
Barua, A., & Mani, D. (2014). Augmenting Conflict Resolution with Informational Response: A Holistic View of Governance Choice in Business Process Outsourcing. *Journal of Management Information Systems, 31*(3), 72–105. https://doi.org/10.1080/07421222.2014.995530
Benford, R. D., & Snow, D. A. (2000). Framing Processes and Social Movements: An Overview and Assessment. *Annual Review of Sociology, 26*, 611–639.
Brancheau, J. C., & Wetherbe, J. C. (1987). Key Issues in Information Systems Management. *MIS Quarterly, 11*(1), 23–36. https://doi.org/10.4018/jgim.2010100102
Cornelissen, J. P., & Werner, M. D. (2014). Putting Framing in Perspective: A Review of Framing and Frame Analysis Across the Management and Organizational Literature. *Academy of Management Annals, 8*(1), 181–235. https://doi.org/10.1080/19416520.2014.875669
Davidson, E. J. (2002). Technology Frames and Framing: A Socio-Cognitive Investigation of Requirements Determination. *MIS Quarterly, 26*(4), 329–358. https://doi.org/10.2307/4132312
Deloitte. (2017). *Global Shared Services*. https://www2.deloitte.com/content/dam/deloitte/us/Documents/process-and-operations/us-global-shared-services-report.pdf. Accessed 1st October 2019.
Dhillon, G. (2004). Dimensions of Power and IS Implementation. *Information and Management, 41*(5), 635–644. https://doi.org/10.1016/j.im.2003.02.001
Eisenhardt, K. M. (1989). Building Theories from Case Study Research. *Academy of Management Review, 14*(4), 532–550. https://doi.org/10.5465/AMR.1989.4308385
Försterling, F. (2001). *Attribution: An Introduction to Theories, Research, and Applications*. Psychology Press.
Goffman, E. (1974). *Frame Analysis: An Essay on the Organization of Experience*. Harper & Row.

Gospel, H., & Sako, M. (2010). The Unbundling of Corporate Functions: The Evolution of Shared Services and Outsourcing in Human Resource Management. *Industrial and Corporate Change, 19*(5), 1367–1396. https://doi.org/10.1093/icc/dtq002

Hahl, O., Kacperczyk, A. O., & Davis, J. P. (2016). Knowledge Asymmetry and Brokerage: Linking Network Perception to Position in Structural Holes. *Strategic Organization, 14*(2), 118–143. https://doi.org/10.1177/1476127015624274

Hardy, C. (1985). The Nature of Unobtrusive Power. *Journal of Management Studies, 22*(4), 384–399. https://doi.org/10.1111/j.1467-6486.1985.tb00004.x

Hardy, C. (1996). Understanding Power: Bringing About Strategic Change. *British Journal of Management, 7*(s1), S3–S16. https://doi.org/10.1111/j.1467-8551.1996.tb00144.x

Harvey, P., Madison, K., Martinko, M., Crook, T. R., & Crook, T. A. (2014). Attribution Theory in the Organizational Sciences: The Road Travelled and the Path Ahead. *Academy of Management Perspectives, 28*(2), 128–146. https://doi.org/10.5465/amp.2012.0175

Hinds, P. J., Neeley, T. B., & Cramton, C. D. (2014). Language as a Lightning Rod: Power Contests, Emotion Regulation, and Subgroup Dynamics in Global Teams. *Journal of International Business Studies, 45*(5), 536–561. https://doi.org/10.1057/jibs.2013.62

Howcroft, D., & Light, B. (2006). Reflections on Issues of Power in Packaged Software Selection. *Information Systems Journal, 16*(3), 215–235. https://doi.org/10.1111/j.1365-2575.2006.00216.x

Ivaturi, K., & Chua, C. (2019). Framing Norms in Online Communities. *Information and Management, 56*(1), 15–27. https://doi.org/10.1016/j.im.2018.05.015

Jain, R. P., Simon, J. C., & Poston, R. S. (2011). Mitigating Vendor Silence in Offshore Outsourcing: An Empirical Investigation. *Journal of Management Information Systems, 27*(4), 261–297. https://doi.org/10.2753/MIS0742-1222270409

Jasperson, J. S., Carte, T. A., Saunders, C. S., Butler, B. S., Croes, H. J., & Zheng, W. (2002). Review: Power and Information Technology Research: A Metatriangulation Review. *MIS Quarterly, 26*, 397–459.

Kaplan, S. (2008). Framing Contests: Strategy Making Under Uncertainty. *Organization Science, 19*(5), 729–752. https://doi.org/10.1287/orsc.1070.0340

Koppman, S., Mattarelli, E., & Gupta, A. (2016). Third-World "Sloggers" or Elite Global Professionals? Using Organizational Toolkits to Redefine Work Identity in Information Technology Offshore Outsourcing. *Organization Science, 27*(4), 825–845. https://doi.org/10.1287/orsc.2016.1068

KPMG. (2016). *Exploring the Future: Global Business Services in Consumer Markets.* https://assets.kpmg/content/dam/kpmg/be/pdf/exploring-the-future.pdf. Accessed 1 October 2019.

Lacity, M. C., Khan, S. A., & Yan, A. (2016). Review of the Empirical Business Services Sourcing Literature: An Update and Future Directions. *Journal of Information Technology (palgrave Macmillan), 31*(3), 269–328. https://doi.org/10.1057/jit.2016.2

Leonardi, P. M. (2011). Innovation Blindness: Culture, Frames, and Cross-Boundary Problem Construction in the Development of New Technology Concepts. *Organization Science, 22*(2), 347–369. https://doi.org/10.1287/orsc.1100.0529

Leonardi, P. M., & Bailey, D. E. (2017). Recognizing and Selling Good Ideas: Network Articulation and the Making of an Offshore Innovation Hub. *Academy of Management Discoveries, 3*(2), 116–144. https://doi.org/10.5465/amd.2015.0151

Leonardi, P. M., & Rodriguez-Lluesma, C. (2013). Occupational Stereotypes, Perceived Status Differences, and Intercultural Communication in Global Organizations. *Communication Monographs, 80*(4), 478–502. https://doi.org/10.1080/03637751.2013.828155

Levina, N., & Orlikowski, W. J. (2009). Understanding Shifting Power Relations Within and Across Organizations: A Critical Genre Analysis. *Academy of Management Journal, 52*(4), 672–703. https://doi.org/10.5465/amj.2009.43669902

Levina, N., & Vaast, E. (2008). Innovating or Doing as Told? Status Differences and Overlapping Boundaries in Offshore Collaboration. *MIS Quarterly, 32*(2), 307. https://doi.org/10.2307/25148842

Lindenberg, S., & Foss, N. J. (2011). Managing Joint Production Motivation: The Role of Goal Framing and Governance Mechanisms. *Academy of Management Review, 36*(3), 500–525. https://doi.org/10.5465/AMR.2011.61031808

Litrico, J. B., & David, R. J. (2017). The Evolution of Issue Interpretation Within Organizational Fields: Actor Positions, Framing Trajectories, and Field Settlement. *Academy of Management Journal, 60*(3), 986–1015. https://doi.org/10.5465/amj.2013.0156

Maitlis, S., & Christianson, M. (2014). Sensemaking in Organizations: Taking Stock and Moving Forward. *Academy of Management Annals, 8*(1), 57–125.

Mani, D., Srikanth, K., & Bharadwaj, A. (2014). Efficacy of R & D Work in Offshore Captive Centers : An Empirical Study of Task Characteristics, Coordination. *Information Systems Research, 25*(4), 846–864.

Marabelli, M., & Galliers, R. D. (2017). A Reflection on Information Systems Strategizing: The Role of Power and Everyday Practices. *Information Systems Journal, 27*(3), 347–366. https://doi.org/10.1111/isj.12110

Markus, M. L. (1983). Power, Politics, and MIS Implementation. *Communications of the ACM, 26*, 430–444. https://doi.org/10.1145/358141.358148

Metiu, A. (2006). Owning the Code: Status Closure in Distributed Groups. *Organization Science, 17*(4), 418–435. https://doi.org/10.1287/orsc.1060.0195

O'Leary, M., & Mortensen, M. (2010). Go (Con)figure: Subgroups, Imbalance, and Isolates in Geographically Dispersed Teams. *Organization Science, 21*(1), 115–131.

Pfeffer, J. F. (1981). *Power in Organizations*. Ballinger.

Pinjani, P., & Palvia, P. (2013). Trust and Knowledge Sharing in Diverse Global Virtual Teams. *Information & Management, 50*(4), 144–153. https://doi.org/10.1016/j.im.2012.10.002

Ravishankar, M. N. (2015). The Realignment of Offshoring Frame Disputes (OFD): An Ethnographic 'Cultural' Analysis. *European Journal of Information Systems, 24*(3), 234–246. https://doi.org/10.1057/ejis.2014.5

Reay, T., Golden-Biddle, K., & Germann, K. (2006). Legitimizing a New Role: Small Wins and Microprocesses of Change. *Academy of Management Journal, 49*(5), 977–998. https://doi.org/10.5465/AMJ.2006.22798178

Sandeep, M. S., & Ravishankar, M. N. (2015). Impact Sourcing Ventures and Local Communities: A Frame Alignment Perspective. *Information Systems Journal*. https://doi.org/10.1111/isj.12057

Smith, W., Erez, M., Jarvenpaa, S., Lewis, M. W., & Tracey, P. (2017). Adding Complexity to Theories of Paradox, Tensions, and Dualities of Innovation and Change: Introduction to Organization Studies Special Issue on Paradox, Tensions, and Dualities of Innovation and Change. *Organization Studies, 38*(3–4), 303–317. https://doi.org/10.1177/0170840617693560

Strauss, A. L., & Corbin, J. M. (1998). *Basics of Qualitative Research* (2nd ed.). Sage.

Su, N. (2015). Cultural Sensemaking in Offshore Information Technology Service Suppliers: A Cultural Frame Perspective. *MIS Quarterly, 39*(4), 959–983. https://doi.org/10.25300/MISQ/2015/39.4.10

Swan, J., & Scarbrough, H. (2005). The Politics of Networked Innovation. *Human Relations, 58*(7), 913–943. https://doi.org/10.1177/0018726705057811

Tiwana, A., & Keil, M. (2007). Does Peripheral Knowledge Complement Control? An Empirical Test in Technology Outsourcing Alliances. *Strategic Management Journal, 28*(6), 623–634. https://doi.org/10.1002/smj.623

Werner, M. D., & Cornelissen, J. P. (2014). Framing the Change: Switching and Blending Frames and Their Role in Instigating Institutional Change. *Organization Studies, 35*(10), 1449–1472. https://doi.org/10.1177/0170840614539314

Zilber, T. B. (2009). Institutional Maintenance as Narrative Acts. In T. B. Lawrence, R. Suddaby, & B. Leca (Eds.), *Institutional Work: Actors and Agency in Institutional Studies of Organizations* (pp. 205–235). Cambridge University Press.

Zimmermann, A., & Ravishankar, M. N. (2016). A Systems Perspective on Offshoring Strategy and Motivational Drivers Amongst Onshore and Offshore Employees. *Journal of World Business, 51*(4), 548–567. https://doi.org/10.1016/j.jwb.2016.01.005

Part III
Shifting from Traditional Sourcing to Digital Services

9

The Evolution of Intelligent Automation as a Sourcing Option

Leslie Willcocks and Mary Lacity

Introduction

This chapter looks at the evolution of automation as a service option and is based on a much revised and updated interview conducted by Gabe Piccoli, then *MIS Quarterly Executive Editor* in Chief. He initially asked Mary Lacity and Leslie Willcocks to discuss their six-year research program, with the goal of consolidating what is known about Robotic Process Automation (RPA) and Cognitive Automation (CA) Which, in

---

This chapter is revised, updated and synthesized from Lacity, M., & Willcocks, L. (2021). Becoming Strategic with Intelligent Automation. *MIS Quarterly Executive, 20*(2), 169–182, and Lacity, M., Willcocks, L., & Gozman, D. (2021). Influencing Information Systems Practice: The Action Principles Approach Applied to Robotic Process and Cognitive Automation. *Journal of Information Technology, 36*(3), 216–240. https://doi.org/10.1177/0268396221990778.

L. Willcocks (✉)
LSE, London, UK
e-mail: willcockslp@aol.com

M. Lacity
University of Arkansas, Fayetteville, NC, USA

combination are often today called Intelligent Automation (IA) and even included as Artificial Intelligence (AI). The chapter has been extended to cover also the 2021–2023 period to take into account more recent consolidating research. The authors also identify the challenges and ways forward for digital systems leaders, and a research agenda for academics in this field.

By 2023 the hype levels around AI and its impacts were higher than ever before. This chapter uses evidence from organizations to provide a more sober and complex picture than that feeding into the popular imagination.

The Terminology Challenge

We are going to reflect on the overall findings and most impactful lessons from the authors' nine-year research program. It is useful to start by dealing with the confusing terminology used in the automation field.

The research focuses on how enterprises automate services using a variety of digital technologies. When we began studying this space back in 2014, we encountered a dizzying array of automation products marketed as scripting tools, software robots, robotic process automation, artificial intelligence, desktop automation, cognitive computing, process mining, business process management automation and machine learning, to name but a few. The market was very confusing to practitioners, academics and to us.

To make sense of the space, we looked at how these tools worked, the type of data used as input, how they processed data and the type of results produced. From this work, we identified a continuum of automation tools, with the realm of robotic process automation (RPA) at one end and the realm of cognitive automation (CA) at the other. Many now commonly call the latter "artificial intelligence" (AI).

The realm of RPA consists of tools that automate tasks that have clearly defined rules for processing structured data to produce deterministic outcomes. For example, a "software robot" can be configured to process tasks the way humans do, by giving it a logon ID, password and playbook for executing processes. RPA tools are ideally suited for automating those mindless "swivel chair" chores performed by humans, like taking structured data from spreadsheets and applying some rules to update an ERP system. We had the early insight that RPA tools "*take the robot out of the human,*" meaning that the tedious parts of a person's job could be automated, leaving the human to do more interesting work that requires judgment and social skills. This insight resonated so much with practitioners, that we had to chase down more than one supplier and conference organizer who adopted the phrase as their marketing slogan without crediting us. The top RPA providers by market share as of 2023 were Automation Anywhere, Blue Prism and UiPath.

It is important to note that, because of the consequences for ease of scaling, these software providers do not all provide the same thing. There are variants of RPA ranging from desktop-assisted RPA, through enterprise RPA, self-development packages to cloud-based services.

The realm of cognitive automation consists of more powerful software suites that automate or augment tasks that do not have clearly defined rules. We do not like to call such software "artificial intelligence" because we believe the AI label over-states what these tools do. With CA technologies, inference-based algorithms process data to produce probabilistic outcomes. The realm of CA includes a variety of tools, such as tools that analyze data based on supervised and unsupervised machine learning, and deep learning algorithms. Some of the algorithms have been around for decades, but the computational power and memory needed to execute them on big data have only recently become available.

The input data for CA tools is often unstructured, such as free-form text, either written or spoken. For example, at Deakin University, CA was used to answer natural language inquiries from students. However, the input data can also be highly structured, such as the pixels in an image. Google's Machine Learning Kit, IPsoft's Amelia, IBM's Watson suite and Expert Systems' Cogito are examples of CA tools, likewise ChatGTP and similar software suites based on large language models (LLM—a type of artificial intelligence (AI) algorithm that uses deep learning techniques and massively large data sets to understand, summarize, generate and predict new content).

People refer to "strong" AI as using computers to do what human minds can do.[1] The vast majority of organizations are a long way off that! In our view, however, "AI" is widely and misleadingly used, especially by vendors, as an umbrella terms for RPA and CA, as well as for much more advanced software that has not even made it out of the laboratory. The claims by vendors are not helped by the misleading metaphor of comparing the human brain with computing. Most "AI applications" in businesses today can be described as *"weak, weak AI"*—algorithms driven by massive computing power. This is not "intelligence"; it is machine learning—we call it "statistics on steroids" (Fersht, 2012; Willcocks, 2020b).

Though the realm of CA is vast, our research examined how the tools were used to automate or augment back-office processes and customer-facing services, in line with our early interest in RPA. Typical examples we witnessed included processing medical claims, answering customer queries and categorizing user requests to route them to the humans who could help.

The Recent Evolution of Automation

A quick history of RPA is useful at this point. In 2012, Phil Fersht, founder of the outsourcing consulting firm Horses for Sources (HFS), used the term RPA in a provocative report entitled *Greetings from Robotistan, outsourcing's cheapest new destination*. This is a nice idea as it encapsulates automation's ability to replace human labor—the standard selling point of outsourcing vendors—by cheaper, quicker, more accurate machines. It highlighted a UK-based start-up called Blue Prism, which was founded in 2001. Blue Prism did not become well-known until its chief marketing officer, Patrick Geary, started calling its product "robotic process automation" sometime in 2012. That term really resonated with practitioners, so much so, that other automation companies started

---

[1] For a more comprehensive coverage of the types of strong and weak AI, see Benbya, H., Davenport, T. H. and Pachidi, S. (2020), "Special Issue Editorial: Artificial Intelligence in Organizations: Current State and Future Opportunities," *MIS Quarterly Executive* (19:4), December, available at: https://aisel.aisnet.org/misqe/vol19/iss4/4.

rebranding their tools as RPA. By 2016, there were over two dozen companies saying they provided RPA tools, with a claimed market size of $600 million (Fersht & Snowdon, 2018).

There was a desperate need for RPA standards, so Lee Coulter, then CEO of Ascension Shared Services, started an initiative at IEEE, and in December 2016 became the chair of the IEEE Working Group on Standards in Intelligent Process Automation. The group published the first standard in 2017, which distinguished between enterprise RPA designed for an organization and robotic desktop automation (RDA) designed for a single desktop user (IEEE, 2017). Blue Prism began as an RPA provider; Automation Anywhere began as an RDA provider. Both companies' products have evolved into more sophisticated platforms that include natural language processing and machine-learning features.

The RPA market was between $US2 billion and $US4 billion in 2020, depending on which consulting report you read.[2] Nearly every source predicts the annual growth rate will be between 30 and 50% for the foreseeable future.[3] C-suite priorities for emerging technologies have shifted rapidly because of Covid-19. Though the pandemic prompted many enterprises to postpone horizon technologies like edge computing and blockchains, they became laser-focused on technologies that produce rapid return-on-investments (ROIs), and the top of that list was process automation (KPMG, 2020). However, RPA has become a quite small proportion of the overall combined market for RPA, Intelligent Automation and "AI." On a Research and Markets estimate the global artificial intelligence market size was US$136.55 billion in 2022 and expected to reach US$1,812 billion by 2030, expanding at a CAGR of 37.3 percent from 2023 to 2030.

---

[2] See: (1) Robotic process automation (RPA) market revenues worldwide from 2017 to 2023, Statista, January 2020, available at https://www.statista.com/statistics/740440/worldwide-robotic-process-automation-market-size/; and (2) Fersht and Snowdon (2018).

[3] Allied Market Research, reporting on 13 October 2020, forecast that the RPA market at end of 2027 will be $19.53 billion—an annual compound growth rate of 36.4%. A Deloitte survey reporting in December 2020 predicted the RPA market would grow at 40.6% per year to reach $25.6 billion by 2027.

Emerging Challenges

Organizations find it difficult to adapt CA tools designed for a specific context like chess, Jeopardy or Go for use in other contexts like processing health records, mortgage applications and calls to helpdesks. The early enterprise adopters experienced painful and expensive implementations, mostly due to the data challenge. Our case companies adopted CA tools with supervised machine learning, which needs thousands of labeled data examples to enable the machine-learning algorithms to reach an acceptable level of proficiency. However, as much as 80% of an organization's data is "dark," meaning that the data is un-locatable, untapped or untagged. Enterprises adopters of CA tools first had to create new data and clean up dirty data that was missing, duplicated, incorrect, inconsistent or outdated. They also struggled with "difficult data," which we define as accurate and valid data that is hard for a machine to read—for example, a fuzzy image, unexpected data types or sophisticated natural language text. In our CA cases, much of the work to sort out data problems was done by tedious human review.

But we did find examples of organizations that eventually got value from their CA adoptions, including Deakin University, Zurich Insurance and KPMG. As best practices emerge, more organizations are finding success, though CA implementations still tend to be islands of automation rather than enterprise-wide deployments. The size of the CA market in 2020 was reported to be somewhere between $US50 billion and $US150 billion.[4]

RPA and CA have different histories that, from around 2018, have been now converging to what practitioners are calling "intelligent automation." The idea of intelligent automation is to institutionalize a well-designed automation program using a platform for pluggable tools that are best-in-class. In our case studies, business value was not derived

---

[4] See, for example: (1) *Artificial Intelligence Market Size, Share & Trends Analysis Report, Grand View Research By Solution (Hardware, Software, Services), By Technology (Deep Learning, Machine Learning), By End Use, By Region, And Segment Forecasts, 2020–2027, July* 2020, available at https://www.grandviewresearch.com/industry-analysis/artificial-intelligence-ai-market; and (2) *IDC Forecasts Strong 12.3% Growth for AI Market in 2020 Amidst Challenging Circumstances, IDC,* August 2020, Available at https://www.idc.com/getdoc.jsp?containerId=prUS46757920.

from the selection of one technology or service provider, but through the ability to identify and connect different technologies that maximize the full potential of modern automation technologies. At present, though, software providers are at different stages in developing automation platforms that can harness both RPA and CA technologies. Some enterprises buy best-in-class tools and use their own platforms to integrate them internally.

IBM is a good example. IBM's global IT outsourcing services business combined the Blue Prism RPA software with components of IBM's Watson technology. In one service (Global Technology Services Technology, Innovation & Automation), IBM has well over 1,000 customers, and a range of automation tools, including 200 RPA software licenses provided through its London and Amsterdam offices.

One process that IBM automated by integrating technologies was email ticket triage. IBM's customers have email task IDs they can use to send support requests to IBM. The requests are typically things like "Hey, my printer is not working" or "I've forgotten my password." Any emailed support request needs to be logged into the ticketing system and routed to the correct group for resolution. This task used to be done by humans, but was taken on in 2017 by an RPA software robot. The robot uses its logon ID to log into the ticketing system. It retrieves an email, logs it into the ticketing system and engages the CA tool, which categorizes the issue: "this is a network support request" or "this is a telephony request." The CA tool typically has a high degree of certainty, having been trained on thousands of historical tickets. When confidence is low, the ticket is escalated to a human for routing and the label fed back to the CA tool for learning. The RPA tool closes the loop by identifying the appropriate team and routing the ticket to the correct group.

That example is just one of many. Increasingly, we see CA tools feed into RPA software, which acts as the execution engine, especially in banking, insurance and financial services organizations. A bank, for example, will have an interactive front-end chatbot for dialogue with customers, but it will draw on RPA to get the information it needs to be able to have a more accurate conversation with the customer, for example, about a stolen credit card. In the future, we will see even more, better integration of RPA and CA software, leading to automation exchange platforms that are increasingly cloud-based. By 2023 the challenge we had identified is how these automation efforts link with all the other digital technologies that might form part of an organization's digital transformation efforts (Willcocks et al., 2023).

Getting Business Value

We, and others, have studied implementations with outcomes ranging from what we describe as "triple-wins" to complete failures. We think it's most useful to focus on success stories because practitioners like to learn from, and hopefully mimic, the achievements of early adopters. But we also studied failures so we could identify the action principles that differentiate outcomes.

Many of our case study organizations achieved triple-wins by achieving value for three types of stakeholder: the enterprise, customers and—most surprising of all—employees. The Associated Press, BNY Mellon, Bouygues, Deakin University, Ericsson, EY Tax Advisory, KPMG, Mars, Nielsen Holdings, Nokia, nPower, SEC Bank, Shop Direct, Standard Bank, Telefónica O2, the VHA, Xchanging and Zurich Insurance are examples of companies that achieved at least one source of value from each category. Aggregating these findings, we have listed the specific benefits and sources of enterprise, customer and employee value that RPA and CA has delivered across our case study companies (see Fig. 9.1).

If this list seems too good to be true, keep in mind that we initially studied known successes, to see if there was any "there" there! Our Telefónica O2 case identified the value to the company in terms of cost savings, the value to customers who received faster services and the value to internal employees, who were released from dreary work to focus on more interesting tasks. The Deakin University case provided details of a triple win for three stakeholders: the university raised its global brand awareness; students gained faster access to critical services; and staff were able to focus on more interesting tasks. Further evidence from other companies is in several other published studies, both by us and other

Fig. 9.1 Triple-Wins of service automation value are evident across multiple RPA and CA implementations

authors (as examples only see Asatiani & Penttinen, 2016; Davenport & Kirby, 2016; Hallikainen et al., 2018; Lacity & Willcocks, 2016; Lacity et al., 2015; Lowes & Cannata, 2017; Schatsky et al., 2016; Watson, 2017; Willcocks et al., 2019).

What do the failures look like? We purposefully started researching failures for our second book, *Robotic Process Automation and Risk Mitigation: The Definitive Guide*. It's always hard to find companies willing to talk about their blunders, though there are quite a few accounts of the limitations as well as the benefits of the automation we are describing.[5] The software providers and consulting firms we were working with at the time, including Alsbridge (now part of ISG), Blue Prism, Everest Group, HfS, ISG and KPMG, helped us identify failure cases. We studied many enterprises where their RPA implementations had failed to deliver value. Problems included: employee sabotage resulting from inappropriate human resource (HR) policies; functional failures due to poor change management; and implementations that irritated, rather than delighted, customers. Some organizations had localized successes with a few projects, but they never succeeded in scaling and maturing the RPA capability across the enterprise.

What was enlightening to practitioners was to discover that material risks, that is risks that could seriously affect business value, occurred

---

[5] Examples of successes and failures can be found in: (1) Davenport (2018), (2) Smith (2019), (3) Broussard (2018), (4) Smith (2018), and (5) Russell (2019).

throughout the automation lifecycle. These were not plug and play technologies; they needed constant management attention. Given our book theme, let's look at sourcing risks more closely (Fig. 9.2).

The main approach we saw was the DIY plus consultancy support option. However, to be truly effective, this has to be a sustained approach to build internal automation capabilities that link with wider digital transformation efforts over a three-year time line. We saw all too many organizations fail to sustain such an investment because of the related challenges that emerged. The result was that even by the early 2020's many automation initiatives had not scaled and become strategically impactful for the organization. That said, the pandemic period did accelerate automation adoption, though often for short-term reasons. One interesting finding was that automation allowed organizations to re-shore work, choosing to go down the automation route internally, rather than outsource on a more traditional basis.

Meanwhile, some organizations chose to utilize their service providers to take over certain work that could be automated. Increasingly, service providers have taken on board utilizing automation themselves, and this has tended to help build their ability to bid for automatable work. In earlier work on sourcing our larger finding was that the low risk approach is to outsource only those activities that are stable, understood and you can write a detailed management contract for. Following this logic, automation is best managed by building up an internal capability first, and outsourcing later when it has become a commodified set of activities (see also this book's preface).

Meanwhile, with the coming of "Robotistan" outsourcing vendors have found themselves from 2015 increasingly in a double bind—firstly not able to depend so heavily on their selling of human labor at low cost, and secondly increasingly having to deliver not traditional but digital services. During the 2017–2020 period a significant minority of clients, we surveyed had reduced reliance on their service providers. The major IT and business process outsourcing (BPO) providers were well aware that their labor arbitrage business model was severely under threat by automation—they feared losing long-time customers who needed fewer services from outsiders after automation. One provider, OpusCapita, made the strategic decision to build up a significant RPA capability

9 The Evolution of Intelligent Automation ... 337

Automation Sourcing Options

Do It Yourself, and DIY + Consultancy

Benefits:
- Own the solution
- Maintain independence (no tool lock-in)
- Capture all gains
- Reshoring opportunity in cases of "offshoring fatigue"

Cons:
- Technology learning curve
- Upfront investment costs
- Time/cost to build or acquire skills and capabilities: CoE

Service Provider (BPO or RPA)

Benefits:
- Bypass learning curve
- BPOs may be best positioned to "take the robot out of the human" (they already do the work)
- Providers bring cross-client, cross-industry experience
- Expert at retraining robots when IT or business environment changes
- Receive an integrated, managed service

Cons:
- Tool lock-in
- Benefits shared with BPO provider

Fig. 9.2 Sourcing options for automation

internally, and then extended RPA services to customers (see Asatiani & Pennttinen, 2016; Hallikainen et al., 2018). Many other outsourcing providers have followed suit since.

Establishing Effective Management Actions

More broadly, we were interested in establishing a full suite of management actions that were leading to higher business value from automation deployment. Our initial rich, cross-sectoral research base for developing what we call "action principles," covered robotic process and cognitive automation case studies, and is summarized in Table 9.1. (following increasing adoption activity, this has since expanded to over 1,020 RPA and CA cases as at 2023).

What did we find? Do some of the classic practices leading to successful IT project completion apply or, taking those as given, are there distinctive practices critical for RPA/CA success? Overall, we identified 39 action principles that were associated with good outcomes (see Fig. 9.3), and these principles continue to be validated through later research projects.

The action principles approach assumes the following:

Assumption 1: Practitioners are thoughtful agents. Practitioners are assumed to be thoughtful agents capable of action based on free will, power, intelligence, emotion, creativity and self-reflection, but who operate within the affordances and confines of their environments (see Giddens, 1984; Lacity, 2019). Furthermore, practitioners are able to express reasons for and consequences of their actions and the actions of others, *if asked*. As Anthony Giddens wrote: "*To be a human being is to be a purposive agent, who both has reasons for his or her activities and is able, if asked, to elaborate discursively upon those reasons*" (Giddens, 1984). From this assumption, it follows that IS researchers must engage in a dialogue with practitioners to learn about the associations they make between actions and results.

Table 9.1 Client adoption journeys

Company name or pseudonym*	Industry	Head-quarters	Adoption location	Realm	First processes automated
1. Ascension Shared Services	Healthcare	US	BO	RPA	Employee record updates; payments
2. Associated Press	Media	US	BO	RPA	Corporate earnings reports
3. Telefónica O2	Telecommunications	UK	BO	RPA	SIM Swaps; pre-calculated credit
4. Xchanging	BPO provider	UK	BO	RPA	Premium advice notices
5. KPMG	Professional Services	US	Innovation Center	CA	Business development; risk assessment; audit
6. Deakin University	Higher Education	Australia	BO	CA	Student queries and engagement
7. SEB Bank	Financial Services	Sweden	IT	CA	IT Services desk; customer services
8. Zurich Insurance	Insurance	Switzerland	BO	CA	Personal injury claims
9. Blue Cross Blue Shield- North Carolina	Healthcare Insurance	US	BO	RPA	Claims processing
10. Biotech*	Biotechnology	Netherlands	BO	RPA	Financial close
11. Building Society*	Financial Services	UK	BO	RPA	Mortgage lending and savings
12. Consulting*	Professional Services	France	BO	RPA	Multiple services
13. Energy*	Natural Gas	Russia	BO	RPA	New customer registration
14. Financial Services*	Financial Services	UK	BO	RPA	Payroll verification

(continued)

Table 9.1 (continued)

Company name or pseudonym*	Industry	Head-quarters	Adoption location	Realm	First processes automated
15. Financial services*	Financial Services	South Africa	BO	RPA/CA	Consumer Credit
16. Healthcare*	Healthcare	UK	BO	RPA	Patient registration
17. IBM Division	Professional and IT services	UK/Netherlands	IT	RPA/CA	Help desk ticketing
18. Insurance*	Insurance Services	UK	IT	RPA	Pension enrollment
19. Manufacturing*	Consumer Goods	Germany	BO	RPA	Back office processing
20. Utility*	Electric and Gas	Germany	BO	RPA	Meter reading feasibility checks
21. VHA	Healthcare	US	IT	RPA	Web crawls for product descriptions
22. Virgin Trains	Transportation	UK	BO	CA	Incoming customer correspondence

Legend: BO = Business Operations; IT = IT Department

Assumption 2: Action principles are guides, not laws. We assume action principles to be useful guides; we do not consider action principles to be "laws" or even "best practices." Consistent with David Hume (1739), we are aware of the limitations of claiming blanket generalizations based on empirical evidence. Whereas "best practices" imply that mimicry is always recommended and will always produce similar results, an action principle may not be effective in every context; it is for the thoughtful practitioner to decide. As such, action principles created from early adopters are offered to future adopters for their consideration and guidance. The thoughtful practitioner decides the usefulness of an action principle depending on the objectives the organization is trying to achieve; whether the organization has the absorptive capacity to implement the action principle effectively; and timing—there are better times than others to act. Such future adopters are presumed capable of assessing the applicability of practices garnered from other contexts; it is for the thoughtful practitioner to decide the timing and extent to which action x would likely produce result y within his or her organizational context. A summary of our research approach can be found in Lacity et al. (2021).

Many of our action principles commonly apply to any type of organizational adoption of technology. Examples include: gain C-suite support to legitimate; support and provide adequate resources for the service automation initiative; get stakeholder buy-in; and follow Pareto's rule by automating the smallest percentage of tasks that account for the greatest volume of transactions. The research shows value in replicating known practices, and reinforces what managers already know about successful technology implementations. Managers need to retain many of their practices in the face of a new technology. But our research did reveal new distinctive practices and some provocative findings (see Fig. 9.3).

Examples of ***distinctive*** findings in Fig. 9.3 include: under Strategy 1, 3, 5; under Program Management 10; under Process selection 13; Under Tool Selection 16, 18; under Stakeholder Buy-in 22; under Design, Build, Test 25, 26, 27; under Run 28, 29, 31; under Maturity 36, 38.

Strategy
1. You get what you pay for: Focus on long-term value rather than short-term ROI (action) to gain the most value from service automation tools (outcome)
2. Strategy drives investments: Include multiple expected benefits in the justification for service automation investments (action) to achieve the greatest value for the organization, employees and customers (outcome)
3. Consider competitors' reactions (action) to prevent mis-messaging to customers (outcome)
4. Use RPA as forward reconnaissance for CA (action) to gradually build automation skills and to use RPA savings to defer some CA costs (outcome)
5. Strategy envisions longer-term human workforce needs (action) and develops automation and HR plans to gradually meet that vision (outcome)
Sourcing
6. Select the best sourcing option (action) to ensure the success of the implementation (outcome)
7. Incentivize a BPO or tool provider to share the benefits of automation (action) to prevent them from taking all of the savings (outcome)
Program Management
8. Manage RPA as a traditional business case (action) to increase returns on investment (outcome)
9. Manage CA as an innovation program (action) to increase experimentation and to rapidly shift direction (outcome)
10. Manage CA as a learning project (action) to adapt quickly to early lessons learned (outcome)
11. Consider the context (action) to decide which unit is best suited to own the automation program (outcome)
12. Find the "Lewis and Clark"[1] program champions (action) who will overcome obstacles to ensure project implementation (outcome)
Process Selection
13. Take the robot out of the human: Use service automation tools to automate mundane tasks (action) to focus employees on more value-adding work (outcome)
14. Aim for triple wins: Develop comprehensive criteria to identify the best processes to automate (action) to achieve the greatest value for the organization, employees and customers (outcome)
15. Fix discoveries about process flaws before deploying service automation (action) to prevent merely performing a bad process more efficiently (outcome)
Tool Selection
16. Use a controlled experiment to assess tools (action) to select the tool that delivers the best financial value (outcome)
17. Don't look for a "Swiss Army Knife": Select a tool that does a few things well (action) to ensure technical success (outcome)
18. Negotiate the optimal level of client-provider transparency pertaining to machine-learning algorithms (action) to ensure a good relationship (outcome)
19. Expect technical challenges as a first mover (action) to minimize disappointments (outcome)
Stakeholder Buy-in
20. Manage up: Gain C-suite support (action) to legitimate, support and provide resources for the service automation initiative (outcome)
21. Manage down: Communicate the intended effect on jobs early in the process (action) to obtain employee buy-in and to prevent panic and sabotage (outcome)
22. Report financial savings in terms of "hours back to the business," rather than as FTE savings (action) to reinforce that automation is used to liberate employees from routine tasks (outcome)
23. Manage expectations: Be transparent with customers that they are interacting with automation tools (action) to maintain high ethical standards and acceptance (outcome)
Design, Build and Test
24. Follow Pareto's rule: Automate the small number of tasks that account for the greatest volume of transactions (action) to deliver the most business value (outcome)
25. Don't underestimate the data challenge (action) required to get CA tools to perform competently (outcome)
26. Find new data sources if "dirty" data cannot be cleaned (action) to get the CA tool to perform competently (outcome)
27. Compare training the automation tool to training a new employee (action) so that stakeholders expect the tools to be as competent as new employees and not as competent as experts (outcome)
Run
28. Redesign employee scorecards so that they are credited with productivity gains contributed by their robot teammates (action)
29. Invite customers to experiment with the automated service, but keep other channels open (action) to ensure good customer service (outcome)
30. Invite customers to provide feedback (action) to help improve the performance of a CA tool (outcome)
31. Keep subject matter experts continually engaged in data curation (action) to keep the automation relevant (outcome)
32. Robots need supervisors: Supervise the learning of the service automation tool (action) to prevent machines from making new decisions without human direction and approval (outcome)
33. Rethink human talent and skills (action) needed for long-term success (outcomes)
34. Assign clear roles of responsibility (action) to keep the automation operational and relevant (outcome)
Maturity
35. Reuse components (action) to scale quickly and to reduce development costs (outcomes)
36. Multi-skill the robots (action) to extract more business value (outcome)
37. Create a center of excellence (action) to disseminate automation technologies across the organization (outcome).
38. Integrate RPA and CA initiatives (action) to deliver end-to-end service automation (action)
39. Continually innovate (action) to deliver value to customers, employees and shareholder (outcome)

Fig. 9.3 Intelligent automation action principles (*Source* Lacity et al. [2021])[6]

---

[6] The Lewis and Clark Expedition from 31 August 1803 to 25 September 1806 was the US expedition to cross the newly acquired western portion of the country. The expedition leaders had to overcome many new challenges.

Jobs and Automation

Some findings were surprising—at least to us. An example of such a *provocative* finding is worth considering in detail. Many people falsely assume that ROI from automation comes from firing employees. While it's true that the primary source of value from service automation is freeing up human labor, the best way to deliver, measure and communicate this value to the enterprise is "hours back to the business." Think of it as a gift given back to the organization. But what will an organization do with that gift? Most enterprises we studied used the freed-up labor capacity to redeploy people to other tasks within the work unit. Many of these organizations were experiencing high growth, and automation helped them take on more work without hiring proportionally more workers. You can easily imagine how valuable it is to grow efficiently by redeploying existing employees rather than searching for, vetting, onboarding and training new ones.

Let's differentiate "hours back to the business" from what we normally think of as freeing up FTES (full-time equivalents). The two terms are similar, but the messaging is very different. "Hours back to the business" calculations are based on estimating the number of hours it would take if humans still performed the automated tasks. It represents the human capacity that is now free to do different work. Hours back to the business can be converted to FTEs, typically by dividing by 2,000, the average number of hours an employee works per year. For example, EY's US Tax Advisory Business generated 800,000 hours back to the business within 18 months of its RPA implementation. If EY reported that automation saved them 400 FTEs instead of the equivalent 800,000 hours, many may interpret it as: "We no longer need 400 people." But that sends the wrong message, as the labor savings typically come from automating a portion of people's jobs. In practice, saving 400 FTEs is more likely to come from automating 20% of 2,000 people's jobs.

But surely some automation implementations lead to layoffs? Not necessarily. First, we are talking here about time saved that can be used elsewhere in the organization. Second, the time saved is invariably spread across jobs. It's partial task automation, not job loss. Third, people fail to understand that there is an enormous amount of extra work being generated every year in organizations—in one study we suggest between 8 and 12% (Willcocks, 2020a, 2021; see also chapter 13). This arises from the exponential explosion in data volumes, increasing audit and regulation requirements, and bureaucracy, as well as the problems information and communications technologies bring with them—cybersecurity as an obvious example. Increasing workloads allied to skills shortages have forced organizations to turn to automation as a coping mechanism, rather than primarily for headcount reduction.

Of course, we did document some layoffs, but—perhaps surprisingly—layoffs have not been as widespread as one might think, especially during the time frame of our study (2015–2023). Other researchers have also documented this perhaps counter-intuitive insight. Davenport and Rananki found that replacing administrative employees was neither a primary objective nor a common outcome of deploying RPA (Davenport, 2018). They found that only 22% of executives sought headcount reduction as the primary objective of "AI." KPMG found that, of the employees displaced by "AI," only 14% were let go, with the rest retrained to deal with data, or for AI-related tasks, or to work on a specific process or in an industry domain, or to service new business needs.[7]

More generally, Manyinka and Burghin (2018) identified three simultaneous "AI" impacts: jobs lost, jobs gained and jobs changed. In their mid-point scenario, jobs lost by 2030 could displace 400 million workers, but these losses would be more than compensated for by between 555 and 890 million jobs gained. They also predict that many more jobs would be changed by automation than would be lost.

It's worth sharing the findings from two surveys we conducted—one in 2017 of 124 senior managers and one in 2018 of 60 service automation adopters. We asked respondents, "What does your organization do with the labor savings generated from automation?" Only 22% of the respondents in the 2017 survey and 15% of the respondents in the 2018

---

[7] *Easing the pressure points: The state of intelligent automation,* KPMG International (in collaboration with HFS Research), March 2019, available at https://assets.kpmg/content/dam/kpmg/xx/pdf/2019/03/easing-pressure-points-the-state-of-intelligent-automation.pdf.

survey indicated that their organizations laid off employees as a consequence of automation. Other enterprises did reduce headcount, but not through layoffs. Instead, they took a gentler approach to ratcheting down headcount gradually through natural attrition, or by slowing recruitment or offering early retirement.

Our research found that, certainly on 2017/2018 plans, service automation technologies were most commonly used to free up employees from dreary, repetitive work enabling them to focus on more value-adding tasks. Specifically, most enterprises used the freed-up time to redeploy people to other tasks within the work unit or to other work units within the company, for example to reduce the backlog of work or to take on more work without adding more headcount. This was particularly evident in shared service organizations that were under pressure to take on more services without adding more employees. A lot of these organizations were assigning employees to more customer-facing roles and also combining tasks to redefine what constituted a "job."

There was a further surprising finding—at least to us. Before the field research, we had assumed employees would be threatened by automation. Instead, we found that those who embraced automation[8] developed highly valued skills, and many of them were either promoted or went on to join or start consulting companies.

The lesson we derived is that human resources (HR) needs to be involved in RPA/CA automation projects if enterprises want to retain their talent. HR can help with new job descriptions, better compensation packages and opportunities for employees to grow. This has been particularly pertinent following the Covid-19 crisis. Following automation, HR may need to redesign employee scorecards. If they don't, an individual's productivity metric might decline after automation because the employee will focus on more complex work as the robots take over the easy tasks. For example, in one case study on healthcare

---

[8] Many employees so welcomed automation that they anthropomorphized their software robots by providing them with names, personalities and depictions. We first encountered this back in 2014 at Xchanging (now DXC Technologies), and soon found the phenomenon at other sites. For an account, see Lacity, M. C. and Willcocks, L. (2015) *What Knowledge Workers Stand to Gain from Automation,* Harvard Business Review online, June 19,, available at https://hbr.org/2015/06/what-knowledge-workers-stand-to-gain-from-automation.

claims processing, on average, each person processed 12 claims per hour before automation. After automation, this fell to about seven claims per hour—simply because they were now working just on the complex claims. The employees were obviously unhappy because it looked as if their productivity had dropped from 12 claims per hour to seven. The healthcare company understood and adjusted expectations and employee compensation.

Automation Strategy Recommendations

Is there other advice emerging from the research, to help those who are starting or progressing through their RPA/CA journeys? For those just starting their journeys, we summarize the action principles with this advice: *think big, start small, institutionalize fast and innovate continually.*

By *thinking big*, we mean that enterprises need to develop an intelligent automation capability to thrive in the twenty-first century. They need to think strategically about automation from the start by focusing on value-driven triple-wins—for the enterprise, its customers and employees. On our 2023 evidence they also need to align automation deployment with the wider digital strategy, and digital transformation efforts (Willcocks et al., 2023).

Enterprises can *start small* with a pilot, but they likely do not need to do a proof-of-concept; the technology has already been proven, particularly for RPA. A pilot should include a business sponsor, IT security, IT operations, compliance teams and HR so that the automation will be designed for production from the start. There are also plenty of competent advisory firms that can help. Starting small quite quickly must link up with the overall digital strategy, and involve integration with the organization's technical architecture blueprint, and its governance arrangements.

Institutionalize fast refers to creating an organizational structure and change-management capability to mature and scale intelligent automation throughout the enterprise. Many companies initially set up a RPA/

CA center of excellence. We have seen such centers evolve into automation, then digital centers of excellence, thus expanding digital governance alongside digital ambition (Willcocks et al., 2023).

Finally, automations need to be managed and continually improved—software robots are like digital employees: they need to be retrained when business rules change and their proficiency can be improved with more feedback. But our most recent research shows a further evolution where automation can lead to process and business innovations. Thus as RPA and CA become an integrated part of the digital platform, so much more is enabled in terms of processes, new services, new customer experiences and ultimately even new business models (Willcocks et al., 2023).

Our advice for progressing an RPA/CA journey is encapsulated in our action principles for running and maturing service automation capabilities. We discuss these and how they were developed in an evidence-based way in Lacity et al., (2021—see also note 16 above). But let us here highlight a few critical ones.

Particularly for CA deployments in customer-facing services, initial performance will not be perfect because, as we have already pointed out, CA tools produce probabilistic outcomes rather than deterministic results. No matter how much organizations tested a CA tool in their sandbox environments, it never precisely predicted how customers would actually interact with the technology after it went live. SEB Bank learned to warn customers that a virtual software assistant would make the first attempt at answering their query and provided quick access to a human if they grew frustrated. Initially at the bank, IPsoft's Amelia handled about 50% of text chat conversations without needing human intervention. By continually analyzing the live customer interactions, SEB Bank trained the tool to perform better over time.

Another key piece of advice is to multi-skill the robots. Initially, many organizations were buying one software license—i.e., one software robot per automation process. This meant that several robots would be idle during different times of the working day. Though employees tend to have specialist skills that cannot be dynamically re-routed to balance out demand fluctuations from across the enterprise, and also require rest periods, a software robot can be programmed to run different tasks and operate 24 hours a day. It took a while before managers realized that they could program a single software robot to automate several processes, provided they scheduled them at different times. The RPA providers do not like that insight because it results in fewer software licenses being purchased.

Beyond these, smart organizations are now looking to integrate automation into a much bigger digital transformation, and RPA and CA are actually fundamental to such transformations, not a useful "quick-win" appendage. But then automation becomes even more difficult, because digital transformation is a large-scale, long-term, complex process in any sizeable long-standing organization (Wade & Shan, 2020).

Today's Automation Challenges

As they enter the Mid-2020s what are organizations struggling with when it comes to sourcing automation? We have identified several areas where managers and organizations really need help. The first is that they struggle to scale their automation. By the end of 2019, only 13% had scaled and industrialized their RPA deployment and only 12% had an enterprise approach to automation. We looked at this again in late 2020, and while the top software providers had lots of customers, very few of those customers had more than 100 software robots.[9] Let's move to late 2022. Looking just at the 80 plus major "connected-RPA" (RPA plus intelligent automation) suppliers, most clients had between 1 and 80 RPA "robots" (licenses). Few (25%) had scaled to 81–100, let alone a higher number. This has been changing in the last year, but reflects scaling, strategic investment and benefits aspiration challenges.

We think this is partly because the cost of getting to the next stage looks steep, though we have evidence that suggests the benefits can be exponential. Second, there are problems with integrating RPA technology with existing or new IT, let alone across the enterprise. A big issue is pre-existing process fragmentation. The challenges of RPA deployment

---

[9] In a December 2020 survey by Deloitte of 441 executives, only 13% of organizations had 51 or more robots. See *Automation With Intelligence,* 2020, Deloitte Insights, available at https://www2.deloitte.com/content/dam/Deloitte/tw/Documents/strategy/tw-Automation-with-intelligence.pdf.

are compounded where C-suite executives do not see these technologies as strategic, stay too remote from the programs, and frequently under-invest in automation.

The problems of deploying CA technologies are even greater, and each problem is crying out for research attention from a practice-oriented perspective. If you listen to the AI hype, it's very easy to underestimate how slow and challenging actual progress has been to date. We summarize these challenges with an acronym: BOGSHABIF, which stands for brittle, opaque, greedy, shallow, hackable, amoral, biased, invasive and fakeable. It's a pretty rich list of things that practitioners need help with, and humans will be vital in not only designing better CA but partnering with the technology during operational use.

Interestingly, we have seen recently banks and telecom companies driving digital transformation and automation efforts from different starting points and with different executives. As a result, IA initiatives can get becalmed. Moreover, slow progress on digital transformation can delay integrating transformation with the automation agenda. Organizational silos slow deployments of RPA, CA and all the digital technologies. We call the extreme version, which we have encountered, "the 8-siloed organization"—i.e., an organization with multiple silos in processes, skills, managerial mindsets, strategy, structure, data, technology and culture. Scaling and optimizing RPA and CA in such organizations, let alone achieving digital transformation, is indeed a long haul. A lot of research is still needed in this area.

There has also been little research on "born digital" companies and how they use automation technologies. Have they bypassed the "8-silo" problem, and what can more traditional enterprises learn from them? Finally, lots of studies now show that the Covid-19 pandemic and economic crises have accelerated the deployment of automation, but so far, we have found the technologies have been used differently—e.g., to sweat assets or underpin current business performance—or that the crisis might have slowed the automation strategy. Only a few organizations are really investing strategically (as opposed to tactically) in automation—it may be as little as 20% (Willcocks, 2021a, b). This deserves much more study going forward as we are sure the picture will change dramatically into the mid-2020s.

Conclusion: Future Challenges and Research

This chapter has given a subjective researcher account of the formative period for RPA, cognitive and intelligent automation leading into AI. It has provided insights into the evolution of automation as deployed in our work organizations. But the insights, recommendations and action principles must remain provisional and updateable. Going forward the chapter leads to some important research questions:

- How can organizations scale RPA and CA beyond automation islands?
- How can organizations deal with the dramatic skill shifts needed for increasingly digital and virtual businesses enabled by RPA, CA and other automation technologies?
- What human skills are needed in a workforce that will increasingly rely on or work alongside digital workers?
- What role should automation technologies play within broader digital transformation programs?
- What are the critical practices required by digital leaders to ensure strategic automation provides disproportionate business value?
- What emerging technologies will shift innovation priorities for RPA and CA and disrupt workforce and business models even further?
- How can organizational absorptive capacity avoid being outstripped by the pace of technological innovation?

Let's add to this picture. To date, intelligent automation tools have been adopted within the boundaries of the firm, but the next phase is happening in cooperation with ecosystem partners. For example, inter-organizational data sharing, which requires ecosystem-level solutions, is a great example of the next generation of challenges IT leaders must solve (Wixom & Sebastian, 2020). We are now studying how technologies can automate inter-organizational transactions. The solutions often require integrating a variety of technologies, including Internet of Things (IoT), radio frequency identification (RFID), ERP, blockchains, RPA and machine learning. In our recent case studies on ecosystem-level applications, technologies represented between 20 and 30% of the effort required. Up to 80% of the effort was for trading partners to agree on data and event standards, shared governance models, intellectual property rights and compliance assurance. There's a lot more to investigate in this area, including:

- How can service automation technologies be used to automate inter-organizational transactions?
- Which governance models are effective for shared applications?

Finally, our research method derived the RPA and CA action principles. These principles are based on cumulative evidence thus far, but will need to be revised, extended or retired as organizations gain more experience. We encourage researchers, in particular, to further vet and expand the action principles associated with the maturity phase of adopting intelligent automation.

References

Asatiani, A., & Penttinen, E. (2016). Turning Robotic Process Automation into Commercial Success—Case OpusCapita. *Journal of Information Technology Teaching Cases, 6*(2), 67–74.
Broussard, M. (2018). *Artificial Unintelligence*. The MIT Press.
Davenport, T. H. (2018). *The AI Advantage: How to Put the Artificial Intelligence Revolution to Work*. The MIT Press.
Davenport, T. H., & Kirby, J. (2016). Just How Smart Are Smart Machines? *MIT Sloan Management Review, 57*(3), 21–25.
Davenport, T. H., & Rananki, R. (2018, January-February). Artificial Intelligence for the Real World. *Harvard Business Review.*
Fersht, P. (2012, November 1). *Greetings from Robotistan, Outsourcing's Cheapest New Destination*. Horses for Sources. https://www.horsesforsources.com/robotistan_011112
Fersht, P., & Snowdon, J. (2018, November 30). *RPA Will Reach $2.3bn Next Year and $4.3bn by 2022… as We Revise Our Forecast Upwards*. Horses for Sources. https://www.horsesforsources.com/RPA-forecast-2016-2022_120118.
Giddens, A. (1984). *The Constitution of Society: Outline of the Theory of Structuration*. University of California Press.

Hallikainen, P., Bekkhus, R., & Pan, S. (2018). How OpusCapita Used Internal RPA Capabilities to Offer Services to Clients. *MIS Quarterly Executive, 17*(1), 41–52. https://aisel.aisnet.org/misqe/vol17/iss1/4

Hume, D. (1739). *A Treatise of Human Nature* (Reprinted ed. 1986). Clarendon Press.

IEEE. (2017). *IEEE Guide for Terms and Concepts in Intelligent Process Automation.* https://standards.ieee.org/standard/2755-2017.html

KPMG. (2020). *Enterprise Reboot: Scale Digital Technologies to Grow and Thrive in the New Reality.* KPMG International and HFS Research. https://home.kpmg/xx/en/home/insights/2020/08/enterprise-reboot.html

Lacity, M. (2019). From Theory Worship to Action Principles: A Commentary on Hirschheim's "Against Theory: With Apologies to Feyerabend. *Journal of the Association for Information Systems, 20*(9), 1370–1373.

Lacity, M. C., & Willcocks, L. (2016). A New Approach to Automating Services. *MIT Sloan Management Review, 58*(1), 40–49.

Lacity, M. C., Willcocks, L., & Craig, A. (2015, April). *Robotic Process Automation at Telefónica O2*, Paper 15/02 (The Outsourcing Unit Working Paper Series). London School of Economics, London.

Lacity, M., Willcocks, L., & Gozman,. (2021). Influencing Information Systems Practice: The Action Principles Approach Applied to Robotic Process and Cognitive Automation. *Journal of Information Technology, 36*(3), 216–240. https://DOI.org/10.1177/0268396221990778

Lowes, P., & Cannata, F. (2017). *Automate This: The Business Leader's Guide to Robotic and Intelligent Automation.* Deloitte.

Manyinka, J., & Burghin, J. (2018, October). *The Promise and the Challenge of the Age of Artificial Intelligence.* McKinsey Global Institute. Executive Briefing. https://www.mckinsey.com/featured-insights/artificial-intelligence/the-promise-and-challenge-of-the-age-of-artificial-intelligence

Russell, S. (2019). *Human Compatible: AI and the Problem of Control.* Allen Lane.

Schatsky, D., Muraskin, C., & Iyengar, K. (2016). *Robotic Process Automation: A Path to the Cognitive Enterprise.* Deloitte University Press.

Smith, G. (2018). *The AI Delusion.* Oxford University Press.

Smith, R. E. (2019). *Rage Inside the Machine.* Bloomsbury Business.

Wade, M., & Shan, J. (2020, September). Covid-19 Has Accelerated Digital Transformation, but May Have Made it Harder Not Easier. *MIS Quarterly Executive,19*(3), 213–220. https://aisel.aisnet.org/misqe/vol19/iss3/7

Watson, H. (2017). Preparing For the Cognitive Generation of Decision Support. *MIS Quarterly Executive, 16*(3), 153–169.

Willcocks, L. (2020a). Robo-Apocalypse Cancelled? Reframing the Automation and Future of Work Debate. *Journal of Information Technology, 35*(4), 286–302.

Willcocks, L. (2020b, April 23). Why Misleading Metaphors Are Fooling Managers About The Use of AI. *Forbes.* https://www.forbes.com/sites/londonschoolofeconomics/2020/04/23/why-misleading-metaphors-are-fooling-managers-about-the-use-of-ai/?sh=7ec5fec5de1f

Willcocks, L. (2021a). *Global Business: Management.* SB Publishing.

Willcocks, L. (2021b). Robo-Apocalypse? Response and Outlook on the Post-COVID-19 Future of Work. *Journal of Information Technology, 36*(2), 188–194.

Willcocks, L., Hindle, J., & Lacity, M. C. (2019). *Becoming Strategic with Robotic Process Automation.* SB Publishing.

Willcocks, L., Hindle, J., Stanton, M., & Smith, J. (2023). *Maximizing Value with Automation and Digital Transformation: A Realist's Guide.* Palgrave Macmillan.

Wixom, B., & Sebastian, I. (2020). *Data Sharing Across Company Boundaries.* MIT Center for Information Systems Research. https://cisr.mit.edu/content/data-sharing-across-company-boundaries

10

Formal and Relational Outsourcing Governance of Artificial Intelligence and Algorithms

Erik Beulen, Albert Plugge, and Jos van Hillegersberg

Introduction

Today, emerging technologies, such as machine learning, robotic process automation and complex algorithms, referred to as Artificial Intelligence (AI), are expected to impact organisations significantly (Willcocks, 2020;

An earlier version of this chapter was published as Beulen, E., Plugge, A., & van Hillegersberg, J. (2022). Formal and Relational Governance of Artificial Intelligence Outsourcing. *Information Systems and e-Business Management, 20,* 719–748. This is a much revised and updated version.

E. Beulen (✉)
AMBS, University of Manchester, Manchester, United Kingdom
e-mail: erik.beulen@manchester.ac.uk

A. Plugge
Nyenrode Business University, Breukelen, The Netherlands

J. van Hillegersberg
Faculty of Behavioural Management and Social Sciences (BMS), Industrial Engineering and Business Information Systems (IEBIS), University of Twente, Enschede, The Netherlands

see also chapter 9). Recent studies on AI reveal its potential to help solve current problems in the field of data processing and business process optimisation. There are many reports on the AI market and what follows is indicative only. Market research by consultancies and research agencies shows that the 2025 market size of AI will grow to $232 Billion (KPMG, 2018). A market survey on AI conducted by McKinsey's (2020) shows that AI adoption is highest in service development and service operations. In a similar vein, Gartner (2020) indicated that *"by the end of 2024, 75% of enterprises will shift from piloting to operationalising AI, driving a 5 × increase in streaming data and analytics infrastructures"*. This fits within the service-oriented approach of organisations today to improve internal business services (Plugge et al., 2020). Literature shows that there is no consensus on a common definition of AI (Legg & Hutter, 2007; Wang, 2019; see also Chapter 9). Dwivedi et al. (2021, p. 2) argue that *"the common thread amongst AI definitions is the increasing capability of machines to perform specific roles and tasks currently performed by humans within the workplace and society in general"*, see also (Jaiswal et al., 2022; Khan et al., 2023). This description includes machines that mimic cognitive functions, like learning (Russell & Norvig, 2016) and the ability to independently interpret and learn from external data (Kaplan & Haenlein, 2019; Zhang, 2021). However, concerns are raised about the potential of AI to support wrong decision-making (Dignum, 2018; Floridi et al., 2018). This is part of a broader digital transformation outsourcing trend (Beulen, 2016; Beulen & Ribbers, 2020).

In AI services the development and maintenance of algorithms are an important element. An essential element in outsourcing algorithms is the potential competitive risks. Organisations need to be mindful of protecting their interest and avoid that vendors are not replicating and re-using knowledge and experience for competitors of their organisation—for example in pricing algorithms (Harrington, 2022). Secondly, privacy preservations need to be addressed, monitored and audited by organisations that outsource algorithms (Jiang & Fu, 2020). Furthermore many organisations are focusing on becoming data-driven. Data quality is still slowing down the adoption of data-driven decision-making. Algorithms are instrumental to improve data quality and to speed up the implementation of data-driven decision-making (Tajammal et al., 2021).

Leading vendors in this field include Accenture, Atos, Boston Consulting Group, EY, HCL, KPMG, McKinsey and Tata Consultancy Services, as well as many other established and niche vendors. As the impact of AI on business is of strategic importance, AI and algorithms outsourcing needs to be carefully governed. Kranz (2021) argues that there is statistical evidence that contractual governance plays a key role in IS arrangements. However, there is no research on how formal AI contracts are established. Moreover, the way clients and vendors cope with relational governance, including psychological contracts (Argyris, 1960; Levinson et al., 1962), in the context of AI and algorithms is unknown. Our aim is to fill this research gap by conducting a study that examines the governance of AI and algorithms outsourcing in an in-depth, qualitative manner. To broaden our view on governance for AI and algorithms outsourcing, we examine formal and relational governance elements, including a psychological contract, as part of the client-vendor outsourcing arrangement. These elements have to be taken into account, not only by clients and vendors, but also by IS sourcing advisors. To the best of our knowledge, this is the first study that examines formal and informal governance in the context of AI and algorithms outsourcing. Consequently, we answer the call of Kranz (2021) to study the implementation of contractual models and its effect on governance and relationship outcomes. Moreover, we extend the study by Linden and Rosenkranz (2019) on relational governance in the context of AI and algorithms outsourcing. Hence, the main research question of this study is:

> How are formal and relational governance used in Artificial Intelligence and algorithms outsourcing?

We contribute to the literature by making an inventory of the current AI and algorithms outsourcing practices by focusing on formal and relational governance. Our chapter is organised as follows. First, we describe the theoretical background addressing the concepts of governance for AI and algorithms outsourcing. Next, we introduce a research framework, based on the Lioliou et al. (2014) outsourcing governance framework. Subsequently, the research method is presented, then the data analysis and results are described. Finally, we present a discussion and conclusions.

Theoretical Background

Artificial Intelligence

Kaplan and Haenlein (2019) argue that, while the academic discipline of AI was established already in the 1950s, "*AI remained an area of relative scientific obscurity and limited practical interest for over half a century*" (p. 5). Literature shows that AI has been studied from an augmentation perspective, arguing that AI should support humans in decision-making (Duan et al., 2020; Miller, 2018). Moreover, Davenport and Ronanki (2018) argue that AI systems are not able to explain the reasoning process of decision-making, and as such are supportive of human judgement. The authors address the role of deep learning as a means to learn from large volumes of labelled data. However, it is almost impossible to understand the models that are designed to execute its functionality. The AI "black box" may cause issues, for instance in regulated sectors, as regulators insist on knowing why and how decisions are made. Hence, AI can be perceived as an awareness system that is supportive of humans in order to increase the visibility of events or states (Krancher et al., 2018) that may add business value to organisations by means of technology (Sabherwal & Jeyaray, 2015).

Tarafdar et al. (2019) demonstrate in their study on AI that successful organisations, which are able to create value, radically improved their business processes. Consequently, AI aids organisations to process more data that support human decision-making. When AI systems, such as intelligent Information Technology (IT) service management systems (Zhang, 2021), rely on fragmented and missing or inconsistent data, conventional organisations are challenged by successfully integrating data, which in turn may result in biased or incorrect decision-making. When involving vendors, ensuring this has become more difficult, as AI services in outsourcing are performed at arms-length. Managing compliance regulations, which is perceived to be a business challenge (Dwivedi et al., 2021; Haenlein & Kaplan, 2019), is influenced by the degree of AI complexity. This may create compliance issues. Recently, Coombs et al. (2020, p. 13) found that *"there is limited research that examines how organisations design governance arrangements and structures associated with Intelligent Automation decision-making"*. By applying an IS governance lens, organisations may develop strategies to overcome compliance challenges and contribute to support AI decision-making.

Algorithms

Algorithms are step-by-step procedures or sets of rules for solving a particular problem. They are fundamental in computer science and form the building blocks of software development as well as artificial intelligence (Lindsell et al., 2020). For governmental organisations there is an additional ethical consideration of "fairness" to be taken into account when using algorithms (Fernández, 2023; Wang et al., 2023), as for any organisation (Bankins & Formosa, 2023). The ownership of the algorithms needs to be addressed by organisations that are collaborating with vendors. Organisations need to develop Intellectual Properties (IP) strategies (Alexy et al., 2009). Most organisations apply a defensive strategy, which predominantly rely on formal contracts, but also there are strategies with a combination of formal and informal contracts (Grimaldi et al., 2021).

IS Governance

We conducted a literature review to identify attributes that correspond to Information Systems (IS) governance. Our review demonstrates that IS governance, taking formal and relational attributes into account, has been extensively researched. Importantly, there does not appear to be a single accepted definition of IS governance—which makes it difficult to formulate an exact description. Our definition is that *"IS governance is an integral part of corporate governance [that] addresses the definition and implementation of information system processes, structures and relational mechanisms in the organisation, enabling both business and IS people to execute their responsibilities in support of business/IS alignment and the creation of business value from IS-enabled business investments*" [adapted from Van Grembergen and De Haes (2009)]. Literature reveals two main research streams that include formal and relational governance.

Scholars have studied formal governance that aims to coordinate activities between outsourcing partners to prevent opportunistic behaviour through mutually agreed and legally binding behaviours (Beulen & Ribbers, 2007, 2021); Chang et al., 2017). Rai et al. (2012) considered relationships in which the work of Macneil (1980) is used as a starting point. Relational governance attempts to address some of the deficiencies in contract governance: the failure to account for social structures within which the inter-organisation exchanges are embedded, as well as the overestimation of hazardous elements in the exchange (Xiao et al., 2012). Recently, literature on IS governance demonstrates more dynamic interrelationships between formal and relational governance than the previously assumed dichotomy of complementarity and substitution (Kranz, 2021; Lacity et al., 2016; Oshri et al., 2015). These studies address the role of relation-specific boundary conditions. As a result, formal and relational governance mechanisms can act as substitutes (Rai et al., 2012), and may simultaneously work as substitutes and complements (Lioliou et al., 2014; Tiwana, 2010) or have an impact that may change over time (Huber et al., 2013).

Formal IS Governance

Formal IS governance addresses the necessity to include contract mechanisms to monitor and enforce contractual commitments (Lacity et al., 2016). Common formal governance-related attributes address contracts (Oshri et al., 2015), Service Level Agreements (SLAs) and Key Performance Indicators (KPIs) (Lioliou & Willcocks, 2019) and flexibility (Goo et al., 2009). In addition, pricing mechanisms, such as Time and Materials contracts and Fixed Price contracts, are also relevant formal attributes (Oshri et al., 2015). More recently, contracts may include profit-sharing, also known as gainsharing, as a pricing mechanism (Lioliou & Willcocks, 2019). A recent study of Kranz (2021) looked at formal and relational IS governance in the field of innovation IT outsourcing. Based on his study it seems that contractual mechanisms primarily determine joint performance. The author observed that "*while relationship learning profited from higher levels of alignment between the two governance modes (e.g. formal and relational), joint innovation is highest when contractual governance is high and relational governance is at a medium level* (p. 13)". Importantly, a remaining question that is still unanswered in the research is to understand how control- and coordination-focused clauses affect governance and relationship outcomes. Our aim is to explore this question in the context of Artificial Intelligence outsourcing.

Relational IS Governance

The IS literature shows five common attributes to relationships in sourcing, namely: (1) trust, (2) commitment, (3) dependency, (4) communication and (5) psychological contract. Trust between the client and vendor is essential (Lacity et al., 2016; Li et al., 2010) to achieve agreed outcomes. Closely related to trust is commitment (Goo et al., 2009; Kranz, 2021; Lioliou et al., 2014), as a two-sided approach drives achieving results and will contribute to trust. Dependency contributes only if there is a vendor dependency or a mutual dependency (Lioliou et al., 2014). Communication, on the other hand, enables proactive responses from both the vendor and the client (Lacity et al., 2016; Lioliou & Willcocks, 2019). Finally, psychological contracts are considered as a set of beliefs and perceptions that correspond to contractual obligations (Robinson & Rousseau, 1994) to solve the limitations of formal contracting and as such, create flexibility for the client as well as the vendor (Han et al., 2017). Linden and Rosenkranz (2019), who studied the relational IS governance perspective, address the importance of third-party advisors in IT outsourcing engagements. This novel study on third-party advisors shows that relational mechanisms are perceived to be essential in building the relationship between client and vendor.

However, this valuable study does not include the role of vendors. In our research we focus on vendors explicitly and as such, contribute to literature.

AI Outsourcing Governance Research Framework

As we study AI in the context of outsourcing, the unit of analysis in this research is the vendor side. Based on our research we will gain a better understanding on how IS governance for AI is structured. IS governance and its embedded attributes (formal governance, relational governance and psychological contracts) are used as a moderator. Our framework (see Fig. 10.1) is applicable to IS governance in regular vendor relationships. Our framework is based on the general IS governance framework provided by Lioliou et al. (2014). As AI is an emerging technology, there is additional complexity with regard to IS governance. In this context, trust and collaboration require an increased focus (Hoecht & Trott, 2006). Also there is an increased dependency, due to the client specifics of the AI-outsourced services (Gopalakrishnan & Zhang, 2019). Moreover, protecting IP is essential in innovative services (Cammarano et al., 2019), such as AI services. This complexity also guided the analysis of our expert interviews.

Research Method

As the multifaceted domain of IS governance for AI can be considered as complex, we decided to adopt an exploratory, case study-based approach. Our basic assumption is that this will give us a deeper understanding of the subject under examination (Yin, 2017). Orlikowski and Iacono (2001) argue that study research is a common method in the field of IS and useful to study "how" and "why" questions (Benbasat et al., 1987). Our approach allowed us to focus on formal governance and relational governance practices of vendors involved in AI-outsourcing contracts. Due to confidentiality, the vendors under study were reluctant

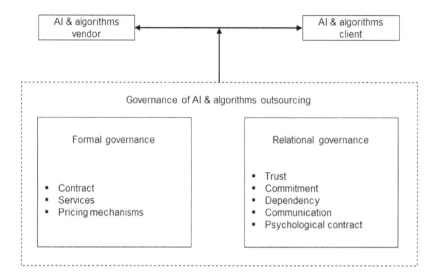

Fig. 10.1 Governance of Artificial Intelligence and algorithms outsourcing research framework (interrelations between formal and relational governance and psychological contract are based on Lioliou et al. (2014 – Fig. 2, p. 520)

to share contractual insights with the researchers. Consequently, we did not have access to contractual obligations between the vendors and their clients. Through an extensive research protocol protecting the interests of vendors, we were able to interview various vendor representatives. To select vendors, we used two main criteria. First, we made a distinction with regard to the range of a vendor's portfolio regarding AI services. Second, some vendors only focus on client engagements, while others provide solutions to multiple partners. We selected eight vendors offering a variety of AI services, supplemented with two market research advisors to understand the market better, the two criteria outlined above are met.

Data Collection

A two-phased approach was used to collect primary and secondary data by means of an interview protocol. We started by collecting publicly available data related to the type of IS outsourcing vendors for AI. The data collection is based on two sources: (1) desk research and (2) direct observations. We examined documentation that included website information, whitepapers, factsheets and public webinars. Next, we interviewed two market research advisors (interviewees 16, 17 and 18). In addition, we drafted field notes during the interviews. In the second phase, we conducted a number of online and telephone interviews. The interviews were semi-structured and based on a protocol that included open questions (see Appendix A) that contribute to the consistency and reliability of the results (Denzin 1978). In all, 18 in-depth interviews were conducted with vendor representatives in which we combined two key roles in each interview, namely, a vendor senior representative (partners, directors, senior vice presidents) and AI and algorithms Subject Matter Experts (SMEs). All interviewees were selected based on their involvement in establishing AI-related services towards their clients. The interviewees 1–4, 6, 8, 10, 12, 14–18 have C-level and C-level-1 leadership positions in global leading vendors and +20 years of experience, and are leading global AI and algorithms engagements. The interviews 5, 7, 9, 11 and 13 are senior AI and algorithms SMEs delivering engagements to global top-tier clients with +10 years of experience.

Due to confidentiality, the names and roles of the interviewees in the organisation are anonymised (see Table 10.1). The interviews were held between November 2020 and May 2021 and lasted between 30 and 90 minutes. They were all digitally recorded and transcribed. Next, the transcripts were sent to the participants for confirmation. A research database was built to ensure a reliable data analysis.

Data Analysis

The data was analysed in a number of systematic steps to make sure the process was replicable. As a first step, we studied the context-related information from a broader organisational client-vendor relationship. The aim was to create a basic understanding of what type of AI services are provided by vendors. As a second step, we thoroughly analysed the interview transcripts and archival data, verifying the data as needed via follow-up telephone calls and e-mails. As a third step, we triangulated the interview transcripts with supplementary key documents (e.g.

Table 10.1 Overview of interviewed experts in case organisations

Expert	Type of vendor	Company	Function interviewee	Interview time
1		BCG	Managing Director and Partner	30 minutes
2	Strategy advisor	BCG	Managing Director and Partner	30 minutes
3		McKinsey	Client Partner	30 minutes
4		EY	Client Partner	60 minutes
5	Accounting & Consulting firm	EY	AI subject matter expert	60 minutes
6	(Big 4)	KPMG	Senior Manager	60 minutes
7		KPMG	AI subject matter expert	60 minutes
8		Accenture	Client Partner	60 minutes
9		Accenture	AI subject matter expert	60 minutes
10		Atos	Client Partner	60 minutes
11	Technology vendor	Atos	AI subject matter expert	60 minutes
12		HCL	Senior Vice President	60 minutes
13		HCL	AI subject matter expert	60 minutes
14		TCS	Vice President & Global Head	45 minutes
15		TCS	Chief Technology Officer	45 minutes
16		Gartner	Client Partner	60 minutes
17	Market research advisor	Gartner	AI subject matter expert	60 minutes
18		Horses for Sources	Senior Vice President	90 minutes

webinar input, whitepapers, factsheets, field notes) (Denzin, 2009). In doing so, we were able to validate the research steps and ensure internal validity of the expert interviews. All interview data were subject to cross-examination by the research team (three researchers), while correcting errors that contributed to the triangulation of available data. Coding and clustering techniques (Yin, 2017) were used, and next we followed Miles and Huberman (1994) advice and divided coding among two researchers, who each coded the interview notes. We applied Atlas.ti to code and combine interview data of the 18 respondents and created concept maps which resulted in a total of 141 codes. In total, we conducted four rounds of concept aggregation. During the first three rounds, a number of concepts that are closely aligned were aggregated into a single code. Moreover, we reduced the number of codes by ignoring concepts that are perceived as influencing attributes. In round four, we identified 42 codes (concepts) that represent the most important elements of our research framework (see Appendix B). As a next step, findings were discussed and disagreements were clarified. Finally, we draw conclusions on what types of AI were provided by the vendors under study and how they handle the governance of AI and algorithms outsourcing.

Findings

In the following sections, we highlight the governance attributes by answering our research question: *How are formal and relational outsourcing governance used for Artificial Intelligence and Algorithms*? We clustered our findings by means of the governance of AI and algorithms outsourcing and its embedded elements, indicated in italics, and have summarised embedded elements in (Table. 10.1).

Client–Vendor AI Outsourcing Arrangement

Interviews show that the initiator of AI and algorithms at the client side often varies across various departments, such as data analytics, data science, innovation, IS and business intelligence. Interviewees argue that clients' business processes and IS-enabled systems are interrelated and can be perceived as a prerequisite to discuss and apply AI solutions and implement algorithms. With regard to clients' AI approach, we distinguish two phases. The first phase corresponds to clients that establish a multidisciplinary team which includes both business and IS representatives exploring the potential of AI opportunities. Potential business process candidates that can be supported by AI and algorithms are analysed from different perspectives, such as risk, compliance, privacy and legality.

Two interviewees mentioned that:

> Clients' IT and innovation teams often lack the knowledge of what's really important for business processes, which procedures need to be applied, and how to avoid pitfalls and failures. But it's not that they already have that within their background. And we don't pretend that all our data scientists know this already, but we do have people specialised in industries and if we work together with them, we can already bring in the right teams. (source: Technology vendor-Accenture-Client Partner)
>
> The typical set of profiles of clients involved in AI is 50% business stakeholders and 50% technology experts. However we see more and more clients initiating AI initiatives from a business side. (source: Market research advisory firm-Gartner-Client Partner)

Second, the multidisciplinary team is responsible for building, testing and deploying the AI solution by applying an agile (sprint) approach. By using proof-of-concepts, AI functionality is tested in practice. An interviewee mentioned that:

> Start small initiatives, and focus on continuous improvement. What is important is to monitor the availability of capabilities closely from the start. The ability to scale up is an important success factor. (source: Market research advisory firm-Gartner-AI SME)

The interviews consistently show that applying an agile approach is a better practice in the current emerging market maturity for AI.

Formal Governance of AI and Algorithm Outsourcing

Contract

We observed two findings that relate to Intellectual Property (IP) and Terms and Conditions. We noticed that vendors argue that AI- and algorithm-related IP should be owned by their clients as they are responsible for applying AI and Algorithms solutions. Technology vendors in contrast made a distinction between commodity and customised type of IP, in which the latter should be owned by the client. One of the interviewees mentioned that:

> Essentially we are bounded by the contract that we agreed with. If we build an AI algorithm, then the client wants us to sign that we do not build the same algorithm for the other clients. So, IP is transferred to the client. (source: Technology vendor-Accenture-AI SME)

Similar to software development, if a vendor includes their IP in AI and algorithms, they grant a perpetual licence to protect their interest. Importantly, vendors also provide clients the opportunity to co-develop AI services and algorithms. In these circumstances, both the client and vendor draft specific contractual clauses on how to deal with IP-related topics. One of the interviewees mentioned that:

By co-creating IP, we are able to monetarise our client's assets that affect their balance sheet positively. In case we co-develop IP with a client we may come to an agreement that this IP can be used in other client engagements. If that's the case, the original client receives a royalty fee. (source: Technology vendor-HCL-SVP)

Our interviews demonstrate that standard T&Cs are used in AI-related contracts. Some vendors argue that existing frameworks are used to contract AI and therefore standard T&Cs are applied. However, more specific AI solutions are embedded in the underpinning AI solution and algorithm developments and maintenance Statements of Work. Interestingly, none of the interviewees argued that decreased liability caps were applied in contracts for AI services and algorithms. Apparently, vendors do not recognise extra risks when provisioning AI and algorithms or have instead incorporated the additional risks into their fees.

Services—SLAs and KPIs

Findings regarding the attribute *services* show that find that existing framework agreements are used. Vendors argue that existing SLAs are applied to measure AI and algorithms performance. We noticed that the vast majority of engagements are based on a project approach (e.g. design, build, test and deploy). By applying a project approach, service agreements reflect the skills of data designers, data engineers and project lead times. Importantly, vendors may agree on applying experience-driven xLAs with their clients. This finding demonstrates their ability to focus on AI solution outcomes in contrast to technical availability. One of the interviewees mentioned that:

> We see a shift towards xLAs (experience-driven service levels). Based on the insights that we gain during AI tests we can predict how AI will perform in practice. That means that we are willing to apply a service level driven by experience. (source: Technology vendor-TCS-VP & Global Head)

Based on the interviews we did not find examples of experience penalty clauses for underperforming service levels when providing AI services and algorithms. Hence, there are no observations related to contractual KPIs, only SLA measurements that include a penalty for missing the agreed-upon service level.

Pricing Mechanisms

The third formal governance attribute corresponds to *pricing mechanisms*. Interviews reveal that pricing mechanisms can be categorised into transaction-based (e.g. Fixed Price, Time and Materials, consumption) and outcome-based (e.g. bonus/malus) mechanisms. Fixed Price agreements are often performed in project-based activities to decrease the degree of risks, such as setting up a proof-of-concept to test and validate an AI solution. In case the degree of uncertainty (e.g. risks) of a project increases, clients and vendors agree to apply the Time and Materials mechanism. An example corresponds to an unknown number of sprints that are required to develop, test and deploy AI, as well as algorithms. One of the interviewees mentioned that:

> Considering our AI support the financial model is based on a fixed fee type of model. If the degree of uncertainty in a project is difficult to calculate, we use a time and materials model. We do not use or see risk and reward types of financial models in practice. (source: Accounting and Consulting firm-KPMG-Senior Manager)

Technology vendors that offer "AI & algorithms as a Service" apply a more consumption-driven approach. Depending on the number of client users and types of AI solutions and algorithms, the degree of consumption affects the price immediately. We find that two technology vendors offer outcome-based pricing agreements (e.g. HCL and TCS). After co-developing a solution, AI and algorithms performance is measured for a certain period, and based on the performance and learnings, an agreement is made for the desired outcome. These vendors applied a bonus/malus mechanism which is based on the provided outcome. The interviews reveal that strategy advisors apply the identification of relevant use cases for their AI and algorithms, which is a similar principle as for their other offerings-potential benefit / investment ratio. One of the interviewees said:

> We will not touch anything which is less than 10X, and on average we typically pitch for opportunities between 50 to 100X, both in terms of benefit/investment ratio. (source: Strategic advisor-McKinsey-Client Partner)

Relational Governance of AI and Algorithms Outsourcing

Trust

The interviews show that the attribute *trust* in vendor capabilities is perceived as critical. All vendors applied practical frameworks that are used to support AI solutions and algorithms, for instance for design, development and implementation. Generally considered factors that are discussed corresponds to risks (e.g. data, design, performance), technology, ethics, reliability, accountability and social impact. One interviewee commented that:

> Importantly, we developed criteria to assure the quality of our work. In case we develop AI for clients, we also apply our internal AI quality framework. We share and discuss this quality framework with our clients and provide full transparency as an extra guarantee. Next, the client accepts our product and becomes responsible for the use of the AI solution, such as an algorithm. (source: Accounting & Consulting firm-KPMG-AI SME)

All vendors explicitly address the importance of ethics in delivering AI and algorithms. Continuously monitoring ethical compliance is perceived to be important. One of the interviewees said:

> Of course, everyone agrees that ethics is important, but how do you really implement it? Actually, when you look at certain elements that

are relevant for ethics and fairness, and then testing your output among different groups that isn't rocket science. But you can also make it transparent. That will contribute to trust. (source: Accounting & Consulting firm—EY—AI SME)

In addition, we noticed that providing AI and algorithms assurance, including ethical compliance, is emerging. Thus one interviewee said:

Going forward, clients might ask for, or even due to regulatory compliance might be in need of, an assurance certification" (source: Market research advisory firm-HfS-SVP) and "Business leaders are increasingly very closely involved in ensuring ethical compliance. (Technology vendor-TCS-VP & Global Head)

Another interviewee commented that:

I think we are five to ten years away from people thinking about it systematically and proactively. However, in all of our engagements we explicitly integrate ethical compliance in our engagements. (source: Strategic advisor-BCG-MD and Partner 2)

One interviewee further mentioned *that:*

We have our set of ethical principles and a set of actionable policies. Any engagement team has to answer 10 yes/no questions to flag risks, potentially followed by a full assessment of 50 questions to assess the ethical risk profile. During the engagement, high-risk cases are closely monitored by a committee. These senior subject matter experts are also guiding engagement teams. (source: Strategic advisor-BCG-MD and Partner 1)

Commitment

Addressing the attribute of *commitment*, our research findings show that relationship management is a key for vendors. We notice that most AI solution initiatives start at the executive level due to the strategic impact that AI may have within organisations. The motivation to create executive-level sponsorship is twofold. First, AI and algorithms may affect an organisation's corporate image seriously, for instance when poor-designed solutions result in wrong decision-making. Second, as AI and algorithms are complex, projects require multiple internal stakeholders (e.g. business representative, designer, developer, data engineer). As a consequence, executive sponsorship is a prerequisite to align internal departments and create insights in both opportunities and risks. By achieving executive commitment vendors are able to build commitment and trust before starting an AI project. Thus one interviewee said:

> AI may have a serious effect within a firm or towards their customers that may be impactful. Therefore, it is important to ensure that executive management is aware of the consequences. That's why we focus on C-level commitment first. (source: Strategic advisor-McKinsey-Client Partner)

No differences were found in the initiation of AI solution engagements across the vendors. AI solution engagements are with both existing clients and with new clients.

Dependencies

When addressing the attribute *dependency*, our analysis shows two relevant dependencies that relate to clients and its vendors. Importantly, when vendors and their clients co-develop IP, the AI solution and algorithms may comprise inconsistencies. One of the interviewees mentioned:

> By co-creating IP we are able to monetarize our client's assets that affect their balance sheet positively. In case we co-develop IP with a client we may come to an agreement that this IP can be used in other client engagements. If that's the case, the original client receives a royalty fee. (source: Technology vendor-HCL-AI SME)

Interviewees stated that data quality (e.g. correctness, completeness, compliance) is a key and can be perceived as the fundament for an AI solution. If an AI solution is functioning incorrectly, data quality may cause a serious dependency. As clients are primarily responsible for their data, the reputation of their vendor may be at risk. One of the interviewees said:

> It does start with the data you know because AI will use available data in which the quality is key. Dependent on the client's data quality, we select a relevant type of AI technology and then start to co-develop. Not just apply the same AI technology because you're used to it, but the client's specific situation will influence the choice of a technology. (source: Accounting & Consulting firm-EY-AI SME)

A second dependency is the demand for skilled professionals. The labour market for AI professionals, such as data scientist and data engineers, is stressed. AI and algorithms skills are in demand by both suppliers and clients. Access to qualified resources is essential for IS governance. Thus an interviewee commented:

> Data scientists and data engineers are in high demand. We see a lot of emphasis on training, also as part of our engagements. (source: Technology vendor-Accenture-AI SME)

We find that educating client staff in AI and algorithms reduces the dependency and improves IS governance.

Communication

Our study reveals that as the number of clients' stakeholders involved in AI solution and algorithms increases, *communication* becomes more intense to align AI and algorithms goals and their expected outcomes. We find examples of agile teams, in which client and vendor representatives collaborated in sprint sessions, and where vendors educated their clients. In addition, bi-weekly management meetings are used to discuss the progress of AI solution and algorithm development. Due to the complexity of designing AI solutions and algorithms, and the number of stakeholders involved, our findings show that proactive communication and collaboration enables trust between a client and their vendor:

I think we quite often make AI and algorithms something that is really far away and is a kind of a black box. But actually, it's a human team that is behind it. And the more you communicate and get involved with the client team that in the end is using it, the more aware you become of AI functionalities. (source: Technology vendor-Atos-Client Partner)

Psychological Contract

Our study shows that as the number of client stakeholders involved in AI solution and algorithms increases, the degree of awareness related to reputational risks also increases. Combined with AI outsourcing contracts, a psychological contract is established. As in any outsourcing contract, there are mutual responsibilities that are addressed in a formal contract as well as in a psychological contract. Interestingly, we observed that vendors' knowledge and experience, combined with their (long-term) client relationship, results in proactive responses to handle incidents regardless of formal agreed responsibilities. Thus:

If my customers get worried that our algorithm is not providing the right results for them anymore, then all the attention will go to fixing it now, and then the question of who is responsible for that is no longer relevant anymore because we just need to fix it. We make it happen. (source: Technology vendor-Atos-Client Partner)

Our findings demonstrate that a psychological contract enables transparency with regard to the obligations between clients and vendors, which in turn supports the governance of AI outsourcing.

Summary

Our findings demonstrate that all vendors confirm the need to implement and apply IS governance. The general understanding was that formal governance and relational governance are interwoven. Importantly, AI is still an innovative technology and both the client and vendor

Attributes/codes	Sub-codes	Events	Expert	Vendor
	Gradual approach (sprints)	12	8,9,10,11,12,13,14,15	Accenture, Atos, HCL, TCS
Client-vendor AI arrangement	AI Proof of Concept	6	8, 10,11, 14,15	Accenture, Atos, TCS
	Multidisciplinaire teams	7	9,11,13,14,15	Accenture, Atos, Gartner, HCL, TCS
	Data strategy, platform and quality	10	8,9,10,11,13,18,7,15	Accenture, Atos, Gartner, HCL, HfS, KPMG, TCS
Contract	Intellectual Property	7	8,10,12,14,15	Accenture, Atos, BCG, HCL, TCS
Services	xLAs	4	12,18,14	HCL, HfS, TCS
	Fixed price model	4	8,10,4,6	Accenture, Atos, EY, KPMG
	Outcome based model	3	12,18,14	HCL, HfS, TCS
Pricing mechanisms	Consumption driven model	3	12,14	HCL, TCS
	Risk/reward model	3	8,10,3	Accenture, Atos, McKinsey
	Time&Material model	4	8,10,6	Accenture, Atos, KPMG
	AI quality framework	5	8,4,6,12	Accenture, EY, KPMG, HCL
Trust	Ethical compliance	5	10,12,14	Atos, HCL, TCS
	AI assurance	6	10,4,3,6	Atos, BCG, EY, McKinsey, KPMG
Commitment	AI co-development with clients (projects)	8	9,11,13,7,15	Accenture, Atos, HCL, KPMG, TCS
	Executive involvement	7	8,10,3,14,15	Accenture, Atos, McKinsey, TCS
Dependency	Co-development of IP (client=owner)	8	8,10,13,7,14	Accenture, Atos, HCL, KPMG, TCS
	Education and training	8	8,9,11,5,13,3	Accenture, Atos, EY, HCL, McKinsey
Communication	Business involvement	6	8,10,11,12,6,14	Accenture, Atos, HCL, KPMG, TCS
Psychological contract	Client relationship	6	8,9,10,12,18,3	Accenture, Atos, HCL, HfS, McKinsey

Fig. 10.2 Overview of core statements and findings

currently have limited experience. More specifically, we find that relational governance is dominant over formal governance. We summarised the core statements and findings in Fig. 10.2.

Discussion

Formal Governance

Our research demonstrates that vendors who co-develop AI solutions and algorithms go beyond the traditional type of outsourcing contract agreements, which are more rigid by nature (Aubert et al., 2015; Lioliou et al., 2014). Our findings on co-development suggest that collaboration between clients and vendors contributes to the creation of common insights that in turn strengthens trust between both parties. Based on trust, clients and vendors are willing to establish an outcome-based model that reflects a desired outcome. This shows the interwoven nature of formal and relational governance. Literature (Bapna et al., 2016) suggests that the outsourcing experience of clients has a negative impact on contract outcome. We expand on Bapna's analysis by demonstrating that co-development positively contributes to establishing an outcome-based contract.

Intellectual Property

Strategic Advisors as well as Accounting & Consulting firms argue that IP of co-developed AI services and algorithms should remain with the client. The technology vendor shares this opinion in the case of customised AI. An efficient way to protect IP is to separate projects into a series of segments given to different suppliers (Lacity & Rottman, 2008). The fact that clients become owner of co-developed IP contributes to future innovations. This finding is in contrast to the fragmented IP approach suggested by Rottman and Lacity (2006). Our findings operationalise a recent study of Kranz (2021) in which contractual mechanisms primarily determine joint innovation performance. Based on our analysis we argue that both formal and relational IS governance contribute to AI and algorithms outsourcing. By establishing a set of beliefs and perceptions (psychological contract), such as AI and algorithms proof-of-concepts and co-development of IP, clients may overcome contract uncertainties. This corresponds to Kranz (2021, p. 12) who argues that "*positively framed contracts offer an alternative instrument for coping with the substantial exchange hazards and uncertainty risks involved in embedded Information Technology Outsourcing (ITO) relationships aimed at co-creating innovation*".

Experience-driven Service Levels

Our analysis shows that experience-driven service levels prevail over metrics-based service levels. We argue that implementing experience-driven service levels may result in a decrease of transaction costs and at the same time limit ex post vendor opportunism by creating incentives for mutual cooperative behaviour (Kranz, 2021). By means of experience-driven service levels, clients and vendors apply a strategy to adapt to changes more easily as contracts evolve over time. Based on co-developing AI solutions and algorithms, both clients and vendors are able to increase the level of trust by applying experience-driven service levels. We argue that experience-driven service levels foster relational governance.

Pricing Mechanisms

Our findings show that different types of pricing mechanisms are applied, which is consistent with previous IS governance studies (Amiri et al., 2021; Oshri et al., 2015). Importantly, two technology vendors apply outcome-based contracts by means of a bonus/malus pricing mechanism. In this case, the technology vendors co-developed AI and the algorithms with their clients and achieved transparency about decision-making principles. This finding provides evidence for the assumption of Oshri et al. (2015) that outcome-based mechanisms *"increase transparency regarding commitment and profit-sharing involved in such a setting"* (p. 213). The decision to include dissimilar resources in the client-vendor relationship contributes to shared value creation, a view that is supported by Vitasek and Manrodt (2012). Our findings on outcome-based pricing models go beyond a recent study of Amiri et al. (2021) who find that pricing models in the context of IS sourcing arrangements are predominantly based on Time and Materials and Fixed Price. The role of a client involved in co-developing AI services may explain our findings. We argue that vendors who collaborate with clients to achieve experience-driven services shift from a transactional type of relationship to a relational type of outsourcing arrangement.

Relational Governance

Our study confirms that well-governed client-vendor outsourcing relationships positively affect the degree of trust between parties in creating AI solutions and algorithms. Our findings are consistent with previous studies with regard to the willingness of parties to share knowledge (e.g. co-develop IP) and invest in trusted inter-organisational relationships (Whitley & Willcocks, 2011). Our study reveals that the development and maintenance of social ties between vendors and clients contributes to building trust and reduces transaction costs (Poppo & Zenger, 2002).

Foster Innovation

Vendors who strive for commitment with clients' management, create reciprocity that stimulates a bilateral approach to joint innovation. We argue that mutual commitment forms a prerequisite in developing AI solutions and algorithms, taking the various stakeholders at client and vendor side into account. Prior research shows that mutual adjustments would fit in the relationship between the client and vendors to cater for unanticipated events (Plugge & Janssen, 2020). Specifically, technology vendors and accounting and consulting firms become mutually dependent on their clients in their collaboration to develop AI solutions and algorithms. This is consistent with a study of Pfeffer and Salancik (1978), who argue that resource concentration is related to the extent in which power and authority are widely dispersed. We conclude that both clients and vendors are equally interdependent on each other. Our analysis demonstrates that vendors who are willing to share research insights or collaborate with client subject matter experts experience communication as a key success factor. An active communication strategy of vendors strengthens a trustworthy relationship with their clients. Moreover, our findings show how vendors build relationships with their clients by providing subject matter AI and algorithms support.

Information Asymmetry

Prior literature (Bapna et al., 2016) showed various devices to reduce information asymmetry between clients and vendors as part of IS outsourcing arrangements such as, vendor reputation, client-vendor prior relationship and technological diversity of the vendor. We suggest that vendors need to be willing to reduce information asymmetry by jointly collaborating with their clients. By co-developing AI solutions and algorithms that are based on mutual adjustments, vendors may overcome information asymmetry risks. This includes a focus on communication and putting in place a psychological contract. The attribute communication aligns with COBIT's suggestion to implement governance boards, as detailed by De Haes et al. (2020). Regarding the psychological contract,

Monquin et al. (2020) suggest to balance the commercial interest of vendors with client interests. Our findings enhanced the model of Linden and Rosenkranz (2019) as we included the vendor view in AI and algorithm outsourcing specifically.

Implications for Governance of AI and Algorithm Outsourcing

Some studies show an increased complexity between formal and relational governance as relationships are affected by interfirm contingencies (Huber et al., 2013; Lioliou et al., 2014; Tiwana, 2010). Our findings concerning vendors show two relevant client contingencies that influence formal and relational governance, including a psychological contract. The first contingency corresponds to the need for clients to co-develop AI and algorithms with vendors. Our findings demonstrate that collaboration between both parties strengthen the degree of trust. Moreover, we indicate a complementarity effect due to the interaction between a contractually agreed activity and the relational mechanism of trust. The second contingency corresponds to the willingness of the client and vendor to apply experience-driven service levels. The contractual agreement to measure service metrics by means of a client's perception underpins the relational governance attribute of dependency. Our results show that formal and relational governance are complementary, as the combined use of both governance mechanisms positively fosters the outsourcing arrangement. Similar to previous research (Goo et al., 2009; Lioliou et al., 2014), relational governance by technology vendors to support client AI solutions enables the effectiveness of formal governance.

Conclusion

As far as we know, this is the first attempt to study the governance of outsourcing from the perspective of vendors. Our study extends previous research on IS governance by examining both formal and relational governance, including a psychological contract. We answer the call of Kranz (2021) to study the implementation of contractual models in an innovation-driven context and enhance the study of Linden and Rosenkranz (2019) by including the role of vendors. Secondly, our study shows various forms of contractual models in which some apply to client needs specifically (e.g. outcome-based, experience-driven agreements). Our analysis acknowledges that AI and algorithms outsourcing shifts the emphasis from a transactional type of arrangement to a relational type of outsourcing arrangement. Third, our study posits that formal and relational governance are complementary in cases where clients and vendors co-develop AI solutions and algorithms. The similar use of both governance mechanisms positively fosters AI and algorithms outsourcing arrangements.

Limitations

Although our study provides important implications for clients and vendors involved in the design and delivery of AI and algorithms solutions, there are also some limitations. As our research is based on a limited number of expert interviews (#18) of eight vendor firms and two market research advisors, the analytical generalisability of the results is limited due to the differences in vendor types. Second, our study focuses on the use of formal and relational governance. However, literature reveals that the context in which a study is conducted matters (Lacity et al., 2016). We have not studied other context-related factors that may influence the client-vendor relationship, and our case studies are based on various types of AI services, market and technology vendors. While these global and leading AI firms can build on a large client base and rich experience, the experiences of client organisations and their view on governance of outsourcing would further enrich the findings presented. Third, in addition to our qualitative research we could have conducted a qualitative study by increasing the number of participants and a simple coherent questionnaire as the basis for a survey.

Future Research

The interviews identify various avenues that require further research. We recommend additional expert interviews to increase the generalisation of the results, which is related to our first research limitation. These additional expert interviews should include interviews with experts from Tier 2 and Tier 3 vendors who are geographically dispersed. We suggest to include case study specific elements such as the AI and algorithms outsourcing contract, service level and audit reports. Secondly, we may assume that the impact of maturing technologies will potentially impact the vendor landscape. We expect that more mature vendors will trigger a gradual exit of the strategy advisors in the market. Future research may identify relevant trends in this field, where we have added the focus on algorithms to this publication (Beulen et al., 2022). Third, we argue that additional research is needed to study the effect of knowledge creation and capturing in case a client and vendor co-develop IP. By using a social capital lens, researchers may explore how co-development of IP may develop mutual trust. These suggestions address the context limitation, which is our second research limitation. Finally, we would recommend, in line with our third research limitation, combining multiple case studies to validate and statistically generalise our findings.

Appendix A: Interview Questions

1. Can you please describe the type(s) of Artificial Intelligence engagements your firm is involved in? Think for example: inventory of AI algorithms, develop AI algorithms, explore potential AI functionality, implement AI, risk assessment and AI algorithm assurance.
2. Can you describe how your clients have implemented relationship management with your firm? Think for example: meeting frequency, agenda topics, seniority and organisational embedding of the contract manager and the authorised contract signer. Does the type of engagement (as listed in the first question) impact the relationship management setup?

3. In our research we identify three types of creators of Artificial Intelligence solutions: (1). A client's internal data scientist team, (2) A client's internal Information Technology department and (3). External service providers. What is the impact of the creator of the Artificial Intelligence solutions on the engagement? Examples relate to: contract, technology, pricing mechanisms and consulting team composition. Please differentiate by engagement type.
4. In our research we identify two type of users of Artificial Intelligence solutions: (1) A client's internal data science team and (2). A client's business department. What is the impact of the use of the Artificial Intelligence solution on the engagement? Examples relate to: contract, technology, pricing mechanisms and consulting team composition. Please differentiate by engagement type.
5. Can you link contract and pricing mechanisms to each type of engagement? Think for example: time & materials, fixed prices or risk & reward.
6. Are there any clauses in the engagement which are different for Artificial Intelligence solution engagements compared to other consulting engagements? Please differentiate by engagement type.

Appendix B: Coding Overview

Construct	Codes	Sub-codes	Events identified	Impact	Vendor
Client-supplier arrangements	Services and functionality	Advisory services	10	Strong	All vendors
	Services and functionality	AI strategy	5	Average	Accenture, HfS, HCL
	Services and functionality	Process optimization	8	Strong	Accenture, Atos, HCL, KPMG, TCS

(continued)

(continued)

Construct	Codes	Sub-codes	Events identified	Impact	Vendor
	Services and functionality	Outsource AI projects/services	7	Strong	Accenture, Atos, EY, KPMG, HCL, TCS
	AI development	In-house development	2	Limited	Accenture, KPMG
	AI development	Hybrid development	2	Limited	KPMG
	AI development	Outsourced development	7	Strong	Accenture, Atos, EY, KPMG, HCL, TCS
	AI development	Use cases (business process)	2	Average	Accenture, KPMG
	AI development	Coding AI data	2	Average	Accenture, KPMG
	AI development	Gradual approach (sprints)	12	Strong	Accenture, Atos, HCL, TCS
	AI development	AI proof of concept	6	Strong	Accenture, Atos, TCS
	AI development	Multidisciplinaire teams	7	Strong	Accenture, Atos, Gartner, HCL, TCS
	AI development	Data strategy, platform and quality	10	Average	Accenture, Atos, Gartner, HCL, HfS, KPMG, TCS
	AI development	Centralised organization	3	Limited	Accenture, McKinsey, KPMG
Formal governance	Contract	Managed service	3	Average	HCL, TCS
		Role of clauses	4	Average	BCG, Accenture, HCL
		Intellectual property	7	Strong	Accenture, Atos, HCL, TCS

(continued)

(continued)

Construct	Codes	Sub-codes	Events identified	Impact	Vendor
	Services	Advanced analytics	2	Average	KPMG
		AIaaS (basic SLAs)	2	Average	HCl, HfS
		xLAs	4	Strong	HCL, HfS, TCS
	Pricing mechanisms	Fixed price model	4	Average	Accenture, Atos, EY, KPMG
		Outcome based model	3	Average	HCL, HfS, TCS
		Consumed driven model	3	Average	HCL, TCS
		Risk/reward model	3	Average	Accenture, Atos, McKinsey
		Time & Material model	4	Average	Accenture, Atos, KPMG
Relational governance	Trust	Trusted advisor	4	Strong	Atos, EY, HdS, KPMG
		People focus (awareness)	4	Average	Accenture, EY
		AI quality framework	5	Strong	Accenture, EY, KPMG, HCL
		Ethical compliance	5	Average	Atos, HCL, TCS
		AI assurance	6	Average	BCG, Atos, EY, McKinsey, KPMG
	Commitment	AI co-development with clients (projects)	8	Strong	Accenture, Atos, HCL, KPMG, TCS
		Executive involvement	7	Strong	Accenture, Atos, McKinsey, TCS
		Governance and control	4	Average	EY, HfS, KPMG, TCS

(continued)

(continued)

Construct	Codes	Sub-codes	Events identified	Impact	Vendor
	Dependency	Trusted advisor	4	Strong	Atos, EY, HdS, KPMG
		Collaborative way	4	Strong	Accenture, HCL, McKinsey
		Co-development of IP (client = owner)	8	Strong	Accenture, Atos, HCL, KPMG, TCS
		Education and training	8	Strong	Accenture, Atos, EY, HCL, McKinsey
		Labour shortage (data specialists)	3	Average	Accenture, Atos
	Communication	Business involvement	6	Strong	Accenture, Atos, HCL, KPMG, TCS
		Weekly meetings	5	Average	Accenture, Atos, HCL
	Psychological contract	Supplier relationship investment	3	Strong	Accenture, McKinsey
		Client relationship	6	Strong	Accenture, Atos, HCL, Hfs, McKinsey

References

Alexy, O., Criscuolo, P., & Salter, A. (2009). Does IP Strategy Have to Cripple Open Innovation? *MIT Sloan Management Review, 51*(1), 71.

Amiri, F., Overbeek, S., Wagenaar, G., et al. (2021). Reconciling Agile Frameworks with IT Sourcing Through an IT Sourcing Dimensions Map and

Structured Decision-Making. *Information System and E-Business Management.* https://doi.org/10.1007/s10257-021-00534-3

Argyris, C. (1960). *Understanding Organizational Behavior.* Dorsey.

Aubert, B. A., Kishore, R., & Iriyama, A. (2015). Exploring and Managing the "Innovation Through Outsourcing" Paradox. *Journal of Strategic Information Systems, 24*(4), 255–269. https://doi.org/10.1016/j.jsis.2015.10.003

Bankins, S., & Formosa, P. (2023). The Ethical Implications of Artificial Intelligence (AI) for Meaningful Work. *Journal of Business Ethics, 185*(4), 725–740.

Bapna, R., Gupta, A., Ray, G., & Singh, S. (2016). Research Note—IT Outsourcing and the Impact of Advisors on Clients and Vendors. *Information Systems Research, 27*(3), 636–647. https://doi.org/10.1287/isre.2016.0645

Benbasat, I., Goldstein, D., & Mead, M. (1987). The Case Research Strategy in Studies of Information Systems. *MIS Quarterly, 11*(3), 368–387. https://doi.org/10.2307/248684

Beulen, E. (2016, February 16–19). Contract Renewal Decisions in IT-Outsourcing: A Survey in the Netherlands. In *Shared Services and Outsourcing: A Contemporary Outlook: 10th Global Sourcing Workshop 2016.* Val d'Isère, France, Revised Selected Papers 10 (pp. 178–192). Springer International Publishing.

Beulen, E., Plugge, A., & van Hillegersberg, J. (2022). Formal and relational governance of artificial intelligence outsourcing. *Information Systems and e-Business Management*, 1–30.

Beulen, E., & Ribbers, P. (2007). Control in Outsourcing Relationships: Governance in Action. In *2007 40th Annual Hawaii International Conference on System Sciences (HICSS'07).* IEEE, New York.

Beulen, E., & Ribbers, P. (Eds.). (2020). *The Routledge Companion to Managing Digital Outsourcing.* Routledge.

Beulen, E., & Ribbers, P. (2021). *Managing IT Outsourcing: Governance in Global Partnerships* (3rd ed.). Routledge.

Cammarano, A., Michelino, F., & Caputo, M. (2019). Open Innovation Practices for Knowledge Acquisition and Their Effects on Innovation Output. *Technology Analysis & Strategic Management, 31*(11), 1297–1313. https://doi.org/10.1080/09537325.2019.1606420

Chang, Y. B., Gurbaxani, V., & Ravindran, K. (2017). Information Technology Outsourcing: Asset Transfer and the Role of Contract. *MIS Quarterly, 41*(3), 959–973.

Coombs, C., Hislop, D., Taneva, S. K., & Barnard, S. (2020). The Strategic Impacts of Intelligent Automation for Knowledge and Service Work: An

Interdisciplinary Review. *The Journal of Strategic Information Systems, 29*(4), 101600. https://doi.org/10.1016/j.jsis.2020.101600

Davenport, T. H., & Ronanki, R. (2018). Artificial Intelligence for the Real World. *Harvard Business Review, 96*(1), 108–116.

De Haes, S., Van Grembergen, W., Joshi, A., & Huygh, T. (2020). *COBIT as a Framework for Enterprise Governance of IT. In: Enterprise Governance of Information Technology* (pp. 125–162). Springer. https://doi.org/10.1007/978-3-030-25918-1_5

Denzin, N. K. (2009). Triangulation 2.0. *Journal of Mixed Methods Research, 6*(2), 80–88. https://doi.org/10.1177/1558689812437186

Dignum, V. (2018). Ethics in Artificial Intelligence: Introduction to the Special Issue. *Ethics and Information Technology, 20*(1), 1–3. https://doi.org/10.1007/s10676-018-9450-z

Duan, W., Zhang, G., Zhu, Z., et al. (2020). Psychological Contract Differences for Different Groups of Employees: Big Date Analysis from China. *Information Systems E-Business Management, 18*, 871–889. https://doi.org/10.1007/s10257-019-00403-0

Dwivedi, Y. K., Hughes, L., Ismagilova, E., et al. (2021). Artificial Intelligence (AI): Multidisciplinary Perspectives on Emerging Challenges, Opportunities, and Agenda for Research, Practice and Policy. *International Journal of Information Management, 57*, 101994. https://doi.org/10.1016/j.ijinfomgt.2019.08.002

Fernández, J. V. (2023). Artificial Intelligence in Government: Risks and Challenges of Algorithmic Governance in the Administrative State. *Indiana Journal of Global Legal Studies, 30*, 65.

Floridi, L., Cowls, J., Beltrametti, M., et al. (2018). AI4people-an Ethical Framework for a Good AI Society: Opportunities, Risks, Principles, and Recommendations. *Minds and Machines, 28*(4), 689–707. https://doi.org/10.1007/s11023-018-9482-5

Gartner. (2020). https://www.gartner.com/smarterwithgartner/gartner-top-10-trends-in-data-and-analytics-for-2020/

Goo, J., Kishore, R., Rao, H., & Nam, K. (2009). The Role of Service Level Agreements in Relational Management of Information Technology Outsourcing: An Empirical Study. *MIS Quarterly, 33*(1), 119–145. https://doi.org/10.2307/20650281

Gopalakrishnan, S., & Zhang, H. (2019). Client dependence: A boon or bane for vendor innovation? A competitive mediation framework in IT outsourcing. *Journal of Business Research, 103*, 407–416.

Grimaldi, M., Greco, M., & Cricelli, L. (2021). A Framework of Intellectual Property Protection Strategies and Open Innovation. *Journal of Business Research, 123*, 156–164.

Haenlein, M., & Kaplan, A. (2019). A Brief History of Artificial Intelligence: On the Past, Present, and Future of Artificial Intelligence. *California Management Review, 61*(4), 5–14. https://doi.org/10.1177/0008125619864925

Han, J., Kim, Y., & Kim, H. (2017). An Integrative Model of Information Security Policy Compliance with Psychological Contract: Examining a Bilateral Perspective. *Computers & Security, 66*, 52–65. https://doi.org/10.1016/J.cose.2016.12.016

Harrington Jr, J. E. (2022). The Effect of Outsourcing Pricing Algorithms on Market Competition. *Management Science, 68*(9), 6889–6906.

Hoecht, A., & Trott, P. (2006). Innovation Risks of Strategic Outsourcing. *Technovation, 26*(5–6), 672–681. https://doi.org/10.1016/j.technovation.2005.02.004

Huber, T. L., Fischer, T. A., Dibbern, J., & Hirschheim, R. (2013). A Process Model of Complementarity and Substitution of Contractual and Relational Governance in IS Outsourcing. *Journal of Management Information Systems, 30*(3), 81–114. https://doi.org/10.2753/MIS0742-1222300304

Jaiswal, A., Arun, C. J., & Varma, A. (2022). Rebooting Employees: Upskilling for Artificial Intelligence in Multinational Corporations. *The International Journal of Human Resource Management, 33*(6), 1179–1208.

Jiang, L., & Fu, Z. (2020). Privacy-preserving Genetic Algorithm Outsourcing in Cloud Computing. *Journal of Cybersecurity, 2*(1), 49.

Kaplan, A., & Haenlein, M. (2019). Siri, Siri, in My Hand: Who's the Fairest in the Land? On the Interpretations, Illustrations, and Implications of Artificial Intelligence. *Business Horizons, 62*(1), 15–25. https://doi.org/10.1016/j.bushor.2018.08.004

Khan, A. A., Laghari, A. A., Li, P., Dootio, M. A., & Karim, S. (2023). The Collaborative Role of Blockchain, Artificial Intelligence, and Industrial Internet of Things in Digitalization of Small and Medium-Size Enterprises. *Scientific Reports, 13*(1), 1656.

KPMG. (2018). *Ready, Set, Fail? Avoiding Setbacks in the Intelligent Automation Race.* https://advisory.kpmg.us/articles/2018/new-study-findings-read-ready-set-fail.html

Krancher, O., Dibbern, J., & Meyer, P. (2018). How Social Media-Enabled Communication Awareness Enhances Project Team Performance. *Journal of the Association for Information Systems, 19*(9), Article 3. https://doi.org/10.17705/1jais.00510

Kranz, J. (2021). Strategic Innovation in IT Outsourcing: Exploring the Differential and Interaction Effects of Contractual and Relational Governance Mechanism. *Journal of Strategic Information Systems, 30*(1), 101656. https://doi.org/10.1016/j.jsis.2021.101656

Lacity, M., Khan, S. A., & Yan, A. (2016). Review of the Empirical Business Services Sourcing Literature: An Update and Future Directions. *Journal of Information Technology, 1*(3), 269–328. https://doi.org/10.1057/jit.2016.2

Lacity, M., & Rottman, J. (2008). Offshore Outsourcing of IT Work. In *Offshore Outsourcing of IT Work. Technology, Work and Globalization*. Palgrave Macmillan.

Legg, S., & Hutter, M. (2007). A Collection of Definitions of Intelligence. Frontiers in Artificial Intelligence and Applications. In *Advances in Artificial Intelligence: Concepts, Architectures, and Algorithms, 157*, 17.

Levinson, H., Price, C. R., Munden, K. J., Mandl, H. J., & Solley, C. M. (1962). *Men, Management, and Mental Health*. Harvard University Press.

Li, J. J., Poppo, L., & Zhou, K. Z. (2010). Relational Mechanisms, Formal Contracts, and Local Knowledge Acquisition by International Subsidiaries. *Strategic Management Journal, 31*(4), 349–370. https://doi.org/10.1002/smj.813

Linden, R., & Rosenkranz, C. (2019). Opening the Black Box of Advisors in Information Technology Outsourcing: An Advisory Activity Model. *Communication of the Association of Information Systems, 44*, Article 37. https://doi.org/10.17705/1CAIS.04437

Lindsell, C. J., Stead, W. W., & Johnson, K. B. (2020). Action-informed Artificial Intelligence—Matching the Algorithm to the Problem. *JAMA, 323*(21), 2141–2142.

Lioliou, E., & Willcocks, L. P. (2019). *Global Outsourcing Discourse: Exploring Modes of IT Governance*. Palgrave Macmillan.

Lioliou, E., Zimmermann, A., Willcocks, L. P., & Gao, L. (2014). Formal and Relational Governance in IT Outsourcing: Substitution, Complementarity and the Role of the Psychological Contract. *Information Systems Journal, 24*(6), 503–535. https://doi.org/10.1111/isj.12038

Macneil, I. R. (1980). *The New Social Contract: An Inquiry into Modern Contractual Relations*. Yale University Press.

McKinsey Research. (2020). https://www.mckinsey.com/business-functions/mckinsey-analytics/our-insights/global-survey-the-state-of-ai-in-2020

Miles, M., & Huberman, A. (1994). *Qualitative Data Analysis*. Sage.

Miller, S. (2018). AI: Augmentation, More so than Automation. *Asian Management Insights, 5*(1), 1–20.

Moquin, R. (2020). Psychological Contract in IT: A Qualitative Exploration of Missed Expectations. *The Journal of the Southern Association for Information Systems, 7*, 1–20. https://doi.org/10.17705/3JSIS.00014

Orlikowski, W. J., & Iacono, C. S. (2001). Research Commentary: Desperately Seeking the "IT" in IT Research: A Call to Theorizing the IT Artifact. *Information Systems Research, 12*(2), 121–134. https://doi.org/10.1287/isre.12.2.121.9700

Oshri, I., Kotlarsky, J., & Gerbasi, A. (2015). Strategic Innovation Through Outsourcing: The Role of Relational and Contractual Governance. *Journal of Strategic Information Systems, 24*(3), 203–216. https://doi.org/10.1016/j.jsis.2015.08.001

Pfeffer, J., & Salancik, G. R. (1978). *The External Control of Organizations*. Harper & Row.

Plugge, A. G., & Janssen, W. F. W. A. H. (2020). Governing and Orchestrating Multi-sourcing Relationships. In E. Beulen, P. Ribbers, & J. Roos (Eds.), *The Routledge Companion to Managing Digital Outsourcing*. Routledge.

Plugge, A. G., Nikou, S., & Bouwman, W. A. G. A. (2020). The Revitalization of Service-Orientation: A Business Services Model. *Business Process Management Journal, 27*(8), 1–24. https://doi.org/10.1108/BPMJ-02-2020-0052

Poppo, L., & Zenger, T. (2002). Do Formal Contracts and Relational Governance Function as Substitutes or Complements? *Strategic Management Journal, 23*(8), 707–725. https://doi.org/10.1002/smj.249

Rai, A., Keil, M., Hornyak, R., & Wüllenweber, K. (2012). Hybrid Relational-Contractual Governance for Business Process Outsourcing. *Journal of Management Information Systems, 29*(2), 213–256. https://doi.org/10.2753/MIS0742-1222290208

Robinson, S. L., & Rousseau, D. M. (1994). Violating the Psychological Contract: Not the Exception But the Norm. *Journal of Organizational Behavior, 15*(3), 245–259. https://doi.org/10.1002/job.4030150306

Rottman, J., & Lacity, M. C. (2006). Proven Practices for Effectively Offshoring IT Work. *Sloan Management Review, 47*(3), 56–63.

Russell, S. J., & Norvig, P. (2016). *Artificial Intelligence: A Modern Approach*. Pearson Education Limited.

Sabherwal, R., & Jeyaray, A. (2015). Information Technology Impacts on Firm Performance: An Extension of Kohli and Devaraj (2003). *MIS Quarterly, 39*(4), 809–836. https://www.jstor.org/stable/26628653

Tajammul, M., Shaw, R. N., Ghosh, A., & Parveen, R. (2021). Error Detection Algorithm for Cloud Outsourced Big Data. *Advances in Applications of Data-Driven Computing* (pp. 105–116). Springer.

Tarafdar, M., Beath, C. M., & Ross, J. W. (2019). Using AI to Enhance Business Operations. *Sloan Management Review, 60*(4), 37–44.

Tiwana, A. (2010). Systems Development Ambidexterity: Explaining the Complementary and Substitutive Roles of Formal and Informal Controls. *Journal of Management Information Systems, 27*(2), 87–126. https://doi.org/10.2753/MIS0742-1222270203

Van Grembergen, W., & De Haes, S. (2009). *Enterprise Governance of Information Technology: Achieving Strategic Alignment and Value.* Springer.

Vitasek, K., & Manrodt, K. (2012). Vested Outsourcing: A Flexible Framework for Collaborative Outsourcing. *Strategic Outsourcing: An International Journal, 5*(1), 4–14. https://doi.org/10.1108/17538291211221924

Wang, G., Guo, Y., Zhang, W., Xie, S., & Chen, Q. (2023). What Type of Algorithm Is Perceived as Fairer and More Acceptable? A Comparative Analysis of Rule-Driven Versus Data-Driven Algorithmic Decision-Making in Public Affairs. *Government Information Quarterly*, 101803.

Wang, P. (2019). On Defining Artificial Intelligence. *Journal of Artificial General Intelligence, 10*(2), 1–37. https://doi.org/10.2478/jagi-2019-0002

Whitley, E. A., & Willcocks, L. P. (2011). Achieving Step-Change in Outsourcing Maturity: Toward Collaborative Innovation. *MISQ Executive, 10*(3), 95–107.

Willcocks, L. P. (2020). Robo-Apocalypse Cancelled? Reframing the Automation and Future of Work Debate. *Journal of Information Technology.* Published June 10. https://doi.org/10.1177/0268396220925830

Xiao, J., Xie, K., & Hu, Q. (2012). Inter-firm IT Governance in Power-Imbalanced Buyer–Supplier Dyads: Exploring How It Works and Why It Lasts. *European Journal of Information Systems, 22*(5), 512–528. https://doi.org/10.1057/ejis.2012.40

Yin, R. K. (2017). *Case Study Research and Applications: Design and Methods.* Sage.

Zhang, F. (2021). Construction of Internal Management System of Business Strategic Planning Based on Artificial Intelligence. *Information Systems E-Business Management.* https://doi.org/10.1007/s10257-021-00510-x

11

Internet-Based Sourcing: Cloud and Crowdsourcing as Delivery Models

Ilan Oshri, Julia Kotlarsky, and Leslie Willcocks

Introduction

Cloud services and crowdsourcing are increasingly popular sourcing models based on Internet delivery of products or services. In practice, each of these high-level sourcing models can be implemented in different ways in terms of specific operational and commercial aspects of service provision. In this chapter we build on our commentary on

---

Chapter 11 is a more developed version of a chapter from the authors' textbook: Oshri, I., Kotlarsky, J., & Willcocks, L. P. (2023). Internet Delivery Sourcing Models. In I. Oshri, J. Kotlarsky, & L. P. Willcocks (Eds.), *The Handbook of Global Outsourcing and Offshoring* (4th ed., pp. 39–65). Palgrave Macmillan

---

I. Oshri (✉) · J. Kotlarsky
University of Auckland, Auckland, New Zealand
e-mail: Ilan.oshri@auckland.ac.nz

J. Kotlarsky
e-mail: j.kotlarsky@auckland.ac.nz

L. Willcocks
LSE, London, UK

cloud sourcing in Chapter 1, and set up the work on crowdsourcing in Chapter 12 by describing the key principles of these two Internet-based sourcing models, giving examples of how they have been adopted by client firms.

Cloud Computing Services

Cloud sourcing typically involves the delivery of a growing range of on-demand computing services—from applications to storage and processing power—over the Internet. When a third-party provider is involved, this occurs on a rental or pay-as-you-go basis. In the global sourcing marketplace, cloud computing has taken the form of cloud services (or cloud computing services) such as IT resources, business applications, infrastructures or platforms, which are delivered on demand, using public, community, private or hybrid infrastructures. The metaphor of the cloud draws on the way the Internet is depicted in computer network diagrams and represents an abstraction of the complex infrastructure it conceals. In other words, cloud computing allows users to access technology-enabled services on the Internet without having to know or understand the technology infrastructure that supports them. But nor do users have much control over it, with continuing security and privacy concerns as a result. That said, the cloud services market has grown rapidly over the last ten years, as comprehensively detailed in Chapter 1. All reports we have accessed predict healthy future growth in the various cloud markets.

The key benefit of cloud computing is that it provides on-demand access to supercomputer-level power, even from a smartphone or laptop, enabling massively scalable services. For example, those logging on to Facebook or searching for flights online are taking advantage of cloud computing to connect to large volumes of data stored in remote clusters or networks of computers. Another example of cloud computing is Google and all its services.

The key properties of cloud services are[1]:

- On-demand computing and self-service provisioning;
- Resource pooling;
- Scalability and rapid elasticity;
- Pay-per-user pricing;
- Measured service;
- Resiliency and availability;
- Security;
- Broad network access;
- Ever-growing range of services, e.g., software, infrastructure, storage, digital workforce, platform, all delivered 'as-a-service'.

Cloud services can be hosted and configured for single or multiple client organisations, and even hosted privately within the organisation or provided over a virtual private network (VPN). Four basic types of cloud infrastructure characterise cloud-deployment strategies[2]:

- *Private clouds*, which are operated solely for the use of a single organisation servicing multiple consumers (e.g., Business Units) within the organisation
- *Public clouds*, which use cloud infrastructure available for the use of the general public (i.e., referred to as public network)
- *Hybrid clouds*, which combine the infrastructure of two or more clouds (public, community and private) that remain unique entities but are connected in such a way as to enable data and application portability
- *Multiclouds*, which are made up of more than one cloud service, from more than one cloud vendor—public or private. All hybrid clouds are multiclouds but not all multiclouds are hybrid clouds. Following the COVID-19 outbreak, KPMG/HFS (2020) reported that 70% of executives expected hybrid and/or multicloud to be the predominant cloud infrastructure going forward (see also Chapter 1).

---

[1] https://www.techtarget.com/searchcloudcomputing/feature/7-key-characteristics-of-Cloud-Computing.
[2] https://www.redhat.com/en/topics/cloud-computing/public-cloud-vs-private-cloud-and-hybrid-cloud.

The main distinction between cloud infrastructures are restrictions regarding the specific group of consumers who can access the cloud (i.e., one organisation, cross-organisational community or public). In terms of ownership of the infrastructure, any type of cloud may be owned, managed and operated by a business, academic or government organisation, a third party or some combination of these, and it may exist on or off premises.

While many organisations were initially reluctant to use cloud services, the general public have embraced them in the form of search engines, for example, and social media platforms such as Facebook, Twitter, LinkedIn, Pinterest and YouTube, among others. Many such services are in fact relatively free at the point of use, relying on advertising revenue and the value of user-provided data. Consumer demand for easy-to-use, intuitive, accessible applications—accessed via a browser—has spread upwards through many organisations as employees expect the same ease of use from employer in-house systems.

As the ongoing COVID-19 pandemic necessitated long and repeated lockdowns, this forced enterprises to embrace remote working on a global scale, thus accelerating the adoption of cloud computing services. According to a relatively recent forecast from Gartner,[3] the worldwide end-user spending on public cloud services was forecasted to grow 20.4% in 2022 to total US$494.7bn, up from US$410.9bn in 2021. In 2023, end-user spending was expected to reach nearly US$600bn (see also Chapter 1). Fundamentally, the drivers for cloud services adoption during and after the COVID-19 pandemic have not significantly changed.[4] Enterprise has remained focused on the need to improve efficiency, streamline operations and cut costs, even those who previously believed cloud services to be the preserve of small and medium-sized organisations. However, a 2022 McKinsey survey pointed to a much greater focus on cybersecurity and investments in cloud technologies—even as most companies continued transforming their core architecture and infrastructure in tandem. Today these investments have become

---

[3] https://gulfbusiness.com/worldwide-public-cloud-end-user-spending-to-reach-nearly-500bn-in-2022-gartner/.
[4] https://www.forbes.com/sites/forbestechcouncil/2021/01/15/how-the-pandemic-has-accelerated-cloud-adoption/?sh=6acc7f406621.

a competitive necessity. The competitive divide between winners and the rest has only grown during the pandemic. Compared with the IT organisations at other companies, top performers have made much more progress in their cyber, digital and cloud moves (McKinsey, 2022; Willcocks et al., 2023).

While the primary driver for corporates to investigate cloud computing has tended to be cost savings, by the early 2020s, all organisations came to realise that the cloud promised a lot more in the form of operational efficiency, reduced waste and increased business agility, partly because clients can begin to relieve themselves of the onerous on-premise software and hardware upgrade cycle. Cloud computing has also become a strategic necessity, providing a more flexible infrastructure, speeding up technology deployment, improving customer engagement across a wider base and getting digital products and services to market more quickly. The cloud also represents a massive opportunity. McKinsey Digital (2021) estimated that by 2030 cloud adoption could provide US$430 billion more value through IT cost optimisation, risk reduction and core operations digitisation, a further $US770 billion through innovation-driven growth, accelerated product development and hyper scalability, as well as additional opportunities from early adoption of cloud technologies, not least enabling future technology deployment such as quantum computing, mixed reality technologies, blockchain and digital fabrication.

In summary, with the growth in cloud services, there is increased demand for enterprise cloud solutions among clients. As discussed, by the early to mid-2020s the enterprise cloud solution market had entered a high-growth phase and held considerable potential for enterprises and suppliers alike.

Cloud-Based Sourcing Models

In terms of commercial sourcing models, cloud services are far from being a single-template solution. Although we have now reached the point when one can envisage a world of nearly everything-as-a-service (EaaS), typically, there are three main forms: platform as a service (PaaS), infrastructure as a service (IaaS) and software as a service (SaaS) (see also Chapter 1). These services can be delivered over public, community, private or hybrid infrastructures and can also be combined to create various forms of business platform as a service (BPaaS) offerings. To build on Chapter 1:

- *PaaS* provides a development platform for creating end-user solutions. Google's App Engine and Microsoft Azure are examples of this.
- *IaaS* supplies storage and processing capabilities as services over the network. Capacity is pooled and made available to handle workloads that range from application components to high-performance applications. Amazon's cloud is an example of an IaaS platform.
- *SaaS*, meanwhile, provides a complete application as a service on demand. The software runs in a/the cloud and may service multiple end-users or client organisations. The most widely known example, and a pioneer of the model, is Salesforce.com; although, it now also provides a platform and an ecosystem of hosted business applications. A number of other solutions like Microsoft Office 365 and Google Apps offer a range of day-to-day business applications. Apple's own walled-garden approach offers an alternative ecosystem used by millions of consumers. Many types of software are well-suited to the SaaS model for customers with little interest or capability in software deployment, but with substantial computing needs. The model can be applied within different segments of the market. At the higher end of the market, suppliers may offer applications such as ERP, CRM and e-commerce, as well as selected industry-specific solutions. Low-end applications include solutions for small and medium enterprises that users can easily configure.

Different commercial cloud models offer different types of cloud services that can be consumed in multiple ways. Some examples of the services requested under different models and usage scenarios are included in Table 11.1.

Table 11.1 Cloud consumer and cloud provider activities

Service models	Examples of services available	Cloud consumer activities	Provider activities
SaaS	ERP, billing, sales, CRM, collaboration, HR, email and office productivity, content management, social networks, financials, document management	Uses application/ service for business process operations	Installs, manages, maintains and supports the software application on a cloud infrastructure
PaaS	Business intelligence, application deployment, database, integration, development and testing	Develops, tests, deploys, and manages applications hosted in a cloud system	Provisions and manages cloud infrastructure and middleware for the platform consumers; provides development, deployment, and administration tools to platform consumers
IaaS	Service management, platform hosting, storage, compute, backup and recovery	Creates/installs, manages and monitors services for IT infrastructure operations	Provisions and manages the physical processing, storage, networking, and the hosting environment and cloud infrastructure for IaaS consumers

Source Based on NIST (2020)

Case Studies—Cloud-Based Digital Workforces

Robotic process automation and intelligent automation applications have been available for some time and are being further developed and integrated with other digital technologies (See Chapter 9). Increasingly clients are utilising them as digital workforces made available from the cloud—a sourcing development referred to in Chapter 9 as Robotistan.

Take **TransUnion**, a leading global risk and information solutions provider. Having established a long track record of innovation, TransUnion was looking to improve its service and information delivery. But the information they handle is highly sensitive and there are strict guidelines that govern how and when it can be released. TransUnion had already identified intelligent automation as a likely candidate to help them improve their service and delivery outputs. But the question remained, *Could intelligent automation over the Cloud be deployed while still maintaining absolute confidence in information security?* Following an analysis of the opportunities by TransUnion and Blue Prism teams, customer on-boarding was identified as the best place to start. TransUnion was receiving upwards of 55 new corporate subscriber applications a day. Agents had to manually assess which products a customer could access, in line with strict regulations. This information was passed to service teams who manually rekeyed the entries into a host of disparate systems, opening up the possibility for errors that could lead to further delays. A Blue Prism intelligent digital workforce was trained to handle these initial assessments. As a result, up to 70% of the target transactions were automated within weeks, with digital workers now on the job 24 hours a day.

First2Protect is a specialist property insurer in the UK. Traditionally, when a customer needs insurance for a new property, a broker can't extend an offer for cover until the specific property has been rented or purchased. First2Protect shortcuts this delay, providing a rapid quote and giving customers peace of mind that their insurance is sorted before they move in. But to maintain this advantage, First2Protect had to process applications quickly. On average, each application took eight minutes to manually compile and dispatch. Making matters worse, the volume of applications peaked towards the end of each month, putting the team under increased pressure.

After identifying where the bottlenecks were, First2Protect deployed a Blue Prism intelligent digital workforce. Within a month of automating the issuing of new policies, First2Protect had already saved 100 hours, a saving that will continue to grow as more parts of the process are transferred to the digital workers. First2Protect is now able to process applications 24 hours a day. Moreover, as the workload peaks towards the end of each month, First2Protect can deploy more digital workers without having to add additional headcount.

Consider the case of **Nasdaq**. From 2021, Finnish company Digital Workforce has deployed its Azure Cloud-based Roboshore service for dozens of large organisations. Roboshore deploys RPA automations from the cloud and delivers automation maintenance as one managed service. With usage-based pricing and no long-term commitments, customers can optimise and scale the use of their RPA assets up and down as needed. Roboshore delivers all the leading RPA technologies, including UiPath, Blue Prism, Automation Anywhere and Microsoft Power Automate. But compared to more traditional RPA services, where the customer buys RPA based on their maximum capacity needs—usually with one year's minimum commitment—Roboshore helps maximise utilisation and eliminates the struggle with underused licences. With Roboshore, customers pay per value as opposed to being tied to fixed capacity.

Nasdaq, a global technology company began their RPA journey in 2018 in their finance department. They later selected Roboshore because it is more scalable and flexible than other approaches. Furthermore, to support their growth aspirations Nasdaq wanted a solid maintenance function to ensure maximum uptime from the digital workforce. Given cloud security concerns, Roboshore complies with the ISO/IEC 20,001:2011 structure and processes and the cloud platform is being used successfully by organisations with strict information security requirements, including banks, healthcare organisations and government entities.[5]

On-Premise vs. Cloud Solutions

With the maturing of cloud services, most organisations face the dilemma of whether to continue investing in on-premise solutions. One of the main challenges is technology legacy and the internal support

---
[5] Sources: Eloise Jeffrey, Blue Prism, and https://www.realwire.com/releases/Roboshore-optimizes-RPA-usage-and-makes-it-more-transparent-than-ever, 9/2/2021.

structures that have grown up around it over many years. Many senior IT strategists now accept that given the opportunity to start from scratch, they would do things very differently. The challenge for those IT strategists, therefore, is to become more business- and information-focused.

A key differentiator between traditional on-premise solutions and cloud computing is control. On-premise solutions give clients complete control over their assets—licensing issues aside—while leaving them with capital outlay and support headaches. In contrast, the cloud model demands a different mindset by requiring the client to relinquish some control and potentially share assets in exchange for greater scalability, more rapid deployment and reduced costs. Lock-in is an issue here, as has already been explored.

Some organisations adopt a hybrid approach where the solution spans both on-premise and cloud elements. Many organisations retain core/critical systems and applications in-house, while moving non-critical and replicable business process tasks outside of the organisation. Here, cloud services are seen as analogous to outsourcing by many client firms. Other organisations preserve their current IT assets on premise while investing for their future needs in the cloud.

Furthermore, it is important to consider who the different actors are, their roles in the cloud marketplace and the key components in a cloud computing architecture. The National Institute of Standards and Technology (NIST, 2020[6]) has developed cloud federation reference architecture (on the basis of the 2011 NIST cloud reference architecture), which outlines the roles of the five major actors involved in the delivery and consumption of cloud services, and the 11 components of cloud architecture. These roles (described in Fig. 11.1) can be used as a tool for discussing the requirements, structures and operations of cloud computing.

---

[6] https://www.nist.gov/publications/nist-cloud-federation-reference-architecture.

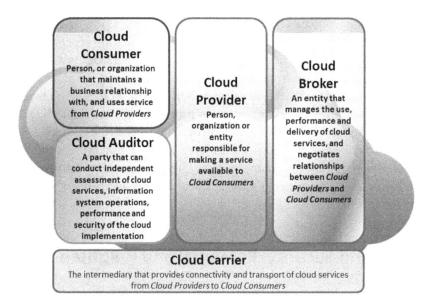

Fig. 11.1 Actors in the NIST cloud computing reference architecture

Business, Data and Financial Factors

In research conducted by the authors, client organisations were asked to rate how business and financial factors influenced their choice of cloud-based enterprise solutions. Generally speaking, client organisations and suppliers shared the same perspectives on most business and financial considerations. However, while suppliers believed that scalability was one of the key influences for the adoption of enterprise cloud services, client organisations did not share this view very strongly.

Firms were asked to rate other business factors enabling and hindering the adoption of enterprise cloud solutions. Both client organisations and suppliers rated cost management as one of the key influencers of the adoption of cloud solutions. Interestingly, while clients perceived productivity to be a key element, suppliers did not share this view. The top factor hindering enterprise cloud adoption was information security, while the least important factor was performance.

Firms were also asked to rate the factors that added value. The research revealed that suppliers overestimated the importance of experimenting with new ideas, while client organisations needed persuading that hard business outcomes would be delivered.

It is understandable why suppliers might choose to focus on obvious enterprise concerns like cost and innovation during the initial stages of cloud adoption. However, the enterprise cloud market has matured to a stage where other business drivers have equal, if not more weight in an enterprise's decision-making process. Suppliers need to refocus their marketing efforts to better align with these changes in customer attitudes and behaviour.

Cloud and Security: Perennial and Heightened Concerns

Even in 2014, Willcocks, Venters and Whitley found sufficient concern on multiple aspects of security that they devoted an extra chapter on the subject in their book '*Moving to the Cloud Corporation*'. By 2021, cybersecurity had emerged as the most common technology transformation companies were pursuing and planning to pursue in the future.

One root of the problem is the misleading terminology. Rather than being somehow 'out there' worldwide, cloud services actually reside in hardware—data centres—that are located on land and therefore subject to national laws, including those concerning data hosting, processing and transfer, in both the client and supplier territories. However, privacy and confidentiality remain a concern, especially when clients use service providers in a different country, where the local law may allow the government of that country to access certain data stored on hosted servers.

There are also security implications of a different kind inherent in supplier lock-in. Being reliant on any single supplier to host data remotely, and potentially also computing platforms and core business applications, means becoming a hostage to that supplier's fortunes, good customer relations, employees and internal security regime.

Suppliers need to be transparent about the security regimes they provide. Due diligence is essential for clients, who should also discuss with potential suppliers what both sides can do to implement better data security. Regarding supplier credibility, suppliers need to move away from the use of generic references to bolster their credibility. It has become clear that enterprises need recommendations from a trusted source.

Organisations planning to include the cloud as part of their IT portfolio need to have a comprehensive IT and business strategy in place to deal with the differences they will encounter on their journey to the cloud. The whole organisation will need to be trained in best practices for ensuring data security.

Recent studies have added to these generic concerns and recommendations. One macro-concern is that too much of the cloud market is in the hands of three main cloud providers: Amazon Web Services, Microsoft Azure and Google Cloud. What happens if any one or all fail? Meanwhile, at the organisational level, Kazemargi and Spagnoletti (2020) provide valuable insights. They point out that the primary focus of IT security has shifted from physical threats (i.e., in-house security threats) to logical cyber threats. Moreover, cloud service providers may subcontract some services to third parties. This makes control over data, already difficult, even more challenging. Also, data is not static in data centres, but rather in transit or in process from one layer to another, or from one application to another, creating vulnerabilities.

They suggest major barriers to adopting cloud sourcing are lack of full control over data and IT infrastructure, and emerging new security vulnerabilities characterised by cloud service levels and deployment models. Previous research has suggested other factors, such as business context, the level of sensitivity of data, and the nature of business processes that influence organisational decisions related to what resources can be moved to cloud. As examples, banking, aerospace and healthcare sectors are more reluctant to adopt cloud solutions due to the high sensitivity of their data.

Kazemargi and Spagnoletti (2020) add weight to a number of mitigating practices. The internal security skills of the client firm are critical, not least to negotiate contracts, SLAs and the security levels needed.

More importantly, they see the need for a paradigm shift in how IT governance of the non-physical assets is managed. They also emphasise the crucial role of regulatory bodies in developing standards and formal procedures that influence strategic decisions within organisations.

Operationally, Harvey (2021) summarises some major practical recommendations:

- Understand your shared responsibility model;
- Ask the cloud provider detailed security questions;
- Deploy an identity and access management solution;
- Train your staff;
- Establish and enforce cloud security policies;
- Secure endpoints;
- Encrypt data in motion and at rest;
- Use intrusion detection and prevention technology;
- Deploy cloud access security broker tools built to enforce cloud security policies;
- Double check compliance requirements;
- Conduct audits and penetration testing;
- Enable security logs.

Vendor Selection

Since security and lack of confidence in the supplier are two main factors hindering cloud adoption, client organisations need to have a robust vetting and selection process where they review and validate the credentials of their potential cloud services supplier. Omale (2018), a Gartner analyst, suggests five priorities. Firstly, clients should research the critical features and capabilities offered by leading cloud providers. They should also consider how the supplier's technical architecture will integrate with their workflows, now and in the future. Secondly, clients need to understand how cloud offerings stack up against their key requirements and criteria. Thirdly, clients should use planning and controls to mitigate security and compliance risks, and fourthly, focus on developing a structured framework for acquiring cloud management platforms tools. Finally, clients need to know their own process and architecture options for implementing cloud governance. Organisations often prioritise time-to-functionality decisions over planning for long-term scalability and support. However, it is essential for organisations to take the time to prepare for the much bigger cloud future.

Cloud Sourcing Management

In their research, Willcocks et al. (2014) made the case for developing further the Feeny and Willcocks (1998) retained core capabilities model and applying it for cloud sourcing management. The model sees retained capabilities needed to elicit and deliver on business requirements, achieve architecture planning and design and ensure delivery of technology services. This requires nine internal capabilities: technology leadership, informed buying technology architecting, technology fixing, business systems thinking, relationship building with the business, contract facilitation, contract monitoring and vendor development. For cloud management these capabilities would deliver governance, cloud architecture, business know-how and innovation and specialist sourcing capability. Informed buying would need to take into account that the whole idea behind the cloud is that things are going to be agile. The cloud also requires the ability to source different technologies and services from a multi-supplier base on a more dynamic, frequently pay-for-use and pay-as-you-go basis. Getting rid of architecture planning and design and technology 'fixing' capabilities is tempting but very wrong-headed when moving into a cloud environment. Moreover, governance, coordination, business facing and innovating, delivery of service and interfacing capabilities remain as critical as ever. All these capabilities help to progress the change in ethos needed to move from more traditional ways of managing IT to an 'evolution with cloud' or even 'cloud first' approach.

The difficulties are considerable, not least the formidable technology integration challenge, security and legal risks, and maintaining strategic corporate control over computing and going digital. As Willcocks et al.

(2014) note, it is not just about contracting for cloud services. While the cloud brings its own challenges, it is also part of long-term strategic moves towards becoming digital businesses. Although companies are transitioning more workloads to the public cloud, missteps in coordination are costing the average company 14% more than planned, and 38% of firms have experienced cloud migration delays of more than three months (Balakrishnan et al., 2021). Aggregated cost overruns at the global level have been estimated to exceed $US100 billion over the course of three-year cloud migrations, potentially also endangering $US500 billion of shareholder value.

To meet companies' cloud ambitions, staffing needs to move from 35% in-house to 50% in-house. This means organisations around the world will be looking to hire or reskill over one million new cloud developers over the next three years. Not surprisingly, companies are turning to external labour and service providers to fill gaps arising from tightening labour markets. However, service providers have become the single most cited source of cost overruns outside of change management.

What is the way forward? Clearly building the retained management capabilities outlined above is critical. Analysis by Balakrishnan et al. (2021) shows that the high performing companies are 32% more likely than others to have active CEO sponsors, and 9% more likely to develop the full implementation road map up front, including the security and compliance framework, rather than funding a series of one-off initiatives. Furthermore, they are 57% more likely to hire for advanced skill sets (such as DevOps and FinOps). More importantly, they are also more willing to make drop decisions on data-centre funding to focus on financing cloud migration, even if it means paying early termination fees.

Crowdsourcing Delivery over the Internet

Since the early 2000s, technological developments have fuelled the emergence of new organisational sourcing models such as crowdsourcing. *Crowdsourcing* describes the act of a company or institution taking a function once performed by employees and outsourcing it to an undefined (and generally large) network of people in the form of an open call (Howe, 2008). It enables organisations to reach beyond their immediate resources to tap into new knowledge and skills (Fréry et al., 2015). Fuelled by the growth of Internet-based platforms that provided its technological foundation, and by the need for an agile and uniquely skilled workforce, crowdsourcing has grown from the grassroots (Nevo & Kotlarsky, 2020). This sourcing model has been widely adopted in the open innovation movement (e.g., by Innocentive, TekScout, IdeaConnection, among many other open innovation marketplaces and communities). A large number of new business ventures have emerged through crowdsourcing, mainly by creating an opportunity for anybody to submit an idea (examples are products such as photos, videos and illustrations to iStock.com or t-shirt designs to Threadless.com) and then letting the community of users or potential buyers decide whether a particular creation is worth buying. Crowdsourcing projects rely on the contributions of individuals or a collective of people who are not necessarily motivated by monetary incentives. Psychological motivations, such as self-fulfilment, sense of contribution and the pleasure of solving problems are other motivating factors no less important than monetary rewards.

Similar to the emergence of large numbers of business-to-customer and customer-to-customer online marketplaces bringing together buyers and sellers (e.g., Amazon and Ebay), online marketplaces for sourcing customised products and services have also emerged. Such marketplaces allow customers to contract a supplier (an individual or a company) to develop and deliver a product or service based on the customer's specific needs. Different from online auctions such as eBay and e-malls like Amazon, which sell ready-made goods, online sourcing marketplaces provide clients with a suitable supplier of a product or service. Marketplaces such as Freelancer, Amazon Mechanical Turk (MTurk), Guru and Upwork serve as intermediaries, providing legal and project management support in the form of standard contracts that include copyright protection, payment protection and basic project management stages to facilitate interactions between clients and suppliers who are essentially members of the crowd. Registered crowd members can be individuals or firms. Such marketplaces (also referred to as 'crowdsourcing platforms') often have reputation for particular types of services, which reflects skills and interests of a crowd registered with the specific marketplace. For example, Amazon Mechanical Turk offers a wide range of services, from conducting simple data validation and research to more subjective tasks like survey participation and content moderation; Upwork specialises in creative design work, writing and translation as well as a range of back-office and support services, such as legal, administration, sales and marketing, accounting. IT-related skills are most commonly represented on different platforms, and it is not uncommon that the same supplier (individual or organisation) is registered with more than one crowdsourcing platform.

This sourcing model is usually suitable for relatively small and well-defined tasks[7] such as website design, the development of specialised applications or software development to implement small product features, proofreading or indexing. Clients and suppliers rely exclusively on online interactions and usually never meet face to face.

The following case study by Onook Oh and Rajiv Kishore, and reproduced from Oshri et al. (2023) describes the crowdsourcing phenomenon and provides an example of the InnoCentive crowdsourcing platform.

Case Study: The Crowdsourcing Phenomenon

With the development of Web 2.0 technologies, entrepreneurs are continually creating and experimenting with innovative e-business models. One e-business model that has gained popularity and recognition within a short time span is crowdsourcing. This business model harnesses the potential of a heterogeneous and globally dispersed online crowd to meet a variety of business needs, and to give opportunity to consumers (directly or indirectly) to participate in co-creating the goods

---

[7] This sourcing model is also referred to as 'microsourcing' and is seen as a way to break down projects into 'microtasks' that can be distributed to workers over the Internet.

and services they consume. As a result, the line between producer and consumer has become blurry in the crowdsourcing phenomenon.

Crowdsourcing may best be understood as a variant of the outsourcing phenomenon, in that both sourcing mechanisms utilise resources from outside the organisation's boundaries to meet internal business needs. However, a major difference between the two sourcing mechanisms is that while traditional outsourcing relies predominantly on a handful of established professional services firms, crowdsourcing turns to a much larger heterogeneous, online crowd of individuals to meet internal business needs. The main driver for crowdsourcing has been the ability to reach a multitude of potential virtual workers made possible through the collection of Web 2.0 technologies that enable individuals to actively participate and engage in co-creation activities via the 24/7 interconnected virtual technological environment. Furthermore, this highly connected technological environment makes it possible for organisations to aggregate individual profiles from the crowd and create a large virtual workforce of varied skill sets that they can search and match to specific business needs and then contract with specific individuals, and all in real time.

Innocentive

The Oil Spill Recovery Institute (OSRI) was formed in response to the catastrophic 1989 Exxon Valdez oil spill in Alaska to find ways to remove oil from contaminated areas. While dozens of barges have diligently pumped oil from iceberg cracks into barge tanks, the mixture of pumped water and oil quickly freezes to a sticky state, making it difficult to separate the oil and water. In 2007, OSRI posted a challenge relating to this issue on the InnoCentive website. Within two weeks, a cement expert, John Davis, came up with a simple solution that surprised OSRI scientists. John applied tools and techniques widely used in the concrete industry, where a vibration tool is used to keep cement from becoming solid during massive cement pours. John's solution was to attach a long pole to the vibration tool and then insert the pole into the oil recovery tanks and vibrate it to prevent the oil and water from freezing. Using this simple vibrating tool, OSRI could now remove oil from water, and the challenge solver John was rewarded with US$20,000.

The InnoCentive website is the meeting point for solvers and seekers—corporations or non-profit organisations that post their Research and Development (R&D) challenges to InnoCentive's open innovation marketplace. Each challenge has a solution submission deadline and is assigned a cash reward ranging from US$5,000 to more than US$1 Million. Any registered InnoCentive solver can enter the online project room to gain access to the posted challenges and work on any project that he or she may want to solve. The seeker reviews the submitted solutions after the deadline has passed, awards the cash reward to the best solver and pays an agreed commission to InnoCentive.

In 2022, InnoCentive's website reports 80% success with crowdsourcing projects, with over two-hundred thousand solutions captured and over US$60M in awards. InnoCentive is using the crowd's collective creativity and the power of the scale of the knowledge community to solve problems. It counts Proctor & Gamble, Boeing, DuPont, LG and other large and famous brand names among its seeker customers.

How Crowdsourcing Environments and Marketplaces Work

Despite the growing popularity of crowdsourcing, it is often considered as a phenomenon detached from (out)sourcing. Yet, we believe that sourcing professionals in client and vendor organisations could benefit significantly from understanding how crowdsourcing could be used to complement traditional sourcing models. Already in 2014 Nevo and Kotlarsky highlighted that sub-contracting specific parts of outsourced work, which is what most vendors do, could take the form of crowdsourcing. Clients too can directly engage with a crowd for specific, smaller-scale tasks.

Crowdsourcing represents a somewhat unknown slice of the global sourcing landscape which can be characterised as an Online Sourcing Environment (OSE), i.e., an online space where buyers and suppliers of services can meet, offer and apply for jobs (see Chapter 13); carry out project-related tasks; and conduct financial transactions.

All OSEs have three main stakeholders: buyers, suppliers who form the 'crowd' and online platforms. Buyers are companies or individuals who come to OSEs because they are interested in outsourcing a part of their workload. Historically, most OSE buyers have been small—usually entrepreneurs and small firms with fewer than 100 employees, and mostly from English-speaking countries. Suppliers are also represented primarily by small service firms and individuals, with the latter being either moonlighters or independent professionals. They participate in OSEs to market their skills and services to potential buyers. The population of suppliers is more geographically distributed than that of buyers, with the USA still contributing a significant portion. In addition, certain countries have become somewhat specialised in specific project types—for example, India and Pakistan dominate the IT category. The third stakeholder is the intermediary, the crowdsourcing marketplace itself, which takes the shape of an *online platform*. These are the websites that provide an environment where buyers and suppliers can interact.

A new project in an OSE usually starts with the buyer formalising its work needs and converting them into project requirements. These requirements are then communicated to suppliers, typically in the form of a job, project that can be advertised as a request for bid, or as a competition announcement. The former, *tender-based* approach to crowdsourcing (also referred to as '*micro-sourcing*') implies that crowd member(s) is/are selected based on their bids. They assume work only after the fees have been agreed. The later, *tournament-based* approach relies on competitions/contests. It is commonly employed in creative and knowledge-intensive tasks such as R&D, and analytics and involves crowd members self-selecting to work on projects, with the best solution chosen as the winner. Given that only winners are being paid, crowdsourcing using tournament-based approach needs to be designed in such a way that it attracts crowd members willing to complete work for free (i.e., to invest their time and resourcing in the project) knowing that they will only be paid if their submission is selected as a winner of the contest. Therefore well-known brands that easily attract attention of large crowds are well positioned to utilise tournament-based crowdsourcing due to their popularity. One example is Starbucks launching a crowdsourcing campaign asking its customers to paint their traditional white cups with any design they want and share its picture with the #WhiteCupContest hashtag.[8] Another example is 'Space Poop Challenge' by the US National Aeronautics and Space Administration (NASA) that was seeking an in-suit waste management system that would be beneficial for contingency scenarios or for any long duration tasks.[9]

After proposals (bids) have been submitted by interested suppliers, the buyer selects a supplier to work on the project. Once the job is awarded, the buyer oversees its completion and, when the final deliverable is deemed acceptable, pays the supplier for services rendered. The final step in the buyer workflow is to rate the supplier and, sometimes, provide additional qualitative feedback on the project.

Suppliers register with OSEs by building a personal profile. Most OSEs today allow rich supplier profiles that include personal and contact information, educational and employment history, job history on the platform and, in many cases, skills evaluation data (tested or self-reported). Once the profile is in place, the supplier can start searching and applying for relevant job or project announcements.

The mechanics of the application process may vary from one OSE platform to another, but usually it is set up as either a reverse auction or a competition. Once selected, the supplier starts working on the project. The work is usually facilitated by the platform, which provides communication, collaboration and project management tools. Once the job is completed, the supplier collects the payment and provides feedback on the buyer.

We distinguish three main types of OSEs: *directories*, which provide listings of projects, supplier profiles and contact information, but where deals are usually done offline; *marketplaces*, which connect buyers and suppliers and facilitate their interaction throughout the entire sourcing life cycle; and *communities*, which aim to build a network of talented and skilled individuals in a particular field, such as creative design or

---

[8] https://consumervaluecreation.com/2019/02/28/using-A-white-cup-for-crowdsourcing-A-starbucks-initiative/.

[9] See details and outcomes of the NASA's Space Poop Challenge here https://www.nasa.gov/feature/space-poop-challenge.

computer programming. Their key characteristics are summarised in Table 11.2.

Boundaries between the three OSE types often blur or change over time. For example, a platform may start out as a directory, but over time features are added with the objective of gradually evolving into a marketplace. Similarly, some platforms in the marketplace category are starting to adopt elements from the community category. For example, marketplace platforms Elance and oDesk have made significant efforts to engage with and foster the community of suppliers (e.g., both platforms maintain blogs and are active on Twitter), until they merged and re-branded as Upwork[10] in 2015.

Scholars have attempted to develop typologies of crowdsourcing platforms by distinguishing platform characteristics, such as whether the nature of collaboration is explicit or implicit (Doan et al., 2011) and whether the user contribution is active or passive (Cook, 2008). In the context of outsourcing, a typology by Kaganer et al. (2013) that distinguishes between different roles—the facilitator, arbitrator, aggregator and governor—that an intermediary platform can play in mediating relationship between buyers and the crowd (i.e., suppliers) is of particular relevance. The *facilitator* refers to crowdsourcing platforms (e.g., Upwork and Freelancer) that provide relatively transparent mechanisms allowing both project initiators and suppliers (crowd members) to view each other's expertise, credibility and past experience in order to make decisions. In a facilitator contract, usually the client is expected to select one supplier who can be an individual or a firm. The fees are agreed between the client and the supplier in advance, before the supplier commences the project. With respect to the *arbitrator*, suppliers compete with each other and provide deliverables that they submit without an advanced promise of a payment (e.g., crowdspring). The project initiator selects only one deliverable that best fulfils its need and only the wining supplier gets paid. The *aggregator* platform usually engages with a large number of suppliers to deliver a huge amount of simple, repetitive tasks and there is no coordination need among suppliers (e.g., CrowdFlower). For each supplier, the payment procedure is the same as with the facilitator model.

---

[10] https://en.wikipedia.org/wiki/upwork.

Table 11.2 Characteristics of online sourcing environments

	Directories	Marketplaces	Communities
Main focus or objective	Help buyers discover suppliers by providing supplier listings with profile and contact information	Connects buyers and suppliers of services throughout all stages of the work flow	Helps members (i.e., suppliers) develop professionally through community interaction and paid client (i.e., buyer) engagements
Nature or structure of deals	Deals are done offline; the platform is not involved	Deals are done online, usually through a reverse-auction type of process; the platform is involved in both legal and financial aspects of the deal	Deals are done online and usually structured as contests or competitions; the platform is involved in both legal and financial aspects of the deal
Platform's role in facilitating buyer-supplier interaction	No buyer-supplier interaction takes place on the platform; buyers may have an option of posting projects online, but all the ensuing activities take place outside of the platform	The platform facilitates buyer-supplier interaction with a focus on project completion	The platform facilitates buyer-supplier interaction with a focus on learning and community building

(continued)

Table 11.2 (continued)

	Directories	Marketplaces	Communities
Revenue model	Advertising, sponsorship	Project commission paid by suppliers; buyers and suppliers may sign up for premium membership	Project commission/ fee paid by buyers
Platform examples	Procurementfreelancers.com Chinasourcing	Guru, Upwork, Freelancer, MTurk	Crowdspring, TopCoder

The *governor* crowdsourcing platform provides project governance by employing a combination of human project managers and a sophisticated software-enabled framework for monitoring and coordinating individual tasks. *Governor* platforms provide a thicker layer of project governance, including collecting project requirements from the client, breaking them up into micro-tasks, coordinating completion and sequencing individual tasks, conducting supplier certification and ensuring the quality of the final deliverable (Kaganer et al., 2013).

In addition crowdsourcing is used to support firm-initiated *campaigns* engaging external workforces to achieve particular business purposes. Usually, the firm creates a dedicated online space (supported by a crowdsourcing platform) for the campaign. The crowd gets involved in the campaign in the form of competitions. Unlike the arbitrator model, there are usually multiple ranked winners who get the rewards. For example, LEGO® learns from consumers' creativity through maintaining its own platform Lego Ideas[11] to share design ideas for new LEGO sets, and vote on models submitted by others. Such a model is frequently used for marketing, R&D and customer-research-related business purposes.

---

[11] https://ideas.lego.com.

Why Do Buyers Come to OSEs?

OSEs afford buyers instant global reach, with neither the buyers in search of talented people nor the suppliers bounded by their region or country. Buyers benefit from the low costs resulting from global supplier competition. The differences in bids submitted to the same project description are usually due to the variation in wages and costs across supplier countries or regions. OSE programmers in India, Bangladesh and Pakistan generally submit bids that are much lower than those by their competitors in wealthy nations.

Another advantage OSEs offer to buyers is the ability to quickly launch and scale up projects. Once a buyer posts a project, it is common to get 20–30 proposals from suppliers within the first couple of days.[12] For larger projects, OSEs can help buyers mobilise members of the supplier community to start working in parallel on the individual tasks comprising the project. Community-type platforms like crowdspring and TopCoder do an especially good job at this.

Finally, buyers can take advantage of an established framework provided by OSEs for initiating and managing their sourcing projects (i.e., a comprehensive suite of online tools and services that help buyers manage all aspects of the sourcing relationship).

What Challenges Do OSE Buyers Face?

Trust is key to any successful buyer–supplier relationship, especially in OSEs, which lack personal contact and face-to-face interaction, with cross-cultural and language differences creating additional obstacles. A buyer needs to have confidence that the supplier it selects will complete the project on time and that the final deliverable will be of acceptable quality. The buyer also needs to be assured that if problems arise, effective mechanisms are available within the platform to address the issue. Thus, trust must be established at two levels: the supplier level and the platform level.

---

[12] Some projects attract large number of automated bids, by bots. A buyer needs to be able to distinguish genuine bids from automated ones.

At the supplier level, the general strategy has been to make the OSEs more transparent, open up communication channels between the buyer and supplier and provide tools to monitor project progress. For example, in the early years of OSEs, suppliers had anonymous user profiles and aliases instead of real names. Over time, OSEs realised that this approach was counterproductive in terms of helping the parties build trusting relationships. Today, most platforms allow suppliers to build rich profiles providing detailed personal and contact information, educational and employment history, skills evaluation scores and often a portfolio of previous work. In addition, to make up for the lack of personal recommendations common in traditional offline environments, platforms have introduced sophisticated rating systems and feedback mechanisms. Buyers can also see a complete history of projects the supplier has worked on, along with earnings and project completion statistics.

With respect to opening up communication channels, many crowdsourcing platforms offer built-in online communication services, including chat, discussion forums, Web conferencing and voice integration. These tools can be used to interview a supplier at the selection phase and facilitate collaboration between the two parties throughout the project. Similarly, many platforms offer project management tools that enable buyers to establish milestones and link payments to milestone completion.

At the platform level, fostering trust is based on the idea that since it is virtually impossible to ensure the trustworthiness of each individual supplier in a global context, the platform itself should become the guarantor buyers will trust. Two primary mechanisms are used to accomplish this goal. The first includes initiatives seeking to reduce the perception of risk for the buyer. Escrow accounts (the project payment is held by the platform until the work is completed and approved by the buyer), arbitration services and mandatory intellectual property agreements for suppliers are the most common examples.

The second mechanism focuses on grooming the supplier pool. Here, the rationale is that by weeding out poor suppliers and promoting high-quality ones, the platform will build a trustworthy reputation for itself. For example, Upwork offers buyers to take advantage of its project management tool that provides general project consulting, helps to define project goals, deliverables and KPIs.

In Chapter 12 Hee Rui He, Julia Kotlarsky and Dorit Nevo provided a detailed sample case study of crowdsourcing in action.

Can Outsourcing Suppliers Benefit from Crowdsourcing?

Crowdsourcing offers several potential benefits to outsourcing suppliers, among them an alternative to the onsite-offshore model. This next generation of outsourcing to the 'human cloud', a virtual, on-demand workforce (Kaganer et al., 2013), is enabled through crowdsourcing platforms. As large companies such as Microsoft have been experimenting with crowdsourcing, its growing popularity has stimulated mixed reactions in the outsourcing community. Some established suppliers are ignoring the fact that an 'unknown workforce' is delivering jobs that could have been contracted to them. Others recognise the increasing competition and are attempting to utilise this virtual on-demand workforce for their benefit (Nevo & Kotlarsky, 2014). In particular, during the economic 2008 downturn, when reducing headcount across global delivery centres was seen as one obvious solution to reduce costs, especially fixed costs, the possibility of tapping into a global talent pool to employ required skills on demand created an interesting proposition for established service providers.

While the expected economic benefits of this proposition are significant, it is not clear what effort is required from established IT service providers to successfully leverage crowdsourcing. Kaganer et al. (2013) suggest, for example, that the organisational challenges associated with the human cloud require new management models and skills from the contracting organisation (the buyer). Putting this perspective into the outsourcing context, Nevo and Kotlarsky (2014) argue that service providers engaging in crowdsourcing need to develop new capabilities to successfully utilise crowdsourcing in delivering services to their clients. Based on data collected from focus groups with crowdsourcing leaders at a large multinational technology organisation, the new capabilities identified stem from the need for the traditional service provider to assume a 'client' role in the crowdsourcing context, while still acting as a 'supplier' in providing services to the end-client (for a detailed discussion of new capabilities, see Nevo and Kotlarsky [2014]). Overall, this combination of 'client' and 'supplier' capabilities enables a primary supplier to manage the three stakeholder groups that play an important role in crowdsourced projects:

1. *The client*, who is ultimately the most important stakeholder, with client buy-in needed to ensure their satisfaction. Not all clients contracting a specific organisation may agree to have (parts of) their work crowdsourced.
2. *Internal team members*, who need to design, facilitate and manage crowdsourced work, as well as integrate the crowdsourced deliverable into the services delivered to the end-client.
3. *The crowd*, who need to have appropriate support (e.g., infrastructure) from the primary service provider, and feel motivated to respond to crowdsourcing calls.

Conclusion

This chapter has reviewed Internet-based sourcing models, in particular providing in-depth insight into cloud computing services and crowdsourcing models. The chapter brings together recent developments in cloud computing and examples of the application of crowdsourcing in various business contexts (see also Chapter 12).

Looking at the big picture going forward, it would seem that the cloudification of computing and digital application resources is foundational. MIT Technology Review Insights (2022) argues that cloud-enabled digital capabilities are becoming ever more pervasive and allow governments, businesses and citizens to conduct transactions more efficiently and equitably, accelerating economic progress and increasing equity and sustainability. Their global cloud ecosystem index points to how some nations have marshalled cloud applications, tools and infrastructure to accelerate and transform economic productivity. The countries leading the way are Singapore, Finland Sweden, Denmark, Switzerland, Germany, France, Norway and Luxembourg. In such countries the cloud will be both easier to manage, and more productive to use.

References

Balakrishnan, T., Gnanasambandam, C., Santos, L., & Srivathsan, B. (2021, October). *Cloud Migration Opportunity: Business Value Grows But Missteps Abound*. McKinsey.

Cook, S. (2008). The Contribution Revolution. *Harvard Business Review, 86*(10), 60–69.

Doan, A., Ramakrishnan, R., & Halevy, A. Y. (2011). Crowdsourcing Systems on the World-wide Web. *Communications of the ACM, 54*(4), 86–96.

Feeny, D., & Willcocks, L. (1998). Core IS Capabilities for Exploiting Information Technology. *MIT Sloan Management Review, 31*(3), 9–21.

Fréry, F., Lecocq, X., & Warnier, V. (2015). Competing with Ordinary Resources. *MIT Sloan Management Review, 56*, 69–77.

Harvey, C. (2021, September). Top Twelve Cloud Security Best Practices. *E-Security Planet.*

Howe, J. (2008). *Crowdsourcing: How the Power of the Crowd Is Driving the Future of Business.*

Kaganer, E., Carmel, E., Hirschheim, R., & Olsen, T. (2013). Managing the Human Cloud. *MIT Sloan Management Review, 54*, 23–32.

Kazemargi, N., & Spagnoletti, P. (2020). Cloud Sourcing and Paradigm Shift in IT Governance: Evidence from the Finance Sector. In R. Agrifolio, R. Lambroglia, et al. (Eds.), *Digital Business Transformation Conference Proceedings*. Springer.

KPMG/HFS. (2020, November). *Enterprise Reboot Perspectives*. KPMG.

McKinsey Digital. (2021, February). *Cloud's Trillion Dollar Prize Is Up for Grabs*. McKinsey.

McKinsey Digital. (2022, March). *Prioritizing Digital Transformations to Win*. McKinsey.

MIT Technology Review Insights. (2022). *The Global Cloud Ecosystem Index 2022. MIT Technology Review.* www.MITTechnologyReview.com

Nevo, D., & Kotlarsky, J. (2014). Primary Vendor Capabilities in a Mediated Outsourcing Model: Can IT Service Providers Leverage Crowdsourcing? *Decision Support Systems, 65,* 17–27.

Nevo, D., & Kotlarsky, J. (2020). Crowdsourcing as a Strategic IS Sourcing Phenomenon: Critical Review and Insights for Future Research. *The Journal of Strategic Information Systems, 29*(4), 1–22.

Omale, G. (2018). *Five Priorities When Buying and Deploying Cloud Offerings.* Gartner.

Oshri, I., Kotlarsky, J., & Willcocks, L. P. (2023). *The Handbook of Global Outsourcing and Offshoring* (4th ed.). ISBN 978-3-031-12034-3

Willcocks, L., Hindle, J., Stanton, M., & Smith, J. (2023). *Maximizing the Value of Automation and Digital Transformation: A Realist's Guide.* Palgrave Macmillan.

Willcocks, L., Venters, W., & Whitley, E. (2014). *Moving to the Cloud Corporation.* Palgrave Macmillan.

12

A Process Perspective on Emerging Value in Tournament-Based and Collaborative Crowdsourcing

Hee Rui He, Julia Kotlarsky, and Dorit Nevo

Introduction

As detailed in Chapter 11, crowdsourcing, which refers to the engagement of external crowds in projects via online crowdsourcing platforms (Howe, 2006), is gaining recognition for its contribution to value creation in organizations. This value is attributed to outcomes such as reducing time to market, reducing costs, improving quality through

---

This chapter is based on the conference paper: He, R.-H., Kotlarsky, J., & Nevo, D. (2021). A Process Perspective on Emerging Value in Tournament-Based and Collaborative Crowdsourcing. Proceedings of the HICSS-54, Hawaii.

H. R. He
Wenzhou Business College, Wenzhou, China

J. Kotlarsky (✉)
University of Auckland, Auckland, New Zealand
e-mail: j.kotlarsky@auckland.ac.nz

D. Nevo
Lally School of Management, Rensselaer Polytechnic Institute, Troy, NY, USA

© The Editor(s) (if applicable) and The Author(s), under exclusive licence to Springer Nature Switzerland AG 2024
L. Willcocks et al. (eds.), *Transformation in Global Outsourcing*, Technology, Work and Globalization, https://doi.org/10.1007/978-3-031-61022-6_12

broad participation, generating alternate solutions with increased creativity, and enabling the employment of specialists on an ad hoc basis (LaToza & van der Hoek, 2016).

The literature on value creation through crowdsourcing is still in its infancy, and somewhat fragmented. Some papers focus on the ability of the crowd to generate value, for example, by studying whether crowd members can compete with professionals in new product development ideas (Poetz & Schreier, 2012). Other examples consider crowdsourcing as enhancing the competitive ability of lean start-ups (Erkinheimo et al., 2015), or enabling organizations to compete with ordinary resources (Fréry et al., 2015).

At a higher level, Kohler (2015) studied crowdsourcing-based business models to explore how value is created by each model. Analyzing crowdsourcing business models at varying levels of success, he addresses specific challenges to value creation and prescribes actions for organizations. This higher level of analysis of the business value of crowdsourcing is useful in that it can be generalized over different crowdsourcing settings. In this chapter we take a similar path toward a more generalizable examination of value creation in crowdsourcing. Specifically, we take a stakeholders' approach to value generation, and we focus on the process of value creation through interactions between a project's stakeholders. This approach is motivated by a desire for a deeper understanding of the unique value that crowdsourcing can provide both firms and crowd members in comparison to other sourcing models. Specifically, while expected outcomes of productivity and creative ideas (for the firm) or monetary rewards and accomplishments (for the crowd) can also be associated with other sourcing models, we are interested in the distinctive value that is created through unique features of crowdsourcing. In this work we study in depth two crowdsourcing forms: tournament-based and collaborative, and we elicit value beyond what is typically expected. Further, we follow one crowdsourcing project over time. We believe that taking a longitudinal approach can provide a temporal perspective on emerging value and distinguish between value for firm and value for crowd. In doing so, we address an observed gap in the literature which lacks an overarching understanding of crowdsourcing value creation process.

Theoretical Background

Three value-related constructs provide the necessary backdrop for our work. The first two originate in the marketing literature and concern the economic meaning of *value*: value-in-exchange occurs when value is created by the firm and distributed in the market (i.e. through exchange of goods and money); value-in-use implies that value is continuously co-created through interactions between firms and customers (Vargo et al., 2008). The third construct comes from the IS literature and concerns the business value of IT.

It considers the performance impacts of information technology in terms of efficiency and competitiveness (Nevo & Wade, 2010). Taken together these value definitions imply three key actors are involved in the creation of value: the firm, the customers, and the technology artifact. In this work we examine a fourth value creating actor in the form of the sub-contractor, which, in the case of crowdsourcing, is represented by the crowd.

Depending on the specific crowdsourcing model employed, the crowd can play different roles in creating value. In Wikipedia, for example, the crowd's role is similar to that of the firm, generating value-in-exchange: crowd members create content, which is then consumed by Wikipedia readers. In Threadless, the crowd's role is similar to that of consumers generating value-in-use by generating and evaluating designs in a series of interactions among themselves, or with the platform. Finally, Kohler (2015) discusses a product platform crowdsourcing business model that aligns with the business value of IT. Here, creators build on to a technology or a basic product and sell the resulting products to customers. This is an example where value creation can be attributed to interactions between the crowd and the technology platform, highlighting its business value.

Our work proposes a different view of these three value types by examining interactions among them. When crowd members perform a specific task contracted out by the firm, part of the value is created in the exchange, through the creation of the desired deliverables (e.g. Afua & Tucci, 2012). Additional value is created in use, through interactions that are shared between the company and the crowd (e.g. Chiu et al., 2010).

And yet additional value is created through the features of the technology platform. This calls for new models and strategies of value creation and capture, to account for the contribution of all value-creating participants (Kohler, 2015). Hence, the first objective of our work is *to study the process of value creation, specifically, how value is co-created by stakeholders over the life of the crowdsourcing project.*

A second foundational literature that we examined concerns specific benefits that both firms and crowd expect to obtain through crowdsourcing participation. From the firm's perspective, crowdsourcing has been shown to contribute both tangible and intangible values. For example, Poetz and Schreier (2012) compared the quality of ideas generated by a firm's professionals to those submitted by users in an idea generation contest. They found that the best ideas were concentrated among users rather than professionals. Similarly, Nishikawa et al. (2017) show that labeling crowdsourced new products as such increases the product's actual market performance by up to 20%, and that this effect can be attributed to perceptions of increased quality perceptions. Additional examples of tangible benefits include increased accuracy and performance (e.g. Glaeser et al., 2016; Jame et al., 2016), lower costs, and reduced time to solution (e.g. Ye & Kankanhalli, 2013). Intangible benefits include the ability to leverage outside capabilities and skills, increased knowledge diversity, understanding of customer preferences, and externalization of project risk (you only pay for results you are happy with) (Ye & Kankanhalli, 2013). Further, crowdsourcing may result in unexpected outcomes that can provide opportunities for the firm and generally positive effects (Gatzweiler et al., 2017).

From the crowd's perspective, insights on expected value can be obtained through literature on crowd members' motivation to participate and contribute to crowdsourcing projects. Studies here explore extrinsic motivation factors, such as career opportunities, payment, and personal need for innovations (Deng & Joshi, 2016; Frey et al., 2011). Morgan and Wang (2010), for example, describe one contributor who was having a hard time finding a job in R&D. Participating in an innovation challenge provided him with a $25K reward as well as re-affirming his confidence in himself. Beyond extrinsic motivation, intrinsic factors are also important for participation. Such factors include the fun and enjoyment of developing solutions and satisfying intellectual curiosity (Frey et al., 2011), feelings of pride and respect (Boons et al., 2015), having a flexible work environment and job autonomy, working on varied tasks, and experiencing personal growth (Deng & Joshi, 2016).

The above benefits of crowdsourcing are perceived at a single point in time, either prior to the project start or after its completion. What is missing from this literature is a more continuous view of project value as it unfolds. Therefore, our second objective is *to add a temporal dimension to this body of literature and to track specific value outcomes as they unfold over the life of the crowdsourcing project.*

To address these two objectives, we conducted a longitudinal qualitative case study following a crowdsourcing project by one of the leading Chinese escape room gaming houses.

Research Method

This inductive theory-building research was designed as an in-depth longitudinal qualitative study of a crowdsourcing project. The first author spent 2.5 months at the case site following the project from its inception in June 2016 through to completion in August 2016. The project was subsequently tracked until implementation of the final outcome in 2017. We collected process data (Langley, 1999; Langley et al., 2013) that focuses on understanding interactions and engagement between the firm and crowd actors; specifically, how they interact and what value they experience as they interact.

Data Collection and Analysis

Data for this study was collected from multiple sources, including: (1) interviews; (2) internal company and online documents; (3) direct observations (e.g. daily operations and weekly team meetings); and (4) informal conversations with members of the PM team. We conducted 12 formal interviews with three members of the Games Company, spanning over multiple milestones throughout the project life cycle. Each interview lasted for 45 minutes on average. We also interviewed 3 winners when the project was completed. Each interview lasted for 60 minutes on average. In total, over 720 minutes formal interviews were recorded. In addition, the first author was on site at the GamesCo. Recorded documents included online working logs on the platform, documents provided by the focal firm, important information collected via informal chats and observations, snapshots of 15 collected game designs and meeting minutes. In total, over 120 pages of documents were collected. Overview of the data sources and list of the interviewees, their roles, and interview contents are summarized in Tables 12.1 and 12.2, accordingly.

In our data analysis we relied on temporal bracketing and visual mapping approaches (Langley, 1999) recommended for process decomposition and representation by Langley et al. (2013) and employed Gioia's methodology (Gioia et al., 2013) to concept development. Before embarking on with-case analysis, multiple sources of data were integrated and organized in a chronological order to reflect the life cycle of the crowdsourcing project. According to Gioia's methodology the first-order analysis focused on established concepts (e.g. monetary rewards, learning about the industry, two completed designs) directly from original transcripts. In the second-order analysis, we tried to gain thorough understanding toward the investigated phenomenon from the perspective of informants, and then carefully translated it into the perspective of researchers. The first-order concepts were associated with themes summarized from the literature review (e.g. value-in-use, value-in-exchange). During the third-order analysis, the second-order themes were aggregated into dimensions (e.g. expected value, emergent value, and realized

Table 12.1 Data sources

Interview	12 formal interviews with 3 members of the local firm
	3 formal interviews with 3 crowd members
Observation	Daily observation spanning 13/06/16 – 24/07/16
	Informal chats with 3 members of the local firm during observations
Documentation	Online documentation on the platform
	Offline documentation recorded by the members of the local firm

Table 12.2 The list of interviewees

Interviewee	Role	Interview content
Vincent	- Top manager - Game designer and market researcher on the internal design team - Member of the PM team	Weekly interviews with each member of the PM team Interviews focused on: - Project preparation, initiation - Deliverable reviews 1st, 2nd, and 3rd weeks - Online and offline phases
Max	- Top manager - Game designer and market researcher on the internal design team - Member of the PM team	
Joe	- Store manager - Game designer and engineer on the internal design team - Member of the PM team	
The Gamer	- One of the three winning online crowd members (submission #4) - One of the two winning offline crowd members	- Online and offline phases
The Historian	- One of the three winning online crowd members (submission #5)	- Online phase
The Musician	- One of the three winning online crowd members (submission #8) - One of the two winning offline crowd members	- Online and offline phases

value). We then followed the guidance for the process theory development (Langley et al., 2013) to structure identified concepts, themes, and dimensions.

Game Design Project: Background

Background on the Gamesco and Local Market

The field of *live escape room games* is relatively young but fast-growing within China's entertainment industry. An escape room gaming venue provides players with a locked adytum, a storyline, and a series of well-designed puzzles and tricks. The basic game principle is that a group of players follow the storyline and solve the puzzles and tricks in order to get out of the room. Established in 2013, GamesCo is one of the most successful entertainment companies in the local escape room market in China. At the time of data collection it had three stores employing about 45 people and containing 15 gaming rooms, and an annual revenue of more than 3,000,000 CNY.

As an early entrant to the field, GamesCo competitive advantages span investments, game design, human resources, and brand awareness. It was ranked the #1 escape room gaming house by local consumers and had accumulated very positive feedback on mainstream consumer-oriented commentator websites. To maintain their competitive edge the two co-investors, Vincent and Max, who held the top management roles in GamesCo, started thinking about new game designs. As managers, they believed that advanced technologies (e.g. 3D effects, artificial intelligence, and virtual reality) and facilities (e.g. lighting systems, acoustic effects, and operational machineries) are crucial to enhance the consumer's experience.

Background of the Game Design Crowdsourcing Project.

Initially, GamesCo intended to design the new games internally. The company had a design team comprising of professional game designers, market researchers, and engineers able to conduct the entire game design process, including market research, theme and storyline design, puzzles and tricks design, and gaming room construction planning. Apart from its own game designs, the GamesCo purchased copyrights from an American entertainment company as an additional source of game designs.

Of the existing 15 gaming rooms, eight were designed by the internal team, and the rest were modified from purchased packages. However, during a design team meeting, Max came up with the idea of crowdsourcing. The team agreed with the suggestion, realizing that interesting new game designs might be found at a relatively low cost.

The major purpose of the crowdsourcing (CS) project was to collect ideas for escape room game designs from the crowd. As Vincent explained, *"The starting point is the most difficult [...] A promising idea is all we need."* In seeking promising ideas, the team also took knowledge protection issues into consideration. On the selected crowdsourcing platform, it was expected that winning ideas will be made public as evidence of fairness and transparency. It would therefore be possible for industry competitors to see and take advantage of these ideas. After several rounds of discussions, the team clarified that they should not expect complete game designs from the crowd, but rather promising ideas worthy of further development.[1] With this in mind, the firm advertised on the CS platform,[2] specifying escape room game designs with interesting themes, storylines, and three to five embedded puzzles and tricks. It was agreed that after the winning ideas were chosen, the internal team would further develop promising ideas offline with the winning participants. The firm set a three-week period during which time it accepted bids from the crowd. Finally, the amount of prize money offered as reward was much higher than the market average level, in an attempt to attract more high-quality submissions. For the first, *online* phase of the project, each of the

---

[1] A complete game design consists of one theme with storylines, 10 to 15 puzzles and tricks, and a construction plan. The creation of an interesting story theme with storylines and embedded puzzles and tricks are the most creative and challenging aspects of game design. A theme, with its accompanying storylines, has to be very engaging in order to trigger consumer interest. Usually, the GamesCo selects up-to-date and popular story themes. Storylines, as containers of puzzles and tricks, elaborate on how the story unfolds. Well-designed puzzles and tricks have to be gripping, logical, highly playable and with appropriate levels of difficulty (not so simple as to reduce playability, and not so difficult as to affect the consumer's experience). Construction plans consider the practical issues of building the game design and attempt to maximize the consumer's experience.

[2] The selected platform was a well-known CS platform, which had been operating in China for 10 years.

three winners would receive a prize of 1,500 CNY. The second, *offline*[3] phase of the project offered another 1,500 CNY for each winner.

The quality of the deliverables would be judged by the project management (PM) team members based on the story themes, storylines, tricks and puzzles designs, estimated construction difficulties, estimated budget, and other concerns. The team expected to find at least two high-standard deliverables from the online phase of the competition, which could then hopefully be developed into two sophisticated game designs through offline cooperation.

Management of the Game Design Project

The management team for the CS project comprised three members: Vincent, Max, and Joe, all of whom were involved in design and construction of the previous 15 game rooms. They also had definitive roles in the internal game design team. They agreed to make decisions jointly during weekly meetings.

The project was advertised as a tournament CS project with guaranteed rewards for the three top designs. At the end of the *online* phase, the PM team decided on the winning entries and authorized payment to the three winning crowd members. These were: the Gamer, the Historian, and the Musician. During the second, *offline* phase of the project, GamesCo involved two crowd members in their internal game design processes. The internal design team engaged with and worked closely with the Gamer and the Musician (separately) to further develop their winning game designs into final products—physical escape rooms.

In the next section, we present our findings and analysis of interactions between GamesCo and the crowd members with the intention to capture the emerging value, as perceived by the focal firm and crowd members.

---

[3] Respondents refer to the two phases of the project as *online* and *offline* phase. In our analysis we distinguished them as *tournament-based* phase and *collaborative* phase.

Findings and Analysis

The actions of the Game Design PM team and their interactions with crowd members were driven by the expected outcome—two promising designs for new escape rooms. As Vincent commented, they wanted *"at least two promising packages which can be further developed into more mature packages [...] Our goal is not about the average quality of all received deliverables, but the best ones."*

Once the project was posted on the platform, the crowd members who decided to participate had their own expectations, as revealed in interviews:

The Gamer: After all, I work for monetary rewards, therefore the chances of winning were important to me. Moreover, I was willing to face challenges. I thought I could learn something new through participation.

The Historian: Firstly, I was capable of accomplishing the project. It was fun to have a try. In addition, the project offered monetary rewards and extra opportunities, which was appealing.

The Musician: The monetary rewards, of course, mattered. I am an online worker, looking for feasible projects. I make a better living this way. However, I did like this project. I did it for fun, learning and altruism. These were the major motivations for my participation.

Online (Tournament) Phase

During the period when the project was open for submissions, crowd members worked on their designs individually. During this time, they experienced emerging value of an intrinsic nature. As the three winning crowd members described:

The Gamer: The designing procedure was mentally challenging. It felt good when I was trying hard. I enjoyed the process since I learnt about how to design real escape room games.

The Historian: I was making efforts to create the game design. As time went by, it felt more and more interesting. Every day it was encouraging to see my progresses. Every day I was able to learn new knowledge. I had a sense of accomplishment.

The Musician: The game design came into being through hard work. I felt a sense of accomplishment and pride.

At the three-week deadline, GamesCo collected contributions submitted by 15 crowd members. To evaluate these 15 submissions 3 members of the management team reviewed each submission individually, and then compared their individual assessments jointly decide on the best 3 submissions. As Vincent, Joe, and Max reviewed and assessed submissions, they commented on the value they saw in different submissions, as summarized in Table 12.3.

As the PM team decided on the winning deliverables, Vincent reflected on the value they gained from the outcome of the online phase: "The value of the online part was mainly about selecting promising deliverables. #4 and #8 are good ones." In addition to the winning designs, they indicated value related to the learning. For example, Max elaborated:

> Through analyzing nicely conceived story themes and storylines, and well-designed puzzles and tricks, I have already learnt from the designers' conceptions. Because of the learning process, I felt something new.

In a similar vein Joe explained:

> I feel that value reflects in the quality of deliverables. I think there are at least three kinds of deliverable with three kinds of value. The first type of value, as seen in the #4 and #8 deliverables, is the type we desire. It fulfils our needs in terms of quality and creativity, which are core values. The second kind of deliverable has certain aspects that we feel are interesting and inspiring, for example a specific puzzle design. This kind of deliverable is valuable, but as a side value, not a core value. In the last kind, for instance #1 deliverable, no value was perceived.

Table 12.3 Value of submission (illustrative quotes)

#4, the Gamer
- Wonderful! This is a very interesting deliverable. There are integrated storylines. The puzzles and tricks are well embedded in the storylines. I think such a design is worth much more than 1500 CHY. ... Descriptions are very attractive. ... some suggestions on design are given, for example the map puzzle. The only aspect I am worried about is the cost of construction. This is a visionary design, with various imaginary elements. Building a grand environment must involve a huge cost. But I still feel confident. In general, I regard this deliverable very highly. Analyzing this deliverable is a kind of learning. I feel that the designer's logic and control over background elements are worth pondering. I enjoyed it. (Joe)
- This is the most mature design we have had till now. All basic requirements are fulfilled, even beyond my expectation. ... this theme will not have issues related to sales. ... With further development, this design may well be the new gaming room in the new store. (Max)
- Among the four deliverables, I think this one is the best. This design is excellent in terms of story theme, storyline, and puzzle design… Working in this industry for a long time, logic becomes fixed. ... This deliverable inspired me a lot in terms of its logic breakthrough. It also made me rethink the direction of Takagism game designs… I think this is an outstanding design. …. (Vincent)

#5, the Historian
- Of course, there is some value. The logic of the game design is good. ... A breakthrough of this design is that hints accumulated in previous storylines will be used in later storylines. This is creative in its logic. It enhances the fun of playing…This game design offers me some inspirations, which could be applied in new game designs." (Vincent)

(continued)

Table 12.3 (continued)

#8, the Musician
- The major advantage and value of this deliverable is the outstanding puzzle design. ... Accomplishing actual construction will not be hard. I think this is one of the top deliverables among all we have received. There are sufficient reasons to further develop it. This could be a very good project. (Joe)
- It is very refreshing, I have never considered or known similar designs. This is a creative design. When I was solving the puzzles, it felt very interesting... I am not good at this field, but it is interesting. In addition, the puzzles have operability and are interactive, which requires teamwork. I think this deliverable will be one of the final winners. This is the game design I desire. (Max)
- The design style is relaxed and elegant, and so very different to our previous logic. ... This deliverable inspires me a lot in terms of logic breakthrough. It also makes me rethink the direction of escape room game design, it can become more diversified. As a theme, it has a wide range of potential audiences. ...The game design is totally different from existing styles. ... The logic of this deliverable inspires me a lot. ...Another point worth discussing is that this deliverable has the same advantage as a previous deliverable. It is the continuity of hints. Hints gained from previous storylines can be used in later storylines. I think this is an outstanding design. I like it very much. I would definitely further develop this design. (Vincent)

#9: It has evident flaws: ... It will not be chosen as one of the winners. But it is not absolutely without value. Some of the puzzle designs are inspiring (Joe)

#10: We have not used such a story theme before. It may enrich our diversity. This could be the value of this deliverable. In terms of puzzle design, I think it is not good enough, and requires more work. (Max)

#11: The only valuable aspect is that it considers teamwork factors. (Max)

#14: Some aspects could be transplanted into suitable designs. This is the value I perceive. (Max)

Offline (Collaborative) Phase

Re-evaluating Expected Outcomes

At the end of the first phase, three top game designs were rewarded, however only the Gamer and the Musician were invited to engage with GamesCo in further design and construction of the actual escape rooms. As Vincent explained: *"When it came to the offline part of the project, we believed in the relationship [between us and crowd members]. The growing relationship started working. We chose to trust our candidates; therefore, we did not set any formal contract or fixed agreement. Instead, we offered great flexibility, which encouraged them [the Musician and the Gamer] to innovate and to produce better game designs."*

To kick off the second phase, the PM team discussed game designs and working plans with the selected crowd members via webcam meetings. As all three managers (respectively) commented:

> There were great points raised in the meeting; for example, using a unique story theme. His [the Musician's] idea is forward thinking and inspiring. Compared with his pre-design research, it seems that we are too conservative. What we have learned from an external designer is to think outside the box. It is time to rethink our in-house game design processes and get rid of routines. (Joe)
>
> The conversation was delightful. He [the Gamer] is a lovely guy. He knows how to communicate with people. During the meeting, he was very active and informative… After talking with him, we formed a mutual trust. He is the right person to deliver our game design. (Max)
>
> They were great guys. Through webcam meetings we got to know each other better. I think they are easy-going, knowledgeable, and very positive. I felt confident after communicating with them. Especially, the Gamer left me very positive impressions. It was surprising to find that he was very knowledgeable about takagism games. (Vincent)

The Musician and the Gamer, who were invited to collaborate with GamesCo, also saw additional value beyond the monetary reward they received. This additional value was expressed in their sense of appreciation about being selected and invited to collaborate. They also described the potential future value that would result from this collaboration. They commented on their feelings, and the learning opportunities and professional development they expected to gain from participation in the offline phase of the project:

> *The Gamer:* The manager expressed willingness to further develop my game design. Of course I was happy about it. […] I was quite motivated because of his encouragement and admiration. It was also a crucial opportunity for me to get some professional direction. This guided my later game designs.

> *The Musician:* Talking with professional designers was great. I learned something new about the differences between design and operation. When they criticized one of my puzzle designs, I realized that operability also needs to be considered.[...] "They are nice people. I was encouraged to express my ideas and they respected me. This made me comfortable... I think at that time our relationship became closer. It was valuable in facilitating the effectiveness of our communication.

Interactive Development of Escape Room Designs

The offline phase involved several iterations as the internal design team reviewed game designs further developed by the Gamer and the Musician, providing regular feedback until the internal team was satisfied with the design. The intention was to provide guidance, but in such a way that it would not restrict the creativity and ideas of the crowd members. Max commented:

> As the project progressed, we got more surprises from them. We followed their design logic and joined them on their escape room journey. Sometimes they were inspiring. Sometimes they were funny. Good designs could quickly grip me... Their job was to create novel blueprints. Our job was to help them create blueprints and consider whether they could be made into reality... After all, it was for business purposes. We brainstormed, and conducted further research and analysis to examine feasibility and operability. It was a necessary and crucial process which will serve future operations.

Furthermore, the PM team started to note value associated with the newly developed relationships. As Vincent described:

> When it came to the offline phase, we believed in the relationship. Over time, the relationship started working. A close relationship made collaboration easy. As we became familiar with each other, we could better understand each other's language and intentions. When we worked with them and finally accomplished the final designs, I felt emotions of gratitude, closeness, and trust. (Vincent)

The Musician and the Gamer also felt the importance of the relationship as it was emerging during the offline phase of the project:

> *The Gamer:* We quickly got to know each other and built up mutual trust. That was the foundation for cooperation. My ideas were fully respected and I was encouraged to be creative.
> It was good to expand the network.
> I enjoyed the way they [the team members] managed the project. They did not set any limits to the game design, leaving great room for me to be creative. They trusted me. At the same time, they offered appropriate guidance at the right time.
> *The Musician:* I was motivated by our relationship. It was a kind of payback. They [the team members] trusted me and offered me great opportunities. I really wanted to deliver better designs and, therefore, worked very hard with great patience.
> It was a very comfortable cooperation. There were actually no strict rules or regulations. As I just said, I was motivated by our relationship. I felt strongly that I was part of the activity. I was willing to contribute.

Finally, when the designs were completed, the PM team reflected on their level of satisfaction with the final design. The value they expressed at this final stage of the project was associated with their ability to construct the physical escape room:

> We accomplished two game designs with the candidates. These two designs will be used for our game rooms. I personally like them very much. I am satisfied with the final versions. The two candidates were very thoughtful and smart. Their designs are fluent, logical, and interesting. I am very satisfied with the quality. It was worth spending this amount of money. Later on, our team will systematically analyze them and come up with construction plans. Compared with purchasing copyrights from the American company, it was very cost-effective. Compared with the internal development, we saved time. (Vincent)

When GamesCo made payment to the Musician and the Gamer, Vincent said: "I felt emotions of gratitude, a closer personal relationship, and trust [towards the selected crowd members]."

After the crowd members received their rewards, they shared their reflections on participation in this project:

The Gamer: I think learning under pressure was a valuable experience. I acquired new knowledge, improved my skills and, most importantly, I did it. That is something to be proud of.
   The reward also counts. It was interesting and challenging to work with professional experts in game design while I was the centre of the cooperation.
   The Musician: My design became more mature. I think it could be a good script for a game room. I felt a sense of achievement. I won extra awards for that.

Implementation of the Game Designs

Both designs were indeed implemented. The Gamer's design was used for the fourth store, which opened in December 2016. The Musician's design was used for an existing local store to replace an old gaming room. The reconstruction was completed in June 2017.

Discussion and Contributions

Guided by our research objectives to understand how value emerges as CS projects unfold, and to identify specific value outcomes over the life of a project, we conducted a longitudinal study of interactions between two key stakeholders—firm and crowd. Our findings (1) reveal the emerging nature of *value*, and (2) distinguish between value *for the firm* and value *for the crowd*, and extent to which they are related (or not). As a limitation, we note that our findings are seen through the eyes of the project winners, whereas future research might further explore the value perceived by all participants.

In our case study, the CS initiative was driven by what we coin as "expected value." While crowd submissions at the end of the tournament-based phase were evaluated against this expected value to decide whether (or not) they met these expectation, additional value emerged for the evaluation process itself, as the firm actors went through the submissions. For example, several submissions that did not meet the required criteria to become winners nevertheless gave firm actors some interesting ideas they had not previously thought about (e.g. the basketball trick in submission #3, and the team factors in #11). Therefore, the value realized by the firm at the end of the tournament-based phase was more extensive than the initial expected value. Crowd members too were driven by expected value that was associated with extrinsic and intrinsic motivational factors. Two out of three winning crowd members, those who were invited to participate in the next phase and design their ideas further, reflected that value associated with the reward and the invitation went beyond their initial expectations.

After the first phase, firm actors refined their expectations by making more detailed and concrete requirements regarding new escape room designs they were interested in. Then, through interactive and collaborative engagement with the selected crowd members, they gained additional value associated with learning from the crowd's expertise (in music and history, respectively), and intrinsic value associated with the trust and inter-personal relationships they developed with these crowd members. Similarly, the selected crowd members expressed appreciation of the value associated with learning about game design, gaining new skills important for their professional development, and a high level of satisfaction with the relationship developed with managers of GamesCo.

This emerging nature of value—from the initial, *expected value* that is then refined and complemented by value associated with learning and the developing relationship as the parties interact—is evident for both firm and crowd stakeholders. However, it is important to distinguish between value *for the firm* and value *for the crowd*, which are essentially different when the two parties engage in a CS project—the crowd is expecting extrinsic and intrinsic value, while the firm is expecting a business-related value. However, when the crowdsourcing project is designed to include collaborative engagement with crowd members (e.g. offline phase of the Games design project), the value that emerges through the interactions between the stakeholders is a *shared* value that demonstrates mutual benefits and appreciation.

Moreover, our study demonstrates that CS could be designed to rely on value *creation* or value *co-creation*. Value creation is evident in tournament-based CS, as crowd members work independently to create value for the firm. In the end, the firm decides whether the value has been created or not, and selects winners to be rewarded for the value they have created. Value co-creation is, however, a joint endeavor. It implies an element of collaboration between the parties through which value is created jointly (i.e. co-created). Thus, it is only in collaborative CS projects that value is co-created through interactions between the different stakeholders. In our study, we observed value co-creation during the second phase of the Games Design project. In the literature there are examples of CS projects where crowd members collaborate between themselves and/or with the firm. The Treadless example mentioned earlier also illustrates value co-creation, as crowd members vote for their favorite designs.

In Table 12.4 we summarize firm and crowd perspectives on value during different phases of the CS project. This table distinguishes between different dimensions of the value. In Table 12.5 we illustrate how value is emerging through what we coin as value-related processes: starting from *value expectation* that firm and crowd members do individually, followed by *value creation* when crowd is working individually creating value (or rather hoping that client will recognize value in their submission), and/or *value co-creation* which relies on interactive, collaborative efforts of between firm and crowd stakeholders. CS projects may include only value creation or value co-creation processes, or both (as in our case study). *Value appreciation* process is associated with the final stage of a CS project when all stakeholders reflect on the value gained through CS. While firm and crowd reflect on their own value, they also appreciate shared value from the CS experience.

Conclusion

The main contribution of this study is to the growing body of the crowdsourcing literature. We offer a process perspective on emerging value and distinguish between *value for firm* and *value for crowd* (as depicted

Table 12.4 Value dimensions over time: Firm and crowd perspectives

	Before CS	During CS		After CS
		Tournament phase	Collaborative phase	
Firm	**Business value** Expected core value is agreed between project management team: two new game designs	After submissions are evaluated at the end of the online phase expected core value is *refined*, more details are desired *Learning value* Also firm have learnt new things and how to think outside the box from the other, non-winning submissions	Expected core value is *constantly refined* during interactions with crowd members and regular feedback *Relationship value* The importance of the *relationship* with each crowd member is stated. The *evolving relationship* and *trust* are highly valued	Project concludes when expected core value is achieved Established relationship and trust are noticed as important feelings associated with the project
Crowd	Monetary value Intrinsic value	*Learning value*	New monetary value Refined intrinsic value	

(continued)

Table 12.4 (continued)

Before CS	During CS		After CS
	Tournament phase	Collaborative phase	
Crowd members are looking for *monetary rewards* and *interesting* project to work on	At the end of the tournament-based phase winning crowd members appreciate monetary reward, value associated with learning, and intrinsic value	Selected crowd members are offered new *monetary reward* and to continue working on the *interesting* project	At the end of offline phase selected crowd members appreciate monetary reward, value associated with learning, and intrinsic value
		Relationship value	
		During offline phase evolving relationship is highly appreciated and associated with intrinsic value	Established relationship and trust are noticed as important feelings associated with the project

in Fig. 12.1). In doing so, we address an observed gap in the literature, which lacks an overarching understanding of crowdsourcing value creation process. Given that the Games Design project involved two different CS models—tournament-based and collaborative—we were able to compare and contrast similarities and differences between the two models in terms of implications for value (co-)creation, and to see how they are related when combined in the same CS initiative.

In line with the first objective of our work, we studied *the process of value creation and transitions from value-in-exchange to value co-creation over the life of the project*. During the tournament-based phase, value-in-exchange took the form of monetary value expectations (by the crowd)

Table 12.5 Value-Related processes over Time

	Before	Tournament phase	Collaborative phase	After
Firm vs crowd relationship with the value	Each party has own expectations regarding the value expected from participation in crowdsourcing	Crowd members work *individually* creating something that would be (not) considered of value by the firm	Crowd members work *together* with the firm co-creating value that meets firm's evolving expectations	Each party evaluate (and appreciate) value(s) gained from the project
Value-related process	- > Value expectation (crowd *and* firm, *independently*)	- > Value creation (crowd *for* firm, whether the value was created or not depends on firm's evaluation)	- > Value co-creation (crowd *with* firm, through interactive and collaborative efforts)	- > Value appreciation (crowd and firm *individually* and *jointly*)

in exchange for game ideas (for the firm). Since value-in-exchange is set by the project parameters prior to initiating the project, there is a potential challenge in setting the monetary amount as the client firm cannot foresee the true value of the ideas they might receive. During this phase, stakeholders experienced value-in-use that took the form of some (limited) learning outcomes for both firm and crowd. However, in comparison to the value-in-use that was experienced in the next, collaborative phase, value-in-use during the tournament-based phase was not so significant due to a definition of project parameters that limited interactions.

In the second, collaborative phase, value-in-exchange was also associated with monetary reward. However at this stage, the firm had a better idea of what they would receive (i.e. detailed game designs), so the exchange was more accurately estimated. The selected crowd members

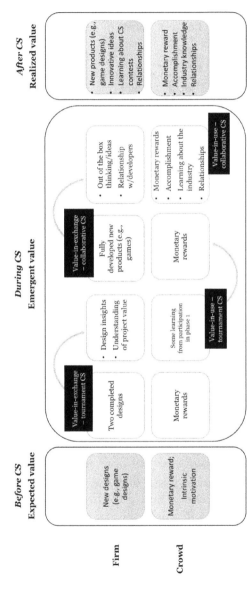

Fig. 12.1 A process perspective on emerging value in tournament-based and collaborative crowdsourcing

also had a good understanding of what was required from them in exchange for the (guaranteed) reward. Therefore in this phase, value-in-exchange closely reflected the value expectations held by each party prior to engaging in the collaborative work. We therefore find that the value-in-exchange for the collaborative CS phase was more accurate than for the tournament-based phase, due to some learning experiences on both sides. During the collaborative phase, there was significant value-in-use in terms of the learning and relationship development that we previously noted. The interactive nature of this phase enabled true value co-creation where value-in-use was mutual and shared between the parties.

In line with our second objective *to add a temporal dimension to this body of literature and track specific value outcomes as they unfold over the life of the project*, in Fig. 12.1, we depict our findings and attempt to make them applicable to various CS contexts. This figure illustrates how value transforms from *expected* to *emergent* and then to *realized*, building on the notion of value-in-exchange and value-in-use experienced by the project stakeholders.

References

Afuah, A., & Tucci, C. L. (2012). Crowdsourcing as a Solution to Distant Search. Academy of Management. *The Academy of Management Review, 37*, 355–375.

Bonabeau, E. (2009). Decisions 2.0: The Power of Collective Intelligence. *MIT Sloan Management Review, 50*, 45–52.

Boons, M., Stam, D., & Barkema, H. G. (2015). Feelings of Pride and Respect as Drivers of Ongoing Member Activity on Crowdsourcing Platforms. *The Journal of Management Studies, 52*, 717–741.

Chiu, C.-M., Liang, T.-P., & Turban, E. (2014). What can Crowdsourcing do for Decision Support? *Decision Support Systems, 65*, 40–49.

Deng, X., & Joshi, K. D. (2016). Why Individuals Participate in Micro-task Crowdsourcing Work Environment: Revealing Crowdworkers' Perceptions. *Journal of the Association for Information Systems, 17*, 648–673.

Erkinheimo, P., Jussila, J., & Kärkkäinen, H. (2015). Lean Start-up Companies by Means of Crowdsourcing. *Journal of Innovation Management, 3*, 17–20.

Fréry, F., Lecocq, X., & Warnier, V. (2015). Competing With Ordinary Resources. *MIT Sloan Management Review, 56*, 69–77.
Frey, K., Lüthje, C., & Haag, S. (2011). Whom should Firms Attract to Open Innovation Platforms? The Role of Knowledge Diversity and Motivation. *Long Range Planning, 44*, 397–420.
Gatzweiler, A., Blazevic, V., & Piller, F. T. (2017). Dark Side or Bright Light: Destructive and Constructive Deviant Content in Consumer Ideation Contests. *The Journal of Product Innovation Management, 34*, 772–789.
Gioia, D. A., Corley, K. G., & Hamilton, A. L. (2013). Seeking Qualitative Rigor In Inductive Research Notes on The Gioia Methodology. *Organizational Research Methods, 16*, 15–31.
Glaeser, E. L., Hillis, A., Kominers, S. D., & Luca, M. (2016). Crowdsourcing City Government: Using Tournaments to Improve Inspection Accuracy. *The American Economic Review, 106*, 114–118.
Gol, E. S., Stein, M-K., & Avital, M. (2019). Crowdwork Platform Governance toward Organizational Value Creation. *The Journal of Strategic Information Systems, 28*(2), https://doi.org/10.1016/j.jsis.2019.01.001
Hofstetter, R., Zhang, J. Z., & Herrmann, A. (2018). Successive Open Innovation Contests and Incentives: Winner-Take-All or Multiple Prizes? *Journal of Product Innovation Management, 35*, 492–517.
Howe, J. (2006). The Rise of Crowdsourcing. *Wired Magazine*, 14.
Jame, R., Johnston, R., Markov, S., & Wolfe, M. C. (2016). The Value of Crowdsourced Earnings Forecasts. *Journal of Accounting Research, 54*, 1077–1110.
Kohler, T. (2015). Crowdsourcing-Based Business Models: How to Create and Capture Value. *California Management Review, 57*, 63–84.
Langley, A. (1999). Strategies for Theorizing from Process Data. *Academy of Management Review, 24*, 691–710.
Langley, A., Smallman, C., Tsoukas, H., & Van de Ven, A. (2013). Process Studies of Change in Organization and Management: Unveiling Temporality, Activity, and Flow. *Academy of Management Journal, 56*, 1–13.
LaToza, T. D., & van der Hoek, A. (2016). Crowdsourcing in Software Engineering: Models, Motivations, and Challenges. *IEEE Software, 33*, 74–80.
Morgan, J., & Wang, R. (2010). Tournaments for Ideas. *California Management Review, 52*, 77–97.
Nevo, S., & Wade, M. (2010). The Formation and Value of IT-enabled Resources: Antecedents and Consequences of Synergistic Relationships. *MIS Quarterly, 34*, 163–183.

Nishikawa, H., Schreier, M., Fuchs, C., & Ogawa, S. (2017). The Value of Marketing Crowdsourced New Products as Such: Evidence from Two Randomized Field Experiments. *Journal of Marketing Research, 54*, 525–539.
Poetz, M. K., & Schreier, M. (2012). The Value of Crowdsourcing: Can Users Really Compete with Professionals in Generating New Product Ideas? *The Journal of Product Innovation Management, 29*, 245–256.
Vargo, S. L., Maglio, P. P., & Akaka, M. A. (2008). On value and value co-creation: A service systems and service logic perspective. *European Management Journal, 26*, 145–152.
Ye, H., & Kankanhalli, A. (2013). Leveraging Crowdsourcing for Organizational Value Co-Creation. *Communications of the Association for Information Systems, 33*: article 13.

13

Digitalised Flexible Organisations: Towards the Sourcing Future of Work

Leslie Willcocks

Introduction

In the second decade of this century work, and its posited futures, has been through a fraught period. From mid-2020 we witnessed the pandemic-induced shifts to remote and home working, by 2023 more than twice as prevalent than before COVID-19. By that date some 76% of companies had adopted hybrid working, though many were still not sure of the optimal home-office work balance to adopt.

From mid-2022 there followed the 'Great Resignation'—ostensibly many people in the developed economies giving up work and not taking up new employment. By late 2022 and into 2023 the topic of overreach

---

This chapter synthesises and updates a number of research papers and articles by Leslie Willcocks. The notion of the digital flexible organisation first appears in Willcocks, L. (2021). Robo-Apocalypse? Response and outlook on the post-COVID-19 future of work. Journal of Information Technology, 36(2), 188–194.

L. Willcocks (✉)
LSE, London, UK
e-mail: willcockslp@aol.com

© The Editor(s) (if applicable) and The Author(s), under exclusive licence to Springer Nature Switzerland AG 2024
L. Willcocks et al. (eds.), *Transformation in Global Outsourcing*, Technology, Work and Globalization, https://doi.org/10.1007/978-3-031-61022-6_13

set in, with major companies in hi-tech, banking, management consultancy—and Amazon—sacking thousands of workers because they had overestimated post-COVID economic pickup and demand trends.

On a longer time-scale, going back to 2014, there were fears of massive job loss from accelerating automation and digitalisation of work. But most recent reports downplayed this, predicting that, between 2019 and 2030, the net global job loss was likely to be around one per cent. Then generative AI and ChatGPT set off new alarm bells. By March 2023 the BBC reported Goldman Sachs claiming that '*AI could replace equivalent of 300 million jobs*'. No timeline given, and a global extrapolation from US and European data. But, looking behind the headlines, the report comments: '*The good news is that worker displacement from automation has historically been offset by creation of new jobs, and the emergence of new occupations following technological innovations accounts for the vast majority of long-run employment growth*'. The report itself points to labour cost savings, new job creation and higher productivity for non-displaced workers likely increasing productivity and economic growth 'substantially'—again no timeline given, but very much in line with most post-COVID-19 studies on the subject.

Meanwhile, across 2023, organisations in the 21 leading economies regularly reported staffing and skills shortages even in the face of conditions of deflated economic growth. Major labour sourcing questions arose: Would new advanced technologies, harnessed to improve productivity and cut costs, finally lead to large-scale job loss? How could skills shortages be ameliorated? Would extending the labour market ever further, virtually and globally, remedy labour problems? What policies towards different forms of labour would be optimal? This chapter finds evidence-based answers to these questions, and points to both an emerging way forward—a digitalised flexible labour model—but also its inherent challenges. Taking the period to 2030, we investigate first the extent to which digital technologies are likely to replace human labour, the exponential rise in the amount of work to be done, and how far distinctively human skills are future-proofed, and therefore likely to be in short supply. The evidence is then assessed for a permanent switch to home and remote working enabled by emerging technologies. Given the 2020s context, the chapter goes on to assess the business, digital and labour strategies of work organisations and identifies and points to the promise and challenges presented by a dominant trend towards a digitally enabled flexible labour model heavily dependent on contractual arrangements and external labour.

Digital Futures: Not a Job Apocalypse

Is this the decade when technology replaces labour as the dominant source of input value across sectors? Will this result in massive job loss globally? The notion of a jobs 'Robo-Apocalypse' has steered the future of work debate for a very long time (Willcocks, 2020a). Looking at the big picture it is not easy to pick your way through the media representations of the debate. Sources and multiple studies are, in fact, very variable in quality, evidence and rigour. Nevertheless, media narratives seem to polarise around two storylines—hype and fear. 'Hype' tells us that it is largely going to be fine and most of us are going to live in a well-run technologised world—'Automotopia'—with more than enough goods, services and leisure. Meanwhile the other, 'fear' vision of 'Robo-Apocalypse' is essentially dystopian. This polarised narrative also assumes quick and pervasive adoption of the technology, but sees it as displacing a huge number of physical and cognitive-based jobs across industries, geographies and at most levels in the organisation.

Unsurprisingly, so-called artificial intelligence (AI) as job killer has been the focus of disproportionate media attention. It is a story too good to be false. Unfortunately, an anchor study by Frey and Osborne (2013) is still used to support this narrative, with the often-quoted headline figure of 47% of US jobs highly automatable. However, the researchers do not try to specify the speed of technology development, nor a time period for the loss of jobs—*'some unspecified number of years, perhaps a decade or two'*, they say (page 38). Nor do they attempt to predict the number of jobs lost, nor jobs created through automation. The study also does not look at the key bottleneck of how commercially feasible, viable and organisationally adoptable the emerging technologies are, i.e.

the long road to diffusion of innovation dilemma is ignored. These self-confessed omissions are all but factored out in media representations of the findings.

The media have also been slow to pick up on later studies richer in data, and more fine-tuned in their analysis. For example, Forrester Research (2017) suggested robots would take 24.7 million US jobs, but create 14.9 million new jobs by 2027, leading to a net loss of 9.8 million jobs, about 7% of the US workforce. An OECD study by Arntz, Gregory and Zierahn (2016) suggested that 9% of US individuals faced high job automatability, and, on average, 9% of OECD jobs (UK 10%) would become highly automated within a decade.

By 2019, the picture of high job loss had changed dramatically, though not necessarily in the headlines. The World Economic Forum (2018), for 2018–2022, found automation replacing 0.98 million jobs while creating 1.74 million new ones. The Asia Development Bank (2018) came out as positive on net job creation from automation. Price Waterhouse Coopers (2018) estimated that the net job effect of automation in the UK from 2017 to 2037 would be a slight gain of 168,000 jobs (7.176 million created, 7.008 million displaced). MGI (2018a and 2018b) suggested that: *'overall, the adoption of AI may not have a significant impact on net employment in the long term…. Our average global scenario suggests that total full-time equivalent employment may remain flat at best compared with today'* (pages 44 and 45).

Then COVID-19 was meant to see a wave of job-killing automation. But by 2023 there was little evidence of this. In practice OECD countries generally were experiencing an abnormally large number of unfulfilled vacancies, even as near recessionary conditions loomed. The rate of decline in the supposedly more easily automatable jobs actually slowed during the pandemic. In mid-2023 the Economist was reporting that in the previous decade the average rich-world unemployment rate had halved, and the share of working-age people in employment was at an all-time high. Countries with the highest rates of automation and robotics, such as Japan, South Korea and Singapore, had the least unemployment. The Economist calculated that if more than 50% of jobs were automated or jobs were eliminated as they were automated, this could mean a net loss of 15% of US jobs. But this, the Economist suggested, was unlikely to happen, as historically job destruction happens far more slowly (The Economist, 2023; see also Willcocks, 2020a).

What is startling here is that as time has gone by, the estimates for net job loss from automation have been disappearing to the point of being negligible—though of course, the net figures mask considerable disruption and skills shifts. There have to be serious qualifications to the Robo-Apocalypse and job loss narrative.

In a comprehensive review, Willcocks (2020a) showed that many assumptions imbedded in the Robo-Apocalypse narrative are highly questionable: that automation creates few jobs short or long term; that whole jobs can be automated; that the technology is perfectible; that organisations can seamlessly and quickly deploy AI; that humans are machines that can be replicated; that it is politically, socially and economically feasible to apply these technologies. Then there are the macro factors. With ageing populations, productivity gaps and skills shortages predicted across many G20 countries, the danger might be too little, rather than too much labour. Ironically, far from taking over, automation will be, most likely, just helping organisations to cope.

Finally, let us return to the issue of speed of adoption of these technologies. The most recent studies suggest that the pandemic and ensuing economic crisis will accelerate automation and digitalisation. However, this does not mean that the eight qualifiers outlined in Willcocks (2020a) suddenly become redundant. In particular, the third qualifier (technology is never a fire-and-forget missile), the fourth qualifier (technology is never that perfectible) and the fifth qualifier (distinctive human strengths are needed at work) present considerable challenges to those embarking on accelerated digital and automation programmes. Somewhere among these is a much under-rated factor—the limited organisational capacity to change, adopt and institutionalise digital technologies. In practice, organisations have a great deal of information technology legacy and are also heavily siloed. In research into over 400 organisations, Willcocks et al. (2023) found all too many enterprises lagging behind their automation intentions due to some or all eight inhibiting siloes—structure, process, data, technology, culture, managerial mindset, strategy and skill sets. As digital transformation efforts have demonstrated over the last 10 years, this is a difficult series of challenges to navigate, at a time when many organisations have declining absorptive capacity to innovate and do something new, in any major way. Moreover, after the pandemic, many organisations will have to return to the basics—re-establish finances, recover customers, refresh products and services, re-engage the workforce. For many, this will distract them from big investments in technology for some time to come. McKinsey and Company (2020) surveyed major clients and found them suggesting that COVID-19 had accelerated digitalisation on a number of fronts—notably remote working, migrating assets to the cloud, data security, responding to changing customer expectations and demand for online purchasing and services and more advanced technology use in operations and decision-making. A majority were convinced that remote working, online purchasing and changed customer expectations were the most likely to persist after the pandemic. Our own research suggests that only about 20% of enterprises lead in digital transformation. Indeed, these are likely to move even faster, not least because they have a better starting point, the experience and usually the better financial performances to do so. But this means that some 80% of organisations are not, and probably will not be, great performers on digital transformation (Willcocks, 2021; Willcocks et al., 2023). All this is likely to slow job loss (and gain) from automation and digitalisation, and slow skill changes as well.

The Ghost in the Automation and Work Debate

Willcocks (2020a) and Willcocks et al. (2023) reinforce immensely this contention by identifying a critical factor neglected by all previous studies. Despite assumptions, and hidden in plain sight, the amount of work to be done is not remaining stable; it is growing across sectors, year on year, dramatically, and inexorably. Work intensification would seem to have been increasing, especially since the financial crisis of 2008. Organisations have sought to increase productivity and the amount of work done by 'sweating the assets' and attempting to do more with less using the same labour base and partly through applying digital technologies.

This phenomenon is very under-researched. However, some studies are indicative.

Thus Felstead, Gallie et al. (2013) found that the percentage of UK jobs needing hard work moved from 31.5% in 1992 to 45.3% in 2012. Since 2006 both the speed of work has quickened and the pressures of working to tight deadlines have also risen to record highs. Korunka and Kubicek (2017) collected a range of research papers recording work intensification over the last ten years across several economies. In our own research we very frequently found that, apart from the many other benefits, a major reason for automation was a range of stakeholders experiencing a rising tide of work to be done (Lacity & Willcocks, 2017, 2018; Lacity et al., 2021; Willcocks & Lacity, 2016; Willcocks et al., 2019). The limits to working smarter and of high-performance practices were being tested and the practices often found wanting. ServiceNow's 2017 multi-country survey found 70% of some 1,874 corporate respondents registering that the pace of work grew by at least 10% in 2016; nearly half said it grew by 20% or more. It found that by 2018 46% of companies were going to need greater automation to handle the volume of tasks being generated. By 2020, without more automation, 86% of organisations believed they would reach their break point soon, and dealing with the volume of work would no longer be sustainable.

But where is this dramatic increase in the amount of work coming from? Almost all studies to date routinely leave out three key factors. Willcocks et al. (2023) suggest that, combined, these factors probably account for a 10–12% annual growth in the amount of work to be done, depending on sector and country.

The Exponential Data Explosion. ServiceNow (2017) found, for example, that nearly 80% of respondents reported that data from mobile devices and the Internet of Things was accelerating the pace of work. Some estimates suggest that 90% of the world's digital data that we try to process, was created in the last two years, and that the amount of digital data grows by 50% a year. Ganz, Reinzel et al. (2017) estimated that by 2025 there would be ten times the data generated in 2016. Even if these are only ball park figures, they still raise the fundamental question: how are we going to collect, store, process, analyse and use data arriving in such colossal volumes? It implies a massive explosion of work, especially as data seems to create more data. Maybe we really do need more automation just to cope.

Cross-sectoral growth of audit, regulation and bureaucracy, amplified by the data explosion and the application of modern information and communication technologies. We have been creating, we would argue, a veritable witches brew of data, technology and bureaucracy. Graeber (2015, 2018) had been one of the few to pinpoint the importance of this development for the future of both work, and the capitalist system itself. But even he probably understated the degree to which audit and regulation inevitably accompany high levels of distrust, the likelihood of market failure and increased demands for transparency. Such work may not be seen as particularly productive, but it is dramatically increasing across government agencies, business sectors and economies almost everywhere. The Economist (2023) adds to the picture by pointing out that generative AI could act as a drain on productivity, being able to generate objections and counter-arguments to, for example planning applications, in minutes. In an AI heavy world lawyers and legal actions are likely to multiply. Also most of the jobs at risk from AI are in heavily regulated sectors, often with much state involvement such as education, healthcare, housing and policing. One can envisage multiple ways in which audit, regulation and bureaucracy could slow down productivity enhancing impacts of automation, and indeed how automation could enhance the ability to extend audit, regulation and bureaucracy even further, thus creating more work.

Technology: Both Solution and Problem. A third source of more work is technology's double-edged capacity to provide solutions that also create additional problems. If you create more data, that then raises the work-creating problem of how to process, store, analyse, then use it. Then there are unanticipated work-making consequences. For example, the Internet has created cybersecurity issues. The cost of cyberattacks was estimated at $445 billion in 2013 and continued to rise dramatically to beyond $600 billion into 2018. This has led to further technology solutions, of course—with the cybersecurity market being $75 billion in 2015 and also growing much faster since then to reach $US 223.7 billion in 2023 and potentially $US 338.84 billion in 2027 at a CAGR of 10.9% (Research & Markets, 2023). As another example, concerns about fake news through social media had, by 2019, led to Facebook employing fact checkers in 20 countries.

There is also increasing evidence for the addictive properties of mobile devices, games, the internet, email and related technologies and applications (see for example Alter, 2017; Aiken, 2016). Much has been made of the productivity enhancing potential of these and 'AI' technologies. But such technologies are often deliberately designed to support multitasking and constant interruption at considerable cost to real productivity at work.

The emerging evidence is that task switching, being constantly interrupted and multi-tasking result in substantial performance costs. For peak performance, the goal should be sustained, focused and singular attention. But the modern worker is all too easily distracted from task performance by irrelevant information and suffers interruption by attempting to pursue simultaneous multiple goals, aided and abetted by technologies such as email, social media, the internet and mobile devices. These distractions and interruptions can come from outside or be self-generated.

Modern technologies also allow a worker to easily elide work and non-work, while ostensibly at work. Some indicative examples. A CareerBuilder survey found the smartphone, internet, social media and email among the five most cited workplace disrupters and productivity killers.[1] A 2018 Udemy survey found a third of Generation Z employees admitting to using their smartphones for personal activities up to 2 hours in the work day.[2]

Alter (2017) cites studies showing that 70% of office emails are read within six seconds of arriving. This is hugely disruptive; on one estimate it can take up to 25 minutes to become re-immersed in an interrupted task. Gazzaley and Rosen (2016) found that multi-tasking and task switching incur notable performance costs in disengaging from a task, focusing on the new task, then disengaging and re-entering the original work. A pre-smartphone study they cite found that when office workers

---

[1] Chad Brooks in Business News Daily, April 16, 2015.
[2] David Shimkus in HR Technologist.com downloaded April 6, 2018.

are interrupted as often as eleven times an hour, it costs the USA $558 billion a year in lost productivity. Wajcman and Rose (2011) found workers spending only half their day on actual 'work episodes' with two-thirds of interruptions self-generated and most involving a mediated communication through a technological device. Meanwhile most workers have access to email and other communications networks, and about 45% of the world's population own a mobile phone (Gazzaley & Rosen, 2016).

In these ways more technology is undoubtedly having complex, even contradictory effects, including a significant, if largely unresearched, adverse impact on productivity and on the time required to accomplish work tasks. While more technology is the frequently touted answer to personal, social and business problems, we can find ourselves on an endless treadmill of technological solutions and the new problems they also generate.

Automation Sourcing and Skills Revisited

Recent research, by the author and others, suggests that dramatic skills shifts and shortages will be the most impactful challenges to productivity, technology adoption and economic growth through to 2030.

The dominant trend emerging from recent research is shown in Fig. 13.1. (Willcocks, 2021; Willcocks et al., 2023). There will be a move away from low skills—physical, repetitive, non-technical, non-cognitive basic human skills—towards digital, technical cognitive, distinctively human, medium/high skills. On several estimates low-skilled workers will go from 44 to 32% of the global workforce in the 2019–2030 period. By the early 2020s the global labour force probably had 95 million surplus low-skilled workers, but a 90 million shortage in medium/high- skilled workers (Willcocks et al., 2023).

These major skills gaps will widen without government, corporate and individual intervention, and it is fairly obvious that the inequality divides arising from automation and digitalisation will require labour market institutional changes. An overlooked aspect is that if the requisite skills to support and complement automation and new technologies are

Skills Demand Shift: 2019–2030

2019	Skills Gap →	2030
Repetitive	To	Non-Repetitive
Physical	To	Digital
Non-technical	To	Technical (STEM)
Non-cognitive	To	Cognitive
Basic human	To	Distinctive human
Low skills	To	Medium/high skills

1. Significant decline but not elimination of skills on left side. Easy automation targets
2. Emerging supply-demand gap and skills shortages developing at varying rates across sectors
3. Automation technologies also moving into right side skills.

Fig. 13.1 The skills demand shift 2019–2030 (*Source* author)

not forthcoming, the much-touted technological changes will be further delayed.

An under-appreciated factor remains how limited the applicability of the technology might be. The analysis here builds upon the work of MGI (2017), Lacity and Willcocks (2018), Willcocks (2021) and composite sources. MGI identified 18 generic sets of skills used in the workplace (see Fig. 13.2).

Looking ahead to 2030, it is likely that some eight skill sets will remain as largely human capabilities in the workplace, three are dependent on choices or technological advances and some seven skill sets are automatable (though that does not mean they will be). Distinctively human skills like empathy, teambuilding, leadership, critical thinking and imagination are both valuable in work organisations, and exceedingly difficult to replicate or replace. Looking at Fig. 13.2, over the next 10 years there will probably be large and small gains for human work in some areas, and some large, new work gains for machines. This would suggest that the Frey and Osborne (2013, 2017) study, together with Frey (2019) have considerably over-estimated the automatability of jobs and work to be done, at least for the 2019–2030 period.

SKILLS*	Machine vs Human**
Sensory Perception	Machine
Cognitive Capabilities	
• Retrieving information	Machine+
• Recognizing known patterns/categories	Machine +
• Generating novel patterns/categories	Human +
• Logical reasoning/problem solving	Human+
• Optimizing/planning	Machine+
• Creativity	Human+
• Articulating/display output	Machine
• Coordination with multiple agents	Depends on agents
Natural Language Processing	
• Generation	Machine
• Understanding	Depends on advances
Social and Emotional Capabilities	
• Sensing	Human++
• Reasoning (about socio-emotional states)	Human++
• Output (speech, body language)	Human++
Physical Capabilities	
• Fine motor skills/dexterity	Human+
• Gross motor skills	Mixed
• Navigation	Depends on AI R&D
• Mobility	Human

ACTIVITIES***

Large new work gains for humans
- Applying expertise (18% automatable)
- Interfacing with stakeholders (20% automatable)
- Managing and developing people (9% automatable)

Small new work gains for humans
- Unpredictable physical activities (26% automatable)

Large new work gains for machines
- Processing data (69%)
- Collecting data (64%)
- Predictable physical activities (81%)

* MGI (2017)
** LSE Analysis May 2019
*** Composite sources and MGI

Fig. 13.2 Automatable and human work skills 2019–2030

Home and Remote Working

Working from home is a subset of remote working—working potentially from any location. Will remote working become the dominant mode, as many have suggested? Not surprisingly, we have seen a rising uptake in both remote and home working over the last 10 years, not least because of improvements in enabling technologies. MGI (2020b) noted that the potential for remote work is highly concentrated in a handful of sectors, such as information and technology, finance and insurance and management, and executives surveyed from those sectors show greater intent to deploy their employees remotely. But the study also pointed out that more than 60% of workers in the US economy, for example, cannot work remotely, particularly blue-collar workers, but many 'knowledge workers' as well. Their jobs require at least some physical presence—such as standing on a meat-processing line, helping customers in a store or providing healthcare services. In less developed economies, the share of workers unable to work remotely is even higher. There is also the role of executive decision. McKinsey found some support for allowing a minority of workers to work remotely for two days a week post-COVID-19, but from late 2022 across 2023 many executives became more cautious about the challenges and economics, and productivity implications of managing home and remote working (Forsdick, 2022; McKinsey, 2023).

Is virtual working so productive? Apart from distractions and social conditions in the home, several studies showed that virtual communication could curb ideas generation, and that firm-wide remote work caused the collaboration network of workers to become more static and siloed, with fewer bridges between disparate parts. Furthermore, there was a decrease in synchronous communication and an increase in asynchronous communication. Together, these effects made it harder for employees to acquire and share new information across the network (Brucks & Levav, 2022; Yang et al., 2022). After the necessary remote working during the pandemic years, Forsdick (2022) found that less attractive economic conditions raised concerns over remote worker productivity, and restricting home working became a symptom of executives re-asserting control. McKinsey (2023) estimated that 20–25% of workforces in advanced economies could work from home in the range of three to five days a week (which would be four times more remote work than pre-COVID-19). But not all work that can be done remotely should be, e.g. negotiations, brainstorming, giving sensitive feedback. This supports the broader point that Brown and Duguid (2017) make about the social life of information—that we have to look beyond mere information to the social context that creates and gives meaning to it.

Remote working is not just a practical but also an economic and social issue. We already know that the net productivity from remote working has proven to be quite strong and is likely to be even better if done at a greater scale. However, there is the chance that quite a lot of work will be included that is not suitable for remote working, and there may be some fallout when unanticipated costs arise. This is where social and cultural factors kick in. These can be societal (acceptable norms, social legislation); organisational (applicable to which kinds of workers; impact on culture, does work need more interpersonal contact); or individual level (worker preferences, type of job, home situation). Figure 13.3 suggests that, post-pandemic, economic factors are likely to win out, at least for a while, but remote working will only greatly accelerate if the social factors are fully supportive (Willcocks, 2020b). In some sectors, with some kind of work, it may well be that businesses will experience limited change, or even a return to pre-pandemic arrangements and levels. The economics of remote and home working will be the clincher for all businesses, and assuming the technology will be readily available, the two key issues will be: Is it more productive? And does it cost less? One then has to add in some critical moderating social factors, for example, specific employee circumstances, social responsibility and legislation issues, childcare arrangements, and impact on the firm's wider culture.

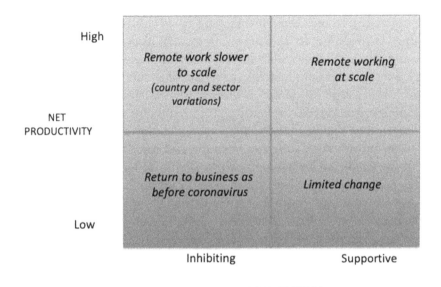

Fig. 13.3 Remote working—Four scenarios

Towards the Digitally Enabled Flexible Labour Organisation

How to make sense of all these complex trends? How have employers been responding? According to an MIT/Deloitte 2021 report, a pre-COVID and, we find, continuing trend is 'workforce eco-systems'—trying to find multiple sources of internal and external skills by using various contractual arrangements, global markets and reward systems, and by forming communities of connected and interdependent workforces and organisations. Not only are organisations placing significant value on gaining ideas and skills from contributors who do not work for the organisation; they intend to rely increasingly on external participants and draw on on-line platforms to secure talent (Altman et al., 2021).

However, this approach has been insufficiently conceptualised, and needs a lot more detail if it has to be represented as a strategic approach. Research at the LSE together with Knowledge Capital Partners shows most organisations adopting key elements of a 'core-peripheries' model for organising labour, though they tend to do this on an ad hoc basis, mainly in response to short-term factors (Willcocks, 2023a). These include labour shortages, need to keep costs low, and attempts to harness digital technologies productively, for example to support home working during the recent pandemic. Willcocks (2023b) found some 65% of organisations surveyed in January 2023 adopting short-term tactical approaches to digital investments, either 'sweating the assets' in order to focus on cash flow, customer retention and cost cutting, or investing limitedly in digital technologies to 'underpin today's business'. Some 35% of organisations had longer-term plans for digital investments and developing their business strategies, though over half of these were delaying strategy in order to respond to 2023 economic conditions.

As long ago as 1984, John Atkinson posited a core/periphery model to provide an organisation with functional, numerical and financial flexibility. With the addition of much more enabling technology, the model is uncannily representative of how businesses and government agencies intend to utilise labour over the next two decades (Atkinson, 1984; Willcocks, 2021). Overall, we will, in the author's view, see accelerating, more strategic moves towards what has already been done on this in the last 35 years.

The overall objective is to achieve responsiveness and agility through creating three types of flexibility—**functional, numerical and financial**. The core workers represent the key skills, and are viewed as long stay employees with favourable terms and conditions in exchange for which they will be functionally flexible, supported by training and development, and new technologies. The first peripheral group may also be full time or part time but do the less key work and tend to have less good terms and conditions.

Then there are multiple, other, more transactional relationships as the organisation draws on agency workers, sub-contractors, outsourcing firms, self-employed workers, including the technologically enabled 'open talent' economy and 'ghost workers' making high, medium and/or low skills available globally depending on requirement, on more or less favourable labour contracts (see Gray & Sun, 2019; Winsor & Paik, 2024). These relationships give some functional flexibility, but mainly numerical and financial flexibility. In recent years digital technologies have given three more types of flexibility—**locational** (think remote working) **temporal** (think 24 × 7) and **labour replacement/enhancement** flexibility (through automation and online 'robo-sourcing').

This means there will continue to be core full-time primary, internal workers who are integral to the functionality of the organisation. These will be functionally flexible and difficult to replace, due to high-level skills, knowledge and experience. These workers will have a big say in the degree to which they move to remote working, and how digital technologies will be utilised in their work. Meanwhile, there will be different types of peripheral workers. One (first peripheral) group will be low-skilled, often part time and flexible. A second peripheral group will experience a mix of short-term contracting, being public subsidy trainees, job sharing or be part time. Another group will comprise large volumes of agency staff, self-employed, outsourcing vendor staff and subcontractors. We can already see many such external market-based workers operating in traditional functions such as cleaning and catering, but also in the gig economy and remote work contracting. Although not direct employees of the organisation, they are important to its functioning. However, these and the first and second peripheral groups of workers have little bargaining power, not least over whether technology will be controlling, 'informating' or displacing in their workplaces. Where it makes economic sense to the organisation, managers will use remote working as the cheapest, optimal alternative for harnessing these 'peripheral' and market-based labour pools. In so doing, managers will have to take into account some real challenges—on modes of control, security issues, motivational challenges and also corporate social responsibility concerns.

Challenges and Ways Forward

So far so impressive. However, MIT/Deloitte (2021) reported that over three quarters of respondents were not sufficiently prepared to manage a workforce consisting mainly of external participants. Our ongoing research is more granular and is discovering emerging, unanticipated challenges:

1. If the model is assembled through a series of short-term responses, sooner rather than later organisations 'run out of road'. There needs to be a strategic intent to look after the sustainability of the business over a moving five-year time horizon.
2. Core workers are key as they carry the culture, core skills and provide vital agility in today's volatile, uncertain environment. However, there are signs that the model in practice is eroding organisational cultures, and also that not only employees do not behave as core workers—too often they seek to leave the organisation in search of career progression—but nor do employers treat their employees as core—thus the renewed emphasis during 2023 on Employee Experience to right this trend.
3. The peripheral arrangements tend to be transactional and contractual in character—this does not breed key cultural values among these workers. Furthermore, as we found when looking at outsourcing, the management and transaction costs of operating contractually can be surprisingly high.
4. The model needs to be operated as a strategic approach to labour utilisation, with a core group responsible for ensuring that both core and peripheral workers are properly treated and trained to do the tasks allocated to them. There are indications that HR functions are not up to this task in most organisations. If not, then it is definitely an area to be worked on.
5. Does this mode of operating respond sufficiently to skills shortages? Clearly, it makes labour utilisation more flexible, and can draw on a wider, even global talent base. It can also harness the expanding possibilities of automating work, human–machine work design and cloud-sourcing a digital workforce. In the best versions, core workers will receive substantial training and development. But old habits of cutting training budgets first die hard, especially when the organisation is struggling, or at least acting early to lower costs, protect the balance sheet, and spending more on resilience, for example in cybersecurity and supply chains. Historically, 'peripheral' workers have been left to fend much more for themselves, while 'the war for talent' has been less about training and development, and much more about

competitive hoovering up skills at the market price. That tends to create winners and losers, not skills surpluses.

There are some constructive ways forward. One view is that retaining and building the core workforce has to be the priority target. There has to be strategic clarity around that objective. One part is defining a core worker in the light of strategy and changing contexts. This is, in practice, by no means easy to do if organisations do not have great clarity about their purpose, operating model and values. Many do not.

Internal labour markets and high velocity horizontal fast tracks can do much to encourage and develop core workforce members. This was a big practice among major Japanese companies in the 1980s, when they were at the height of their success.

There is a lot of evidence that organising into small cross-functional teams given discretion on how to achieve measurable goals and performance is a productive use of core labour, and indeed some other peripheral workforce members.

Peripheral workers need to be drawn closer into the main organisation and its culture. For example, adopting across the organisation principles of economic integrity, societal equity and environmental integrity and fair reward, might well help here. One of the important findings on remote workers is that they experience work-home interference, poor communication procrastination and loneliness. Closer monitoring and intensifying the work load tend to undermine rather than make such workers more productive. Meanwhile, much more social support, including some 1–2 days in the work office seems to have the most beneficial effects.

Conclusion

These are just some observations. Dramatic skills shifts require major actions and interventions by governments, educational systems, businesses and workers themselves, sustained over time. But how the flexible labour organisation is managed will have a lot of consequences for labour attraction, retention, building the skills base, the utilisation of technology and the levels of productivity achieved.

On a broader front, Willcocks (2020d) aimed to provide the evidence that, beyond the 'hype-fear' polarisation in media headlines and passing also into some academic studies, a much more complex and nuanced set of changes were underway under the headings of automation and 'AI'. This polarisation is still with us because it attracts attention. For example, Susskind (2020) published a book entitled 'A World Without Work'. In practice, its contents largely refute the title. Indeed, the author himself says on page 5, '*if you picked up this book expecting an account of a dramatic technological big bang in the next few decades, after which lots of people suddenly wake up to find themselves without work, you will be disappointed. That is not likely to happen*'. So what is happening? '*The demand for the work of human beings is likely to wither away, gradually. Eventually what is left will not be enough to provide everyone who wants it with traditional well-paid employment*'. Note the careful phrasing.

We need to move on from the rhetoric and reality of 'Robo-Apocalypse'. Willcocks (2020a) suggested that 'Robo-Apocalypse' was neither likely, cancelled nor postponed, but a misdirected narrative framing. Robot myths form a persistent way of thinking about anxieties and machines very relevant to our rising dependence on information and communication technologies. From this perspective, it is interesting that automation as robotics and the automation of knowledge work have been conflated throughout the debate with the much bigger phenomenon of digitalisation, involving at least ten sets of major digital technologies. Robots represent a narrative, symbol and repository for our anxieties, fears and hopes when it comes to relating to our self-created machines (Willcocks, 2020c). As the technology becomes more virtual, opaque and less visible, so humans feel the need to make sense of the machines by rendering them in physical form. This appears to be a deep-set, human psychological need, not easily circumvented, or substituted for. In the author's view, it is misleading to think in this way, and dangerous to allow such beliefs to inform policies. COVID-19 has clarified that there are much bigger anxieties to be had concerning the future of work, to which technology may contribute, but also help reduce.

References

Aiken, M. (2016). *The Cyber Effect*. John Murray.
Alter, A. (2017). *Irresistible*. Random House.
Altman, E., Schwarz, J., Kiron, D., Jones, R., & Kearns-Manolatos, D. (2021). *Workforce Ecosystems: A New Strategic Approach to the Future of Work*. MIT/Deloitte 2021 Future of the Workforce Global Executive Study and Research Report. Deloitte/MIT.
Arntz, M., Gregory, T., & Zierahn, U. (2016) *The Risk of Automation for Jobs in OECD Countries: A Comparative Analysis*. OECD Social Employment, and Migration Working Papers no. 189. Paris: OECD Library.
Asian Development Bank. (2018). *Asian Development Outlook 2018: How Technology Affects Jobs*. Asian Development Bank.
Atkinson, J. (1984). Manpower Strategies for Flexible Organizations. *Personnel Management, 16*, 28–31.
Brown, J., & Duguid, P. (2017). *The Social Life Of Information*. Harvard Business.
Brucks, M., & Levav, J. (2022). Virtual Communication Curbs Creative Ideas Generation. *Nature, 606*, published online 27th April.
Dery, K., Van Der Meulen, N., & Sebastian, I. (2018). Employee Experience: Enabling your Future Workforce Strategy. *MIT Sloan Center for Information Systems Research* XVIII(9). https://sloanreview.mit.edu/article/using-ai-toenhance-busi-ness-operations/. Accessed 12 May 2020.
Felstead, A, Gallie, D, Green, F., & Inanc, H. (2013). *Work Intensification in Britain: First Findings from the Skills and Employment Survey 2012*. Centre for Learning and Life Chances in Knowledge Economies and Societies, Institute of Education.
Forrester Research. (2017). *The Future of Jobs: Working Side-by Side with Robots*. Forrester Research.
Forsdick, S. (2022, December 13). 2023 Trends—the End of Remote Working and the 'Great Return'. *Raconteur*.
Frey, C. (2019). *The Technology Trap*. Oxford University Press.
Frey, C., & Osborne, M. (2013). The Future of Employment: How Susceptible are Jobs to Computerization? *Oxford Working Paper*, Oxford University, Oxford, September.
Frey, C., & Osborne, M. (2017). The Future of Employment: How Susceptible are Jobs to Computerization? *Technological Forecasting and Social Change, 114*, 254–280.

Ganz, J., Reinsel, D., & Rydning, J. (2017). *Data Age 2025: The Evolution of Data to Life-critical. IDC white paper*, April.
Gazzaley, A., & Rosen, L. (2016). *The Distracted Mind: Ancient Brains in a High-tech World*. MIT Press.
Graeber, D. (2015) *The Utopia of Rules: On Technology, Stupidity and the Secret Joys of Bureaucracy*. Melville House, Brooklyn.
Graeber, D. (2018). *Bullshit Jobs*. Penguin Random House.
Gray, M., & Sun, S. (2019). *Ghost Work*. Houghton Mifflin Harcourt.
Karr, J., Loh, K., & San Andres, E. (2020). COVID-19, 4IR and the Future of Work. *APEC Policy Support Unit Brief No. 34*, June. Asia-Pacific Economic Cooperation.
Korunka, C., & Kubicek, B. (Eds.). (2017). *Job Demands in a Changing World of Work*. Springer.
Lacity, M., & Willcocks, L. (2017, September 13). A New Approach to Service Automation. *Sloan Management Review*, 41–49.
Lacity, M., & Willcocks, L. (2018). *Robotic and Cognitive Automation: The Next Phase*. SB Publishing.
Lacity, M., Willcocks, L., & Gozman, D. (2021). Influencing Information Systems Practice: The Action Principles Approach Applied to Robotic Process and Cognitive Automation. *Journal of Information Technology, 36*, 3. https://doi.org/10.1177/0268396221990778
McKinsey, (2020, Octobe 5). How COVID-19 has Pushed Companies over the Technology Tipping Point—and Transformed Business Forever. *McKinsey & Company. Digital and Strategy and Corporate Finance Practices*. McKinsey.com
McKinsey (2023). What is the Future of Work? *McKinsey and Co*, January
McKinsey Global Institute (MGI). (2017). *Jobs Lost, Jobs Gained: Workforce Transitions in a Time of Automation*. McKinsey & Company.
McKinsey Global Institute (MGI). (2018a). *Notes from the AI Frontier: Insights from Hundreds of Use Cases*. McKinsey and Company.
McKinsey Global Institute (MGI). (2018b). *Notes from the AI Frontier: Modeling the Impact of AI on the World Economy*. McKinsey and Company.
McKinsey Global Institute (MGI). (2020a, June). *The Future of Work in Europe: Automation, Workforce Transitions, and the Shifting Geography of Employment*. McKinsey Global Institute.
McKinsey Global Institute (MGI). (2020b, September). *What 800 Executives Envision for the Post-pandemic Workforce*. Paper, McKinsey Global Institute, New York.

Meulen, N., & Sebastian, I. (2018). Employee Experience: Enabling your Future Workforce Strategy. *MIT Sloan Center for Information Systems Research XVIII* (9). https://sloanreview.mit.edu/article/using-ai-toenhance-business-operations/. Accessed 12 May 2020.

Price Waterhouse Coopers. (2017). *UK Economic Outlook: Will Robots Steal Our Jobs?* Price Waterhouse Coopers.

Research and Markets. (2023). *Global Cybersecurity Market Report 2023.* Research and Markets.

Service Now. (2017). *Today's State of Work: At the Breaking Point.* Service Now.

Susskind, D. (2020). *A World Without Work.* Allen Lane.

The Economist. (2023, May 13). The Future Of Work: Your New Colleague, *The Economist,* 59–61.

Wajcman, J., & Rose, E. (2011). (2011) Constant Connectivity: Rethinking interruptions at work', with Emily Rose. *Organization Studies, 32*(7), 941–962.

Willcocks, L. (2020a) Robo-Apocalypse Cancelled?: Reframing the Automation and Future of Work Debate. *Journal of Information Technology,* 36

Willcocks, L. (2020b, April). Remote working—Here to stay? *LSE Business Review.* https://blogs.lse.ac.uk/businessreview/2020/04/02/remote-working-here-to-stay/

Willcocks, L. (2020c, April 23). Why Misleading Metaphors are Fooling Managers about the use of AI. *Forbes.* https://www.forbes.com/sites/londonschoolofeconomics/2020/04/23/

Willcocks, L. (2020d, September). COVID-19 may Exacerbate the Digital Divide Among Businesses. *LSE Business Review.* https://blogs.lse.ac.uk/businessreview/2020/09/03/covid-19-may-exacerbate-the-digitaldivide-among-businesses/

Willcocks, L. (2021). *Global Business: Management.* SB Publishing.

Willcocks, L., & Lacity, M. (2016). *Service Automation Robots and the Future of Work.* SB Publishing.

Willcocks, L., Hindle, J., & Lacity, M. (2019). *Becoming Strategic with Robotic Process Automation.* SB Publishing.

Willcocks, L. (2023a, April 18). Here's How Digitalised Flexible Labour Organizations became the Future of Work. *LSE Business Review.* https://blogs.lse.ac.uk/businessreview/2023/04/18/heres-how-digitalised-flexible-organisations-become-the-future-of-work/

Willcocks, L. (2023b, May 4) *Robotic Process Automation And The Future of Work.* Presentation to the CTO Forum.

Willcocks, L., Hindle, J., Stanton, M., & Smith, J. (2023). *Maximizing Value With Automation and Digital Transformation: A Realist's Guide*. Palgrave.

Winsor, J., & Paik, J. (2024). *Open Talent: Leveraging the Global Workforce to Solve your Biggest Challenges*. Harvard Business Review Press.

World Economic Forum. (2020, January 22). *We need a Global Reskilling Revolution—Here's why*. Briefing Paper, World Economic Forum. Geneva.

Yang, L., Holtz, D. Jaffe, S. et al. (2022, January). The Effects of Remote Work on Collaboration among Information Workers. *Nature Human Behaviour, 6*, 43–54.

14

Emerging Global Sourcing Challenges: Innovation, Net Zero and Digital Transformation

Ilan Oshri, Leslie Willcocks, Heiner Himmerleich, Anthony Vlasic, Hrishi Hrishikesh, and John Hindle

Introduction

The post-COVID-19 world has been going through multiple shocks that require executives and decision-makers to rethink their sourcing strategies. In this chapter we pay close attention to three emerging, critical topics in the business community. The first topic is effective management of innovation ecosystems that have become critical for client firm's ability to accelerate time-to-market and ensure access to critical skills in a timely manner. The second is the growing compliance demands by governments and pressures on enterprises to increase transparency with regard

---

This chapter is based on several studies, and we would like to acknowledge the contributions of Evelien Scherp, Heiner Himmelreich, Hrishi Hrishikesh and Anthony Vlasic to two of these on vendor innovation eco-systems and sustainability. The sections on digital transformation draw upon the original research work of John Hindle of Knowledge Capital Partners and Leslie Willcocks.

I. Oshri (✉)
University of Auckland, Auckland, New Zealand
e-mail: ilan.oshri@auckland.ac.nz

© The Editor(s) (if applicable) and The Author(s), under exclusive licence to Springer Nature Switzerland AG 2024
L. Willcocks et al. (eds.), *Transformation in Global Outsourcing*, Technology, Work and Globalization, https://doi.org/10.1007/978-3-031-61022-6_14

to carbon footprints, as sustainability has taken a central role in corporate responsibility, particularly with regard to environmental issues. The third issue is an all-encompassing one—how organisations can manage their ongoing digital transformations, and the role of external suppliers in this process. All three issues have implications for future client and vendor sourcing strategies.

Winning with Vendor Innovation Ecosystems

Outsourcing innovation, particularly for digital capabilities and processes, may be critical for survival, but it isn't easy to generate results by doing so. As business comes to grips with the growing role of digital technologies in creating and capturing value—a lesson driven home by the COVID-19 pandemic—it is turning to IT and business service providers to create novel digital products and processes, in addition to developing them internally.

This development marks a departure from the way many companies have worked with IT service providers in the past, when they based outsourcing decisions mainly on efficiency-related parameters such as reducing costs or accessing the skills they needed. In spite of this shift, the results have proven to be illusory. According to a recent IDC study,

---

L. Willcocks
LSE, London, UK

H. Himmerleich
BCG, Amsterdam, Netherlands

A. Vlasic
BCG, Sydney, NSW, Australia

H. Hrishikesh
BCG, New York, NY, USA

J. Hindle
Accenture, London, UK

only one in ten companies is satisfied with the outcomes service providers deliver.

To get the best out of IT service providers, Chief Digital Officers (CDOs) and Chief Information Officers (CIOs) are realising that they need to find novel ways of engaging with them. Rather than focusing on individual providers, market leaders are learning to create and orchestrate ecosystems of them (see also Chapter 13). These vendor innovation ecosystems (VIEs) not only provide access to the latest technologies, specialised capabilities and deep expertise, they also offer faster times to market, increased flexibility and greater accountability. Deploying VIEs can also insulate businesses from the 'not invented here' syndrome that often handicaps digital transformations and helps turn IT service providers into trusted innovation partners.

To understand how companies manage these emergent VIEs, we studied the leaders of nearly 200 organisations that pursued innovations through vendor ecosystems. Our analysis suggests that companies create four different types of innovation ecosystems: mixed, multiservice, specialist and internal. Each type delivers its own level of satisfaction, but companies were most happy with mixed ecosystems, which consist of both multiservice and specialised service providers. However, we found that the more multiservice providers in an ecosystem, the less happy companies were with overall performance. In this chapter, we focus on the lessons that can be learned from this first-ever global survey of VIEs.

The Four Types of VIEs

Most companies, especially large corporations, usually work with several IT service providers and systems integrators at the same time, establishing direct connections with each of them. Some have created VIEs around their service providers, connecting them with one another as well as with in-house capabilities. These ecosystems are built around large, multiservice providers and smaller, specialised providers, as well as IT consultancy firms. The four types of VIEs companies create include the following:

Mixed Ecosystems. Many companies (32%) had deployed innovation ecosystems that consist of both multiservice and specialised service providers. Explains the head of one US financial institution: *'We depend on three multiservice providers, with one of them serving as the main partner for innovation along with our internal resources. We also surround ourselves with niche providers that help us accelerate innovation efforts. The niche firms drive innovation around specific pieces of work, while we think of the multiservice provider as the "factory" that drives results.'*

Multiservice Ecosystems. Some companies (31%) had developed ecosystems made up of only multipurpose service providers. Most organisations use multiservice vendors for outsourcing business processes, so they have found it natural to turn to those vendors for innovation as well.

Specialist Ecosystems. Some companies (24%) had orchestrated innovation ecosystems using only specialised service providers, with each focusing on a different problem or different aspects of the same problem. *'Niche firms drive innovation,'* the IT head of an Australian telecommunications company told us. *'We prefer to work directly with them rather than with multiservice providers.'*

Internal Ecosystems. A minority of companies (14%) chose not to depend on IT service providers, preferring instead to use only internal ecosystems to drive innovation efforts.

While the specialist service providers tend to concentrate on innovation, the multiservice ones offer more (or only) standard services. For instance, the survey shows that just 22% of specialist service providers offer only innovation-related services, while 52% provide a mix of innovation-related and standard services. By contrast, 14% of the multiservice providers offer only innovation services, while 21% supply a combination of innovation and standard services. By combining multiservice providers with specialists, companies are undoubtedly able to foster greater innovation.

Three Key Capabilities

Companies should create innovation ecosystems made up of service providers with diverse kinds of capabilities, so they can gain access to a range of competencies. According to our survey, CDOs and CIOs felt that there are three main skill sets to look for in-service providers when creating VIEs. First, providers should be able to productise solutions and platforms (82.5% of executives felt this was the most important capability). Second, they should have business and sectoral expertise (80% felt this was most important). Third, they should have a track record of delivering successful innovation (this was the priority for 80.5% of executives).

To identify the service providers they need, the CDO's starting point should be an understanding of their own organisation's technological abilities. Next, the CDO should consider what technologies and capabilities the company needs to acquire or outsource for innovation and the costs of doing so. Before making choices, companies must also gauge a service provider's ability to deliver technological applications and how well the vendor is likely to work with other providers to develop new products or processes.

The Ecosystems That Work Best

Most companies said they use VIEs to create new products or processes related to cloud-based applications, digital solutions (applications) and cybersecurity. However, they benefit differently from different ecosystems. For instance, the biggest benefit to companies that use mixed ecosystems was better-performing business processes. Those that deployed multiservice or specialist ecosystems, meanwhile, benefitted from being able to introduce new products, but not better-performing processes.

That leads to the critical issue of performance: Which kinds of VIEs work best? According to our survey, most of the companies that were extremely satisfied with their service providers' innovation prowess (59%) had created ecosystems with both multiservice and specialised service providers. In other words, heterogeneity is more critical for success than specialisation, with mixed ecosystems providing access to more skill sets and diverse thinking.

There's a relationship between the number of service providers in an innovation ecosystem and companies' satisfaction with overall performance: companies with the highest level of satisfaction used between six and ten service providers. However, our survey data shows that the trend diverges in the case of multipurpose providers: the more multipurpose providers a company used, the lower its level of satisfaction. With specialised service providers, though, a company's satisfaction didn't change as the number of vendors in an ecosystem rose or fell.

Managing Ecosystems

The biggest risk to any ecosystem is that service providers will try to push their products and services even if they don't fit customer needs. The survey confirms that this is a concern for companies. That's why it's important for them to use their ecosystems to understand what they're buying as well as the limitations of those purchases; a diverse ecosystem will diffuse the risk that companies end up buying brochureware.

Managing VIEs composed of both large and small service providers, some with generic offerings and others with specialised solutions, can be challenging. It requires the ability to manage relationships, products and processes, capabilities that often extend beyond IT functions' normal strengths. Companies have no choice but to cultivate fresh capabilities if they wish to be successful. When asked, they chose three organisational capabilities that, in their experience, are essential to get the most out of VIEs:

- A higher-than-average level of maturity in terms of deploying digital solutions;
- Strong IT service provider management abilities;
- The ability to build close relationships with multiple service providers.

Companies have figured out how to find the right service providers for IT outsourcing, but they haven't developed a similar capability for identifying partners for innovation—yet. As a result, many use multiservice providers to scout for possible innovation partners and speed up the process of creating VIEs. They also use multiservice providers to manage their innovation ecosystems; as many as 26.5% of the companies we surveyed said they preferred that to doing it themselves.

Companies were clear-eyed about how they would make their VIEs perform better over time. Many (38%) agreed that they would use more-specialised service providers to drive innovation, although globally distributed teams would drive the process. Companies also recognised the need for a single governance structure across the organisation to manage service providers and felt that their current technology infrastructures were insufficient to tackle the rising complexity of innovation ecosystems.

At the same time, companies admitted that soft capabilities would not be enough to ensure the success of the innovations that ecosystems produce. Nearly a quarter of the respondents (23%) felt that they would have to reinforce those capabilities with in-house technological knowledge of the solutions, areas and businesses that service providers focus on. In addition, executives felt their organisations needed to hone their own capabilities to translate business needs into technological requirements (17%) to get the best from their service providers. They also needed to integrate knowledge and solutions from service providers into their products or platforms (16.5%) to successfully take innovations developed by their VIEs to market.

It is important to understand why innovation ecosystems, which are a relatively novel governance model, have become critical when using service providers. Many companies have found it difficult to use them for innovation in the past because it's tough to design the right incentives. Service providers can increase margins by innovating, but many innovations tend to generate efficiencies that could reduce the revenue they earn. That's why companies need to create ecosystems in which the roles of the players and the rewards for innovation are both transparent. Organisations must ensure that their innovation ecosystems create value while also managing the risks and optimising the distribution of value in an equitable manner among their partners to sustain their ecosystems. If companies want to use IT service providers for innovation, they have no choice but to organise and orchestrate them into VIEs.

Accelerating Net-Zero Progress with Innovative Technology

Governments and enterprises have been doubling down on the development of their net-zero targets in recent years, seeking to demonstrate ambition and accountability. Timely examples include the European Union's commitment to achieve net zero by 2050, supported by recent actions such as the launch of a new Biomethane Industrial Partnership. The EU also recently announced it intends to ban the sale of fossil fuels for cars beginning in 2035, reinforcing its pledge to deliver on its net-zero roadmap.

At the enterprise level, BAM Group, a leader in the construction space, announced an ambitious 2026 operational emissions net-zero target for its UK and Ireland division. Despite the enterprise progress demonstrated by this example and others, it appears that less than a third of private companies have set net-zero targets.

Devising and announcing net-zero targets is one small part of the process; achieving them is a challenge for the entire value chain of an enterprise (Kotlarsky et al., 2023). According to one respondent:

> There are two lenses through which organisations must look at sustainability. Acting on your own company commitments and driving others to act as well. Head of Sustainability, Global mining company

In many cases, emissions are produced by organisations. Yet they also are produced by consumers and suppliers, creating a complex challenge to overcome. Carbon emissions can be categorised into three scopes:

- **Scope 1**: Emissions a company produces directly;
- **Scope 2**: Emissions a company creates indirectly, such as when energy it purchases for heating buildings is produced on its behalf;

- **Scope 3**: All of the emissions a company is indirectly responsible for throughout the value chain.

The complicated nature of this mission calls for precise measurement, tracking, and reporting, conducted in an ongoing, end-to-end manner. Technology is vital to any company's value chain and plays a critical role in effectively tackling emissions. This includes large-scale deployments of products like SAP Carbon Footprint Analytics to more targeted solutions like BCG's own CO2 AI.

Business leaders must review their net-zero strategies through a technology lens, with an understanding that technology itself also contributes to emissions. Here we will review how enterprises are preparing to deliver on their net-zero pledges and how technology providers intend to support them. A four-phase approach will be offered, designed to guide leaders to harness technology to their advantage.

Assessing Enterprise Progress

We gained insights from more than 30 executives at major multinational enterprises and those from technology service providers with two key goals in mind: to assess the net-zero strategies of large multinationals and to closely examine the role of technology in this lengthy and crucial process.

Respondents emphasised the widespread importance of the climate and sustainability issue, with a majority having established targets in a top-down manner. We identified fragility, however, in the approaches of most sample companies, many of which placed a disproportionate focus on Scope 1 and Scope 2, while struggling with Scope 3.

When examining the difficulties organisations face in addressing Scope 3, it became clear that many still need to collect and build the necessary data foundations pertaining to the wider value chain. This indicates a capability gap where sophisticated technology is required, specifically in the form of solutions that can capture, collate and analyse large amounts of data in real time.

Challenges associated with Scope 3 also vary by sector, with some organisations unclear on how to reduce their indirect emissions. Some banks expressed difficulty in determining appropriate loan recipients, telecom companies could sometimes be unsure of which equipment to procure, and retailers struggled to select the most environmentally friendly waste reduction techniques. The industry body associated with the chemicals space, Together for Sustainability (TfS), is a specific example of an organisation created to help define standards for Scope 3 calculations. Standards help visibility and, according to one respondent:

> Visibility creates the ability to improve, and technology makes this possible across the supply chain in an end-to-end way. Head of Procurement, European banking services provider

We also discovered that most of the respondent enterprises have introduced a dedicated sustainability role, but this was commonly found to be a recent step taken in the last two to three years. It also became clear in the majority of cases that businesses have not yet allocated additional dedicated funds to help meet the net-zero targets they set, despite frequently being incorporated in business KPIs. These metrics tend to be in the top-level business category, as we found that they are rarely embedded at the business unit and operational levels.

There are some encouraging signs that organisations are beginning to make meaningful progress, with instances of net-zero plans being communicated and implemented at the BU level. However, support functions like IT are still commonly excluded. Some are also beginning to explore the use of data analytics to enhance measurement capabilities, and others are looking to data centres to help reduce emissions associated with technology itself.

The organisations that have started their journey to net zero stated that it is easier to map a pathway to reducing carbon footprints if sustainability speaks the language of the business. On this basis, there may be value in using quantified cost and benefit assessments to evaluate alternatives, in the same way a company would typically assess other investments.

Technology and the Net-Zero Journey

When it comes to digital for net zero, value creation is twofold. Not only is it a source of ecological value—with tech and data reducing carbon emissions by more than 30%—digital is also a driver of economic value, helping companies realise sustainability as a new form of competitive advantage.

Building this "EcoDigital Advantage" requires driving three levels of system impact. The first level, "Decarbonise IT," addresses the vital need to reduce emissions created by technology itself. "Decarbonise operations" supports emissions reduction across the value chain. The third level, "Decarbonise industry," is instrumental in developing open-data collaborations and digital products to aggregate and monitor relevant information and provide new opportunities for innovation.

Decarbonising IT calls for infrastructure optimisation and the implementation of cloud-native architecture, enhanced by sustainable software engineering. Sustainable tech vendor sourcing is a critical aspect of this process and ensures that emissions are being reduced both directly and indirectly. Cutting down on IT-related emissions will require a strong focus on Scope 3 and greater visibility of emissions generated by data centres and devices.

When it comes to decarbonising business operations, there should be considerable focus on simplifying IT processes across the value chain. The integration of digital platforms and IoT is also of paramount importance. These capabilities form the basis of digitalised processes and data visualisation, which will equip organisations to measure emissions and their sources with greater precision and to remove unnecessary steps in the process. Next-gen supplier management is also critical, alongside the application of digital enablement techniques. Above all, having simplified processes, higher-quality data sharing and measurement capabilities, and the right internal incentives and standards will promote the meaningful decarbonisation of operations.

Reducing industry emissions calls for better data sharing and a distributed architecture. Having the appropriate digital products and services is important, but so is encouraging behaviours that will bring about a cultural shift towards achieving net-zero goals. Finally, the use of an ecosystem operating model and platform ventures will also be an effective tool in driving widespread progress. Past research found that maximising the return on supplier innovation requires an ecosystem of both multiservice and specialist suppliers. Addressing Scope 3 net-zero targets requires the same discipline.

The Vision for Technology Providers

When speaking with technology providers, we found a widely shared view among executives that they have an important role to play in assisting enterprises in delivering on net-zero goals. All of the tech provider executives included in our study had taken steps to tailor their propositions to enterprises pursuing ambitious sustainability targets—from reducing their own emissions to carbon footprint transparency in support of Scope 3. Many are also developing industry-specific solutions designed to solve the key challenges linked to different verticals. One vendor manager remarked:

> We know that it is a trillion-dollar investment market between now and 2030, but we are still trying to work on how to convince clients to spend.
> VP Sustainability, Technology vendor

At present, the insights from our study demonstrate that there is not yet a strong willingness among enterprises to adopt specialised solutions offered by technology providers. However, there is an exception in the case of cloud-based solutions, with enterprises proving significantly more receptive to this approach. For technology suppliers to be successful in supporting clients, they will need to continue refining their offerings. As a starting point, this should include sharing their own emissions data with clients as a basis for data-driven sustainability.

On reflection, the key considerations for technology providers include:

- Providing industry-specific solutions that meet client needs, e.g., focusing on energy consumption with more effective cooling technologies or new chip designs with significantly less energy consumption for comparable compute power;
- Gathering and sharing internal data across the value chain with clients;
- Having clear and transparent policies that clients will understand;
- Providing demonstrable evidence of delivery on commitments;
- Pushing for partnerships rather than transactional vendor relationships.

Plotting a Path to Net-Zero Success

Leveraging our analysis, we established a four-phase strategy to enable enterprises to create a plan for their net-zero journey. A comprehensive plan that harnesses the power of technology offers the most robust, data-driven approach to achieving real net-zero success.

Phase 1 involves the development of a baseline. Establishing a firm foundation upon which to build is vital. To do this, enterprises must appoint both a sustainability leader and an oversight committee. In support of this step, data sources need to be harnessed and measured systematically to create a baseline for the three key net-zero scopes, before being aligned with existing carbon emissions. In compliance with the scopes, accurately assessing the direct, indirect and value chain emissions are all essential to the success of this phase. For example, an interviewee described a three-step process of recording, reporting, and reducing, commenting that:

> You can't reduce emissions effectively without a baseline measurement you can trust. Executive of Energy and Climate Change, Industrial goods

For precise and ongoing measurement to be possible, the sustainability lead and oversight committee must work with the wider enterprise to select and adopt carbon emissions calculators. This will require consultations with technology suppliers and standard-setting organisations to determine which data tools will be the most effective. The next step in Phase 1 is to identify 10 to 15 suppliers that can drive the biggest impact on emissions reduction. This should be conducted as early in the process as possible. The success of this approach relies on alignment among the biggest contributors in Scope 3, as their data will be essential for baselining and selecting the right tools.

Phase 2 is centred around the development of targets. After building solid foundations in terms of data tools and an initial supplier-base in Phase 1, the organisation must agree on short-, medium- and long-term targets. This includes setting the overarching target for achieving net zero, but the target must be based on intermediate objectives that compartmentalise the extensive task and ensure it is achievable. It is also critical to factor in reporting targets.

Next, targets should be implemented across all business units, with KPIs embedded and with the emissions reduction treated as any other primary business objective. Lastly, supplier working groups from within the supply chain should be established to form ecosystems that will aid the deployment of technology, education, and progress monitoring. Client companies also have a role:

> We have a responsibility to help our suppliers to develop. Head of Procurement, Industrial goods

Phase 3 is dedicated to delivering on long-term net-zero ambitions. At the heart of this phase is establishing working groups and a governance framework to ensure that progress is sustainable. Working groups should be set up within business units and tasked with devising individual plans to handle ownership and delivery. A funding pool should also be put in place to support delivery, and it should be viewed as part of the cost of doing business.

As part of this phase, suppliers from the supply chain should be brought into the loop and assigned targets for which they should be supported. Two leading companies told us that they have implemented an internal carbon pricing scheme to deliver on this phase, with one even setting different tax rates depending on the source of CO_2 in question.

Phase 4 is an opportunity to implement monitoring, and optimise the entire system. Setting up a systematic approach to monitoring is critical, as this will form the basis of progress tracking. Consulting industry bodies, standards bodies and government agencies is the first port of call, ensuring that the enterprise is prepared for ongoing compliance. This also provides important access to new sources of innovation, which will help organisations deliver on their targets. The transformation of internal and external processes must also be considered in this phase, such as the introduction of carbon tax to drive more responsible behaviour. Developing a dashboard to capture lead indicators is also important, as it will provide timely information about the state of net-zero targets across all three scopes.

Managing Digital Transformation

Our final overarching issue goes to the heart of the future of global sourcing of IT and business services: how organisations can best manage their digital transformations over the next 3–5 years, and how external service suppliers are best leveraged as part of this process. We have already provided insight into the critical role of vendor ecosystems (see above). Meanwhile, in Chapter 11, we detailed the key internal capabilities needed for IT and cloud sourcing management. Our Preface also provided five perennial lessons on global sourcing practice that are relevant for at least the rest of the 2020s. Here we focus on the vital component that founds client global sourcing strategy, namely the core internal capabilities needed to elicit and deliver on business requirements, develop the IT-business process platform, and leverage external suppliers, in order to evolve towards digital transformation.

But first it is useful to take a macro view. Willcocks (2021) defines digital transformation as whole-organisation, large-scale change. It sees radical changes in business activities, processes, competencies and models to fully leverage the changes in and opportunities provided by digital technologies. The goal is to become a digitally enabled business. By the mid-2020s nearly all organisations were trying to progress on this path, but many have underestimated the length of time required, and the management challenges along the way. Extensive and long-term research into over 1,100 organisations by the London School of Economics and Knowledge Capital Partners suggests that support from the global services market is valuable, but that seven core capabilities are needed in-house for digital transformation to be successful (Willcocks et al., 2023). These capabilities, suitably integrated, form a **core competence of digital transformation**, measured by total net business value gained.

These core capabilities are shown in Fig. 14.1. It is worth looking at these in more detail, as they have emerged with much more clarity more recently, and some may be unfamiliar.

Business strategy is an integrated set of commitments and actions designed to exploit core competencies and gain competitive advantage. Digital strategy is part of business strategy and establishes how to maximise the combined business benefits of data assets and technology-focused initiatives. Digital strategy sees the application of digital technologies to enable new and differentiating business models and capabilities. Central to today's organisation, digital strategy is required for its delivery of Digital Transformation. Therefore, **digital transformation maturity** reflects advanced alignment of strategy; integrated planning; program governance; imbedded culture; digital platform; change management; and navigation capabilities. Let us look at these in more detail.

1. **Strategy Capability:** *'establishes the vision and direction for digital businesses.'* This represents the ability to establish sustainable competitive, customer-focused short-, mid- and long-term business direction informed by digital technology developments, driven by business imperatives and steered by c-suite executives pursuing an organisational transformation agenda.
2. **Integrated Planning Capability:** *'details and dynamically updates how digital transformation strategy is enacted.'* This consists of a detailed set of organisation-wide processes designed to dynamically align strategy with operations, and coordinate developments in data, technology, processes and people to deliver a digital transformation agenda.

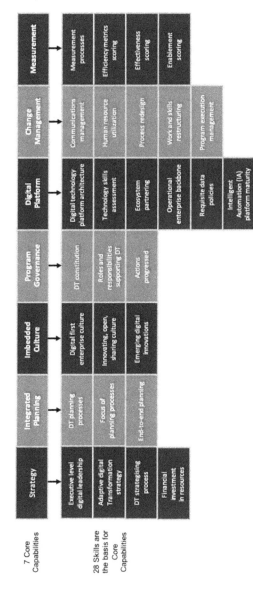

Fig. 14.1 Digital transformation capabilities (Source Leslie Willcocks and John Hindle, 2023)

3. **Imbedded Culture Capability:** *'shared "digital first" norms, beliefs and behaviours that underpin strategic and operational practices.'* The 'digital first' culture fosters constant innovation for business impact, speed in execution, openness to and sharing of diverse sources of information and insight, and allows people high levels of discretion on what needs to be done.
4. **Program Governance Capability:** *'draws up the decision-making rules and processes for digital transformation.'* This capability sees the establishment of a digital transformation constitution for how decisions get made, resources get allocated and how duties and responsibilities and deliverables are assigned.
5. **Digital Platform Capability:** *'the founding and continuous improvement of the enablement platform for digital business.'* This consists of design and development that integrates on an evolutionary basis, through architecture, the use of data and multiple digital technologies with legacy business applications in order to support business strategic direction and operational excellence.
6. **Change Management Capability:** *'the absorptive capacity of the organisation to dynamically innovate using automation and digital technologies.'* *This capability ensures that* change management integrates SMAC/BRAIDA technologies optimally with requisite developments in skills, processes, structure, culture, reward systems, management orientations, team-building and strategic direction.
7. **Navigation Capability:** *'measuring to keep strategy on course.'* This capability provides a set of processes that establishes **Efficiency** ('doing things right'), **Effectiveness** ('doing the right things') and **Enablement** ('doing new things') metrics designed to monitor and apply the learning from the business value gained from automation and digital transformation activities.

Clearly, even very large organisations will be drawing upon external as well as internal resources to build these capabilities. The advice here is that clients should do this on a 'buy-in' and partnering rather than a transactional 'outsourcing' basis. For our purposes in this book, the area that particularly relates to the external services market in terms of ITO and BPO is digital platform capability, and the role of external suppliers in building future-ready digital platforms.

Making Digital Platforms Future-Ready

Digital transformation needs, firstly, foundations. To succeed in the emerging digital economy, organisations will need to deploy intelligent automation (see Chapter 9) as the foundation of a digital enterprise platform, to accelerate responsiveness and time to market, galvanise customer experience, provide agility and resilience, virtualise their operating and business models, offer ongoing strategic options and support business value creation, at speed and scale. Among a very few digital leaders, this has already been happening. But for others, there are ways of catching up, by accelerating the process.

Above we identified seven essential capabilities for digital transformation. While all seven are critical for success, Strategy and Digital Platform are critical requirements at the outset of the transformation journey. Today, aligning Strategy and Platform is not enough; they must be developed dialectically. Let's look at this proposition.

The Strategy-Platform Dialectic

Strategy capability establishes and dynamically updates the vision and direction for the digital business—its competitive differentiation. It defines products and services, markets, customers, channels, as well as the resources (including talent, financial, technological, material) needed to enable the strategy. It incorporates the digital strategy—the key technologies that will enable new and differentiating business models and capabilities.

A **digital platform** is a repository of business, technology and data components facilitating rapid innovation and enhancement of digital offerings for customer experience and operational efficiency. The raw material of digital offerings and processes is a set of software components. To facilitate development of both new and enhanced offerings and processes, organisations need robust platforms that make reusable business and technology components available for reconfiguration. Among digital leaders, modularity is a constant design imperative.

Many practitioners and vendors define such platforms in ways that give them limited scope, e.g., a sales platform, a procurement platform. In our macro view a matured digital platform can deliver transformed customer experiences, performance jumps in operational efficiency, and be the foundations for multiple interlinked business platforms.

As intimated above, Digital Platform capability sees the design, building and continuous improvement of the technology platform for strategy realisation. The foundation of the Digital Platform is a robust intelligent automation infrastructure for executing operating processes. It consists of enterprise-grade RPA platform, augmented by an ever-expanding range of AI tools and capabilities—machine learning (ML), natural language processing (NLP), optical character recognition (OCR), decision agents, etc.—connecting and unifying a diverse range of internal and external human and digital resources (employees, customers, suppliers, partners, data resources, etc.) to enable and deliver the strategy. But the digital platform is developed by further combining and optimising emerging digital technologies for business purpose.

The goal is a business-led modular technology and data platform. Willcocks et al. (2023) found that putting in place a fit-for-purpose modern technology architecture driven by business needs and strategic imperatives is one of the top success factors, enabling secure, scalable performance, rapid change and deployment, together with reliable ecosystem integration.

In dynamic technology and business environments, moreover, the ability to continuously reconfigure and align enterprise capabilities and resources with commercial opportunities is key. But there is no endpoint. And strategy-platform alignment must now become fusion. This requires a continuous and conscious 'dialectic' between Strategy and Platform—Strategy informs and shapes Platform choices, and Platform enables and shapes Strategy options. Platform, in effect, becomes the physical and conceptual instantiation of Strategy. And in a digital operating environment, both Strategy and Platform must be dynamic and open-ended, not fixed and immutable.

We have observed much of this among digital leaders. Furthermore, when making platform choices and decisions, these leaders consider two frames of reference and participation:

1. **Internal**—an agile platform infrastructure that enables and accelerates continuous development and innovation by standardising enterprise component interfaces and interactions across operating functions and management entities—e.g., common data units/formats, hardware interfaces and software APIs for building applications in a 'building block' model, including enabling rules for access and utilisation.
2. **External**—a multi-function platform infrastructure that enables secure direct and third-party integrations with multiple entities and resources in the 'extended enterprise' (customers, partners, suppliers, developers, influencers, etc.) across diverse media, data types and content sources.

The key characteristics and performance dimensions that leaders consider and evaluate when building a foundation platform for digital transformation include:

- **Compatibility**—backwards/forwards, internal/external, 'open' across multiple sub- and third-party platforms—the ability to accommodate relevant protocols and interface standards for various data entities, content and media types (industry-specific or media-specific).
- **Extensibility**—the ability to scale (up or down) easily and cost-effectively, at both hardware and software levels, in near-real time, to create and respond to demand; cloud is an obvious strategy/solution.
- **Control**—the ability to monitor and manage access and performance actively across all elements of the extended platform—technology, data, security, even human resources.
- **Congeniality**—ease of use, both at the 'builder' level (designing and building solutions) and the 'customer' or 'consumption' level (users, partners, suppliers, etc.)

In addition to these technology management characteristics, there exists a third digital platform level of talent development—acquiring, developing and training the human software needed to build and run the above. Human talent is integral to the digital platform.

Using a case study, we illustrate below how organisations can apply these principles in the context of digital transformation.

Bank Case Study: Making Platform Progress

The earlier financial services companies got into computing, the more complicated their digital integration challenges today. Banks have lived through and embody multiple generations of technologies—from mainframes, desktops, client server and internet-based technologies, and applications, not least varieties of enterprise planning database and cloud applications. Becoming digital, each bank has its unique starting points, and each its distinctive journey. We see lots of impressive digital strategies. Then we look at what passes for the digital platform and know it's not going to go too well. This is not surprising. The integration challenges are formidable. But there are ways forward. Each has to build the same seven core capabilities for digital transformation to happen. Let's see what can be done by looking at one large bank, and its ways forward. Our focus is digital platform capability.

In 2023 this bank was among the sector leaders on digital strategy, was advanced on integrated planning, change management, embedded digital culture and digital platform, and average for program governance and measurement.

> **Digital technology platform architecture and blueprint.** The bank had moved from developing an architecture incrementally with overall governance and integration by IT towards a well-developed architecture and blueprint for an agile enterprise digital technology platform. In this they were ahead of probably 60% of the organisations in their sector. The potential problem is becoming wedded to the existing plan and technologies while new technologies and uses are emerging rapidly

and continuously. They needed to ensure that design of the technology platform is open and can incorporate new technologies quickly.

Technology and skills assessment. From relying on HR and third-party advisors for staff training and assessment, and on IT for technical tool evaluation, the bank is moving towards having strong central capability in assessment of tools, skills and technical demands for platform design, construction and operation. The bank will be able to drive much progress with these in place; the problem will be retaining skilled personnel, paying them enough and providing sufficient interest. Ambitious projects attract high performers, who need to be serviced and supported well.

Ecosystem partnering. The bank is less good at working with external technology suppliers. It works with various vendors and external advisors, depending on the functional processes under development. Partnering decisions are made and managed by individual business units. Using the external services market on this selective sourcing 'horses for courses' basis needs a more strategically inclined sourcing function that links with and helps deliver the overall DT strategy. Digital transformation needs a strong internal technology sourcing capability to build a network of technology partners that is requisite, updated regularly, and is utilised synergistically with internal resources.

Operational enterprise technology backbone. This is also a weaker component. The bank has been operating across a number of local technology platforms and infrastructures, and has been relying on IT to manage platform integration across multiple acquisitions and service providers. As with many others in financial services, this bank still has too many platforms, and too many applications and really do need to develop a blue print on how to standardise data and technologies, and limit the number of IT service providers.

Requisite data policies. Unlike many we have researched, this bank is relatively strong here. The Bank developed an overall digital data strategy and architecture to protect and provide access to enterprise data, and to ensure data integrity and accuracy. The bank is well advanced on integrated development, curation and ethical use of digital data. In this respect it has made good progress in an area most executives overlook and neglect. But the bank needs to keep

focusing on data policies as a core activity rather than shifting focus on something that seems to need more urgent attention.
Intelligent automation execution. The bank is advanced, especially on delivery and service model, but is not yet a leader in its use of intelligent automation. The main catch-up work needs to be done in the areas of pipeline, technology and the pace of development here and the ambitions over the next year are aligned with overall digital strategy maturity.

This bank is among the top 30% globally in its digital transformation efforts. It demonstrates serious work-in-progress driven by ambitious targets. Technology transformations are notoriously difficult and complex. In the large, it has avoided the top mistakes of being too piecemeal and limited in scope, not connecting technology to business value, being too dependent on external service suppliers and finding transformation too expensive to sustain. It has become much more future-ready in its management approach. What does this mean?

Future-Ready Digital Platforms

Facing today's environmental dynamism, connectedness and uncertainty, together with rising, increasingly unpredictable competition, organisations need to become not just digital but also agile and adaptable—that is, 'future-ready.' As several commentators point out, this means building an ambidextrous organisation and digital platform for both **exploitation**—efficient leveraging of existing resources and capabilities through continually improved processes—and **exploration**—combining resources and capabilities in new ways to create further capabilities and opportunities (Ross et al., 2019).

Tensions between exploitation and exploration will occur. The crucial point is that organisational ambidexterity is not enough. To be future-ready, business ambidexterity must have digital foundations, and operate through data and digital processes. MIT academics Jeanne Ross and colleagues have put it another way: in designing for digital there is a simultaneous need for a digital componentised operational backbone (to underpin exploitation), and for digital services platforms (for speed, flexibility and experimentation, i.e., exploration) (Ross et al., 2019). And, of course, this design logic of digital ambidexterity is increasingly facilitated by today's multi-layered technology architecture, supported by modularised components, API-enabled connectivity and scalable cloud usage.

Tensions within the digital platform between exploitation and exploration can be managed through a multi-layered technology architecture with an API-based integration layer that connects core infrastructure with customer facing services and content.

The overall vision here is of a business-IT-digital fusion, with business IT and digital strategies highly interlinked, and with technology increasingly driving business innovation. In a step towards being even more future-ready, some suggest that tensions in bridging Business and IT can be managed by re-organising around **business capability platforms** run by autonomous cross-functional teams and coordinated by automated processes and platform standards. However, most organisations will not be in a position to make this step yet. So, what can they do be doing?

Getting to 'Future-Ready'

Looking across our research and composite sources, organisations that are building 'future-ready' can be found working on three components:

- The first is a reimagined role for technology that is tightly focused on and fused with the business strategy. The business-technology gap has been a perennial issue in transformation initiatives, and has been closing slowly, over several decades. But now, *digital is becoming the business*. Therefore, what has been called 'tech-forward' business strategy is critical, together with integrated bus-tech management and stewardship of the digital user experience.
- Secondly, enterprises need to continue to reinvent technology delivery. This means agile-at-scale software delivery, modularisation, adoption of next generation infrastructure services (e.g., cloud, end-to-end automation, NoOps, PaaS), technology skills excellence (internal and

external) and flexible technology partnerships. Our earlier advice on vendor innovation ecosystems is highly relevant here.
- The third component is future-proofing the foundations—that is, the digital platform. The target state here is, firstly, a flexible, business-backed architecture developed iteratively and continuously to renew core systems so they support new digital functionalities. The process will see multiple, even daily, production releases and frequent upgrades. The flexible architecture will consist of self-contained applications connected with easy-to-configure application programming interfaces (APIs). Secondly, the technology core will include data and analytics systems that provide technology teams across the enterprise with the high-quality information and tools they need to anticipate customer and employee preferences, design innovative applications and enrich user experiences. Thirdly, security and privacy protections need to be integrated into solutions from the start, rather than added subsequently. This approach can accelerate delivery while improving information security.

For digital platforms, there are many routes to future-ready. Woerner et al. (2022) found only 22% of companies future-ready (in 2021), and identified four pathways to improvement that were particularly effective, producing an average net operating margin 19.3% points higher than the industry average.

1. Where customer experience was uncompetitive, organisations first focused technologically on creating an integrated customer experience and better digital offerings. MBank in Poland did this, then needed operations to get up to speed, so implemented a new customer-at-the-centre banking platform.
2. Organisations with poor operational efficiency focused first on industrialising their technology platform, then on further improving the customer experience. Danske Bank and Commonwealth Bank of Australia adopted this approach.
3. A third pathway took small 'balancing steps'—alternating focus on operations and customer experience—over several iterations. A key success factor is to have an overall transformation roadmap that

informs each of the separate efforts. Without this coordination, digital initiatives tend to lose their way, and the overall digital transformation project loses momentum.
4. A fourth, more radical, pathway is to start a new future-ready company with a digital platform and all the advantages built in. This is a sensible option if the competition is fierce, and management cannot see how to change the culture, customer experience and operations fast enough to survive.

Of course, it is quite possible to take more than one of these routes. The digital leaders that make up 18–25% of organisations in their sector frequently do choose multiple pathways, or complete one, then take up another. For example, Bancolombia internally transformed customer engagement and operations systems but also created its own digital-only banking entity—Nequi—as a test bed and internal competitor. By late 2021 80% of Bancolombia's own customers were digital users, and Nequi was made a separate business to grow and exploit its technology.

Conclusion

Following the significant uptick in enterprises announcing their net-zero commitments and targets, we can expect to see significant progress taking place from 2023. As organisations seek to demonstrate sustainability progress, innovative solutions will be increasingly in demand—and technology providers must understand how to best provide effective solutions. One senior manager told us:

> Forget about the cost of net zero, your business will disappear if you don't do it right. Head of Diversity, Equity, and Inclusion, Pharmaceutical Company

We expect to see a clearer, stronger pattern emerging in terms of partnerships between enterprises and suppliers, and the types of solutions in which they are engaging.

Both vendor innovation ecosystems and sustainability practices have to become part of the larger digital transformation efforts all organisations were engaged in by the mid-2020s. Digital transformation has also been transforming what external service providers do and how they relate to their clients. All the research points to how difficult the overall task is, with serious disruptions and question marks along the way. In most sectors, value migration is constant. And when the game changes, the winners are, like Wayne Gretzky pursuing the ice hockey puck, the ones who migrate to where the value will be. We hope this book contributes to understanding the trends, and how organisations can become future-ready in both their digital transformation efforts, and in their global sourcing strategies.

References

Kotlarsky, J., Oshri, I., & Sekulic, N. (2023). Digital Sustainability in Information Systems Research: Conceptual Foundations and Future Directions. *Journal of the Association for Information Systems, 24*(4), 936–952.

Ross, J., Beath, C., & Mocker, M. (2019). *Designed For Digital: How to Architect Your Business for Sustained Success*. MIT Press.

Willcocks, L. (2021). *Global Business: Management*. SB Publishing.

Willcocks, L., Hindle, J., Stanton, M., & Smith, J. (2023). *Maximizing Value With Automation and Digital Transformation: A Realist's Guide*. Palgrave Macmillan.

Woerner, S., Weill, P., & Sebastian, I. (2022). *The Four Pathways To Creating Digital Value*. Harvard Business Review Press.

Index

A
Accommodating conflict handling style, 149, 150, 154, 157
Action principles, 334, 338, 341, 342, 346, 347, 350, 351
Adidas, 114, 115, 118, 120, 127–136
AI adoption, 356
AI governance, xx
Algorithms outsourcing, 357, 363, 365, 366, 370, 376, 380, 381
Alignment of objectives, 132, 134–136, 138
Alignment of processes, 132–136
Applications development, 5
Architectural integration, 81, 98
Architectural knowledge, 64–66, 68, 71–78, 81, 83, 88–91, 93–103
Artificial Intelligence (AI), 7, 8, 11, 13, 328, 329, 331, 355–359, 361–373, 375–377, 379–382, 454, 455, 457, 460, 461, 472
Aspirational performance, 254
Audit, regulation and bureaucracy, 460
Automation, 1, 6–8, 13, 454–460, 462, 469, 472
Automation continuum, 328
Automation evolution, 327, 330, 350
Automation sourcing, 462

B
Backsourcing, xviii, xix, 250–253, 255–260, 264, 265, 268, 269, 271–275
Behavioral theory, 250, 254
Behavioral uncertainty, 113, 115–117, 120, 123, 125, 129–132, 135, 136, 140
Bilateral outcome control, 20, 21, 24, 25, 27–30, 34, 36–42, 44, 46–51, 53
British Airways, 62, 64
Business process optimisation, 356
Business process outsourcing, 1, 2, 6–8

Business services, 2–4, 9
Business services outsourcing, 147–152, 157, 158, 160–162, 164–170, 172, 174, 177–191, 195
Business units, 282, 283, 285–287, 291, 310, 311, 313, 314
Business value, 332, 334, 335, 338, 350

C

Capabilities, 3–5, 12–14
Carbon footprints, 478, 486
Centre of excellence, 128
Client adoption journeys, 339
Client success in multisourcing, 25
Client-vendor dyad, 23, 25–27, 33
Cloud services, viii, xxi, 393–398, 401–406, 408
Cloud sourcing, v, vi, 7–9
Coalitions in firms, 254
Cognitive automation, 327–329, 338
Cognitive functions, 356
Collaboration, 286, 313, 315
Collaboration willingness, 206
Collaborative crowdsourcing, xxi
Collaborative engagement, 443
Collaborative opportunities, 207, 215
Collaborative practices, 207, 232, 233, 238, 240, 241
Collective outcome control, 20, 21, 24, 25, 27–32, 34, 36, 37, 39–51, 53
Commercial aspects, 393
Commercial conflict stories, 168
Competitive risks, 356
Complementary objectives, 205
Complex algorithms, 355
Compliance demands, 477
Compromising conflict handling style, 149, 150, 154, 157

Conflict avoidance, 254
Conflict management procedures, 21, 24, 25, 27, 30, 31, 36, 37, 39, 40, 42–45, 47–52, 54
Conflict resolution, 21, 31, 48, 149–160, 162–165, 167, 169, 172, 177, 180–182, 186, 187, 191, 195
Conflict resolution style
 accommodating/smoothing/ obliging, 149, 150, 159, 160, 162, 164, 165
 avoiding/withdrawal, 150, 159, 160, 163, 165
 collaborating/ problem solving/ integrating, 159, 160
 competing/dominating/ forcing, 150, 159, 160, 162, 163, 165, 187
 compromising/sharing, 149, 150, 157, 159, 160
 switching, 160, 162
Conflict types
 commercial, 148, 151, 158, 162, 163, 167, 168, 178, 179, 183, 186
 relationship, 151, 157, 158, 162, 164, 167, 174, 175, 178, 186
 service, 148, 151, 158, 162–164, 167, 172, 178, 183
Contractual governance, 4, 5
Co-opetition, 112, 113, 135
Coordination issues, 206
Core-periphery digitalised labour model, 468
Corporate responsibility, 478
Cost-benefit analysis, 271
Covid-19, 453, 454, 456, 458, 465, 466, 472
Covid-19 crisis, 345
Critical skills, 477

Crowdsourcing, vi, xxi, xxii, 425–430, 432, 433, 443, 444, 446–448
Crowdsourcing models, 421
Customer value, 334
Cybersecurity, 460, 470

D
Data-driven decision making, 356, 357
Data explosion, 459, 460
Data processing, 356
Data quality, 356, 372, 373
Decarbonizing operations, 487
Decision-making, 287, 288, 293
Defensive behaviors, 207, 211, 218, 223, 225, 233, 235, 236, 239
Developmental conflict, 207
Digital futures, 455
Digitalized flexible organisation, 453–467
Digital services, ix, xv, xix
Digital technologies, v, vii, xxii, xxiii
Digital transformation, vii, xx, xxiii, 457, 458, 478, 479, 491–493, 495, 497–500, 503, 504
Dissatisfaction, 250, 251, 254–258, 260, 265, 268, 271–274
Distributed work, 282, 283, 287, 289, 313, 318

E
Economic value, 427
Emerging technologies, 355, 362
Employee value, 334
Enterprise value, 343
Expectations, 250, 251, 253–259, 268, 269, 271, 272
Expected value, 428, 430, 442, 443
Exponential growth in work, 454
Extrinsic motivation, 428

F
Financial slack, 251, 255, 260, 263, 268, 269, 272–274
Flexible labour model, 454, 455
Flexible organisation challenges, 454
Formal governance, 360, 362, 367, 369, 374, 375, 379
Formal governance in multisourcing, 23, 25
Frame analysis, 283
Frame contest, 284, 309, 311
Frame disputes, 282–287, 290, 306, 307, 309–312
Framing theory, 284
Future of work, 455, 472

G
Gainshare, 163, 171
Gig economy, 469
Globally distributed work, xviii, 205–210, 212, 213, 216, 219, 232–241
Global outsourcing, v, viii
Global sourcing, 3, 4, 8, 14, 285, 286
Governance, 62, 64–66, 68–77, 81, 82, 88, 89, 94–98, 100–104, 357–362, 365–367, 369, 370, 373–380
Governance efficiency, 20, 22, 26–31, 36–39, 42–44, 48, 50, 51, 55
Governance mechanisms, 20, 22, 24, 44, 46, 48–52
'Great Resignation', 453
Guardian vendor, 62–65, 67, 69, 73–77, 82, 94, 95, 97, 98, 101–104

H
High-status units, 283, 286, 287, 293, 307–311, 313

Home/remote working, 454, 458, 465
Human work skills, 464
Hybrid clouds, 395

I
Identity threats, 206, 208–210, 232, 238
Implementation challenges, 287
Information Processing View (IPV), 65, 66, 68–71, 74, 76, 77, 81, 88, 95, 102, 104
Information systems multisourcing, 19, 20
Information technology outsourcing, 1, 2, 7, 8
Infrastructure-as-a-service, 8–10
In-house delivery, vi
Innovation, vii, viii
Innovation eco-systems, xxii, 477, 502, 504
Insourcing, vi
Integrating conflict handling style, 149, 154, 157
Intellectual Properties (IP), 359, 367, 376
Intelligent automation, 328, 331, 332, 342, 346, 348, 350, 351
Interaction of governance mechanisms, 50
Interdependencies, 20, 22, 23, 26, 27, 31, 45–47, 51, 61, 62, 64, 66, 72, 73, 95, 96, 100, 101
Internal ecosystems, 480
Internal uncertainty, 116, 123, 129, 133, 139
Internet, 460, 461
Internet-based sourcing, 394, 421
Internet delivery, 393
Internet service delivery, xxi
Inter-organisational relationships, 148

Inter-vendor governance, 64, 68–76, 94–98, 100–102, 104
Intrinsic motivation, 443
IP capacity, 64–77, 88, 94–98, 102
IT and business services, xv
IT-enabled tasks, 281–283, 288–290, 306, 313
IT infrastructure, 6, 10
IT offshoring, 284, 286, 312
IT services provider, 118

J
Job displacement, 454
Jobs and automation, 343
Joint performance, 20, 26–31, 33, 37–39, 42–48, 50, 51, 55, 62–64, 66–78, 80, 83, 88–91, 94–100, 104

K
Knowledge asymmetries, 206, 208, 217, 232, 233, 235

L
Learning algorithms, 355
Low-status unit, 283, 287, 292, 308–311, 313

M
Machine learning, 8, 11, 355
Mixed ecosystems, 479–482
Multiservice ecosystems, 480
Multisourcing, vii, viii, xv–xvii, 61–73, 75, 77, 79, 95, 96, 100–103, 111–115, 119, 122, 127, 131, 135
Multisourcing risks, 112, 117
Multisourcing success, 20, 21, 25–31, 38, 43, 49–52
Multi-tasking, 461

N
Net-zero targets, 484, 486, 488, 491

O
Offshore outsourcing, xviii
Offshoring, v, vii, xix
Online platforms, 430
Operational aspects, 393
Opportunistic behavior, 112–117, 119, 120, 123, 129–138
Opportunistic propensity, 116, 117, 120, 122, 123, 129, 131, 139
Organisational strategy, 314
Organizational behavior, 254
Outcome control, 20, 21, 24, 28
Out-tasking, vi

P
Paradoxical complexities, 208
Pay-per-user pricing, 395
Performance goals, 255
Platform-as-a-service, 8, 9, 12, 13
Political support, 250, 251, 254, 259, 269
Power asymmetries, 206, 208, 209, 232, 238, 241
Power dynamics, 283, 313
Primary core internal workers, 469
Privacy preservations, 356
Problemistic search, 250, 254, 256, 268
Professional IT services, 6
Psychological contract, 357, 361–363, 374, 376, 378–380

R
Relational governance, 4, 5, 23, 357, 360–363, 370, 374–377, 379, 380
Relationship conflict stories, 174
Resiliency, 395
Resource allocation, 272
Resource pooling, 395
Risk management, 254, 260
Risk mitigation, 335
Robo-Apocalypse, 455, 457, 472
Robotic process automation, 7, 13, 327–336, 338, 343–351, 355
Robots, 456, 472

S
Scope 1, 2, 3 (emissions), 484
Service automation, 335, 341, 343–345, 347, 351
Service conflict stories, 172
Service development, 356
Service Level Agreements (SLAs), 62, 104
Service operations, 356
Siloed organisation, 457, 465
Skills demand, 463
SMAC/BRAIDA technologies, viii
Software-as-a-service, 6, 8–11
Sourcing decisions, 249–252, 257, 259, 271–273
Sourcing options, 337
Sourcing strategies, 477, 478, 504
Specialist ecosystems, 480, 481
Speed of adoption (automation), 457
Stakeholders, 426, 428, 442–444, 447, 449
Status differentials, 283, 285–288, 290, 291, 295, 302, 306–309, 311, 313, 314
Strategic decisions, 282
Strategic partnering, vii
Structural changes, 207, 226, 238
Subcontractors, 469
Support units, 281, 282, 285, 286, 311, 313, 314
Sustainability, 478, 485–489, 503, 504

T

Task migration, 282, 283, 285–290, 294, 296, 298, 299, 302, 305–315, 317, 318
Task migration strategies, 283, 285, 286, 307, 312, 313
Technology
  solution and problem, 460
Technology artifact, 427
Time-to-market, 477
Tournament-based crowdsourcing, xxi
Traditional outsourcing arrangements, 19
Transaction Cost Economics (TCE), 113, 115, 116, 118–120, 135
Transaction costs, 114, 118, 128
Triadic client-vendors level, 22
'Triple Win', 334, 335
Types of flexibility
  financial, 468
  functional, 468
  labour replacement/enhancement, 469
  locational, 469
  numerical, 468
  temporal, 469

U

Uncertainty, 112, 113, 115, 116, 119, 120, 123, 125, 129–131, 133–136, 139, 140

V

Value appreciation, 444
Value co-creation, 444, 446, 449
Value creation, 425–428, 444, 446
Value-destroying conflict, 206
Value-related processes, 444, 447
Vendor cooperation, 70, 71
Vendor Innovation Ecosystems (VIEs), 478, 479
Vendor relationships, 362, 364, 377, 380

Printed in the USA
CPSIA information can be obtained
at www.ICGtesting.com
CBHW072018280824
13694CB00009B/101